Canadian Edition

2023 Year A

Workbook for Lectors, Gospel Readers, and Proclaimers of the Word®

Catherine Cory

Peter O'Leary

Stephen S. Wilbricht, CSC

LTP
LITURGY
TRAINING
PUBLICATIONS

CONTENTS

Liturgy Training Publications
3949 South Racine Avenue
Chicago IL 60609
800-933-1800
Fax: 800-933-7094
orders@ltp.org, www.LTP.org

CCCB Publications
Canadian Conference
of Catholic Bishops
2500 Don Reid Drive
Ottawa, Ontario Canada K1H 2J2
613-241-7538
800-769-1147
Fax: 613-241-5090
www.cccbpublications.ca

This book was edited by Christina N. Condyles. Christian Rocha was the production editor, Anna Manhart was the designer, and Kari Nicholls was the production artist.

Cover art: Barbara Simcoe

Printed in the United States of America

ISBN (CANADA):
978-0-88997-929-1

ISBN (USA): 978-1-61671-666-0

CANADIAN CODE: 184-983

WL23C

(continues on next page)

Ordinary Time

MESSAGE AND PROCLAMATION

According to the *Catechism of the Catholic Church*, the liturgy is an "action" of the *whole Christ*, one that recapitulates the eternal drama in which "the Spirit and the Church enable us to participate whenever we celebrate the mystery of salvation in the sacraments" (1139). It is a celebration of the whole community: participative, connective, and joyful. Crucial to the celebration is the Liturgy of the Word, through which the Holy Spirit awakens faith, offering signs—in the lectionary and the book of the Gospels; in procession, incense, and candles; and in the place of proclamation at the ambo—and instruction—through the proclamation itself of the Word of God to the faithfully assembled. As the *Catechism* puts it, "The Spirit makes present and communicates the Father's work, fulfilled by the beloved Son" (1155).

To read the Word of God is an act of proclamation. What is being proclaimed? The faith itself. *Kerygma* is the Greek word for proclamation; it appears multiple times in the New Testament, in Paul's letters and in the Acts of the Apostles, for instance, to refer to both the act and the content of proclaiming the good news. In Paul's first letter to the Corinthians, he confesses, "When I came to you, brothers and sisters, I did not come *proclaiming* the mystery of God to you in lofty words or wisdom. For I decided to know nothing among you except Jesus Christ, and him crucified. And I came to you in weakness and in fear and in much trembling. My speech and my *proclamation* were not with plausible words of wisdom, but with a demonstration of the Spirit and of power, so that your faith might rest not on human wisdom but on the power of God" (1 Corinthians 2.1–5; emphasis added). Paul doesn't want to be persuasive; rather, he wants his proclamation to reflect the spirit of God's power that fills him. When you proclaim, you reflect this spirit of the power of God.

In his Apostolic Exhortation *Evangelii gaudium*, Pope Francis insists that evangelization relies on a deeper understanding of proclamation. Francis refers to proclamation (he calls it *kerygma*, using the Greek term) as the "first announcement," whose essential confidence brings us deeper into the mystery of faith. (It is first because it is primary.) Francis is thinking of the importance of instruction when he writes that the formation of Christians is grounded upon the proclamation of the Good News

and our ongoing immersion in it; this is the basis for catechesis at any level (165). But this catechesis, which means simply a ministry of the word (catechesis, which means "instruction," comes from the Greek word *katechein*, which means "echo"), has an instructive social element you involve yourself in

---

The word of God constantly proclaimed in the Liturgy is always a living and effective word through the power of the Holy Spirit. It expresses the Father's love that never fails in its effectiveness toward us.

---

whenever you attend Mass and whenever you participate as a proclaimer of the Word. Francis insists that the Good News of Jesus Christ always calls us to be in community (177). Engagement with the community and deepening your life in that community are precisely what you accomplish as a lector, Gospel reader, and proclaimer of the Word.

Alpha and Omega

"I am the Alpha and the Omega." Thus says the Lord in the Revelation to John. Twice, in fact: in the opening chapter and in the twenty-second. It's one of the most potent and memorable phrases in all of the New Testament. Among its many interpretations and purposes, it might usefully serve as a motto for all proclaimers of the Word in the Church: lectors, deacons, and priests. One way to paraphrase this claim is that God is saying, "I am the alphabet."

Language, of course, is the medium you use as a lector, the instrument you play. Effective proclaiming is like effective piano playing. As every music teacher knows, some students are no good at playing the piano because they don't practise and don't have a good feel for the instrument. Other students are pretty good because they practise and have learned how to read music and to play the notes in the proper order. A few students are superb because they combine the discipline of practice with an intimate and immediately audible feel for the instrument, combining voicing, pauses, skill, and poise. Proclamation involves a similar skill set. Practice is important, but so is developing as good a feel for language—your instrument—as you can.

How do we develop a feel for language? One of the main ways that meaning is conveyed when modern English is spoken is through the interplay of syntax (the order of words in a sentence or phrase) and stress (the emphasis in speech that falls on one part of a word or phrase over another). Poetry is the literary form most attentive to syntax and stress. Poetry in English is qualitative, which means that it relies on the repetition of strong stresses in words to convey its patterns and meanings. This is called meter.

Scripture is organized by book, chapter, and verse. This system of organization is modern, coming into use in the sixteenth century. It was first used in English when the *Geneva Bible* was published in 1560. Verses refer, in the main, to sentences, since most of Scripture is written in prose. Some verses are poetic verse, including especially the Psalms but also the prophetic books in the Old Testament. Nevertheless, because the use and study of verse in English involve descriptive terminology, it is helpful to think about proclaiming the Word as a lector, deacon, or priest in terms of reading poetry aloud.

There are five basic metrical units in English, the names for which are all borrowed from Greek. A metrical unit is a pattern of stressed (DA) and unstressed (da) syllables. The five basic units, with examples of words that follow each pattern, are

iamb—da-DA (Baddeck);

trochee—DA-da (London);

anapest—da-da-DA (Montreal);

dactyl—DA-da-da (Edmonton);

and spondee—DA-DA (Moose Jaw).

There are other metres, of course, but it's useful to have a sense of these five basic units when you are reading anything aloud, including Scripture, much of which, even in English translation, comes through as poetry.

You will note that the two longest of these metrical units have only three syllables. This means, practically speaking, that every two or three syllables, when you read something aloud, there should be a stress, an emphasis. Identifying these stresses does not exaggerate the sound of the phrase; instead, it enhances the phrase, highlighting its natural expressiveness.

> It is necessary that those who exercise the ministry of reader . . . be truly suited and carefully prepared, so that the faithful may develop a warm and living love for Sacred Scripture from listening to the sacred readings.

Consider again, "I am the Alpha and the Omega." This statement, one of the boldest of all in the New Testament, doesn't require any exaggeration or intensification on your part beyond identifying where the stresses in this statement lie. First, in the personal pronoun. Second, in the first syllable of Alpha. And third, in the second syllable of Omega. You could write the statement out this way, using capital letters to emphasize the stresses:

I am the ALpha and the oMEGa.

That captures the stresses. However, it doesn't entirely capture the most effective pace for proclaiming this statement.

Thinking about metrical units in English, you can identify where the pauses in this statement might usefully lie. The pauses in your speaking set the pace. Every two or three syllables, when speaking aloud, there is an opportunity for a pause, even if it's only a slight hesitation that allows you to enhance the stresses. We can use this symbol | to indicate pauses, however slight, and rewrite the statement from Revelation this way:

I | am the ALpha | and | the oMEGa.

An alternative reading would eliminate the third pause:

I | am the ALpha | and the oMEGa.

In the first version, the line has four beats:

1) I; 2) am the ALpha; 3) and; 4) the oMEGa.

The second version has three beats:

1) I; 2) am the ALpha; 3) and the oMEGa.

In the first version, the third pause, after "and," allows you to emphasize the parallel being drawn between the beginning and the end in the Lord's statement. In the second version, you speed ever so noticeably quicker to Omega, which is the word in the verse imbuing it with ominous power.

The Sacred Scriptures, above all in their liturgical proclamation, are the source of life and strength.

Both versions are effective. Both, if you speak them aloud (as practice), can be suited to your speaking style. And both possible readings reinforce one of the most helpful strategies for effective proclaiming: read slowly enough that stresses and emphases can be heard by the congregation. A good rule of thumb, easy to remember, when reading anything aloud is:

Read twice as loud and at half the pace that you normally speak.

Most lectors will be reading into a microphone, which means you need not increase your volume in the way you would without a microphone. However, the rule of thumb above can serve as a reminder that you are reading in front of an audience, your congregation, and the more clearly you proclaim, the more likely it is that they will pay attention. Like a teacher coming into a classroom and raising their voice above the level of the din or a coach blowing a whistle to get the attention of the team, you can command the attention of your congregation by the pitch and volume of your voice. Don't be afraid to use it.

Likewise, read slowly. Depending on the architecture of your church, it's likely that your amplified voice will echo. Reading slowly allows your words to be heard and absorbed, rather than reflected and distorted.

Similarly, the more clearly you read, while paying attention to where the stresses lie in the passage from Scripture you are reading, the more intelligible and available your proclaiming will be. You do not need to act out any of the phrases by changing the pitch of your voice or feigning emotion. Scripture already contains all the drama and power required for its proper expression. You need merely to voice it.

"Less is more" might be a useful axiom for proclaiming, but you don't want to excuse yourself from the work of proclaiming, which requires your presence for maximum effect. Your presence includes your voice, which allows you to announce the Word of God, but also your attention, which shows you where the stresses and emphases in the passage you are proclaiming lie. Simone Weil, the twentieth-century activist and mystic, wrote, "Absolutely unmixed attention is prayer." The attention you bring to your proclaiming enables you then to pray the Word of God with your congregation.

Readings Old and New

The Liturgy of the Word typically consists of a reading from the Old Testament, a reading from the New Testament (often one of the letters of Paul), and a reading from the Gospels. In the case of Year A, which this workbook covers, almost all of the Gospel readings, with exceptions on some of the feasts, come from Matthew.

Gospel readings during Ordinary Time tend to go more or less in order. In Year A, they start from early in Matthew and work toward the Gospel's end. Readings on feast days, as well as during the seasons of Advent, Christmas, Lent, and Easter, are selected specifically for those Sundays and don't necessarily follow a sequential order. The first reading—again, typically from the Old Testament—is selected to harmonize with the Gospel reading.

The second reading—again, often from one of the letters of Paul, but not always—is more deliberately instructive. Usually, from week to week at Sunday Mass, you will notice that one Sunday's second reading picks up where the previous week's left off.

Each of these parts of Scripture can be proclaimed differently, with subtle but valuable effects. First readings tend to be more poetic than second readings. You can effectively infuse your first reading with forms of poetic attention, being mindful especially of pauses, but also of some of the other rhetorical features that make Scripture so rich. These include

anaphora, which is the use of the repetition of a word or phrase;

parallel structure, in which an entire phrase is repeated with slight variation;

the imperative voice, in which the speaker commands the audience to do something, usually to listen, to hear, and to heed; and

the power of questions, in which the speaker asks forceful questions not necessarily easy or comfortable to answer.

Each of these rhetorical features serves to enhance the power of the words and phrases in the reading.

Consider the first reading for the Twenty-Fourth Sunday in Ordinary Time, from the twenty-eighth chapter of Sirach. This reading is in the imperative voice, spoken directly to the listener, making stern but earnest pronouncements the speaker expects the listener to take to heart:

Forgive your neighbour the wrong that is done, and then your sins will be pardoned when you pray.
Does anyone harbour anger against another, and expect healing from the Lord?
If one has no mercy toward another like oneself,
can one then seek pardon for one's own sins?
If one who is but flesh harbours wrath, who will make an atoning sacrifice for that person's sins?
(Sirach 28.2–5)

The whole reading relies on repeated parallel structures in which a claim or question is made in the first line and then advanced or fulfilled in the line immediately following. So, "Forgive your neighbour the wrong that is done" is followed by its completion, "and then your sins will be pardoned when you pray." The three verses that are questions are similarly structured, with two of them making use of the anaphora of "If one." And finally, as indicated above, the imperative voice is used, which augments the urgency of the advice being given. Recognizing these patterns can show you how best to proclaim these verses and where to lay the emphasis.

The Gospel for the Twenty-Fourth Sunday in Ordinary Time comes amid a series of Gospel readings from Matthew in which Jesus uses parables to instruct his listeners about discipleship and the kingdom of God. It connects to the reading from Sirach because it concerns forgiveness and the way we treat others. In response to Peter's question about how often he must forgive someone, Jesus shares a parable about forgiveness freely given and wrathfully taken back. A servant who owes his master a great sum of money is forgiven his debt, yet shortly after the servant refuses to show mercy to another servant who owes him money. The first servant is punished by the master for not extending the same mercy he was offered. Jesus concludes the parable by suggesting that this is how God in heaven will treat those who fail to be forgiving. Note how the message of the first reading and the Gospel reinforce each other.

God's word shows us what we should hope for with such a longing that in this changing world our hearts will be set on the place where our true joys lie.

The second reading for the Twenty-Fourth Sunday in Ordinary Time offers a succinct and beautiful reading from the Letter to the Romans. It follows a long stretch of sequential (but not continuous) readings from Romans that begin on the Eleventh Sunday in Ordinary Time this year. With this reading, Paul's teachings from Romans are concluded for this liturgical cycle. The reading makes use of an especially vivid and pointed contrast between living and dying, and what it means to live and die for the Lord.

Where the first reading is often poetic, the second reading is typically instructive. It's also almost always a shorter reading. You should proclaim it as an instruction. Read slowly, take your time presenting its argument, and emphasize its point, which will come in the last sentence or two of the reading.

First and second readings always conclude with the phrase "The word of the Lord." Try to pause a moment before you read this conclusion. Likewise, don't rush through the phrase. It will blur, sounding like "word Lord." Instead, break the phrase into two units, reading it like this: The WORD | of the LORD. It's effective to pause for two or three beats after you say this before stepping away from the ambo.

Preparation and Execution

It helps to practise. You should read through your assigned reading at least a few times, once silently to yourself to get its sense and two or three times aloud to get a feel for its rhythm and pace, as well as any unusual words, names, or place names. (The marginal pronunciation guides will help you with these.)

If you are assigned to proclaim the first reading, read the Gospel for that week as well. They will be connected in thematic ways. If you are assigned to proclaim the second reading, take a look at the previous week's second reading as well as the following week's to see where the second reading is coming from and where it is going. This will give you some context for the insights it contains.

For many of us, our main experience reading aloud comes from reading to children. Proclaiming Scripture is something different. When you practise reading aloud, it's better to read in as straightforward a way as possible than to try to dramatize your reading through inflection, pitch, or voicing in the way you might if you were reading something to a child. Scripture is unusually powerful in its expressiveness, symbolism, and language. If you read in a steady, evenly pitched, and articulate voice, its power will come through your reading. You will be, during Mass, the instrument of its power.

For many people, it can be a little intimidating to stand before a congregation and proclaim. You might find it helpful to place one of your index fingers in the margin of the lectionary to remind you of your place. You might also find it helpful to place your other hand on the ambo to steady yourself. This has the effect of giving you the appearance of an open posture.

As you read, try to look up from time to time and make eye contact. Choose faces in different places of the assembled congregation to focus on when you look up: sometimes close by, sometimes farther back, and sometimes from one side to the other. This simple gesture has an inclusive effect; you are not merely reading *to* the congregation; you are reading *for* it and *with* it. If you use your index finger to keep your place in the lectionary, you will not worry about getting lost whenever you look up.

That said, you are not performing. You don't need to smile unnecessarily, you don't need to emote beyond what the words themselves suggest, and you don't need somehow to exemplify the words in your comportment or your presentation. The words of Scripture are utterly endowed with power. You are the instrument to voice that power. A sincere and plainspoken proclamation will invariably convey that power to your fellow congregants.

In addition to the margin notes and pronunciation guides that accompany each reading, many words have been bolded to aid in your preparation for proclaiming the Word of God. In each reading, there are a handful of key terms that set the tone and characterize the instruction that the reading contains. Nevertheless, you will find that many more words are bolded than just these key terms. All of these bolded words are there as guides, or landmarks, for your proclamation. They give you a sense of where

---

The Church is nourished spiritually at the twofold table of God's word and of the Eucharist: from the one it grows in wisdom and from the other in holiness.

---

you are in the reading, and they serve to remind you how to measure your spoken expression while you are proclaiming. They are not meant to be overly stressed! Bolded words simply indicate the natural places where the stresses in a given phrase or sentence lie, as well as words and phrases that enhance the message of the reading. Sometimes this means that prepositions get some extra stress. (Consider: "**Through** him, **with** him, and **in** him . . .") At other times, it means that the proper names of Prophets or the disciples or place names get emphasis. And at still other times, it means otherwise ordinary words get stressed because the rhythm of the proclamation compels it. If you practise your reading and test your proclamation against these bolded words, you will have a clear guide for how to proceed through the reading in a way that enhances your natural powers of spoken expression without obliging you to exaggerate your vocal mannerisms as you proclaim. It is important to note, again, that Scripture is already full of power. Your ministry is in service of this Word of God. You don't need to add anything to that power for it to ring out to your assembly. Instead, pay attention to stresses and emphases, as indicated in the bolded texts, and remember to proclaim twice as loud and at half the pace that you normally speak.

Participation

For inspiration, consider these words by Pierre Teilhard de Chardin, from *The Divine Milieu*, his "essay on the interior life."

> We may, perhaps, imagine that the Creation was finished long ago. But that would be quite wrong. It continues still more magnificently, and in the highest zones of the world. *Omnis creatura adhuc ingemescit et parturit.* And we serve to complete it, even by the humblest work of our hands. That is, ultimately, the meaning and value of our acts. Owing to the inter-relation between matter, soul, and Christ, we lead part of the being which He desires back to God in whatever we do. With each one of our works, we labour—atomically, but no less really—to build the Pleroma; that is to say, to bring to Christ a little fulfillment. (Pierre Teilhard de Chardin, *The Divine Milieu*, ed. Bernard Wall [New York: Harper & Brothers, 1960], 31)

For Teilhard, "Pleroma" means the mysterious fullness of creation. The Latin phrase, *omnis creatura adhuc ingemescit et parturit*, refers to Romans 8.22, "the whole creation has been groaning in labour pains until now." We are still in the process of creation; whenever you participate in the Mass, you are adding to that work. And whenever you proclaim at Mass, you are helping, by the humblest work of your voice, to bring to Christ a little fulfillment.

Pull-out quotations throughout this article are from the introduction to the *Lectionary for Mass*.

Peter O'Leary

The Authors

Catherine Cory is professor emerita of theology at the University of St. Thomas in St. Paul, MN. She holds a doctorate in New Testament studies with subspecialties in Old Testament and early Church. Her research interests are in the Gospel of John and Revelation. She has edited and authored several books including *The Christian Theological Tradition, A Voyage through the New Testament* and *The Book of Revelation* in the New Collegeville Bible Commentary series. In addition to her academic teaching at the undergraduate and graduate level, she enjoys doing adult education presentations at local parishes.

Peter O'Leary studied religion and literature at the Divinity School of the University of Chicago, where he received his doctorate. He has written several books of poetry, most recently, *Earth Is Best*, as well as two books of literary criticism, most recently, *Thick and Dazzling Darkness: Religious Poetry in a Secular Age*. He teaches at the School of the Art Institute of Chicago and lives with his family in Oak Park, IL.

Stephen S. Wilbricht, CSC, is associate professor in the Religious Studies and Theology Department at Stonehill College in Easton, MA. He holds a doctorate in sacred theology from the Catholic University of America in Washington, DC, and has served in two parishes in the Southwest. He is the author of several books, including *Baptismal Ecclesiology and the Order of Christian Funerals* (LTP, 2018), *The Role of the Priest in Christian Initiation* (LTP, 2017), and *Rehearsing God's Just Kingdom: The Eucharistic Vision of Mark Searle* (Liturgical Press, 2013). He is also a team member for LTP's Catechumeneon.

The authors' initials appear at the end of the Scripture commentaries.

An Option to Consider

The third edition of *The Roman Missal* encourages ministers of the Word to chant the introduction and conclusion to the readings ("A reading from . . . "; "The word of the Lord"). For those parishes wishing to use these chants, they are demonstrated in audio files that may be accessed either through the QR codes given here (with a smartphone) or through the URL indicated beneath the code. Be careful to distinguish between the letter l (lowercase L) and the numeral 1.

The first QR code contains the tones for the first reading in both a male and a female voice.

http://bit.ly/l2mjeG

The second QR code contains the tones for the second reading in both a male and a female voice.

http://bit.ly/krwEYy

The third QR code contains the simple tone for the Gospel.

http://bit.ly/iZZvSg

The fourth QR code contains the solemn tone for the Gospel.

http://bit.ly/lwf6Hh

A fuller explanation of this practice, along with musical notation for the chants, is provided in a downloadable PDF file found under the supplement tab on the product's webpage: http://www.ltp.org /products/details /WL23.

Pronunciation Key

bait = bayt
cat = kat
sang = sang
father = FAH-ther
care = kayr
paw = paw
jar = jahr
easy = EE-zee
her = her
let = let
queen = kween
delude = deh-LOOD
when = hwen
ice = īs
if = if
finesse = fih-NES

thin = thin
vision = VIZH*n
ship = ship
sir = ser
gloat = gloht
cot = kot
noise = noyz
poison = POY-z*n
plow = plow
although = ahl-THOH
church = cherch
fun = fuhn
fur = fer
flute = floot
foot = foot

Shorter Readings

In the Scripture readings reproduced in this book, shorter readings are indicated by brackets and a citation given at the end of the reading.

FIRST SUNDAY OF ADVENT

LECTIONARY #1

READING I   Isaiah 2.1–5

A reading from the book of the Prophet Isaiah.

Isaiah = ī-ZAY-uh

Amoz = AY-muhz

A rhythmical, forceful, and poetic reading.

Judah = JOO-duh

The **word** that **Isaiah** son of **Amoz saw**
concerning **Judah** and **Jerusalem**.
In **days** to **come**
the **mountain** of the **Lord's house**
shall be **established** as the **highest** of the **mountains**,
and shall be **raised** above the **hills**;
all the **nations** shall **stream** to it.
Many **peoples** shall **come** and **say**,

At "Come," the forcefulness of the reading intensifies. Raise your voice ever so slightly.

"**Come**, let us go **up** to the **mountain** of the **Lord**,
to the **house** of the **God** of **Jacob**;
that he may **teach** us his **ways**
and that we may **walk** in his **paths**."
For out of **Zion** shall go forth **instruction**,

Zion = zī-uhn or zī-ahn

and the **word** of the **Lord** from **Jerusalem**.
He shall **judge** between the **nations**,
and shall **arbitrate** for many **peoples**;

Emphasis on "swords" and "ploughshares"; "spears" and "pruning hooks."

they shall **beat** their **swords** into **ploughshares**,
and their **spears** into **pruning hooks**;
nation shall not lift up **sword** against **nation**,
neither shall they **learn war** any **more**.
O **house** of **Jacob**, **come**,
let us **walk** in the **light** of the **Lord**!

READING I | Isaiah's role as Prophet is to be interpreted in light of the Babylonian Exile, which spanned roughly the years 586 to 539 BC. Many of the exiled Israelites who had witnessed the destruction of Jerusalem were still alive when Isaiah tried to call the people back to their land. This was an unenviable task, as many of the Israelites had come to discover peace and prosperity in Babylon. What within the rubble of a destroyed Jerusalem could possibly entice them to return?

Isaiah's prophecy responds to this dilemma by proclaiming that, "in days to come," Jerusalem will be raised higher than any other nation on earth. It will be the envy of every nation, as all peoples will "stream to it." Although the timeframe suggested by the words "in days to come" points to an eschatological reality, there is an urgency about Isaiah's vision. A return to the remnants of Jerusalem will offer the Israelites an opportunity to be instructed in the way of the Lord.

The instruction that the Lord will provide is not simply for the comfort and security of Israel as a restored nation. Instead, it is meant to radiate outward to all the nations. Israel will know its redemption not only by taking possession of the land once more but also by being an example of God's justice that will turn "swords into ploughshares" and "spears into pruning hooks." Instead of focusing on war, the nations of this world will learn to walk in the Lord's light. Thus, the prophecy of Isaiah is designed to make the restored nation of Israel a Prophet itself.

READING II | In his correspondence with the church in Rome, Paul uses a variety of images to communicate

1

For meditation and context:

RESPONSORIAL PSALM   Psalm 122.1–2, 4–5, 6–7, 8–9 (R. see 1)

R. Let us go rejoicing to the house of the Lord.

I was glad when they said to me,
"Let us go to the house of the Lord!"
Our feet are standing
within your gates, O Jerusalem.

To it the tribes go up, the tribes of the Lord,
as was decreed for Israel, to give thanks to
    the name of the Lord.
For there the thrones for judgment
    were set up,
the thrones of the house of David.

Pray for the peace of Jerusalem:
"May they prosper who love you.
Peace be within your walls,
and security within your towers."

For the sake of my relatives and friends
I will say, "Peace be within you."
For the sake of the house of the Lord
    our God,
I will seek your good.

READING II   Romans 13.11–14

A reading from the Letter of Saint Paul to the Romans.

This reading is in the form of a personal address. Familiarity is what makes it forceful.

Brothers and **sisters**,
you **know** what **time** it is,
how it is **now** the moment for you to **wake** from **sleep**.
For **salvation** is **nearer** to us **now**
than when we became **believers**;
the **night** is far **gone**, the **day** is **near**.

Note the parallels: "aside" and "darkness"; "on" and "light."

Let us then lay **aside** the works of **darkness**
and put **on** the **armour** of **light**;
let us live **honourably** as in the **day**,

Note the pairings. Give them emphasis.

not in **revelling** and **drunkenness**,
not in **debauchery** and **licentiousness**,
not in **quarrelling** and **jealousy**.
Instead, put on the **Lord Jesus Christ**,
and make **no** provision for the **flesh**, to **gratify** its **desires**.

---

the importance of making "watchfulness" a foundational attitude of Christianity. These images include awakening from sleep, the contrast between night and day, the "armour of light," and various immoral activities. Paul's challenge for Christians to live fully awake in this world and not to involve themselves in lewd conduct stems from the belief that the parousia is near. Therefore, everyone is to live as though *this* is the hour of Christ's victorious return.

The images Paul uses to communicate the need for vigilance first suggest that such waiting is comparable to engaging in battle with an enemy. The "armour of light" is necessary to keep believers awake and ready to defend themselves from the temptations of the world. Note that Paul addresses the community as a whole, saying "let us" cast off evil deeds, rather than directly challenging individuals (as in, "you" cast off sin). The work to remain alert and ready for the coming of the Lord is that of the church as a whole.

After shocking his readers with the words chosen to illustrate the way of immorality—and therefore activities of the night ("works of darkness")—the reading ends with Paul's command to recognize a Christian's union with Christ. The one who has been baptized has been clothed in the robe of salvation and already lives in the time of promised salvation. Nevertheless, the mandate to "put on the Lord Jesus Christ" entails a daily act of clothing oneself, of making the conscious decision to resist the temptations of this world. The way of following the Lord Jesus in this life requires a constant putting to death of fleshly desires. For Paul, the desire is as sinful as the action itself.

Jesus uses an example from Scripture to speak about the present. This creates a vivid ambience.

Note the parallels and repetitions; "two" to "two women" and "one will be taken" to "one will be left."

Emphasis on "awake," but don't overdo it.

Note the repetition, reinforcing the message.

GOSPEL   Matthew 24.37–44

A reading from the holy Gospel according to Matthew.

Jesus spoke to his **disciples**:
"As the **days** of **Noah** were,
so will be the **coming** of the **Son** of **Man**.
For as **in** those days **before** the **flood**
they were **eating** and **drinking**,
marrying and giving in **marriage**,
until the **day Noah entered** the **ark**,
and they knew **nothing**
until the **flood came** and swept them **all away**,
so too will be the **coming** of the **Son** of **Man**.
Then **two** will be in the **field**;
one will be **taken** and **one** will be **left**.
Two women will be **grinding meal together**;
one will be **taken** and **one** will be **left**.
Keep **awake**, therefore,
for you **do not know** on what **day** your Lord is **coming**.
But understand **this**:
if the **owner** of the **house** had **known**
in **what part** of the **night** the **thief** was **coming**,
he would have **stayed awake**
and would **not** have let his **house** be broken **into**.
Therefore you also must be **ready**,
for the **Son** of **Man** is **coming** at an **unexpected hour**."

TO KEEP IN MIND
The words in bold are suggestions for ways to express the meaning of the reading. Consider using them as you practise the reading, then choose to stress them or to find your own way of proclaiming.

GOSPEL Today's Gospel passage opens with the kind of behaviours that Paul, in his letter to the Romans, noted distract Christians from focusing on the parousia. Matthew refers to the time of Noah, when people ignored the call to repentance and continued with their dissolute ways, being focused on eating and drinking and entering into marriage. As a result, they were caught off guard when the flood came and destroyed the face of the earth.

Matthew likens this scene from Noah's day to the present age, as they wait for "the coming of the Son of Man." Unlike the story of Noah, in which all creation was treated the same, Matthew's depiction of the day of the Lord's return suggests the imposition of a judgment. This judgment is one that cannot be foreknown: one out of two men will survive, one out of two women will survive. The only means of survival, implied by Matthew, is the posture of staying awake. The one who is prepared is the one judged fit for God's reign.

Putting this Gospel in context with today's second reading, the theme of staying awake for the Lord is a clear connecting strand. When we consider the Gospel reading in light of Isaiah's prophecy in the first reading, a different theme appears to be emphasized, namely that of vocation. Just as Israel's return to Jerusalem testifies to the world of God's mighty judgment that will impose peace on all the peoples of the earth, so does the Gospel suggest that vigilance for the Lord's return is a commitment undertaken by true disciples. Our responsibility as followers of Christ is not to know *how* the Lord will judge but rather to be ready for that judgment at any hour. S.W.

SECOND SUNDAY OF ADVENT

LECTIONARY #4

READING I   Isaiah 11.1–10

A reading from the book of the Prophet Isaiah.

Isaiah = ī-ZAY-uh

The tone of this potent reading is hopeful.

Jesse = JES-ee

Though not emphasized rhythmically, note how often "shall" is used in this reading. Let this word—and the hopeful, future tense in which it is set—guide your proclamation.

On **that** day:
A **shoot** shall come **out** from the **stump** of **Jesse**,
and a **branch** shall **grow** out of his **roots**.
The **spirit** of the **Lord** shall **rest** on him,
the **spirit** of **wisdom** and **understanding**,
the **spirit** of **counsel** and **might**,
the **spirit** of **knowledge** and the **fear** of the **Lord**.
His **delight** shall be in the **fear** of the **Lord**.
He **shall not judge** by what his **eyes** see,
or **decide** by what his **ears hear**;
but with **righteousness** he shall **judge** the **poor**,
and **decide** with **equity** for the **meek** of the **earth**;
he shall **strike** the **earth** with the **rod** of his **mouth**,
and with the **breath** of his **lips** he shall **kill** the **wicked**.
Righteousness shall be the **belt** around his **waist**,
and **faithfulness** the **belt** around his **loins**.
The **wolf** shall live with the **lamb**,
the **leopard** shall lie **down** with the **kid**,
the **calf** and the **lion** and the **fatling together**,
and a **little child** shall **lead** them.
The **cow** and the **bear** shall **graze**,
their **young** shall lie down **together**;
and the **lion** shall eat **straw** like the **ox**.

The images of animals help to focus the reading, making it vivid.

READING I   Ancient Israelite theology bases the coming of the messiah upon three events. First, the anointed one will come from the line of David. Second, this righteous king will establish justice in the land. Finally, all of creation will be restored to the peace found in the original garden of Eden. In essence, the messianic age will see the establishment of right relationship on earth: right relationship among humans, between humans and God, and within the entire sweep of living things. All creatures will live in the harmony God intended for his creation when he spoke his word and brought life into being.

"The stump of Jesse" that Isaiah refers to in the opening line reveals the present state of the ruling institution in Israel. For too many generations, Israel has known corrupt and self-seeking kings who have proven themselves unfaithful. But God promises to renew this kingship by sending his spirit who will inspire right judgment (counsel, strength, knowledge) and will ensure the king's proper reverence of God (fear of the Lord).

Unlike the wicked and unfaithful kings of recent generations, the spirit-filled king will execute justice throughout the land. This leader will act swiftly to overturn past sins. The poor and the afflicted will receive special attention, while the ruthless and the wicked shall be struck down. This is a king who will not have to use the sword to punish the unjust; rather, his words alone will restore justice. His entire strength will come from his worldview of justice and faithfulness.

Finally, this chosen envoy of God will not only restore right relationship within

Emphasis on "destroy."

The **nursing child** shall **play** over the **hole** of the **asp**,
and the **weaned child** shall put its **hand** on the **adder's den**.
They will not **hurt** or **destroy**
on **all** my holy **mountain**;
for the **earth** will be **full** of the **knowledge** of the **Lord**
as the **waters** cover the **sea**.
On **that day** the **root** of **Jesse** shall **stand**
as a **signal** to the **peoples**;
the **nations** shall **inquire** of him,
and his **dwelling** shall be **glorious**.

Don't overdo the emphasis on "glorious."

For meditation and context:

TO KEEP IN MIND
Read the Scripture passage and its commentary in Workbook. Then read it from your Bible, including what comes before and after it, so that you understand the context.

RESPONSORIAL PSALM Psalm 72.1–2, 7–8, 12–13, 17 (R. see 7)

R. In his days may righteousness flourish, and peace abound forever.

Give the king your justice, O God,
and your righteousness to a king's son.
May he judge your people with
    righteousness,
and your poor with justice.

In his days may righteousness flourish
and peace abound, until the moon
    is no more.
May he have dominion from sea to sea,
and from the River to the ends of the earth.

For he delivers the needy one who calls,
the poor and the one who has no helper.
He has pity on the weak and the needy,
and saves the lives of the needy.

May his name endure forever,
his fame continue as long as the sun.
May all nations be blessed in him;
may they pronounce him happy.

READING II Romans 15.4–9

A reading from the Letter of Saint Paul to the Romans.

Brothers and **sisters**:
Whatever was **written** in **former days**
was **written** for our **instruction**,
so that by **steadfastness**
and by the **encouragement** of the **Scriptures** we might
    have **hope**. »

The tone of this reading is hopeful.

Judea, but he will end wars and discord among every faction on earth. No more will the world be guided by fear of others and by predatory relationships. The curse brought about by the serpent's sin in the garden of Eden (Genesis 2.19) will come to an end as "the cow and the bear shall graze" together. The kingdom of God is founded upon a just order in which no creature competes with another for survival. Instead of functioning according to competition, God's kingdom manifests itself in selfless cooperation. The passage ends with the reminder that "the root of Jesse,"

this just king, will be a sign for all the nations; God's kingdom of right relationship is to extend through all the world.

READING II Chapter 15 of Paul's letter to the Romans aims at replacing dissension within the community with an attitude of harmony. He speaks not merely of Christ-like hospitality but of the way of mercy. The problem the Roman community faces is the divide between the circumcised and the uncircumcised and the debate as to whether circumcision is necessary to become a follower of Christ. This

was a community composed of both Jewish and Gentile members. How were they to follow the Christian way with different ethnic practices?

For Paul, the answer lies in "steadfastness" and through "the encouragement of the Scriptures." The Word of God is filled with examples of divine patience, and it is only fitting that communities discover hope in this Word. Paul suggests that fidelity to the Word will yield a sense of true unity by which the community thinks in harmony and speaks with one voice. It is this harmony that makes for true worship; God's

"May" indicates that Paul is making a petition.

May the **God** of **steadfastness** and **encouragement**
grant you to **live** in **harmony** with one **another**,
in **accordance** with **Christ Jesus**,
so that **together** you may with **one voice**
glorify the **God** and **Father** of our **Lord Jesus Christ**.
Welcome one another, therefore, just as **Christ**
        has welcomed **you**,
for the **glory** of **God**.

"Welcome" redirects the hope to Paul's audience.

circumcised = SER-kuhm-sīz*d

For I **tell** you
that **Christ** has become a **servant** of the **circumcised**
on **behalf** of the **truth** of **God**
in **order** that he might **confirm** the **promises** given
        to the **patriarchs**,

patriarchs = PAY-tree-ahrks

Gentiles = JEN-tīls

Scripture's authority emphasizes the hope.

and in **order** that the **Gentiles** might **glorify God** for his **mercy**.
As it is **written**,
"**Therefore** I will **confess** you among the **Gentiles**,
and sing **praises** to your **name**."

GOSPEL   Matthew 3.1–12

A reading from the holy Gospel according to Matthew.

A very vivid story is told in this Gospel reading.

Judea = joo-DEE-uh or joo-DAY-uh

Isaiah = ī-ZAY-uh

In **those days John** the **Baptist**
appeared in the **wilderness** of **Judea**, **proclaiming**,
"**Repent**, for the **kingdom** of **heaven** has come **near**."
This is the one of whom the **Prophet Isaiah spoke**
when he **said**,
"The **voice** of one crying **out** in the **wilderness**:
'**Prepare** the **way** of the **Lord**,
make his **paths straight**.'"
Now **John** wore **clothing** of **camel's hair**
with a **leather belt around** his **waist**,
and his **food** was **locusts** and **wild honey**.

Slight pause between "belt" and "around."

---

name cannot be glorified if people's hearts are torn apart in discord.

The final portion of this passage alludes to the core problem that separates the community in Rome, namely the status of those members who have not been baptized. Paul suggests that a spirit of welcome is necessary in order to overcome such a division. Furthermore, he writes that Christ came to those who were already circumcised as a sign of God's fidelity to the people of the covenant, but he also has a plan to include the Gentiles according to his gift of mercy. What Paul is saying here is

that the Romans, and in fact all of the Gentiles, are not an afterthought in God's mighty plan of salvation but are very much part of the reason for which God sent his Son into the world. Thus, Paul cites Psalm 18.50 as proof: "Therefore I will confess you among the Gentiles, and sing praises to your name."

GOSPEL In the layout of Matthew's Gospel, the figure of John the Baptist serves as a bridge between the infancy narrative and the inauguration of Jesus' public ministry. While it is clear that

John's ministry was one of calling Israel to repentance and to a baptism that would mark their restored allegiance to God and the coming of the kingdom of heaven, at some point, John became acutely aware that his cousin, Jesus, would play a particularly important role in heralding God's plan of salvation. In other words, while John's preaching did not initially point to Jesus, he became convinced that Jesus is God's revelation.

No matter when John came to believe in the power of Jesus' ministry, it is clear that Matthew wishes to cast John in the role

Pharisees = FAYR-uh-seez
Sadducees = SAD-yoo-seez

Emphasis on "brood" and "vipers."

Slight pause between "up" and "children."

Emphasis on the pronouns as this reading concludes, especially as John the Baptist switches from first to third person.

Then the **people** of **Jerusalem** and **all Judea**
were going **out** to him,
and **all** the **region along** the Jordan,
and they were **baptized** by him in the **river Jordan**,
confessing their **sins**.
But when he **saw** many **Pharisees** and **Sadducees coming**
    for **baptism**,
John **said** to them,
"You **brood** of **vipers**!
Who warned you to **flee** from the **wrath** to **come**?
Bear **fruit** worthy of **repentance**.
Do **not presume** to **say** to **yourselves**,
'We have **Abraham** as our **father**';
for I **tell** you, **God** is able from **these stones**
to **raise up children** to **Abraham**.
Even now the axe is **lying** at the **root** of the **trees**;
every tree therefore that **does not bear good fruit**
is **cut down** and **thrown** into the **fire**.
I baptize you with **water** for **repentance**,
but one who is more **powerful** than **I** is coming **after** me;
I **am not worthy** to **carry** his **sandals**.
He will baptize you with the **Holy Spirit** and fire.
His **winnowing fork** is in his **hand**,
and he will **clear** his **threshing** floor
and will **gather** his **wheat** into the **granary**;
but the **chaff** he will **burn** with unquenchable **fire**."

of a subordinate. It is likely that Matthew wants the reader to see John as a radical outlier—he wears camel hair clothing and eats wild locusts as his diet. Thus, while John the Baptist is the precursor of the Lord, there ought to be no mistake that John is to remain always in the shadow of Jesus.

Interestingly, John attacks two major power players that will later criticize the actions of Jesus, namely the Pharisees and the Sadducees. The Pharisees are best known as strict keepers of the Mosaic law, while the Sadducees represented the priestly class and thus the work of the Temple. Here, in the context of his summoning an attitude of repentance on the part of the people, John uses them as examples of hypocrisy that will surely not give way to the conversion he is calling for. John suggests that even if they are unable to be transformed by the authority of his preaching and ministry of baptism, then they ought to prepare for the power and authority they will face in the one who is to come after him. Thus, the role that John the Baptist plays of bridging the birth of Jesus with his ministry is not simply one of a polite introduction, but rather, his words leave no doubt that the words and work of Jesus will be nothing like the world has ever seen before. Jesus baptizing "with the Holy Spirit and fire" and his figurative clearing of the threshing floor will serve to transform all opposed to the coming of God's kingdom. S.W.

THE IMMACULATE CONCEPTION OF THE BLESSED VIRGIN MARY

LECTIONARY #689

READING I   Genesis 3.9–15, 20

Genesis = JEN-uh-sihs

This reading contains some of the conclusion of one of the foundational narratives of our faith. Because it is a very familiar story, slow your recitation slightly to emphasize its richness.

The shifting of blame from Adam to Eve and then from Eve to the serpent is crucial to the reading's drama. You can locate this shift in the repetition of the word "woman."

Here, the scorn is heaped on the serpent. The punishment God metes out is as cruel as it is deserved.

A reading from the book of Genesis.

When **Adam** had **eaten** from the **tree**,
the Lord God **called** to him, and said, "Where **are** you?"
The man said, "I **heard** the **sound** of you in the **garden**,
and I was **afraid**, because I was **naked**; and I **hid myself**."
God said, "Who **told** you that you were **naked**?
Have you **eaten** from the **tree** of which I **commanded** you
      not to **eat**?"
The man said, "The **woman** whom you gave to be **with** me,
she **gave me fruit** from the **tree**, and I **ate**."
Then the Lord God said to the **woman**,
"What is **this** that you have **done**?"
The woman said, "The **serpent tricked me**, and I **ate**."
The Lord God said to the **serpent**,
"**Because** you have done this,
cursed are you among **all animals**
and among all **wild creatures**;
upon your **belly** you shall **go**,
and **dust** you shall **eat**
all the **days** of your **life**.

READING I Today's reading from Genesis, which focuses on the primeval account of the origins of human sinfulness, opens with God strolling through his beautiful garden. Certainly, some time has passed since Adam and Eve committed their sin of disobedience, since Adam exhibits both fear and shame for being naked. When God begins to question Adam, it is important to notice how the blame is passed from Adam to the woman to the serpent. Thus, in addition to fear and shame, the sin of denial of responsibility, or

the failure to own up to one's mistakes, is revealed in the passing of blame.

With the sins committed in Eden comes the introduction of judgment into the world. Now God must decide a punishment according to participation in the sin. The author of Genesis is very careful to pair the punishment with the life experience of each sinner. God begins by punishing the snake and separating it from all other animals by making it crawl on its belly; it is therefore cursed by a perpetual posture of humility, unable to stand upright. The ser-

pent will no longer hold a persuasive influence over God's human creatures. Between the serpent and the human there will now be "enmity." This state of discord will continue throughout all subsequent generations of the woman's offspring, meaning that humans forever more will have to contend with the ugliness of sin in their lives.

Today's reading omits the verses in which God doles out punishments for both Adam and Eve (Genesis 3.16–19). God turns first to the woman and punishes her with intense pain in childbearing as well as

enmity = EN-mih-tee = mutual hatred

I will put **enmity** between **you** and the **woman**,
and between your **offspring** and hers;
he will **strike** your **head**,
and you will **strike** his **heel**."
The man named his wife "**Eve**,"
because she was the **mother** of **all** the **living**.

The reading ends with Eve being named. The shift from "woman" to "Eve" feels significant. Convey this in your reading.

For meditation and context:

RESPONSORIAL PSALM   Psalm 98.1, 2–3ab, 3cd–4 (R.1a)

R. Sing to the Lord a new song, for he has done marvellous things.

O sing to the Lord a new song,
for he has done marvellous things.
His right hand and his holy arm
have brought him victory.

The Lord has made known his victory;
he has revealed his vindication in the sight
    of the nations.
He has remembered his steadfast love
and faithfulness to the house of Israel.

All the ends of the earth have seen
the victory of our God.
Make a joyful noise to the Lord, all the earth;
break forth into joyous song and sing praises.

READING II   Ephesians 1.3–6, 11–12

A reading from the Letter of Saint Paul to the Ephesians.

Blessed be the **God** and **Father** of our **Lord** Jesus Christ,
who has **blessed** us in Christ
with **every spiritual blessing** in the **heavenly places**,
just as he chose us in **Christ** before the **foundation** of the **world**
to be **holy** and **blameless** before him in **love**.
He **destined** us for **adoption** to **sonship** as his own
through **Jesus** Christ,
according to the **good pleasure** of his will,
to the **praise** of his **glorious** grace
that he **freely bestowed** on us in the **Beloved**. »

Ephesians = ee-FEE-zhuhnz

Blessed = BLES-uhd

An exhortatory reading. Notice the three divisions: "Blessed be the God and Father . . . ," "He destined us . . . ," and "In Christ." Use these divisions to organize your reading.

Slight emphasis on "praise," "glorious," and "grace."

---

having to toil with domination imposed by a husband (Genesis 3.16). Finally, God speaks to Adam and bestows upon him the punishment of having to struggle with the land in order to produce food to eat (Genesis 3.17–19). The story ends on a positive note, as punishment gives way to hope for new life. Adam names the woman Eve, because she will be the "mother of all the living." Thus, even though sin has entered the world and has marred the beauty of perfection with the sins of disobedience, fear, shame, and denial, God will not abandon his creation—life will triumph over sin.

READING II The Letter to the Ephesians is one of several documents that is said to have been written by Paul but most likely was penned by one of his disciples ten or so years after his death. Unlike many of the letters in which Paul writes to a Christian community to challenge their behaviour, the Letter to the Ephesians is constructed to champion several important facets of Christian doctrine.

In this particular portion of Ephesians, the subject matter revolves around the topic of "predestination." The author states that God "chose us in Christ before the

foundation of the world." The intention of this choice is so that we may live lives of holiness. Furthermore, the author suggests that it is not simply a predetermined choice for us to stand before God without stain, but rather, in time God is able to exercise his love by uniting us with his Son. In other words, God's love for us is bestowed as an act of mercy, which we can acknowledge by giving him all praise and glory. Paul challenges the Ephesians to recognize the abundance of God's grace that has been bestowed upon them through their faith in Christ. While they have been chosen, they

This is Paul's point.

You are assuring the assembly of this first hope.

In **Christ** we have **also** obtained an **inheritance**,
having been **destined** according to the **purpose** of him
who **accomplishes** all things according to his **counsel** and **will**,
so that **we**, who were the **first** to set our **hope** on **Christ**,
might **live** for the **praise** of his **glory**.

GOSPEL   Luke 1.26–38

A reading from the holy Gospel according to Luke.

A narrative reading of one of the most solemn passages in the Gospels, which is also one of the most frequently depicted by artists through the centuries. It's very easy to visualize as a result. Treat it like a pageant.

Because these words are so familiar from prayer, they can have a new life in the context of this reading.

"Most High" and "no end" share a rhythmical and thematic echo.

The **Angel Gabriel** was **sent** by God
to a **town** in **Galilee** called **Nazareth**,
to a **virgin engaged** to a man whose name was **Joseph**,
of the **house** of David.
The **virgin's name** was Mary.
And he came to her and said,
"**Hail**, **full** of **grace**! The **Lord** is with **you**."
But she was **much perplexed** by his words
and **pondered** what sort of **greeting** this might be.
The **Angel** said to her,
"Do not be **afraid**, Mary, for you have found **favour** with God.
And now, you will **conceive** in your womb and **bear** a son,
and you will **name him** Jesus.
He will be **great**,
and will be called the Son of the **Most High**,
and the **Lord God** will give to him the **throne**
      of his **father David**.
He will **reign** over the house of **Jacob forever**,
and of his **kingdom** there will be **no end**."

must respond with their gift of constant thanksgiving.

As we celebrate the solemnity of the Immaculate Conception, it is important to reflect upon the abundance of grace that God poured upon Mary, whom he predestined to be the mother of his Son. The Letter to the Ephesians suggests that those chosen in Christ are destined to keep God's will and thereby "live for the praise of his glory." Our purpose as disciples is to radiate the goodness of God every moment of the day. We are invited to contemplate the mystery of Mary's Immaculate Conception,

because in her we see the perfect example of one who exists for nothing other than the praise of God's glory. In the Gospel passage that follows, the Angel Gabriel proclaims Mary to be "full of grace." Although we, unlike Mary, are born into this world with the stain of original sin and struggle to free ourselves of temptation and sin each day, we are also called to discover God's grace in every moment of our lives.

GOSPEL   Both the Gospel of Matthew and the Gospel of Luke contain an infancy narrative that begins with

signs of Jesus' conception. With that said, Matthew and Luke intend to use the signs of the Lord's birth for different purposes. Matthew emphasizes the role of Joseph and his righteousness in preparing for Jesus' birth, whereas in Luke, this role is transferred to Mary. She is the one who receives a message from the Angel and then runs to her cousin Elizabeth to announce to her all of the wonders that God has done for her.

The Gospel passage we read today is Luke's account of the Annunciation, when the Angel Gabriel appears to Mary and reveals God's plan for her. We are led to

This is the good news that Gabriel delivers to Mary.

Mary said to the **Angel**,
"How can this **be**, since I am a **virgin**?"
The Angel **said** to her,
"The **Holy Spirit** will **come upon** you,
and the **power** of the **Most High** will **overshadow** you;
therefore the **child** to be born will be **holy**;
he will be called **Son** of **God**.
And **now**,
your relative **Elizabeth** in her **old age** has **also conceived** a son;
and this is the **sixth month** for her who was said to be **barren**.
For **nothing** will be **impossible** with God."
Then Mary said,
"Here am **I**, the **servant** of the **Lord**;
let it be **done** to me according to **your word**."
Then the **Angel departed** from her.

Mary's declaration defines the role of all believers, including the Church.

TO KEEP IN MIND
Pause after you announce the book of the Bible at the beginning of the reading. Pause again after the reading, before you proclaim the concluding statement ("The word of the Lord" or "The Gospel of the Lord").

---

ponder the grace of Mary's sinlessness by focusing on her humble response to the Angel: "Here am I, the servant of the Lord; let it be done to me according to your word." Mary is the new Eve who is given the fullness of God's grace. However, unlike Eve, Mary remains obedient to God's voice throughout her life. Mary deserved to be fearful at what the Angel spoke to her, but she listened and obeyed.

While it is important to focus on Mary's obedience, this passage also invites us to reflect upon the nature of God. Why does God choose Mary to be the mother of his Son? God chooses a lowly virgin peasant girl to be the one who will bear the most precious gift of God's love, his very Son. If God had wanted, God could have been born among us in a very powerful and successful family. Or he could have manifested his divinity in a fully grown human person. Instead, his grace rested fully upon one who had no standing within her community. As a faithful Jewish girl, Mary was attuned to the working of God within her life. She listened carefully to God's will. Mary spent her life discerning his movement in her life and was well prepared to offer herself as the chosen ark for God's incarnation. Like Mary, we are invited to cooperate fully with God's will, giving our entire lives over in service of his kingdom.
S.W.

THIRD SUNDAY OF ADVENT

LECTIONARY #7

READING I   Isaiah 35.1–6a, 10

A reading from the book of the Prophet Isaiah.

Isaiah = ī-ZAY-uh

The tone of this reading is set by the early repetitions of "rejoice" and "blossom."

The **wilderness** and the **dry land** shall be **glad**,
the **desert** shall rejoice and **blossom**;
like the **crocus** it shall **blossom abundantly**,
and **rejoice** with joy and singing.
The **glory** of **Lebanon** shall be **given** to it,
the **majesty** of **Carmel** and Sharon.

Lebanon = LEB-uh-nuhn
Carmel = KAHR-m*l
Sharon = SHAYR-uhn

They shall **see** the **glory** of the **Lord**,
the **majesty** of our **God**.

Note the shift into imperatives: "strengthen," "make," and "say."

Strengthen the **weak hands**,
and **make** firm the **feeble knees**.
Say to **those** who are of a **fearful heart**,
"Be **strong**, do not **fear**!
Here is your **God**.
He will **come** with **vengeance**,
with **terrible recompense**.
He will **come** and **save** you."
Then the **eyes** of the **blind** shall be **opened**,
and the **ears** of the **deaf unstopped**;
then the **lame** shall **leap** like a **deer**,

Slight pause between "mute" and "sing."

and the **tongue** of the **mute sing** for **joy**.

READING I The thirty-fifth chapter of the Book of Isaiah serves as something of a bridge between First and Second Isaiah. (Scholars typically divide the Book of Isaiah into three main parts, First, Second, and Third Isaiah.) While it continues much of the deliverance material found in the first part of Isaiah, the chapter introduces a theme that will be significant throughout Second Isaiah, namely, the people's journey home after exile. What is portrayed here is a world transformed. Isaiah's prophecy presents a series of grand reversals, images that demonstrate God's power to rejuvenate and fully restore his deflated people.

The desert, through which the people sojourn on their way back to Judea, has been made abundantly beautiful with foliage and the joyful song of the pilgrims. As the Israelites take possession of the land once again, the cities of Lebanon, Carmel, and Sharon radiate God's glory.

Such images of renewal will certainly make strong hands that are weak and hearts that are frightened. Isaiah continues by making clear that God is not blessing his people from a distance. Just as he guided his people through the desert after ratifying the covenant with Moses on Mount Sinai, so now God comes into their midst to save them. At his coming, blind eyes will see, deaf ears will hear, the lame will leap, and all those who return to Jerusalem will sing a song that will serve to overturn "sorrow and sighing" with "joy and gladness." Isaiah beautifully portrays the redeemed people successfully entering the gates of Jerusalem.

READING II Scholars liken the reading to wisdom literature as it contains a variety of loosely connected

And the **ransomed** of the **Lord** shall **return**,
and **come** to **Zion** with **singing**;
everlasting joy shall **be** upon their **heads**;
they shall obtain joy and **gladness**,
and **sorrow** and **sighing** shall flee **away**.

Zion = Zĭ-uhn or Zĭ-ahn

TO KEEP IN MIND
Smile when you share good news.
Nonverbal cues like a smile help the
assembly understand the reading.

For meditation and context:

RESPONSORIAL PSALM   Psalm 146.6c–7, 8–9a, 9b–10 (R. see Isa 35.4)

**R. Lord, come and save us.
or: Alleluia!**

It is the Lord who keeps faith forever,
who executes justice for the oppressed;
who gives food to the hungry.
The Lord sets the prisoners free.

The Lord opens the eyes of the blind
and lifts up those who are bowed down;
the Lord loves the righteous
and watches over the strangers.

The Lord upholds the orphan and the widow,
but the way of the wicked he brings to ruin.
The Lord will reign forever,
your God, O Zion, for all generations.

READING II   James 5.7–10

A reading from the Letter of Saint James.

Be **patient**, **brothers** and **sisters**, until the **coming** of the **Lord**.
The **farmer waits** for the precious **crop** from the **earth**,
being **patient** with it until it **receives** the **early**
            and the **late rains**.
You also must be **patient**.
Strengthen your **hearts**,
for the **coming** of the **Lord** is **near**.
Brothers and **sisters**, do not **grumble against** one **another**,
so that you may **not** be **judged**.
See, the **Judge** is **standing** at the **doors**!
As an example of **suffering** and **patience**, **brothers** and **sisters**,
take the **Prophets** who **spoke** in the **name** of the **Lord**.

The tone of this reading is gentle.

Note the repetitions of "patient."

The tone becomes firmer in the second half
of the reading; allow your proclamation to
reflect this shift.

---

moral exhortations. Much of the material bears a great similarity to the sayings of Jesus found in Matthew and Luke that are attributed to the Q source. The bulk of these exhortations are oriented to turning people away from the ways of the world to seek the wisdom of heaven, where injustice and poverty have no home.

The word "patient" occurs three times in today's short excerpt from the letter. The author exhorts his audience to have the patience of a farmer who has great expectations for the sprouting and growth of the seeds that he has planted. The patience

James calls for is not mere waiting but is a sort of hopeful yearning. There is much hope that the wait will be worth all that is to come. James encourages those who wait patiently to make firm their hearts. Thus, they are not to be distracted by other alluring forces of this world that may draw their attention away from the Lord's return, which "is near."

In a state of expectant waiting, it is possible that someone could become impatient with and cast judgment upon those uninterested in waiting. James cautions against the temptation to complain about

others. Instead, those who await the Lord's return should look to the example provided by the Prophets. The suffering and the hardship of those who attend to the Lord will witness to a world redeemed and living in the justice of God.

GOSPEL   The animated discussion between the disciples of John the Baptist and Jesus embodies the early Church's struggle to understand the nature of Jesus as the Messiah. The disciples of John were concerned with the dawning of God's kingdom and wanted to

GOSPEL   Matthew 11.2–11

A reading from the holy Gospel according to Matthew.

When **John** the **Baptist heard** in **prison** about the **deeds**
    of the **Christ**,
he sent **word** by his **disciples**
who said to **Jesus**,
"Are you the **one** who is to **come**,
or are we to **wait** for **another**?"
Jesus **answered** them,
"Go and tell **John** what you **hear** and **see**:
the **blind** receive their **sight**,
the **lame walk**, the **lepers** are **cleansed**,
the **deaf hear**, the **dead** are **raised**,
and the **poor** have good **news brought** to them.
And **blessed** is **anyone** who takes **no** offence at **me**."
As they went **away**,
Jesus began to **speak** to the **crowds** about **John**:
"**What** did you go **out** into the **wilderness** to **look** at?
A reed **shaken** by the **wind**?
What **then** did you go **out** to **see**?
Someone **dressed** in s**oft robes**?
Look, **those** who wear **soft robes** are in **royal palaces**.
What **then** did you go **out** to **see**?
A **Prophet**?
Yes, I **tell** you, and **more** than a **Prophet**.
This is the one about **whom** it is **written**,
'**See**, I am sending my **messenger ahead** of you,
who will **prepare your way** before you.'
Truly I **tell** you, among those **born** of **women**
no one has arisen **greater** than **John** the **Baptist**;
yet the **least** in the **kingdom** of **heaven** is **greater** than **he**."

The tone in this narrative reading is urgent.

Note the pairs: "blind" and "sight," "lame" and "walk," and so forth.

Slight pause between "good news" and "brought."

blessed = BLES-uhd

Jesus offers a series of urgent questions by way of setting up his praise of John the Baptist.

Slight pause between "way" and "before."

Emphasis on "greater."

stir up a spirit of repentance among the people. Matthew chose these dedicated disciples to be the ones who prompt Jesus to reveal the nature and purpose of his mission. They serve the role of verifying the authority of Jesus at a crucial juncture in Matthew's Gospel, for in the previous chapter Jesus commissions the twelve Apostles to go out into the world in his name, and now, in chapter 11, Jesus begins to face controversy, especially the challenge waged by the Pharisees.

When John's disciples ask Jesus point-blank whether he is "the one who is to come," Jesus does not answer with a straightforward yes or no. Instead, he points to the results of his ministry: the blind see, the crippled walk, the sick are healed, the deaf hear, and the dead are raised to new life. Jesus concludes the list with the statement "And blessed is anyone who takes no offence at me." This suggests that he knows how an influential segment of the population will soon reject his ministry. Jesus manifests a messiah who is compassionate and just. This is far different from the image of the messiah popularized by the religious establishment of that time and from the

one John predicted (Matthew 3.10), who was full of judgment and power.

Jesus then invites the crowds to look beyond their superficial view of John. He calls John the greatest of "those born of women." Nevertheless, Jesus states that "the least in the kingdom of heaven" are even greater than John. Who are the least? They are the ones who have been touched by encounter with Jesus, they are his disciples, they are the ones who take no offense at what he does. S.W.

FOURTH SUNDAY OF ADVENT

LECTIONARY #10

READING I   Isaiah 7.10–14

A reading from the book of the Prophet Isaiah.

The **Lord** spoke to **Ahaz**, saying,
"**Ask** a **sign** of the **Lord** your **God**;
let it be **deep** as **Sheol** or **high** as **heaven**."
But **Ahaz** said, "I **will not ask**,
and I will **not** put the **Lord** to the **test**."
Then **Isaiah** said:
"**Hear** then, O **house** of **David**!
Is it **too little** for **you** to **weary** the **people**,
that you **weary** my God **also**?
Therefore the Lord **himself** will give you a **sign**.
Look, the young **woman** is with **child** and shall **bear a son**,
and shall **name** him **Emmanuel**."

Ahaz = AY-haz
The tone of this reading is prophetic.
It has a solemn, imaginative quality.

Note the repetition of "weary," which you
can emphasize, slightly.

The reading concludes with a prophecy.
Proclaim it in a solemn and straightforward
voice.

Emmanuel = ee-MAN-yoo-el

For meditation and context:

RESPONSORIAL PSALM   Psalm 24.1–2, 3–4ab, 5–6 (R.7c+10b)

R. May the Lord come in; he is king of glory.

The earth is the Lord's and all that is in it,
the world, and those who live in it;
for he has founded it on the seas,
and established it on the rivers.

Who shall ascend the hill of the Lord?
And who shall stand in his holy place?
Someone who has clean hands and a
   pure heart,
who does not lift up their soul to what
   is false.

That person will receive blessing from
   the Lord,
and vindication from the God of their
   salvation.
Such is the company of those who seek him,
who seek the face of the God of Jacob.

READING I The story of Ahaz is situated in an eighth-century BC political conflict. As king of Judah, Ahaz needs to make a critical choice: whether to submit to Assyria and be counted among one of its territories or to join an alliance with the northern tribe of Israel. With the help of Isaiah's prompting, Ahaz makes the decision to rely on the help of God and to act independently of Israel, since Isaiah prophesies that this will lead to destruction.

Isaiah is once again at work with Ahaz as we enter into today's reading. Ahaz has another difficult decision to make: to ask God for a sign of his providence or not. Isaiah suggests that if Ahaz asks for a sign that God is supporting him, it could come in the form of something truly spectacular; it could be something deep within the sea or something as lofty as the skies. Ahaz should not be hesitant to ask for such a sign. However, Ahaz has made up his mind that he will not ask God to provide a sign.

Nevertheless, despite the king's trust in God, Isaiah knows the heart of the people, who yearn for God to prove himself to be providential. Thus, he informs the kingdom of Judah that it will be given a sign, and the sign is to be a virgin giving birth to a son who is to be named "Emmanuel." This name itself, meaning "God-with-us," suggests that God will continue to be with his people. Because this prophecy has been made to the house of David, it takes on a messianic nature that is linked with the Davidic kingdom found in 2 Samuel 7.2–16.

READING II Paul opens his letter to the Romans with a summary statement of the incarnation of the Son of God that proceeds through to his lordship as the resurrected Christ. In his greeting,

READING II   Romans 1.1–7

A reading from the Letter of Saint Paul to the Romans.

From **Paul**, a **servant** of **Jesus Christ**,
called to be an **Apostle**,
set **apart** for the **Gospel** of **God**,
which **God** promised **beforehand**
through his Prophets in the holy **Scriptures**:
the **Gospel** concerning his **Son**,
who was **descended** from **David according** to the **flesh**
and was **declared** to be **Son** of **God** with **power**
according to the **spirit** of **holiness**
by **resurrection** from the **dead**,
Jesus Christ our **Lord**.
Through Christ we have received **grace** and **apostleship**
to bring about the **obedience** of **faith**
among **all** the **Gentiles** for the **sake** of his **name**,
including **yourselves** who are **called** to **belong** to Jesus **Christ**.
To all God's **beloved** in **Rome**,
who are called to be **saints**:
Grace to you and **peace** from **God** our **Father**
and the **Lord** Jesus **Christ**.

The tone of this reading, which begins Paul's letter to the Romans, is unusual. It's a list of qualifications, almost like a spiritual resumé.

Emphasis on "Through Christ."

Even emphasis on "yourselves."

Paul does not simply introduce himself by name, but he provides several indicators of his authority. First, Paul identifies himself as "a servant of Christ Jesus." This does not mean that Paul is held captive against his own will but rather that he has committed himself totally to Christ. Second, Paul refers to himself as an "Apostle," an eyewitness to the Lord's Resurrection. Finally, like the Prophets of old, Paul has been "set apart" for the task of preaching the Gospel. Paul's audience would be foolish to reject his authority.

After Paul gives witness to the authority of Christ, namely that he was born of the flesh according to the line of David but is to be named the "Son of God," being born of the Spirit, Paul proceeds to extend his mission to those who are receiving his letter. Paul tells the Romans that they, too, "have received grace and apostleship." Although they have never seen the resurrected Christ in bodily form, their authority comes from "the obedience of faith." It is this faith that allows the Romans to "belong to Jesus Christ" and to share in the mission "to be saints." In these few lines, Paul has

clearly opened the way for his challenging word to be heard among the Christians at Rome. While he blesses them with the gifts of "grace" and "peace," he will likewise challenge the community to establish unity among Gentile and Jewish members. He writes to a community he calls "God's beloved," the holy ones of Rome; surely they feel a summons to live up to their name.

GOSPEL   Matthew has just finishing detailing the lineage from which Jesus flows, the impressive genealogy

GOSPEL   Matthew 1.18–24

A reading from the holy Gospel according to Matthew.

The **birth** of **Jesus** the **Christ** took **place** in **this way**.
When his **mother Mary** had been **engaged** to **Joseph**,
but **before** they lived **together**,
she was **found** to be with child from the **Holy Spirit**.
Her husband **Joseph**, being a **righteous man**
and **unwilling** to **expose** her to **public disgrace**,
planned to **dismiss** her **quietly**.
But **just** when he had **resolved** to **do** this,
an **Angel** of the **Lord appeared** to him in a **dream** and **said**,
"**Joseph**, son of **David**,
do not be afraid to take **Mary** as your **wife**,
for the child **conceived** in her is from the **Holy Spirit**.
She will **bear** a **son**,
and you are to **name** him **Jesus**,
for he will **save** his **people** from their **sins**."
All this took place
to **fulfill** what had been **spoken** by the **Lord**
        through the **Prophet**:
"**Look**, the **virgin** shall **conceive** and bear a **son**,
and they shall name him **Emmanuel**,"
which means, "**God** is **with** us."
When **Joseph awoke** from **sleep**,
he **did** as the **Angel** of the Lord **commanded** him;
he **took** her as his **wife**.

The rich tone of this familiar story is mysterious. "This way" is the phrase that initiates the mystery.

The word "appeared" initiates the angelic vision of the reading.

Emphasis on "all this took place."

Here, "Look" reinforces the scriptural vision of the events depicted.
Emmanuel = ee-MAN-yoo-el

that ends with the proclamation that Jesus is called the "Christ." Now Matthew continues his theological examination of the Incarnation by demonstrating how Jesus is both Son of God and son of Mary.

At the outset of the reading is the conflict that originates from Mary both being betrothed to Joseph and found to be pregnant. However, unlike those who discovered Mary's pregnancy, we are told of its divine origins, namely that this pregnancy came about "from the Holy Spirit." Nevertheless, we are meant to struggle with the potential outcome of this serious charge. Although

Joseph and Mary were betrothed, they were not married; therefore, this offense could be punished by death. Joseph's decision to quietly divorce her demonstrates his concern to protect Mary from the law. However, his mind is changed when careful discernment of a dream leads him to take Mary as his wife and to bring her into the protection of his home. He must have recognized that God would keep them from all harm.

The passage ends with a bit of commentary from Matthew. He tells us that this encounter between the Angel and Joseph was meant to allow for the fulfillment of

Isaiah's prophecy that a virgin shall give birth to a son and that he will be named "Emmanuel." The beginning of Matthew's Gospel is clearly meant to impress upon his audience that through the bloodline of David and through the obedient listening of one of its own, Joseph, God would be with his people. S.W.

CHRISTMAS: THE NATIVITY OF THE LORD (VIGIL MASS)

LECTIONARY #13

READING I   Isaiah 62.1–5

A reading from the book of the Prophet Isaiah.

For **Zion's** sake I will **not** keep **silent**,
and for **Jerusalem's** sake I will **not rest**,
until her **vindication shines out** like the **dawn**,
and her **salvation** like a **burning torch**.
The **nations** shall **see** your **vindication**,
and all the **kings** your **glory**;
and you shall be **called** by a new **name**
that the **mouth** of the **Lord** will give.
You shall be a **crown of beauty** in the **hand** of the **Lord**,
and a **royal diadem** in the hand of your God.
You shall no more be termed **Forsaken**,
and your land shall no more be termed **Desolate**;
but you shall be called **My Delight Is in Her**,
and your land **Married**;
for the Lord **delights** in you,
and your land shall be **married**.
For as a young man marries a young **woman**,
so shall your **builder** marry you,
and as the **bridegroom rejoices** over the **bride**,
so shall your God rejoice over **you**.

Isaiah = ī-ZAY-uh

Notice the repetitions of the phrase "you shall." Pace your reading with each expression of "you shall" (or its variations) as a marker.

Notice the sound carried from "Zion's" to "silent" to "rest."

diadem = DĪ-uh-dem = crown

Give extra emphasis to each of these four names.

Even emphasis on all the words in this last line, with extra added on "you."

There are options for today's readings. Contact your parish staff to learn which readings will be used.

READING I   The four weeks of Advent serve as a time of preparation for the great feast of the Lord's Nativity, the Christian celebration of the mystery of the Incarnation. While much of our preparation has been meant to be "eschatological," in that we are patiently awaiting for Christ's return at the end time, thereby ushering in the completion of God's kingdom, the final portion of Advent allows us to prepare with joy for the celebration of the birth of Jesus in history. The Masses that constitute Christmas Day, beginning with the Vigil on December 24 through the Mass at Night and continuing through the Mass at Dawn and the Mass during the Day, balance artfully the two themes of eschatological waiting and joyful celebration for God's manifestation in the baby Jesus.

The Vigil's first reading, from the latter part of Isaiah (often referred to as Third or Trito-Isaiah), opens with a sense of victory. The one who witnesses Jerusalem's renewal is incapable of being silent, but instead, must proclaim in speech and in deed that she has been vindicated. Those who shall see the success of the nation are not simply its own citizens but peoples around the world. This restored creation will be a prized possession for God—"a crown of beauty" and "a royal diadem." Unlike the stance of waiting for a future glory to appear, the words of Isaiah represent a form of "realized eschatology," whereby salvation takes place now. The Israelites do not have to look forward to the future for God to prove his allegiance; they are able to see their chosen status in the present evidence.

For meditation and context:

RESPONSORIAL PSALM   Psalm 89.3–4, 15–16, 26+28 (R.1a)

R. Forever I will sing of your steadfast love, O Lord.

You said, "I have made a covenant with my
    chosen one,
I have sworn to my servant David:
I will establish your descendants forever,
and build your throne for all generations."

Blessed are the people who know the
    festal shout,
who walk, O Lord, in the light of
    your countenance;
they exult in your name all day long,
and extol your righteousness.

He shall cry to me, "You are my Father,
my God, and the Rock of my salvation!"
Forever I will keep my steadfast love for him,
and my covenant with him will stand firm.

READING II   Acts 13.16–17, 22–25

A reading from the Acts of the Apostles.

Antioch = AN-tee-ahk

A didactic reading that sets up a prophetic succession, beginning with the Israelites in the wilderness and moving from David to John the Baptist, and finally to Jesus.

When **Paul** arrived in **Antioch**,
he stood up in the synagogue,
held up his hand for silence, and began to speak:
"**Men of Israel**, and others who **fear God**, **listen**.
The God of this people **Israel** chose our **ancestors**
and made the people **great** during their **stay** in the land of Egypt,
and with **uplifted arm** he led them **out** of it.
When God **made David** their **king**,
in his **testimony** about him he said,
'I have found **David**, son of **Jesse**,
to be a **man** after my **heart**,
who will carry out **all** my **wishes**.'
Of this man's posterity
God has brought to Israel a **Saviour**, **Jesus**, as he **promised**;
before his coming
John had **already** proclaimed a **baptism** of **repentance**
to **all** the people of Israel. »

Though Paul is speaking in this reading, he is quoting the words of his predecessors. You can modulate your voice slightly to suggest this shift.

This is especially the case in the way in which the reading closes. Zion is portrayed as God's bride. Jerusalem is now to be called God's "Delight," for the land is his "Married." Such labels for Israel clearly express God's care and compassion for a people who have managed to stay faithful to him throughout the years of exile. The renewal of God's relationship with his people is so great that he approaches them "as a young man marries a young woman." In other translations, "young woman" is translated as "virgin," alluding to the likeness between this new Jerusalem and a virginal

state, without having been touched by another. Just as marriage is a sign of hope for many years of blessing to come, so too is the return of the people a sign of great hope that manifests itself in festal joy.

Our awaiting the perfection of God's kingdom as well as our celebration of God's incarnation in history ought to manifest the same hope and joy to every corner of the earth. As the Christian community gathers in prayer and vigil this night, the proclamation of God's victory ought to be welling up in every heart, preparing every member of the Church to proclaim from every moun-

tain peak and every rooftop that our God has come to save us.

| READING II | This reading opens with the continuing travels of Paul and Barnabas, who, having just left Pamphylia, have now arrived in the port of Antioch. As a major stop along a primary trade route, Antioch was a Roman colony with a significant population of Jewish citizens. Acts makes clear that Paul wastes no time, going immediately to the synagogue to share his message of Christ with the people.

Paul concludes with John the Baptist's memorable phrase about Jesus. A slight emphasis on "sandals" and "feet" will remind the assembly whose words these are.

And as John was finishing his work, he said,
'What do you suppose that I **am**?
I am not he.
No, but one is coming **after** me;
I am not **worthy** to untie the **thong** of the **sandals** on his **feet**.'"

GOSPEL   Matthew 1.1–25

A reading from the holy Gospel according to Matthew.

An account of the **genealogy** of **Jesus** the **Christ**,
the son of **David**, the son of **Abraham**.
Abraham was the father of **Isaac**,
Isaac the father of **Jacob**,
Jacob the father of **Judah** and his **brothers**,
Judah the father of **Perez** and **Zerah** by **Tamar**,
Perez the father of **Hezron**,
Hezron the father of **Aram**,
Aram the father of **Aminadab**,
Aminadab the father of **Nahshon**,
Nahshon the father of **Salmon**,
Salmon the father of **Boaz** by **Rahab**,
Boaz the father of **Obed** by **Ruth**,
Obed the father of **Jesse**,
and **Jesse** the father of **King David**.
And **David** was the father of **Solomon** by the wife of **Uriah**,
Solomon the father of **Rehoboam**,
Rehoboam the father of **Abijah**,
Abijah the father of **Asaph**,
Asaph the father of **Jehoshaphat**,
Jehoshaphat the father of **Joram**,
Joram the father of **Uzziah**,
Uzziah the father of **Jotham**,
Jotham the father of **Ahaz**,

A whopper of a reading. The first part of this reading is a performative, rhythmical incantation, one unusual name leading to the next. It goes from Abraham to David; from David to the Babylonian exile; from the Babylonian exile to Jesus. It's a folding screen with two hinges, each panel of the screen exactly the same size, and the image of Jesus' birth appears on its front.

genealogy = jee-nee-OL-uh-jee
Abraham = AY-bruh-ham; Isaac = Ī-zik
Judah = JOO-duh
Perez = PAYR-ez; Zerah = ZEE-rah

Only five women are included in this list.
Tamar = TAY-mahr
Hezron = HEZ-ruhn
Aram = AIR-am
Aminadab = uh-MIN-uh-dab
Nahshon = NAH-shon
Salmon = SAL-muhn
Boaz = BOH-az
Rahab = RAY-hab
Obed = OH-bed
Jesse = JES-ee
Uriah = yoo-RI-uh
Rehoboam = ree-huh-BOH-uhm
Abijah = uh-BĪ-juh
Asaph = AY-saf
Jehoshaphat = jeh-HOH-shuh-fat
Joram = JOHR-uhm
Uzziah = yuh-ZĪ-uh
Jotham = JOH-thuhm

Speaking to "men of Israel" and "others who fear God," Gentiles, Paul preaches with great poise and dexterity. His method is to trace the hand of God in significant historical events, demonstrating how God consistently acted to support and nurture his people. First, Paul announces that God chose the people of Israel through "our ancestors," with the moment of the exodus from Egypt as a primary example of God's demonstration of preferring Israel to every other nation on earth. Second, God proved himself providential in providing the right king at the right time for the people of

Israel as he replaced Saul by his anointing of David. Finally, God has provided a saviour for the people, Jesus, who has come to them through the lineage of David. Paul leaves no doubt that God has consistently proven his desire to protect and care for his people.

The passage ends with Paul referring to the testimony of John the Baptist. He portrays the Baptist as a trustworthy Prophet who had attracted the attention of "all the people of Israel." His authority was so great that many mistook him for the messiah. However, Paul repeats the familiar saying

of John that he claimed himself too unworthy to unlace the Messiah's sandals. What Paul has done in this fairly short exhortation is to make credible the word that he preaches. First, he has witnessed to the fidelity of God who journeyed with his people and protected them always, and second, God has seen fit to send the redeemer into the world through the bloodline of his chosen people. What God promised in his covenant with Israel has now been revealed in the one who has come to bring true and lasting freedom. The people of Antioch have

Ahaz = AY-haz
Hezekiah = hez-eh-KĪ-uh
Manasseh = muh-NAS-uh
Amos = AY-m*s
Josiah = joh-SĪ-uh
Jechoniah = jek-oh-NĪ-uh
Salathiel = sal-AL-tee-uhl
Zerubbabel = zuh-ROOB-uh-b*l
Abiud = uh-BĪ-uhd
Eliakim = ee-LĪ-uh-kim
Azor = AY-sohr
Zadok = ZAD-uhk
Achim = AH-kim
Eliud = ee-LĪ-uhd
Eleazar = el-ee-AY-zer
Matthan = MATH-uhn

Ahaz the father of **Hezekiah**,
Hezekiah the father of **Manasseh**,
Manasseh the father of **Amos**,
Amos the father of **Josiah**,
and **Josiah** the father of **Jechoniah** and his **brothers**,
at the time of the **deportation** to Babylon.
And after the deportation to **Babylon**:
Jechoniah was the father of **Salathiel**,
Salathiel the father of **Zerubbabel**,
Zerubbabel the father of **Abiud**,
Abiud the father of **Eliakim**,
Eliakim the father of **Azor**,
Azor the father of **Zadok**,
Zadok the father of **Achim**,
Achim the father of **Eliud**,
Eliud the father of **Eleazar**,
Eleazar the father of **Matthan**,
Matthan the father of **Jacob**,
and **Jacob** the father of **Joseph**, the husband of **Mary**,
of whom **Jesus** was born, who is called the **Christ**.
So all the **generations** from **Abraham** to **David**
       are **fourteen** generations;
from **David** to the **deportation** to **Babylon**, **fourteen** generations;
from the **deportation** to **Babylon** to the **Christ**,
       fourteen generations.
Now [the **birth** of Jesus the **Christ** took place in **this way**.
When his mother **Mary** had been engaged to Joseph,
but before they **lived** together,
she was found to be with **child** from the Holy **Spirit**.
Her **husband Joseph**, being a **righteous man**
and unwilling to expose her to **public disgrace**,
planned to **dismiss** her **quietly**.
But **just** when he had resolved to **do** this,
an **Angel** of the Lord appeared to him in a **dream** and said,
"**Joseph**, son of David, »

Now that Jesus' genealogy has been established, the story of his birth can be told. The focus is Joseph, the second-to-last name in the genealogy. Attune the dynamics of your reading to the figure of Joseph, with whom the assembly is meant to identify.

When the Angel says here Joseph's name, it is a summons. Read it that way.

every reason to listen to the message of salvation Paul brings to them.

GOSPEL Similar to Paul's preaching in Acts, which traced the critical events of salvation history that led to the coming of the Messiah, the genealogy at the beginning of Matthew's Gospel serves the function of substantiating the credibility of Jesus. The word *genealogy* comes from the root word *genesis*, which means the origins of someone or something. For example, the Book of Genesis contains the story of the origins of the world's foundation. Matthew opens his Gospel with the family tree of Jesus because he wants his readers to have no doubt that Jesus is in keeping with God's plan of salvation. God acts within the established framework of history.

It is important to consider the context in which Matthew writes his Gospel. Biblical scholars tell us that the composition of this Gospel takes place shortly after the destruction of the Jerusalem Temple by the Romans in AD 70. Matthew writes to a very Jewish audience who were faced with a significant decision: How are we meant to keep the covenant with God now that the Temple and sacrificial worship are no more? Matthew has an answer for them: Come to faith in Jesus, for he fulfills the covenant. No temple is required to follow after Jesus; instead, what is needed is faith in him through baptism and the keeping of his commands. Because Jesus fulfills the covenant, it is necessary that he be firmly positioned within Jewish history. For this reason, the story of Jesus' Nativity is preceded by this lengthy genealogy.

Matthew 1.1–25 is not an easy reading to proclaim, and it is one that many presiders

Joseph awaking is what happens to the assembly at this moment.

do not be afraid to take **Mary** as your wife,
for the child **conceived in her** is from the **Holy Spirit**.
She will **bear** a son,
and you are to name him **Jesus**,
for he will **save** his people from their **sins**."
All this took place
to **fulfill** what had been spoken by the Lord
        through the **Prophet**:
"**Look**, the **virgin** shall conceive and bear a son,
and they shall name him **Emmanuel**,"
which means, "**God is with** us."
When Joseph **awoke** from sleep,
he did as the Angel of the Lord **commanded** him;
he took her as his **wife**,
but had no **marital relations** with her
until she had borne a **son**;
and he **named** him **Jesus**.]

[Shorter: Matthew 1.18–25 (see brackets)]

choose to replace with another of the Gospel passages from the other Christmas Masses. When the four Masses of the Nativity are taken as a whole, the choice to omit the genealogy is rather unfortunate. There is a natural progression that builds up our faith in the mystery of the Incarnation, as we first hear of Jesus' family tree (Vigil), to his birth announced by the Angels under the stars (Night), to the witness of the shepherds who encounter the infant lying in the manger (Dawn), to the theological synthesis of John, who proclaims the coming of the Word into the world as pure light (Day). The story of Jesus' origins plays a crucial role in preparing us for the wonder of his birth and pays honour and respect to all the many names that played a role in his coming into the world.

At the end of the lengthy genealogy, we hear of Joseph's dream in which an Angel tells him to fear not and to take Mary into his home. Joseph is of the household of David, and thus, having just heard of Joseph's family lineage, we are well prepared to trust in Joseph's righteousness. When the child is born to Mary, it is Joseph who provides him with the name "Jesus." This is the same child who will come to be named "Emmanuel," meaning "God-with-us." Thus, the genealogy of Jesus not only provides for us his roots but also tells of the trust that Mary and Joseph have in the authority of God's plan. S.W.

CHRISTMAS: THE NATIVITY OF THE LORD (MASS DURING THE NIGHT)

LECTIONARY #14

READING I   Isaiah 9.2–4, 6–7

A reading from the book of the Prophet Isaiah.

The people who walked in **darkness** have seen a great **light**;
those who lived in a **land** of **deep darkness**—
on them **light** has **shone**.
You have **multiplied** the nation,
you have **increased** its **joy**;
they **rejoice** before you
as with joy at the **harvest**,
as people **exult** when dividing **plunder**.
For the **yoke** of their burden,
and the **bar** across their shoulders,
the **rod** of their oppressor,
you have **broken** as on the day of **Midian**.
For a **child** has been born for us,
a **son** given to us;
authority rests upon his shoulders;
and he is named
Wonderful Counsellor, **Mighty God**,
Everlasting Father, Prince of **Peace**.
His authority shall **grow continually**,
and there shall be **endless peace**
for the **throne** of David and his **kingdom**. »

Isaiah = ī-ZAY-uh

A reading of great joy and mystery. Read with emphasis on the contrasts between light and gloom, battle and peace.

Take note here of the yoke, the bar, and the rod. These lines express parallel images in parallel constructions.

Midian = MID-ee-uhn

These names are the heart of this reading. Give them due emphasis.

There are options for today's readings. Contact your parish staff to learn which readings will be used.

| READING I | This installment of Isaiah's prophecy is part of the dialogue undertaken with King Ahaz of Judah, who has been promised the coming of a great and mighty king who would free the people from foreign rule and would establish a kingdom based upon justice (Isaiah 7—11). When isolated to the context of this eighth-century BC situation, the prophecy

Isaiah utters speaks to the freedom of the northern tribes of Israel from Assyrian occupation. As they have managed to survive a period of oppression, they are now able to enjoy the new life of liberation. The people are described as journeying out of a time of "darkness" into "great light." This light is so bright that it can be likened to the joy of an abundant harvest, when people celebrate the ability to divide the profits. In the context mentioned above, Assyria is meant to be the "yoke," the "bar," and the "rod" that burdened the people with oppression. Israel's victory over the Assyrians is

equivalent to the "day of Midian," when Gideon successfully defeated the pagan Midianites (see Judges 7.15–25).

After rehearsing the powerful victory of the Israelites, Isaiah turns his prophecy to the foretelling of the messiah. "For a child has been born for us," the Prophet announces. This child is to be given the name Emmanuel (Isaiah 7.14). Isaiah's words spoken in the time of Ahaz transcend this immediate context and become the vision for a future child born in the line of King David. The authority of this just ruler is revealed by the names that Isaiah gives

Give each of the pairs in these three lines—establish and uphold; justice and righteousness; onward and forevermore—equal emphasis.

He will **establish** and **uphold** it
with **justice** and with **righteousness**
from **this time** onward and **forevermore**.
The **zeal** of the Lord of **hosts** will **do** this.

For meditation and context:

RESPONSORIAL PSALM   Psalm 96.1–2, 3–4, 11–12, 13 (R. Luke 2.11)

R. Today is born our Saviour, Christ the Lord.

O sing to the Lord a new song;
sing to the Lord, all the earth.
Sing to the Lord, bless his name;
tell of his salvation from day to day.

Declare his glory among the nations,
his marvellous works among all the peoples.
For great is the Lord, and greatly to
    be praised;
he is to be revered above all gods.

Let the heavens be glad, and let the
    earth rejoice;
let the sea roar, and all that fills it;
let the field exult, and everything in it.
Then shall all the trees of the forest sing
    for joy.

Rejoice before the Lord; for he is coming,
for he is coming to judge the earth.
He will judge the world with righteousness,
and the peoples with his truth.

READING II   Titus 2.11–14

Titus = Tī-tuhs
This reading is broken into three parts, beginning with "the grace of God," continuing with "the manifestation of the glory," and concluding with "He it is who gave himself for us." Pace your reading accordingly

Equal emphasis on these three adjectives.

A reading from the Letter of Saint Paul to Titus.

Beloved:
The **grace** of God has appeared, bringing salvation to **all**,
training us to renounce **impiety** and worldly **passions**,
and in the present age to live lives
that are **self-controlled**, **upright**, and **godly**,
while we **wait for** the blessed **hope**
and the **manifestation** of the **glory** of our great **God** and **Saviour**,
Jesus Christ.
He it is who gave himself for **us**
that he might **redeem** us from all **iniquity**
and **purify** for himself a **people** of his own
who are **zealous** for **good deeds**.

Read the phrase "zealous for good deeds" as a Christmas wish.

---

him: "Wonderful Counsellor, Mighty God, Everlasting Father, Prince of Peace." These titles suggest the qualities that will make up the messiah's character: he will be wise (Wonderful Counsellor), strong (Mighty God), caring (Everlasting Father), and just (Prince of Peace). This king will be revered for making his kingdom one of permanent peace and constant justice.

READING II   This reading from the author's correspondence with Titus is proclaimed in the context of a Mass celebrated in the shadows of night,

a time designated for vigilant and prayerful waiting for the dawning of a festival day. We are reminded here of the eschatological waiting that is necessary for the Lord's triumphant return at the end of days, but we too, in vigilant posture, await the joy that is to accompany our celebration of the Lord's Nativity. Both the Incarnation and the Lord's return are referred to in this passage: "the grace of God has appeared" suggests the Incarnation, while the "manifestation of the glory of our great God and Saviour, Jesus Christ" refers to his coming at the end of time.

Paul's major concern in portraying the trajectory from the birth of Jesus until the parousia is to emphasize the importance for Christians to learn how "to renounce impiety and worldly passions." His plan for education on the Christian way involves training in how to live "lives that are self-controlled, upright, and godly." All three attitudes require discipline and focus. One must be carefully attuned to the difficult work of rejecting the ways of the flesh that can draw one's attention away from the life of the Spirit.

GOSPEL   Luke 2.1–16++

A reading from the holy Gospel according to Luke.

In those days a **decree** went out from Caesar Augustus
that **all the world** should be **registered**.
This was the **first** registration
and was taken while Quirinius was governor of Syria.
All went to their **own towns** to be **registered**.
Joseph also went from the town of **Nazareth** in **Galilee** to **Judea**,
to the city of **David** called **Bethlehem**,
because he was descended from the **house** and **family** of David.
He went to be **registered** with **Mary**,
to whom he was engaged and who was **expecting** a **child**.
While they were there,
the time came for **her** to deliver her **child**.
And she gave **birth** to her **firstborn son**
and **wrapped** him in swaddling **clothes**,
and **laid** him in a **manger**,
because there was **no place** for them in the **inn**.
In that region there were **shepherds living** in the fields,
keeping **watch** over their flock by **night**.
Then an **Angel** of the Lord stood before them,
and the **glory** of the Lord shone around them,
and they were **terrified**.
But the Angel **said** to them,
"**Do not be afraid**; for **see**—
I am bringing you **good news** of **great joy** for **all** the people:
to you is **born this day** in the city of **David** a **Saviour**,
who is the **Christ**, the **Lord**.
This will be a sign for you:
you will find a **child wrapped** in swaddling clothes
and **lying** in a **manger**." »

The reading is divided into two parts. The first part tells the story of the census, moving Joseph and Mary from Nazareth to Bethlehem, where Jesus will be born. The second part shifts to the shepherds visited by the Angel of the Lord. Two vivid Christian images come from this reading: the manger of the Nativity and the heavenly host with the Angel proclaiming glory to God, witnessed by the shepherds watching over their flocks. Both images come alive in this reading.

Place emphasis on these lines by slowing your pace just slightly to draw attention to the image.

In this line, each word should have almost equal emphasis.

Give emphasis again to the word "manger."

The author suggests that the way to maintain this devotion is to focus keenly on the "blessed hope" that is the dawning of God's glory. Notice here that by the time this letter was written—one of the latter installments of the Pauline corpus—that "our great God" is not distinguished from the "Saviour, Jesus Christ." Although the Father and Jesus are distinguished one from another, they are considered here as equal in authority. The passage concludes with a reference to redemption that can be likened to the Hebrew liberation from Egyptian slavery: Jesus gave himself to

"redeem us" from the captivity of "iniquity" in order to "purify" a people for himself. The reader might imagine the powerful effects of both the passage through the Red Sea and the saving relationship established in baptism.

GOSPEL   Luke's account of the Lord's birth opens with the portrayal of human authority attempting to keep control over the world. Caesar Augustus has pronounced that the population of "all the world" must be counted. The greater the numbers, the more powerful

the Roman Empire could consider itself. However, it is the context of the census by which God is able to display a power that is much greater than any human authority could wield. To be counted, Joseph and Mary depart from the comfort of their home and go to Bethlehem in Judea. It is during their time in Bethlehem that Mary gives birth to her child.

It is no mistake that Luke wants us to understand that the birth of God's Son takes place in the midst of a social context in which political officials are trying to manage the world. There is simply no preparing

Give slight emphasis to "praising" as a way of characterizing the image arising from the familiar words to follow: pure praise.

And **suddenly** there was with the Angel
a multitude of the heavenly host,
praising God and saying,
"**Glory** to God in the **highest heaven**,
and on **earth peace** among those whom he **favours**!"
When the Angels had **left** them and **gone** into heaven,
the **shepherds** said to one another,
"Let us **go now** to **Bethlehem**
and **see** this thing that has **taken place**,
which the **Lord** has made **known** to us."
So they **went with haste** and found **Mary** and **Joseph**,
and the **child lying** in the manger.

PRAYERFUL READING, OR *LECTIO DIVINA*

1. *Lectio:* Read a Scripture passage aloud slowly. Notice what phrase captures your attention and be attentive to its meaning. Silent pause.

2. *Meditatio:* Read the passage aloud slowly again, reflecting on the passage, allowing God to speak to you through it. Silent pause.

3. *Oratio:* Read it aloud slowly a third time, allowing it to be your prayer or response to God's gift of insight to you. Silent pause.

4. *Contemplatio:* Read it aloud slowly a fourth time, now resting in God's Word.

---

for the grace that God gives to the world. Even Joseph and Mary are caught off guard and away from home when the child is born. They were not able to plan accordingly for Jesus' birth and are forced to use a manger as the place of his delivery. The Holy Family is completely vulnerable when Jesus comes into his world, but God will work through this vulnerability to demonstrate the wonder of his authority.

Thus, while the Jewish people believed that the messiah would come among them as a king, full of power and might, with the ability to free them from the control of the Romans and all other nations, God chooses to act in a way that astonishes all. God selects lowly shepherds to be his ambassadors to the world, bearing a message of "good news of great joy." And this is a message that goes out to all the world and not just to those awaiting the coming of the messiah.

Luke's theology in the story of the Lord's Nativity is abundantly clear. God chooses the lowly to cast the mighty from their positions of power (Luke 1.52). Through the message of the Angels, the epiphany of God's love for the world is made manifest; this is a love that cannot be counted or measured by a human census. The child Jesus may be wrapped in swaddling clothes and lying in a manger, but our eyes of faith are able to behold the King of Kings and Lord of Lords. God enters this world in a way suspected by no one; all are astonished by his grace. S.W.

CHRISTMAS:
THE NATIVITY OF THE LORD
(MASS AT DAWN)

LECTIONARY #15

READING I   Isaiah 62.11–12

Isaiah = ī-ZAY-uh

Read this exhortation as a poem, which is to say slowly and with emphasis on the highlighted words.

recompense = REK-uhm-pens = compensation for wrongs suffered

The word "Redeemed" is focal in this reading.

A reading from the book of the Prophet Isaiah.

The Lord has **proclaimed** to the **end** of the earth:
"Say to daughter Zion,
See, your salvation comes;
his **reward** is **with** him,
and his **recompense before** him.
They shall be **called** 'The Holy **People**,'
'The **Redeemed** of the Lord';
and you shall be called '**Sought Out**,'
'**A City Not Forsaken**.'"

For meditation and context:

RESPONSORIAL PSALM   Psalm 97.1–2, 5–6, 11–12 (R. see 11)

R. A light will shine on us this day: The Lord is born for us.

The Lord is king! Let the earth rejoice;
let the many coastlands be glad!
Clouds and thick darkness are all
    around him;
righteousness and justice are the foundation
    of his throne.

The mountains melt like wax before the Lord,
before the Lord of all the earth.
The heavens proclaim his righteousness;
and all the peoples behold his glory.

Light dawns for the righteous,
and joy for the upright in heart.
Rejoice in the Lord, O you righteous,
and give thanks to his holy name!

TO KEEP IN MIND
Pause to break up separate thoughts, set apart significant statements, or indicate major shifts. Never pause in the middle of a thought. Your primary guide for pauses is punctuation.

There are options for today's readings. Contact your parish staff to learn which readings will be used.

READING I A basic liturgical principle regarding the proclamation of God's Word in the gathered assembly is that when God speaks, something happens. God's Word is meant to be generative and fruitful; it is not meant to fall upon deaf ears with no corresponding action on the part of hearers. This is especially true when it comes to God's Word spoken by the Prophets. The point of prophecy is to elicit a response from those to whom it is directed.

In this short reading from the Prophet Isaiah, the prophecy begins with an active present, using the commands to "say" and "see." The point of these commands is very clear: those who hear this Word must be moved by it. And what is it that Isaiah's hearers are to do? They are to participate in the announcement of the Lord's coming. The evidence for his nearness is to be found in the change of name bestowed upon the people. They are to be called "The Holy People," "the Redeemed." Likewise, the name of the city of Zion is to be changed as well; from now on it will not be seen as desolate or forsaken but instead will bear the name "Sought Out."

God has spoken, and a great transformation will take place. The Lord provides for the renewal of both people and the Land, and the most important achievement of all is the regeneration of the people's faith. Holiness and redemption are the fruit of the Lord speaking his Word and carrying out his plan to be faithful for all generations to come.

Titus = Tī-tuhs

A reading in one long sentence. The lines of the reading form natural pairs. Read each pair of lines as a thought, proceeding from one to the next, offering advice, to conclude with a message of hope.

The rhythm of this line provides this reading with its reverberant note, so allow yourself to slow slightly as you come to this conclusion.

READING II   Titus 3.4–7

A reading from the Letter of Saint Paul to Titus.

When the **goodness** and **loving kindness** of God
      our Saviour appeared,
he saved us,
not because of any **works** of **righteousness** that we had done,
but **according** to his **mercy**,
through the **water** of **rebirth** and **renewal** by the Holy **Spirit**.
This Spirit he **poured** out on us **richly**
through **Jesus** Christ our **Saviour**,
so that, having been **justified** by his **grace**,
we might become **heirs** according to the **hope** of eternal **life**.

READING II   The author of this pastoral letter writes to Christians in Crete. The major theme of the letter is to warn the community to be careful not to follow the instruction of false teachers (see Titus 1.9). The verses of today's excerpt from the letter come from its final chapter. And here the author provides several truths of Christian teaching, which he uses to substantiate why the community should follow his instruction and not that of other false teachers.

First, the author defines the nature of God's grace. It is a gift that is given accord-ing to God's kindness and generosity. It is not something we merit or accomplish through any deed of our own. Second, God's gift of a saviour to the world is a sign of his great mercy. Thus, the mystery of the Incarnation resides solely on the truth that God wishes to provide for his people; his coming into the world has nothing to do with our being deserving of such a gift.

A third truth of the Christian faith is found in his description of how salvation takes place. It begins with the kindness of God that is marked by the ritual of baptism and the "renewal" provided by the Holy Spirit, which proceeds from the Father through the Son. In turn, this regeneration brings the hope of eternal life. Because we have been brought into relationship with Christ through baptism, we are to be "justi-fied" by God's grace.

GOSPEL   Recall that today's first reading from Isaiah opened with the command words "say" and "see." This Gospel passage from Luke is focused on the testimony of the shepherds who were commanded by the Angels to go and see what God revealed in the city of Bethlehem.

GOSPEL   Luke 2.15–20

A reading from the holy Gospel according to Luke.

When the **Angels** had left them and gone into **heaven**,
the **shepherds** said to one another,
"Let us go now to **Bethlehem**
and see **this thing** that has taken place,
which the **Lord** has made **known** to us."
So they went with **haste** and found **Mary** and **Joseph**,
and the **child lying** in the manger.
When they **saw** this,
they made **known** what had been **told them** about this child;
and all who heard it were **amazed**
at what the **shepherds told** them.
But **Mary** treasured all these words
and **pondered** them in her **heart**.
The **shepherds** returned, **glorifying** and **praising** God
for all they had **heard** and **seen**,
as it had been **told** them.

While the focus of this reading is on the infant Jesus lying in the manger, the eyes through which we see him are those of the shepherds. The shepherds modelled Christian devotion from the beginning of our faith.

Amazement is the primary emotion of this story.

The shepherds' glorifying and praising are to be our own.

Such a plan to seek out God's presence is important to Luke, who begins the mysterious circumstances of the Incarnation with Mary running to her cousin Elizabeth, who testifies to the truth she sees: "Blessed are you among women, and blessed is the fruit of your womb" (Luke 1.42).

Luke wants the reader to see that God chooses the non-powerful and non-influential to make known the greatest gift the world has ever seen. Just like Mary ran to her cousin Elizabeth, so a pack of lowly shepherds goes "with haste" to find the infant. How is it that they were able to see such magnificence in an innocent and powerless child? What was it that spoke to them of God's grace present in the child? Whatever it was, Luke tells us that they do not delay in revealing what the Angels had told them about this child, namely that a saviour has been born into the world, the cause for this world's peace (Luke 2.11, 14). So great was the testimony of the shepherds that Luke makes sure to tell us that all who heard were "amazed."

As the shepherds leave the manger, it is important to notice that they go away "glorifying and praising God" for what they had seen. This is very much like the posture of the Angels who approached them in the field and sang "Glory to God in the highest" (Luke 2.14). There should be no doubt that Luke wants us to "see" exactly what the shepherds saw; we who are as lowly as they have been chosen to testify to God's presence among us. "The Lord has proclaimed to the end of the earth: . . . See, your salvation comes" (see the first reading). S.W.

CHRISTMAS:
THE NATIVITY OF THE LORD
(MASS DURING THE DAY)

LECTIONARY #16

READING I   Isaiah 52.7–10

Isaiah = ī-ZAY-uh

A reading of great joy. In reading this, you are bringing glad tidings to the assembly.

A reading from the book of the Prophet Isaiah.

How **beautiful** upon the **mountains**
are the feet of the messenger who **announces peace**,
who brings good **news**,
who announces **salvation**,
who says to Zion, "Your **God reigns**."

"Listen!" is a word with rich Christmas associations. Allow it to resonate in your reading.

Listen! Your watchmen **lift up** their voices,
together they **sing** for **joy**;
for in **plain sight** they see
the **return** of the **Lord** to **Zion**.
Break forth together into singing,
you **ruins** of Jerusalem;
for the **Lord** has comforted his **people**,
he has **redeemed** Jerusalem.
The **Lord** has bared his holy arm
before the **eyes** of all the **nations**;

Allow "salvation" to resonate here. This word is the key to the whole reading.

and **all** the **ends** of the **earth** shall **see** the **salvation** of our **God**.

There are options for today's readings. Contact your parish staff to learn which readings will be used.

READING I Today's reading from the second part of the book of Isaiah provides a variety of vibrant images to express the joyful announcement of salvation to all the world. First, he suggests that the word goes out through the "beautiful" feet of a messenger who bounds throughout the mountaintops shouting the arrival of Zion's king. Next, Isaiah employs the image of sentinels who stand their guard at the city walls. They behold yet another vibrant image of God's victory, namely the reassembly of the city's ruins, which sing together a song of the Lord's gift of salvation. Finally, Isaiah uses the image of the Lord's mighty arm, which is shown for all the world to see.

Isaiah's prophecy is meant to call Israel to be a herald for the message that God has bestowed salvation upon a nation once destroyed and upon the world as a whole. Just as the messenger runs with his message upon the mountaintops, the Israelites are meant to hear and respond to Isaiah's prophecy with a great deal of urgency. There is no room for the people to hesitate; they must proceed with great courage.

And yet imagine how difficult a summons this would be. Those who returned to Jerusalem after the Babylonian Exile were surely overcome by fear for the future. If such destruction had taken place once, what was to keep it from happening again? Why would the people want to take such a risk to rebuild? The answer lies in the fact that they believed God was demanding great things of them to manifest his power.

For meditation and context:

RESPONSORIAL PSALM   Psalm 98.1, 2–3a, 3b–4, 5–6 (R.3bc)

R. All the ends of the earth have seen the victory of our God.

O sing to the Lord a new song,
for he has done marvellous things.
His right hand and his holy arm
have brought him victory.

The Lord has made known his victory;
he has revealed his vindication in the
    sight of the nations.
He has remembered his steadfast love
and faithfulness to the house of Israel.

All the ends of the earth have seen
the victory of our God.
Make a joyful noise to the Lord, all the earth;
break forth into joyous song and
    sing praises.

Sing praises to the Lord with the lyre,
with the lyre and the sound of melody.
With trumpets and the sound of the horn
make a joyful noise before the King,
    the Lord.

READING II   Hebrews 1.1–6

A reading from the Letter to the Hebrews.

Long ago God **spoke** to our **ancestors**
in many and **various** ways by the **Prophets**,
but in these **last days** he has **spoken to us** by the **Son**,
whom he appointed **heir** of **all things**,
through **whom** he **also** created the **ages**.
He is the **reflection** of God's **glory**
and the exact **imprint** of God's very being,
and he **sustains all things** by his **powerful** word.
When he had made **purification** for sins,
he **sat down** at the **right hand** of the **Majesty** on high,
having become as **much superior** to **Angels**
as the **name** he has **inherited** is more **excellent** than theirs.
For to **which** of the **Angels** did **God** ever say,
"**You** are my Son;
today I have begotten **you**"?
Or **again**,
"I will be his **Father**,
and he will be my **Son**"? »

A reading of poetic and argumentative power about the nature and glory of Christ. The reading consists of a long and poetic set-up that yields to an argumentative call and response. Allow the set-up to gather tension in your reading that the call and response releases.

This is celestial language to characterize the Son.

The call and response is like a small theatre piece.

Their fidelity would result in others throughout the whole world coming to believe in God, as we see in the prophecy at the end of this reading.

After having endured the lot of forced slavery, it would have been quite natural for the Israelites to have turned in on themselves. However, this is not the plan of God's salvation. He does not carve out a people for himself simply for their own isolation. Instead, being the chosen people is a gift that comes with the responsibility of proclaiming the good news of salvation to all the earth. Such commissioning belongs to the followers of Christ as well. We are meant to climb to the mountaintops and shout to all peoples that the Lord has come to save us! As Psalm 98, which responds to the first reading, proclaims: "All the ends of the earth have seen the victory of our God."

READING II The author of the Letter to the Hebrews begins his writing by speaking of the nature of God's revelation in the past and in the present age. First, he claims that in the past, God revealed himself in "many" ways. Thus, the prophecy of Isaiah, which we just heard in today's first reading, would be an example of revelation that was one way of many, but not quite complete. However, the author states that "in these last days" God's revelation has been fully bestowed by the giving of his word as it is spoken through his Son. Jesus is the fullness of God's revelation, and with him God's revelation cannot come nearer. The Word God has spoken in his Son is definitive; there can be nothing greater.

Part of these opening verses may have originally been sung as part of a liturgical hymn. They contain a marvellous soteriological portrait of God's working of salvation

And **again**,
when he **brings** the firstborn into the **world**, he says,
"Let **all** God's Angels **worship** him."

GOSPEL   John 1.1–18

A reading from the holy Gospel according to John.

[In the **beginning** was the **Word**,
and the **Word** was with **God**,
and the **Word** was **God**.
He **was** in the **beginning with** God.
All things came into being **through** him,
and **without him** not **one** thing came into being.
What has **come** into being **in him** was **life**,
and the **life** was the **light** of the human **race**.
The light **shines** in the **darkness**,
and the **darkness** did **not** overcome it.]
There was a man sent from **God**, whose name was **John**.
He came as a **witness** to **testify** to the **light**,
so that all might believe **through him**.
He himself was **not** the light,
but he came to **testify** to the light.
[The **true light**, which enlightens **everyone**,
was **coming** into the world.
He was **in** the world,
and the **world** came into being **through** him;
yet the **world** did not **know** him.
He **came** to what was his **own**,
and his **own people** did not **accept** him.

One of the pillars of Christian theology. The emphases in the opening verses are crucial to that theology.

Linger a little at the contrast between light and darkness.

This passage about John links his testimony with the light.

through the giving of his Son, who is his heir, his coworker in the project of creation, and is the "reflection of God's glory." After accomplishing God's mission by destroying the bonds of sin, the Son was seated at the Father's right hand.

Given the fact that the Letter to the Hebrews was written to people of Jewish background, these words, which suggest that the post-resurrected Christ shares fully in God's majesty, being "much superior to Angels," would have seemed very radical indeed. For staunch Jews who continued to cling to God's covenant with Israel, these words would seem to substantiate a great rupture—God has done something decidedly new and different "in these last days." But that is exactly the author's point: he wants to leave no doubt that former ways looked forward to what was to come, but the coming of the Lord into the world has made God's salvation abundantly clear and undeniable for those who honour the relationship between the Father and the Son.

GOSPEL | Ponder for a moment the Gospel passages that have been proclaimed in the three Masses for the Lord's Nativity, leading up to the final celebration of Mass on Christmas Day. The Vigil focused on the genealogy of Jesus from Matthew, the Mass at Night contained Luke's account of the visit by the Angels to the shepherds in the field announcing the glory of God to be revealed to all the world, and, finally, the Mass at Dawn continued Luke's infancy narrative with the shepherds' journey to the manger in Bethlehem. Throughout these Masses, there has been a progression in the theological dimension of God's plan of salvation: from a distinct bloodline in the course of history comes

The Word becoming flesh is the heart of this reading.

But to all who **received** him,
who **believed** in his **name**,
he gave **power** to become **children** of God,
who were born, **not** of **blood**
or of the **will** of the **flesh**
or of the **will** of **man**,
but of **God**.
And the **Word** became **flesh** and **lived among** us,
and we have **seen** his **glory**,
the glory as of a **father's only-begotten** son,
full of **grace** and **truth**.]

And once again, John testifies. His testimony yields revelation. Give proper emphasis to "made him known" at the end of the reading.

John **testified** to him and **cried out**,
"**This** was he of **whom I said**,
'He who comes **after** me ranks **ahead** of me
because he was **before** me.'"
From his **fullness** we have **all** received,
grace upon **grace**.
The **law** indeed was **given** through **Moses**;
grace and **truth** came through Jesus **Christ**.
No one has ever **seen** God.
It is **God** the only-begotten **Son**,
who is close to the Father's heart,
who has **made him known**.

[Shorter: John 1.1–5, 9–14 (see brackets)]

the fulfillment of God's promise of salvation, which is announced to the lowly of this world but is Good News to be shared with every creature on earth. God's Word is creative and enduring; it is meant for all to hear.

The Gospel passage from the Mass during the Day is taken from the prologue of John's Gospel. The last of the four Gospels to be written, the Gospel of John presents us with a very high Christology. This means that John wants to emphasize the divinity of Christ more than his humanity. For example, there is no infancy narrative in John nor is there any evidence of Jesus growing and maturing as a human; instead, Jesus appears at the outset as the fully-grown anointed one of God.

For those who prefer the nativity story, complete with shepherds and Angels, a manger and barnyard animals, these words from the opening of John's Gospel, may seem less than relatable. That is precisely John's method; he wants his hearers to contemplate the seriousness of a theology of the Incarnation, the Word made flesh. The celebration of this Christian mystery presents us with the awesome wonder that God does not save the world from afar; instead, God chooses to experience all that his human creation experiences, except the destructive forces of sin.

John's prologue places before us the symbol of Christ as the true Light of the World. In these days of winter darkness, the Church holds on to the hope that Christ's light will endure; there is no darkness that the light of Christ cannot dispel. Even though much of the world does not know the Son, and even though his own would reject him, his light reveals the totality of God's never-ending and always-abundant grace. S.W.

THE HOLY FAMILY OF JESUS, MARY AND JOSEPH

Sirach = SEER-ak *or* Sī-ruhk

A didactic reading in which each set of phrases offers advice.

Note the parallels established by the repetition of the word "whoever." The word "and" serves a similar purpose. Each of these teachings is meant to be equal.

The advice in the second section, beginning here, is more familial, the words of a father to his son. You can proclaim it in this spirit.

LECTIONARY #17

READING I   Sirach 3.2–6, 12–14

A reading from the book of Sirach.

The Lord **honours** a father above his children,
and he confirms a mother's **rights** over her **sons**.
Whoever **honours** their father **atones** for sins
and gains **preservation** from them;
when they **pray**, they will be **heard**.
Whoever respects their **mother**
is like one who lays up **treasure**.
The person who **honours** their father
will have **joy** in **their own** children,
and when they **pray** they will be **heard**.
Whoever **respects** their father will have a **long life**,
and whoever **honours** their **mother obeys** the Lord.
My child, **help** your father in his old **age**,
and **do not grieve** him as **long** as he lives.
Even if his **mind** fails, be **patient** with him;
because **you** have all **your** faculties,
do **not despise** him all the **days** of his life.
For **kindness** to your father will **not** be **forgotten**,
and will be **credited** to you **against** your **sins**—
a **house** raised in justice for **you**.

There are options for today's readings. Contact your parish staff to learn which readings will be used.

READING I The Book of Sirach, also known as Ecclesiasticus, is composed of fifty chapters of wisdom literature. Written between the years 200 and 175 BC by the Jewish scribe Ben Sira, the book contains ethical themes and poetic sayings that are similar to those found in the Book of Proverbs. Sirach's fundamental outlook on wisdom is that building up the quality of human relationships will result in the realization that the fear of God is a central dynamic of wise relationships. In other words, constructing right relationships between husband and wife, parents and children, the young and the old, the rich and the poor ultimately leads to better reverence of God.

Sirach's pursuit of right relationship is abundantly clear in these short verses that come near the beginning of the book. A father is to command the honour of his children, and a mother is to have authority over her sons. It is not simply that honouring one's parents allows for good order in the present, but it also "atones for sins" made in the past. Furthermore, not only are sins forgiven, but the honouring of one's parents also opens access for God to be able to hear the prayers that one utters. Thus, right relationship restores what has been broken in the past, strengthens bonds in the present moment, and prepares for the action of God in the future.

The wisdom of this reading that is imparted to us is of particular importance for today's families. Many families today are very fragile and are pushed and pulled by forces and commitments outside the

For meditation and context:

RESPONSORIAL PSALM   Psalm 128.1–2, 3, 4–5 (R. 1)

R. Blessed is everyone who fears the Lord.
or: Blessed is everyone who fears the Lord, who walks in his ways.

Blessed is everyone who fears the Lord,
who walks in his ways.
You shall eat the fruit of the labour of
   your hands;
you shall be happy, and it shall go well
   with you.

Your wife will be like a fruitful vine
within your house;
your children will be like olive shoots
around your table.

Thus shall the man be blessed who fears
   the Lord.
The Lord bless you from Zion.
May you see the prosperity of Jerusalem
all the days of your life.

Colossians = kuh-LOSH-uhnz

A reading that speaks of the virtues of building community.

Each of these qualities is worthwhile, deserving emphasis.

READING II   Colossians 3.12–21

A reading from the Letter of Saint Paul to the Colossians.

[Brothers and sisters:
As God's **chosen** ones, **holy** and **beloved**,
clothe yourselves with **compassion**,
kindness, **humility**, **meekness**, and **patience**.
Bear with one another and,
if anyone has a **complaint** against another, **forgive** each other;
just as the **Lord** has forgiven **you**,
so you **also** must forgive.
Above all, **clothe** yourselves with **love**,
which **binds** everything **together** in **perfect** harmony.
And let the **peace** of Christ **rule** in your **hearts**,
to which **indeed** you were called in the one body.
And be **thankful**.
Let the **word** of Christ **dwell** in you richly;
teach and **admonish** one another in all **wisdom**;
and with **gratitude** in your hearts
sing **Psalms**, **hymns**, and spiritual **songs** to God. »

This passage concludes with a note of thanksgiving, a feeling to guide the community as it builds.

---

household. These challenges often make honour and respect difficult to manifest at home. Yet Sirach calls each member of the household to manifest care and concern for familial relationships. The more we work to honour the relationships of our households, the more we will come to revere God—"a house raised in justice for you," God. The same could be said for the "holy family" that is the Church. The more we labour to care for one another and extend compassion, the greater force will our communal prayer have in praising God our Father.

READING II   Paul writes to the infant church in Colossae, a city east of Ephesus. Although he had never visited Colossae, Paul has been provided information that this Christian community is struggling to follow the faith. Specifically, many Christians have resumed former pagan practices and are worshipping false gods. They were also wrestling with the teaching that Jesus is truly divine and not simply the greatest of all Prophets sent by God. Thus, throughout his letter Paul underscores the divine nature of Jesus.

In today's reading from Colossians, Paul reminds them that those who have been baptized in Christ have a new life to live; all former ways of living must be put aside. The attitudes that belong to Christians are the markings of holiness: "compassion, kindness, humility, meekness, and patience," with forgiveness and love being the capstones that lead to perfection. Furthermore, the gifts of peace and thanksgiving belong to those who hold fast to their unity in Christ's body. These Christian attitudes simply cannot coexist with former outlooks on life.

And whatever you **do**, in **word** or **deed**,
do **everything** in the name of the Lord **Jesus**,
giving **thanks** to God the Father **through** him.]
Wives, be **subject** to your husbands, as is fitting in the Lord.
Husbands, love your **wives** and **never** treat them **harshly**.
Children, obey your **parents** in everything,
for this is your **acceptable duty** in the Lord.
Fathers, do not **provoke** your children,
or they may **lose heart**.

A challenging passage to proclaim, in that it reinforces codes of conduct common to Greco-Roman society but which Paul typically disdains. (Most scholars of early Christianity regard these verses as added later by someone other than the original author, likely a scribe.) Probably best to read this in a neutral tone.

GOSPEL   Matthew 2.13–15, 19–23

A reading from the holy Gospel according to Matthew.

After the **wise men** had left,
an Angel of the Lord **appeared** to **Joseph** in a **dream** and said,
"Get **up**, take the **child** and his **mother**, and **flee** to **Egypt**,
and **remain** there until I **tell** you;
for **Herod** is about to **search** for the **child**, to **destroy** him."
Then **Joseph** got **up**, took the **child** and his **mother** by **night**,
and went to **Egypt**,
and **remained** there until the **death** of Herod.
This was to fulfill what had been **spoken** by the **Lord**
        through the **Prophet**,
"**Out** of Egypt I have **called** my **son**."

The tone of this vivid and magical reading is nevertheless ominous—in that it is filled with omens.
Slight pause between "Lord" and "appeared."

Herod = HAYR-uhd

Having established the general characteristics of what it means to pursue a Christian way of life that overflows in gratitude, as displayed in their response of praise and worship, Paul then turns to the relationships found within a family. If peaceful relations are to be found in the Church, then they must be found also in the Christian family. For this reason, Paul uses language such as wives being "subject" to their husbands, husbands avoiding all "harsh" treatment toward their wives, and children obeying parents in all things. Although we might find this language difficult to stomach in the twenty-first century, it is important to recognize that Paul is not interested in patriarchal power and control of wives and children, but rather, he believes that peace and harmony must reign in the domestic Church (the family) as well as in the worshipping assembly.

GOSPEL   Matthew's account of Jesus' Nativity concludes with Joseph's dream that he should take Jesus and Mary to Egypt in order to escape the persecution of Herod. Inclusion of the journey of the Holy Family to and from Egypt in Matthew's Gospel makes perfect sense considering his audience of Jewish Christians. He wants to place the story of Jesus into the framework of the Exodus experience of Israel sojourning in Egypt to avoid famine and returning to Canaan through the guidance of God's grace. Matthew makes it clear that such a story fulfills the prophecy of Hosea, quoting: "Out of Egypt I have called my son" (see Hosea 11.1). Joseph follows God's command to remain in Egypt until all is made safe for their return to Israel, information that is imparted by an Angel to Joseph in yet another dream.

Archelaus = ahr-kuh-LAY-uhs

The omens in dreams guide this reading, leading toward its concluding prophecy.
Galilee = GAL-ih-lee

Nazorean = naz-uh-REE-uhn

TO KEEP IN MIND
Read the Scripture passage and its commentary in Workbook. Then read it from your Bible, including what comes before and after it, so that you understand the context.

When **Herod** died, an Angel of the **Lord suddenly appeared**
in a **dream** to **Joseph** in **Egypt** and **said**,
"Get **up**, take the **child** and his **mother**,
and **go** to the land of **Israel**,
for **those** who were seeking the **child's** life are **dead**."
Then **Joseph** got **up**, took the **child** and his **mother**,
and **went** to the land of **Israel**.
But when he **heard** that **Archelaus** was **ruling** over **Judea**
in **place** of his father **Herod**,
he was afraid to **go** there.
And after being **warned** in a **dream**,
he went **away** to the district of Galilee.
There he made his home in a **town** called **Nazareth**,
so that what had been **spoken** through the **Prophets**
might be **fulfilled**,
"He will be **called** a **Nazorean**."

Matthew does not provide many details regarding the journey to Egypt or the journey to return home. However, he is very clear that Joseph chooses to settle in the little town of Nazareth in order to avoid the danger waged by the new rule in Judea. In the village of Nazareth, located roughly 145 kilometres north of Jerusalem, Jesus will be able to grow in a quiet fashion until he is ready to begin his ministry.

Read in the context of the liturgical celebration of the Holy Family, we are invited to contemplate the righteousness of Joseph. He puts the care of his family above his own well-being, as he trusts God's intervention through the message of an Angel. He is a beloved foster father who listens carefully to the will of God, forsaking his homeland and his work. We pray that our Christian families, bombarded by many voices in this world, may diligently discern the will of God for the good of their households. S.W.

MARY,
THE HOLY MOTHER OF GOD

LECTIONARY #18

READING I · Numbers 6.22–27

A reading from the book of Numbers.

The **Lord** spoke to **Moses**:
Speak to Aaron and his sons, saying,
Thus you shall **bless** the **children** of **Israel**:
You shall **say** to them,
The **Lord bless** you and **keep** you;
the **Lord** make his face to **shine** upon you,
and be **gracious** to you;
the **Lord** lift **up** his **countenance** upon you,
and **give** you **peace**.
So they shall **put** my name on the **children** of Israel,
and I will **bless** them.

A reading built on advice that God gives to Moses. The verbs "speak," "say," and "put" are crucial, as are repetitions of "the Lord." Use these repetitions to guide your proclamation.

Note how the word "bless" is repeated. Note how "bless" echoes in "peace."

READING I   As part of the instructions given by the Lord to Moses on the construction of the Tabernacle in the Book of Exodus, chapters 28 and 29 are devoted to the consecration of priests and the design of the vestments that are to identify their duty as "Holy to the LORD" (Exodus 28.36). Levitical priests made daily burnt offerings as a sign of Israel's fidelity to the covenant. What is not made clear in Exodus is how priests are to relate to their fellow Israelites. Here in the Book of Numbers, which details Israel's beginnings in the Promised Land, we see a glimpse of

the role priests now play with the people. They are to bless the people.

Blessings had long been a part of the Israelite tradition, as the annual Passover, as well as the keeping of the Sabbath, called for God's name to be blessed. However, in this passage from Numbers, the role of blessing people is now reserved for priests, those who are the descendants of Aaron. Thus, we can see that the priesthood has expanded from the duty of performing daily sacrifice to strengthening the people's relationship with the Lord by reminding them of how he cares for them.

Thus, this blessing prayer invokes the name of the Lord over the people three times, as the people learn of his care: first, keeping them as his possession; second, experiencing the graciousness of God's face shining upon them; and third, receiving the gift of God's kindness and peace. The closeness of God to his people is suggested in all three of these invocations, but especially in the second, for Moses saw the face of God and was forever transfigured. The people are not to see the Lord's face, but they are certainly meant to radiate God's

For meditation and context:

RESPONSORIAL PSALM   Psalm 67.1–2, 4–5, 6–7 (R.1a)

R. May God be gracious to us and bless us.

May God be gracious to us and bless us
and make his face to shine upon us,
that your way may be known upon earth,
your saving power among all nations.

Let the nations be glad and sing for joy,
for you judge the peoples with equity
and guide the nations upon earth.
Let the peoples praise you, O God;
let all the peoples praise you.

The earth has yielded its increase;
God, our God, has blessed us.
May God continue to bless us;
let all the ends of the earth revere him.

READING II   Galatians 4.4–7

A reading from the Letter of Saint Paul to the Galatians.

A reading in which Paul connects the members of the early church in Galatia directly to Jesus. He does so in three sentences, introduced by "when," "and," and "so." In short order, he builds his argument and then concludes it.

Brothers and sisters:
When the **fullness** of time had come,
God sent his Son, **born** of a woman,
born under the law,
in order to **redeem** those who were **under** the law,
so that we might **receive** adoption to **sonship**.
And **because** you are **sons** and **daughters**,
God has sent the **Spirit** of his Son into our hearts, crying,
"**Abba**! Father!"
So you are **no longer** slave but **son**,
and if **son** then also **heir**, **through** God.

The conclusion of Paul's argument, that we are no longer slaves but sons and heirs of God, is truly radical. It deserves some astonishment and emphasis.

countenance. God's benefits will be given to all who call upon his name.

READING II In the fourth chapter of his letter to the Galatians, Paul discusses what it means to be an heir of God. He says that until a child matures and comes of age, he or she can be thought of as a slave, but when the proper age is reached, that person is free to inherit all that he or she has been promised. Paul then suggests that those who have been granted God's revelation of his Son through the power of the Spirit are no longer to

be thought of as slaves, but instead, they are now free to inherit what God has promised them.

This passage from Galatians opens with Paul suggesting that the age of maturity arrived in the Incarnation of Jesus, Son of God. This Son performs a twofold mission: first, he is to "redeem," or set free those who subscribe to the Law, and second, he is to provide "adoption" for those set free by his act of liberation. Furthermore, with adoption comes the movement of the Spirit into believers' hearts so that they

might know God and be able to address him as "Father."

Thus, Paul's microscopic portrayal of salvation history suggests a basic change in relationships. Prior to the sending of the Son, people could only relate to God as a slave would to a master. Now, all who have the Spirit in their hearts have a different relationship with God; they are able to see themselves as children in relationship to a father. Because they are now adopted sons and daughters, they are able to inherit all that God promises, namely the fullness of salvation. God's power is ultimately revealed

A reading that concludes the Nativity story. While the focus is on the infant Jesus lying in the manger, the eyes through which we see him are those of the shepherds. The shepherds modelled Christian devotion from the beginning of our faith.

Amazement is the primary emotion of this story.

The shepherds' glorifying and praising are to be our own.

GOSPEL   Luke 2.16–21

A reading from the holy Gospel according to Luke.

The **shepherds** went with haste to **Bethlehem**
and found **Mary** and **Joseph**,
and the **child lying** in the manger.
When they **saw** this,
they made **known** what had been **told** them about this child;
and all who heard it were **amazed**
at what the **shepherds told** them.
But **Mary** treasured all these words
and **pondered** them in her **heart**.
The **shepherds** returned, **glorifying** and **praising** God
for **all** they had **heard** and **seen**,
as it had been **told** them.

After eight days had **passed**,
it was time to **circumcise** the child;
and he was called **Jesus**,
the name **given** by the **Angel**
before he was **conceived** in the **womb**.

TO KEEP IN MIND
Recognize how important your proclamation of the Word of God is. Prepare well and take joy in your ministry.

---

in the relationships he forms with those who have been brought near by his Son by the working of the Spirit.

GOSPEL Today we repeat the proclamation of the Gospel for the Mass of the Nativity at dawn, with the addition of the verse that announces the naming of Jesus at the time of his circumcision. In the context of today's feast, we are meant to focus particular attention on the figure of Mary. Luke reports that "Mary treasured all these words" in her heart, as she receives the message of the Angels through the ambassadorship of the shepherds. Thus, we see Mary, in a very real sense, as the first Christian contemplative. God has communicated with her in a special way, beginning with her own immaculate conception and continuing through the birth of Jesus. Certainly, pondering within her heart led her to marvel at what God might have in store for her next.

In addition to her contemplation of divine mystery, we are also meant to see Mary as the model of obedience. Throughout Luke's initial chapters, Mary listens completely to the message of the Angel and gives herself over to God's will. In reporting that Jesus was circumcised and given the name spoken by the Angel, we see that Mary is faithful not only to God but to her responsibilities as a Jewish mother. Jesus, like his cousin John before him (Luke 1.59), is to be raised in a thoroughly faithful Jewish household. As the *Theotokos* (an ancient Greek title for Mary, as Mother of God), Mary is the exemplar of contemplative obedience. S.W.

EPIPHANY OF THE LORD

LECTIONARY #20

READING I   Isaiah 60.1–6

A reading from the book of the Prophet Isaiah.

Arise, **shine**, for your **light** has **come**,
and the **glory** of the **Lord** has **risen** upon you!
For **darkness** shall cover the earth,
and **thick darkness** the **peoples**;
but the **Lord** will **arise** upon you,
and his **glory** will appear **over** you.
Nations shall come to your **light**,
and **kings** to the **brightness** of your **dawn**.
Lift up your eyes and **look** around;
they all **gather** together, they **come** to you;
your **sons** shall **come** from **far away**,
and your **daughters** shall be **carried** on their **nurses' arms**.
Then you shall **see** and be **radiant**;
your **heart** shall **thrill** and **rejoice**,
because the **abundance** of the sea shall be **brought** to you,
the **wealth** of the **nations** shall **come** to you.
A multitude of **camels** shall cover you,
the young camels of **Midian** and **Ephah**;
all those from **Sheba** shall come.
They shall bring **gold** and **frankincense**,
and shall **proclaim** the **praise** of the **Lord**.

Isaiah = ī-ZAY-uh

A reading filled with rich and poetic images and phrases. Glory, light, gift giving, and praise guide this prophetic passage. Let these words guide your reading.

This passage is addressed to Jerusalem, but because it is written in the second person, it allows you to speak directly to the assembly. "Lift up your eyes and look around . . ."

Midian= MID-ee-uhn
Ephah = EE-fuh

The camels and the gifts they carry prefigure the wise men. Present this passage as a prelude to the Epiphany story.

READING I Today's reading comes from the third part of Isaiah, which focuses on Israel's restoration after years of exile in Babylon. Rather than a prophecy of doom and gloom, Isaiah announces that the time has come for Jerusalem to reclaim its favoured status: "Arise, shine, for your light has come." It had to be an unenviable task to call the people to return to the land that had been ransacked, with its centrepiece—the Temple—in ruins. So many of the Israelites in their land of exile had to debate whether it would be worth the effort to return. But Isaiah tells the people that today is a new day in which the light of God's glory will shine upon a renewed nation and that this light will spread to other nations. In fact, Isaiah suggests that rulers from all over the world will have no trouble seeing the "brightness of your dawn" that comes forth from the newly recreated land of the Israelites.

In an attempt to lure those who resist returning, Isaiah paints the picture of a great throng of people, young and old, journeying to behold the new Jerusalem. Just as the Egyptians gave their gold and silver to the Israelites when they were preparing to make their exodus from their state of slavery (Exodus 12.35–36), so does Isaiah suggest that visitors from foreign lands will pour out their wealth to the people when they see what God's glory has accomplished. Thus, it would be foolish for anyone to remain in Babylon when they are invited to be the recipients of such a great fortune. These foreigners will not only come with gifts of gold and frankincense, but they will also have the praise of God on their lips. A renewed Jerusalem not only benefits its inhabitants but also serves as a means of calling people to belief in God's

For meditation and context:

RESPONSORIAL PSALM   Psalm 72.1–2, 7–8, 10–11, 12–13
(R. see 11b + Psalm 98.3c)

R. Lord, every nation on earth will adore you.

Give the king your justice, O God,
and your righteousness to a king's son.
May he judge your people with
    righteousness,
and your poor with justice.

In his days may righteousness flourish
and peace abound, until the moon is
    no more.
May he have dominion from sea to sea,
and from the River to the ends of the earth.

May the kings of Tarshish and of the isles
    render him tribute,
may the kings of Sheba and Seba bring gifts.
May all kings fall down before him,
all nations give him service.

For he delivers the needy one who calls,
the poor and the one who has no helper.
He has pity on the weak and the needy,
and saves the lives of the needy.

READING II   Ephesians 3.2–3a, 5–6

A reading from the Letter of Saint Paul to the Ephesians.

Brothers and sisters:
Surely you have **already** heard
of the **commission** of God's **grace** that was given **me** for **you**,
and how the **mystery** was made known to me by **revelation**.
In **former** generations
this mystery was **not** made known to **humankind**
as it has **now** been revealed to his **holy Apostles** and **Prophets**
    by the **Spirit**:
that is, the **Gentiles** have become **fellow heirs**,
members of the **same** body,
and **sharers** in the **promise** in Christ **Jesus** through the **Gospel**.

Ephesians = ee-FEE-zhuhnz

A reading in which Paul emphatically includes the Gentile members of the early church in Ephesus into the community of believers. It's in two long sentences, emphasizing revelation and the Gospel respectively.

Emphasize "Gentiles," "heirs," "members," and "sharers" as part of the "same body."

wondrous care. Heard in the context of the celebration of Epiphany, this reading calls our attention to the way that God calls all the faithful to himself, not just those in a particular time or region.

| READING II | The entirety of the Christmas season centres on the chief mystery of the Incarnation, or the mystery of God-made-flesh. Christian faith in Jesus Christ holds fast to the belief that the depths of God's love are made manifest in the gift of his Son. The theology of Christianity's ancient Hebrew ancestors

likewise believed in God's desire to relate personally to his creation and to reveal his goodness to them. However, what is new with God's revelation in Christ is that God does not simply want believers who fall down in awe and worship before him, but he wants humanity to share in his divinity. This is the mystery we seek to contemplate during these days which mark the Lord's Nativity.

The second reading chosen for the Epiphany comes from the Letter to the Ephesians, which is believed to have been authored by someone other than Paul.

However, assuming the name of Paul, this author declares himself to be a steward of God's grace. The mystery of God's providence has been revealed to him so that he might now reveal it to new generations of believers, precisely the Gentiles that dwell in regions far beyond the land upon which Jesus himself walked. Rather than being a gift that serves to carve out a particular people, the grace of God described here is that of a universal gift. The objective is to draw all peoples into Christ in order to unite them together into one body. In the very next chapter of Ephesians, the author will

A reading that tells a rich and mysterious story, one that includes astrology and betrayal, providing a vivid context for the world into which Jesus was born.

The arrival of the wise men sets the scene. Their desire to pay homage to the newborn king prepares the way for our own worship.

homage = HOM-ij

Herod's fear represents doubt and deception, which the subsequent verses elaborate on.

GOSPEL   Matthew 2.1–12

A reading from the holy Gospel according to Matthew.

In the **time** of King **Herod**,
after **Jesus** was born in **Bethlehem** of **Judea**,
wise men from the **East** came to Jerusalem, asking,
"**Where** is the **child** who has been born **king** of the **Jews**?
For we observed his **star** at its **rising**,
and have **come** to pay him **homage**."
When King Herod heard this, he was **frightened**,
and **all Jerusalem** with him;
and calling together
all the chief priests and scribes of the people,
he **inquired** of them **where** the Messiah was to be **born**.
They told him, "In **Bethlehem** of **Judea**;
for **so** it has been **written** by the **Prophet**:
'And **you**, **Bethlehem**, in the land of **Judah**,
are by **no means least** among the **rulers** of Judah;
for from **you** shall **come** a **ruler**
who is to **shepherd** my people **Israel**.' "
Then **Herod secretly** called for the wise men
and learned from them the exact **time**
when the star had **appeared**.
Then he sent them to Bethlehem, saying,
"**Go** and search **diligently** for the **child**;
and when you have **found** him,
bring me **word** so that **I may also go** and pay him homage."
When they had **heard** the king, they set out;
and **there**, ahead of them,
went the **star** that they had seen at its **rising**,
until it **stopped over** the place where the **child** was.
When they **saw** that the **star** had **stopped**,
they were **overwhelmed** with **joy**. »

Pause slightly after "stopped."

challenge the community to preserve the unity they have been given in Christ, for there is "one Lord, one faith" (Ephesians 4.5). All those who hear the Gospel and are called to be "fellow heirs" must recognize that God's grace is revealed in striving for perfect unity.

GOSPEL   Chapter 1 of Matthew's Gospel, which focuses on the genealogy of Jesus as a means of situating his birth firmly within Jewish heritage, concludes with the briefest of mentions of his Nativity and Joseph naming him Jesus

(Matthew 1.25). Matthew is largely unconcerned with how Jesus was born; instead, he wants to underscore the infant's bloodline. Jesus is born in the line of David, and is thus thoroughly Jewish. This is an important detail for Matthew's Gospel because he is writing primarily for a community of Jewish Christians who recently witnessed the destruction of the Temple (AD 70). Thus, he wants his readers to understand Jesus as both fully Jewish and as the true "temple."

Keeping in mind this background information as we examine the story of the Magi's visit to Bethlehem, the encounter

opens with the foreigners' arrival in Jerusalem, as they inquire where they might find the "child who has been born king of the Jews." Notice the lack of dramatic details as well as the fact that the principal character here is really King Herod. Herod was king from 37 to 4 BC. While history portrays him as a powerful leader known for massive construction projects in Judea, Matthew records Herod's cowardice as he calls for a sweeping massacre of all boys under the age of two (Matthew 2.13–18). Thus, the story of the wise men, who come from the ends of the earth, functions to

Awe and wonder authenticate the wise men and their prophetic visions. Their gifts are utterly precious. And their dream of warning is impossible to ignore. Don't sell their departure short. It's what makes this passage so vivid.

On entering the house,
they **saw** the child with **Mary** his mother;
and they **knelt down** and paid him **homage**.
Then, opening their treasure chests,
they offered him gifts of **gold, frankincense**, and **myrrh**.
And having been **warned** in a **dream** not to **return** to Herod,
they **left** for their own country by **another** road.

show how all of Herod's plotting is no match for God's designs.

Furthermore, this passage illustrates the universalism of God's revelation. It is not insiders from the Jewish establishment who recognize and pay homage to the newborn babe; instead, foreigners come "from the East" to offer their gifts of gold, frankincense, and myrrh. Matthew records the Magi prostrating themselves before the child, a posture which we see elsewhere in the Gospel when the Apostles encounter the risen Lord and he charges them to "make disciples of all nations" (Matthew 28.17–20). All the world is meant to recognize the saving power of Jesus.

At the end of this passage, we see that Herod's plan to find and destroy the infant Jesus is foiled, as the wise men are told in a dream not to give a report to Herod. We know from the remaining verses of chapter 2 that Herod will not relent in his search for the child king. Thus, Matthew demonstrates from the very outset of Jesus' birth that his mission upon earth will not be readily welcomed. In fact, Jesus' own people will pose one of the biggest threats to his ministry. We celebrate the Epiphany of the Lord to remember that God's message of salvation is not meant to be the sole possession of any one people; rather, God manifests himself to every nation so that the world will give him homage. S.W.

THE BAPTISM OF THE LORD

LECTIONARY #21

READING I Isaiah 42.1–4, 6–7

A reading from the book of the Prophet Isaiah.

Thus says the **Lord**:
"**Here** is my **servant**, whom I uphold,
my **chosen**, in whom my soul **delights**;
I have **put** my **spirit** upon him;
he will bring forth **justice** to the **nations**.
He will not **cry** or **lift up** his voice,
or make it **heard** in the **street**;
a bruised reed he will not break,
and a **dimly burning wick** he will not **quench**;
he will faithfully bring forth **justice**.
He will not grow **faint** or be **crushed**
until he has established **justice** in the **earth**;
and the **coastlands** wait for his **teaching**.
I am the Lord, I have **called** you in **righteousness**,
I have **taken** you by the **hand** and **kept** you;
I have **given** you as a **covenant** to the people,
a **light** to the nations,
to open the **eyes** that are blind,
to bring out the **prisoners** from the **dungeon**,
from the **prison** those who sit in **darkness**."

Isaiah = ī-ZAY-uh

A reading in which the Lord identifies his servant, characterizing his virtues in terms of his humility and preparedness, followed by a passage in which the Lord shifts from talking about his chosen servant in the third person ("he") to the second person ("you"), which allows you to direct your proclamation to the gathered assembly. Take advantage of this shift in pronouns.

Even stresses on the words in this line, which present a compelling image. A bruised reed is easy to break; why isn't the chosen servant breaking the reed?

Emphasize "taken you by the hand" and "kept you."

The passage ends with images of dire things the Lord will use "you" to correct.

READING I The Book of Isaiah contains four poems that introduce the theme of God sending a "suffering servant," who will sacrifice his dignity and his entire self for the people's redemption. Chapter 42 begins the first of these poems. It opens by employing the Lord's voice to reveal this servant to Israel. The Lord deems this one as "chosen" because he has already pleased the Lord by all he has done. Empowered by God's spirit, the emissary has the task of bringing justice to the world. The Lord suggests that his servant's arrival will be highly anticipated, as even the faraway regions of the earth await his teaching.

From a Christian perspective, we know that the teaching that Jesus brought to the earth was not what his own people wanted to hear. They were hoping for a political figure who would rid Judea of foreign control and would finally establish Israel's reign as supreme on earth. Instead, God has quite a different mission for his chosen servant. Verses 6 and 7 of chapter 42 describe the Lord providing instructions for the one he has chosen to establish God's justice. God calls his anointed one "a cove- nant to the people" and "a light to the nations." The law of the covenant that the faithful servant of God reveals to the peo- ple is one focused on mercy and compas- sion, as he will give sight to the blind, release to prisoners, and light to those trapped in darkness. The Suffering Servant will prove to be victorious not by his politi- cal might but by his loving justice.

READING II Chapter 10 of Acts wit- nesses Peter entering the house of Cornelius, a Roman centurion, and there experiencing a great change of heart.

For meditation and context:

RESPONSORIAL PSALM   Psalm 29.1–2, 3ac–4, 3b+9c–10 (R.11b)

R. The Lord will bless his people with peace.

Ascribe to the Lord, O heavenly beings,
ascribe to the Lord glory and strength.
Ascribe to the Lord the glory of his name;
worship the Lord in holy splendour.

The voice of the Lord is over the waters;
the Lord, over mighty waters.
The voice of the Lord is powerful;
the voice of the Lord is full of majesty.

The God of glory thunders,
and in his temple all say, "Glory!"
The Lord sits enthroned over the flood;
the Lord sits enthroned as king forever.

This reading expresses ancient convictions of the earliest members of the faith.

"Peace," "Christ," and "Lord" express a unified vision of things.

Even emphasis on the words of this line.

Even emphasis here as well, characterizing Jesus' powers.

READING II   Acts 10.34–38

A reading from the Acts of the Apostles.

Peter began to speak:
"I **truly understand** that **God** shows no **partiality**,
but in every nation anyone who **fears** him and does what is **right**
is **acceptable** to him.
You know the **message** he sent to the **people of Israel**,
preaching peace by Jesus **Christ**—he is **Lord** of all.
That message **spread** throughout Judea,
beginning in Galilee after the **baptism** that John announced:
how God **anointed** Jesus of Nazareth
with the **Holy Spirit** and with **power**;
how he went about doing **good**
and healing all who were oppressed by the devil,
for **God** was **with** him."

As a faithful Jew, entering the house of a Gentile would have caused Peter to stand apart from the Law. However, he listens to an Angel in a vision and comes to have a new relationship with this foreign household.

Today's reading begins after Peter discerns the meaning of his vision. He discovers that "God shows no partiality" in bestowing his message of salvation upon all people. Instead of choosing people according to a particular nation, God finds acceptable the one who "fears him and does what is right." Furthermore, Peter deems those in Cornelius' household as "acceptable" to God

precisely because they have heard the word intended for the Israelites but which is now extended to them. Thus, Peter names Jesus "Lord of all."

Our portion of Peter's discourse concludes with a summary statement of all that Jesus had accomplished in the land of Judea. We are right to suggest that Peter sees no partiality in the ministry of Jesus, as his good deeds went out to all who were in need. In a similar way, Peter has come to know that those who have heard the word must also act with impartiality. Herein lies a primary gift of baptism; baptism in the Lord

provides a unity that no human bias can divide.

GOSPEL The entire liturgical season of Christmas might be thought of as a manifestation of divine theophany. A theophany occurs when God is made manifest to humankind. The manger scene, the celebration of Mary as the ark of God's coming into the world, the journey of the wise men to Bethlehem, and today, the baptism of Jesus in the Jordan are all grand theophanies which reveal the depth of God's love breaking into the world.

GOSPEL   Matthew 3.13–17

A reading from the holy Gospel according to Matthew.

Jesus came from **Galilee** to **John** at the Jordan,
to be **baptized** by him.
John would have **prevented** him, saying,
"I need to be **baptized** by **you**,
and do you come to **me**?"
But **Jesus** answered him, "**Let** it be **so** for **now**;
for it is proper for us in **this way** to fulfill all **righteousness**."
Then **John consented**.
And when **Jesus** had been **baptized**,
just as he came **up** from the **water**,
suddenly the **heavens** were **opened** to him
and he saw the Spirit of God **descending** like a dove
and **alighting** on him.
And a **voice** from heaven **said**,
"**This** is my Son, the Beloved,
with **whom** I am **well** pleased."

Galilee = GAL-ih-lee
A reading that emphasizes the simple power of baptism.

Note the shift in the pronouns here, from "I" to "you," then from "you" to "me."

Slight pause between "God" and "descending."

Matthew's account of Jesus' baptism begins with John trying prevent Jesus from being baptized. Obviously, John does not believe that Jesus needs to undergo baptism as a means of repentance and conversion. Instead, he presents himself to Jesus as the one who needs to be baptized. Matthew's resolution to this dilemma is to put this event into the framework of fulfillment, which he frequently employs throughout the Gospel as a whole. In this case, Jesus announces to John that he wishes to be baptized "to fulfill all righteousness," demonstrating total obedience to the will of God.

The theophany which seals the Lord's baptism is symbolized by the descent of a dove upon the head of Jesus. The Spirit provides a visible sign that accompanies the Father's voice in announcing the presence of his Son. Similar to the story of Noah sending the dove forth from the ark to testify to the dried earth (Genesis 8.6–12), so too is a dove associated with the regeneration of creation inaugurated at the Lord's baptism. God chose Israel as his beloved possession, and now God's relationship with Jesus reveals him as the New Covenant; in Jesus God's promise is fulfilled, and the world begins anew. From the manger to the Jordan, God's in-breaking into the world manifests a new creation. S.W.

SECOND SUNDAY IN ORDINARY TIME

LECTIONARY #64

READING I   Isaiah 49.3, 5–6

Isaiah = ī-ZAY-uh

The tone of this reading is encouraging. Slight pause between "Lord" and "said." Emphasis on "you."

Slight pause between "Jacob" and "back."

The reading concludes with God's promise to Isaiah, which is God's promise to his people.

A reading from the book of the Prophet Isaiah.

The **Lord said** to me,
"**You** are my servant, **Israel**, in **whom** I will be glorified."
And **now** the Lord says,
who **formed** me in the **womb** to be his **servant**,
to bring **Jacob back** to him,
and that **Israel** might be **gathered** to him,
for I am **honoured** in the **sight** of the **Lord**,
and my **God** has become my **strength**.
He says,
"It is **too small** a **thing** that you should **be** my **servant**
to raise **up** the tribes of **Jacob**
and to **restore** the **survivors** of **Israel**;
I will give you as a **light** to the **nations**,
that my **salvation** may **reach** to the **end** of the **earth**."

READING I This Sunday marks the end of the first week of the liturgical season called "Ordinary Time" and the beginning of its second week. Ordinary Time is the period of the Church year that stands outside of the all-important Advent/ Christmas and Lent/Easter seasons. However, to call this period "ordinary" is not to say that it is unimportant. Its name shares a root with the Latin term *ordinalis*, meaning "numbered." Thus, the thirty-four weeks of Ordinary Time mark the movement of time as the salvation story unfolds through the year. Green is the liturgical colour for this season, which is appropriate because it represents a time of spiritual growth. The readings for this Second Sunday in Ordinary Time focus on the commissioning of God's servants to reveal God's plan of salvation for the world.

Today's first reading is taken from what is often called "the second servant song" of the Book of Isaiah. Altogether there are four. This servant song describes a commissioning of the servant as a Prophet or spokesperson of God. Although the identity of the servant is sometimes unclear in the Book of Isaiah, here he is clearly identi- fied with Israel. But which Israel? The set- ting for this commissioning is the period after the Babylonian Exile, when King Cyrus of Persia allowed the Judeans to return to their homeland and rebuild their temple. Although we cannot know for certain, it appears that this Prophet is among a small group of Judeans who are persecuted because of their opposition to more power- ful returnees who have a different view of life in Judea after the Exile. Thus, the Prophet, who is personified Israel, is com- missioned to effect a change of heart in the rest of Israel. God responds by saying that

48

For meditation and context:

RESPONSORIAL PSALM   Psalm 40.1+3a, 6, 7–8, 9 (R.7–8)

R. Here I am, Lord; I come to do your will.

I waited patiently for the Lord;
he inclined to me and heard my cry.
He put a new song in my mouth,
a song of praise to our God.

Sacrifice and offering you do not desire,
but you have given me an open ear.
Burnt offering and sin offering
you have not required.

Then I said, "Here I am;
in the scroll of the book it is written of me.
I delight to do your will, O my God;
your law is within my heart."

I have told the glad news of deliverance
in the great congregation;
see, I have not restrained my lips,
as you know, O Lord.

READING II   1 Corinthians 1.1–3

Corinthians = kohr-IN-thee-uhnz

A reading from the first Letter of Saint Paul to the Corinthians.

The tone of this reading is introductory. It involves one long, inclusive sentence followed by a much shorter blessing. Proclaim the first long part, up to "Grace to you . . . ," in the spirit of an introduction, and the second, shorter part in the spirit of a blessing.

From **Paul**, called to be an **Apostle** of **Christ Jesus**
by the **will** of **God**,
and from our **brother Sosthenes**.
To the **Church** of **God** that is in **Corinth**,
to **those** who are **sanctified** in **Christ Jesus**,
called to be **saints**,
together with **all those** who in **every place**
call on the **name** of our **Lord Jesus Christ**,
both **their** Lord and **ours**:
Grace to **you** and **peace** from **God** our **Father**
and the **Lord Jesus Christ**.

---

this restored and true Israel will shine as a beacon, inviting everyone to share in its light.

READING II   Our second reading is taken from the opening section of Paul's First Letter to the Corinthians. The mostly Gentile Christian church at Corinth was founded by Paul. Acts of the Apostles suggests that he spent a year and a half with this community before moving on to evangelize other locations in the Mediterranean (Acts 18.11), so

he knew them well, and the content of this first letter reveals as much. The opening follows the pattern of a first-century letter opening: sender, recipient, greeting. Paul, the sender, describes himself as an "Apostle," that is, "one who is sent" by God's will. He describes the community as set apart for God and called to be "saints" in the fellowship of Christ. But Paul also wants to remind them that they belong to a much larger community of faith who serve the one God and the Lord Jesus Christ. What a good reminder for us, as well.

GOSPEL   Today's Gospel reading is another version of the story of the baptism of Jesus that we heard last Sunday. This version from the Gospel of John is unique insofar as the author uses John the Baptist as the narrator of the baptism event, as he speaks to his own disciples, two of whom will soon shift their allegiance and become followers of Jesus. John the Baptist identifies Jesus as the Lamb of God and testifies that he is the Son of God.

GOSPEL   John 1.29–34

A reading from the holy Gospel according to John.

John the **Baptist** saw **Jesus** coming **toward** him
and **declared**,
"**Here** is the **Lamb** of **God** who **takes away** the sin of the **world**!
This is **he** of whom I **said**,
'After **me** comes a **man** who ranks **ahead** of me
because he was **before** me.'
I **myself** did not **know** him;
but I came **baptizing** with **water** for this reason,
that he might be **revealed** to Israel."
And **John** testified,
"I **saw** the **Spirit descending** from **heaven** like a **dove**,
and **remain** on him.
I **myself** did not **know** him,
but the **one** who **sent** me to **baptize** with **water said** to me,
'**He** on whom you see the **Spirit descend** and **remain**
is the **one** who **baptizes** with the **Holy Spirit**.'
And **I myself** have **seen** and have **testified**
that **this** is the **Son** of God."

This reading begins with a very familiar phrase from the Eucharistic prayer we hear at Mass. Proclaim it with the same reverence you would hear during Mass.

The Baptist's words connect the Mass with the visionary reality he peered into. Speak the words "I saw" clearly. Slight pause between "Spirit" and "descending."

Slight pause between "Spirit" and "descend."

Biblical scholars offer several possible scenarios for understanding the title "Lamb of God." Perhaps it is an allusion to a powerful and victorious lamb like the one depicted in the Book of Revelation, who stands before God's throne (Revelation 5.6–14) and who presides over an army of God's holy ones (Revelation 14.1–5). More likely, it is a reference to the Passover lamb, whose blood was placed on the lintels and door posts of the Israelites' homes in Egypt so that the Angel of death would pass over their homes in the last plague of the Exodus story. Equally possible, "Lamb of God" might be an allusion to Yom Kippur, the Jewish day of atonement, when animal sacrifices were offered at the Jerusalem Temple for the sins of the people.

Notice that this Gospel account does not include the tradition about Jesus and John the Baptist being related to one another (see Luke 1.26–38). Instead, the Baptist recognizes Jesus as Lamb of God and Son of God only because it was revealed to him through the work he was commissioned to do. The baptism which John was sent to perform is not a baptism of repentance like what we see in Matthew and Luke. Rather, its function was revelatory. John was called to reveal Jesus to all of Israel and to witness to the world that he is the Son of God. Finally, notice how the Baptizer knew Jesus' identity. It was because of the Spirit who descended on Jesus and remained on him. The verbs "to remain" and "to abide," in John's Gospel, are symbolic language used to describe discipleship and the special relationship of indwelling that Jesus enjoys with the Father. C.C.

THIRD SUNDAY IN ORDINARY TIME

LECTIONARY #67

READING I   Isaiah 9.1–4

A reading from the book of the Prophet Isaiah.

There will be **no gloom** for **those** who were in **anguish**.
In the **former time** the **Lord** brought into **contempt**
the land of **Zebulun** and the land of **Naphtali**,
but in the **latter time** he will make **glorious**
the **way** of the **sea**,
the **land** beyond the **Jordan**, **Galilee** of the **nations**.
The **people** who walked in **darkness** have **seen** a **great light**;
those who **lived** in a land of **deep darkness**—
on **them** light has **shone**.
You have **multiplied** the **nation**,
you have **increased** its **joy**;
they **rejoice before** you
as with **joy** at the **harvest**,
as people **exult** when dividing **plunder**.
For the **yoke** of their **burden**,
and the **bar** across their **shoulders**,
the **rod** of their **oppressor**,
you have **broken** as on the **day** of **Midian**.

Isaiah = ī-ZAY-uh

The tone of this reading is triumphant and uplifting.

Zebulun = ZEB-yoo-luhn

NAF-tuh-li

Emphasis on "deep darkness."

"Joy" and "rejoice" describe the message of this reading.

Emphasis on "yoke," "bar," and "rod."

Midian = MID-ee-uhn

READING I   On this Third Sunday in Ordinary Time, the theme of today's readings is the same as last Sunday: the commissioning of God's servants to reveal God's salvation to the world.

Our first reading is from the Book of Isaiah. When reading the Prophets, it is important to know as much as we can about the historical context, because, regardless of the meanings we attach to their oracles today, the Prophets were addressing real-life situations in their own time. We cannot be confident of the integrity of our contemporary interpretations of prophetic discourse unless we can connect the circumstances of the past with the present.

Isaiah served as God's Prophet for approximately forty years, during which time he witnessed the Assyrian conquest of the northern kingdom of Israel, also known as Ephraim, beginning in 733 BC and Syria in 732 BC. When the oracle that comprises our first reading was delivered, Ahaz was king of Judah. He was facing considerable pressure from Syria and Israel to join a coalition against Assyria. When he refused, Syria and Israel invaded Judah with the intent of unseating Ahaz—an event known as the Syro-Ephraimite War. Eventually, the entire northern kingdom was decimated by the Assyrians and its people deported in 721 BC, while the southern kingdom of Judah became a vassal of Assyria.

This truly was a dark time in Judah's history. Isaiah attributes the destruction of Israel to God, according to the pattern of Deuteronomistic history: Israel sins; God punishes; Israel repents; God forgives. How does God show forgiveness? The Assyrian provinces of Dor, Gilead, and Megiddo, which were fashioned from land that once belonged to Israel, are allowed to prosper.

For meditation and context:

RESPONSORIAL PSALM   Psalm 27.1, 4, 13–14 (R.1a)

R. The Lord is my light and my salvation.

The Lord is my light and my salvation;
whom shall I fear?
The Lord is the stronghold of my life;
of whom shall I be afraid?

One thing I asked of the Lord, that will I
seek after:
to live in the house of the Lord all the days
of my life,
to behold the beauty of the Lord,
and to inquire in his temple.

I believe that I shall see the goodness of
the Lord
in the land of the living.
Wait for the Lord; be strong,
and let your heart take courage; wait for
the Lord!

READING II   1 Corinthians 1.10–13, 17–18

A reading from the first Letter of Saint Paul to the Corinthians.

Corinthians = kohr-IN-thee-uhnz

The tone of this reading is one of urgency and intensity.

Slight pause between "divisions" and "among."

Chloe = KLOH-ee

Note the shifts in energy from the pronoun "I" to the proper nouns, "Paul," "Apollos," "Cephas," and "Christ."

Apollos = uh-POL-uhs

Cephas = SEE-fuhs

These two questions shape Paul's argument to the Corinthians. Slight pause between "Paul" and "crucified."

I **appeal** to you, **brothers** and **sisters**,
by the **name** of our **Lord** Jesus **Christ**,
that **all** of you be in **agreement**
and that there **be no divisions among** you,
but that you be **united** in the **same mind** and the **same purpose**.
For it has been **reported** to me by **Chloe's people**
that there are **quarrels among** you, my **brothers** and **sisters**.
What I **mean** is that **each** of you says,
"I belong to **Paul**,"
or "I belong to **Apollos**,"
or "I belong to **Cephas**,"
or "I belong to **Christ**."
Has **Christ** been **divided**?
Was **Paul crucified** for **you**?
Or were you **baptized** in the name of **Paul**?

Thus, as the Prophet says, the gloom and darkness will be lifted, and light will shine on the land. The pronoun "you" in this passage refers to God; Isaiah is the speaker. Biblical scholars have described this part of today's reading as a hymn to accompany accession to the throne or a thanksgiving hymn directed to God. The "yoke," "bar," and "rod" are symbols of Assyrian oppression that will one day be thrown off in holy war, as in the day of Midian and as when God destroyed the Israelites' oppressors by the hand of Gideon, one of several judges whose stories are told in the book of Judges (see Judges 6—8).

The remainder of this oracle, which is not part of today's first reading, is presumed to be about the son that would be born to Ahaz, whose name was Hezekiah and who would inherit Judah's throne after Ahaz. The Second Book of Kings and the Second Book of Chronicles portray him as a good and righteous king, in contrast to his father. However, the list of attributes of a good king, the verses that follow today's reading that describe the child to be born, might be intended to describe some future and long-awaited king. Early Christians attributed this description to Jesus, the bringer of peace and the one who will usher in the fullness of God's kingdom.

READING II Today's second reading is the beginning of the body of Paul's First Letter to the Corinthians. Immediately following the thanksgiving (1 Corinthians 1.4–9), Paul exhorts the Corinthian community to unity after hearing a report about divisions that have surfaced among them. The report came from "Chloe's people," who we can assume

For **Christ** did not send me to **baptize**
but to **proclaim** the **Gospel**,
and **not** with eloquent **wisdom**
so that the **Cross** of **Christ** might not be **emptied** of its **power**.
For the **message** about the **Cross**
is **foolishness** to those who are **perishing**,
but to **us** who are being **saved** it is the **power** of **God**.

GOSPEL   Matthew 4.12–23

A reading from the holy Gospel according to Matthew.

[When **Jesus** heard that John had been **arrested**,
he **withdrew** to **Galilee**.
He left **Nazareth** and made his **home** in **Capernaum** by the **sea**,
in the **territory** of **Zebulun** and **Naphtali**,
so that what had been **spoken** through the **Prophet Isaiah**
might be **fulfilled**:
"Land of **Zebulun**, land of **Naphtali**,
on the **road** by the **sea**, across the **Jordan**,
Galilee of the **Gentiles**—
the **people** who sat in **darkness**
have seen a **great light**,
and for **those** who sat in the **region** and **shadow** of **death**
light has **dawned**."
From **that time Jesus** began to proclaim,
"**Repent**, for the **kingdom** of **heaven** has come **near**."]
As he **walked** by the Sea of **Galilee**,
he saw **two brothers**,
Simon, who is called **Peter**, and **Andrew** his brother,
casting a **net** into the **sea**, for they were **fishermen**. »

The tenuousness and excitement of Christ beginning his ministry pervade this reading. For the longer form of the reading, use the word "withdrew" to focus your proclamation.

Capernaum = kuh-PER-nee-*m or kuh-PER-nay-*m or kuh-PER-n*m
Naphtali = NAF-tuh-lī

Slight pause between "death" and "light."

are employees or slaves of this otherwise unknown businesswoman. We can further assume that Chloe and her servants are followers of Jesus. The servants probably visited the community while on a business trip in or through Corinth and then reported to Paul what they had seen and heard.

Paul is understandably concerned about the divisions in the community, because of his understanding of church as *koinonia*, meaning "fellowship or partnership." This is why he urges them to "be united in the same mind and in the same purpose." Apparently, their divisions stem from allegiances that they formed around the person they claim as their spiritual leader. Apollos, who is mentioned here and elsewhere in this letter, is described in Acts of the Apostles as a Jewish rhetorician and Scripture scholar from Alexandria in Egypt, who later became a Christian preacher (Acts 18.24–28). Most likely, the person whom Paul names as Cephas is Peter. Paul uses this same name in his Letter to the Galatians.

In context, the meaning of "I belong to Christ" is not clear, but Paul's response to the community was to fire off a set of rhetorical questions, in which the speaker is not looking for a response because the intended answer is embedded in the question. This is much more easily done in Greek than in English, but the three questions would read something like this: Then you are saying that Christ is divided, aren't you? And you are not saying that Paul was crucified for you, are you? And you cannot be saying that you were baptized in Paul's name, can you?

Paul's argument reaches its climax when he declares the primary purpose of his ministry: to preach the good news

Use "fishers of people" to focus your proclamation for the second half of this reading.

Zebedee = ZEB-uh-dee

Jesus' ministry begins in earnest.

And he **said** to them,
"**Come**, follow **me**, and I will make you **fishers** of people."
Immediately they left their **nets** and followed him.
As he **went** from **there**, he saw **two other brothers**,
James son of **Zebedee** and his brother **John**,
in the **boat** with their father **Zebedee**, **mending** their **nets**,
and he **called** them.
Immediately they left the **boat** and their **father**,
    and **followed** him.
Jesus went throughout **Galilee**,
teaching in their **synagogues**
and proclaiming the **good news** of the **kingdom**
and curing **every disease** and **every sickness among** the **people**.

[Shorter: Matthew 4.12–17 (see brackets)]

of Jesus Christ, even if imperfectly, so that the power of Jesus' crucifixion can be made manifest in their hearts and minds.

GOSPEL Perhaps you know that the lectionary is organized so that the themes of the first reading and the Gospel cohere in some way. Today's first reading and Gospel reading are a perfect example. Notice how the author of Matthew's Gospel situates Jesus' ministry in the region of Galilee and cites an abbreviated version of the prophecy we hear from Isaiah in the first reading. One might deduce from the way that the writer incorporated this quotation that he intends to suggest that Jesus is the light to the nations and the one who will initiate God's coming kingdom.

As an indication of the Gospel writer's Jewish background, he describes Jesus as calling for repentance and saying, "the kingdom of heaven has come near" not "kingdom of God," as we see in the other Gospels. Out of respect for the name of God, our Jewish brothers and sisters do not speak the name aloud. Regardless of whether we use the phrase "kingdom of God" or "kingdom of heaven," it is important to recognize that Jesus is not talking about a place. Instead, we should think about the kingdom as the reign of God, when God's power is fully manifest for all to see and when there is no more hunger or violence, sickness or death in all the world. Such is the good news of Jesus Christ! C.C.

FOURTH SUNDAY IN ORDINARY TIME

LECTIONARY #70

READING I   Zephaniah 2:3; 3:12–13

A reading from the book of the Prophet Zephaniah.

Seek the **Lord**, all you **humble** of the **land**,
who **do** his **commands**;
seek **righteousness**, seek **humility**;
perhaps you may be **hidden** on the **day** of the Lord's **wrath**.
For I will **leave** in the **midst** of you
a people **humble** and **lowly**.
They shall seek **refuge** in the name of the **Lord**—
the **remnant** of **Israel**;
they shall **do no wrong** and **utter no lies**,
nor shall a **deceitful tongue** be **found** in their **mouths**.
Then they will **pasture** and lie **down**,
and **no one** shall **make** them **afraid**.

Zephaniah = zef-uh-Nī-uh

The tone of this reading is stern but hopeful.

remnant = REM-n*nt

Note the parallel between "do no wrong" and "utter no lies."

Emphasis on "no one."

For meditation and context:

RESPONSORIAL PSALM   Psalm 146.6c–7, 8–9a, 9b–10 (R. Mt 5.3)

R. Blessed are the poor in spirit; the kingdom of heaven is theirs!
or: Alleluia!

It is the Lord who keeps faith forever,
who executes justice for the oppressed;
who gives food to the hungry.
The Lord sets the prisoners free.

The Lord opens the eyes of the blind
and lifts up those who are bowed down;
the Lord loves the righteous
and watches over the strangers.

The Lord upholds the orphan and the widow,
but the way of the wicked he brings to ruin.
The Lord will reign forever,
your God, O Zion, for all generations.

READING I Zephaniah prophesied in the land of Judah during the reign of King Josiah (640–609 BC). His writing is part of a group of texts known as the twelve minor Prophets. His work is considered "minor" not because of any lack important content but because the Book of Zephaniah and the other eleven books of the minor Prophets are much shorter in length than those of the Prophets Isaiah, Jeremiah, Ezekiel, and Daniel.

The prophecy of Zephaniah takes place at a time when Babylon was soon to destroy Jerusalem and send the Israelites into exile. Zephaniah accuses the people of Judah of being far too prideful, and so he seeks to counter their arrogance with a message that calls them to reform and humility. The Prophet speaks of a "remnant" who will successfully "seek refuge" in the Lord on the day that he comes to seek vengeance for the nation's wrongdoing. Zephaniah hopes that, on that fateful day, the Lord will discover several contrite lowly ones, whose humility of heart will counter the pride of the people.

Throughout the Old Testament we can see the belief that the people held, that even after suffering a major disaster, such as a famine or a military collapse, some portion of God's chosen people would remain. Isaiah and Jeremiah likewise prophesied that some of the Israelites would be saved as a "remnant," who would one day be redeemed (for example, see Isaiah 6.13 and Jeremiah 31.7–14). It is also important to notice that Zephaniah suggests that salvation will take place by taking refuge in the Lord, not by standing up to warring invaders. Instead, "they will pasture and lie down, and no one shall make them afraid." Thus, Zephaniah calls for a conversion of

---

READING II   1 Corinthians 1.26–31

Corinthians = kohr-IN-thee-uhnz

Paul's tone to the members of the early church in Corinth is critical but encouraging.

A reading from the first Letter of Saint Paul to the Corinthians.

Consider your own **call**, **brothers** and **sisters**:
not **many** of you were **wise** by **human standards**,
not **many** were **powerful**,
not **many** were of noble **birth**.
But **God chose** what is **foolish** in the **world** to **shame** the **wise**;
God chose what is **weak** in the **world** to **shame** the **strong**;
God chose what is **low** and **despised** in the **world**,
things that are **not**,
to reduce to **nothing things** that **are**,
so that **no one** might **boast** in the **presence** of **God**.
God is the **source** of your **life** in **Christ Jesus**,
who **became** for us **wisdom** from **God**,
and **righteousness** and **sanctification** and **redemption**,
in order that, as it is **written**,
"Let the **one** who **boasts**, **boast** in the **Lord**."

Note the repetition of "God chose."

despised = dih-SPĪZd

Slight pause between "nothing" and "things."

righteousness = RĪ-chuhs-nis

sanctification = sangk-tuh-fih-KAY-shuhn

Don't hurry through these three abstract terms.

GOSPEL   Matthew 5.1–12

A reading from the holy Gospel according to Matthew.

When **Jesus** saw the **crowds**, he **went up** the **mountain**;
and after he sat **down**, his disciples **came** to him.
Then he began to **speak**, and **taught** them, **saying**:
"**Blessed** are the **poor** in **spirit**,
for **theirs** is the **kingdom** of **heaven**.
Blessed are **those** who **mourn**,
for **they** will be **comforted**.
Blessed are the **meek**,
for **they** will inherit the **earth**.

Emphasis on "taught." This reading includes some of Jesus' best-known instructions.

The power of this reading depends on the rhythm you establish between the words that anchor the phrases paired in each beatitude. Say "blest" rather than "bless-ed."

---

heart that replaces pride with humility, as the people place their complete dependence upon God.

READING II This reading from 1 Corinthians serves as a perfect bridge between our first reading and the Gospel. In the first reading, we heard how God protects those who are humble, and in the Gospel for today, we will hear how the Lord calls "blessed" those who are meek and humble of heart. The theme of this passage from 1 Corinthians is quite simply that God chooses those whom the world considers to be fools in order to put to shame those who consider themselves to be wise. In all three readings, it is clear that God does not operate according to the standards of this world; belonging to God's kingdom requires selflessness rather than selfishness.

Paul has just finished telling the Corinthians that he preaches Christ crucified, which is considered folly according to the wisdom of the Greeks (1 Corinthians 1.18–25). Now he reminds them that they are considered chosen by God, not because of wisdom or nobility, but rather, because of their faith in Christ, which the world sees as weakness. The mission of those chosen by God is to cling so tight to this faith that others will see that human boastfulness is empty and counts for nothing. What matters is being able to boast of one's faith. Paul employs the beautiful phrase "Let the one who boasts, boast in the Lord," which he will repeat to the Corinthians in his second letter (2 Corinthians 10.17). With this strong faith, and not futile wisdom, the Corinthians may count themselves part of Christ. Relying solely on this wisdom, they know that God has saved them (redemp-

Emphasis on "reward" and "great."

Blessed are those who **hunger** and **thirst** for **righteousness**,
for **they** will be **filled**.
Blessed are the **merciful**,
for **they** will receive **mercy**.
Blessed are the **pure** in **heart**,
for **they** will see **God**.
Blessed are the **peacemakers**,
for **they** will be called **children** of **God**.
Blessed are those who are **persecuted** for **righteousness'** sake,
for **theirs** is the kingdom of **heaven**.
Blessed are you when **people revile** you and **persecute** you
and utter **all kinds** of **evil** against you **falsely** on my **account**.
Rejoice and be **glad**,
for your **reward** is **great** in **heaven**,
for in the **same way** they persecuted the **Prophets**
who were before you."

TO KEEP IN MIND

When you proclaim Word, you participate in catechizing the faithful and those coming to faith. Understand what you proclaim so those hearing you may also understand.

---

tion), freed them from the way of sin (sanctification), and called them to live upright before God (righteousness).

GOSPEL Today's Gospel passage from the beginning of the fifth chapter of Matthew opens a reading of Jesus' Sermon on the Mount (chapters 5 to 7) that will continue for the next several Sundays in Ordinary Time. Jesus' inaugural preaching event takes place on a Galilean hillside to which crowds were coming from near and far (Matthew 4.25). When Jesus sees the crowd, he gathers his disciples closest to him and begins with the pronouncement of the beatitudes, telling them what it means to be counted among the "blessed" in God's kingdom.

While Luke portrays Jesus proclaiming four beatitudes (Luke 6.20–23), Matthew's version contains nine. A major difference between them is that Luke focuses on a preferential option in this life for the poor, the hungry, and those who mourn, while Matthew broadens these categories to make them more about a spirituality centred on the kingdom of heaven. For example, in Matthew, it is not simply the "poor" who are blessed, but the "poor in spirit." It is not simply the "hungry" who are blessed, but those who "hunger and thirst for righteousness." In all the beatitudes, those who are deemed "blessed" are those favoured by God because their suffering in this world will be overturned under the reign of God. Keeping the attitudes of the kingdom in this life will lead to a reward in the heavenly kingdom. S.W.

FIFTH SUNDAY IN ORDINARY TIME

LECTIONARY #73

READING I   Isaiah 58.6–10++

Isaiah = ī-ZAY-uh

This highly poetic reading is in the imperative voice. God is speaking forcefully to the people through Isaiah. Use this to guide your proclamation.

A reading from the book of the Prophet Isaiah.

Thus says the **Lord**:
Is this not the **fast** that I **choose**:
to **loose** the **bonds** of **injustice**,
to **undo** the **thongs** of the **yoke**,
to let the **oppressed** go **free**,
and to **break** every **yoke**?
Is it not to share your **bread** with the **hungry**,
and bring the **homeless poor** into your **house**;
when you see the **naked**, to **cover** them,
and not to **hide** yourself from your own **kin**?

Emphasis on "light" and "break forth."

Then your **light** shall **break forth** like the **dawn**,
and your **healing** shall spring up **quickly**;
your **vindicator** shall go **before** you,
the glory of the **Lord** shall be your rear guard.
Then you shall **call**, and the Lord will **answer**;
you shall cry for **help**, and he will say, **Here** I am.
If you **remove** the **yoke** from **among** you,

Equal emphasis on all the things to be removed: "yoke," "pointing," and "speaking."

the **pointing** of the **finger**, the **speaking** of **evil**,
if you **offer** your **food** to the **hungry**
and **satisfy** the **needs** of the **afflicted**,
then your **light** shall **rise** in the **darkness**
and your **gloom** be like the **noonday**.

READING I | Today's reading comes from the third major section of the Book of Isaiah. This portion of Isaiah differs from the first two sections in that it is addressed to the Israelites who have returned from exile in Babylon and are now charged with the responsibility of building a new nation. Isaiah likens this restored generation to a light that will shine forth for other nations to behold.

While it is clear that political and military concerns will be on the minds of those attempting to rebuild their nation, Isaiah pays particular attention to their treatment of the poor. It is important to locate this reading within the larger framework of the chapter, which focuses on fasting and the need to avoid empty ritualism. Isaiah wants the people to understand that their fasting will be of little consequence if they do not feed the hungry, shelter the homeless, and clothe the naked. These and other acts of compassion will serve to scatter the darkness and reflect the light of God's love.

Moreover, not only will light emanate from Israel, but when their compassion is demonstrated and their underlying spirit of goodness is manifested, then God's glory will guard them. The Prophet speaks of the people being vindicated. As we read these words, we call to mind how God has protected his people in the past. For example, consider how the ancient Israelites were vindicated at the Red Sea, with God's Angel leading the people in cloud by day and in fire by night. In today's reading, we hear Isaiah prophecy, "your vindicator shall go before you, the glory of the Lord shall be your rear guard." For Isaiah, attention to the poor and the oppressed will be like a key that opens the door to success for the former refugees. He envisions the return to

For meditation and context:

RESPONSORIAL PSALM Psalm 112.4–5, 6–7, 8a–9 (R.4)

R. Light rises in the darkness for the upright.
or: Alleluia!

Light rises in the darkness for the upright:
gracious, merciful and righteous.
It is well with the person who deals
      generously and lends,
who conducts their affairs with justice.

For the righteous person will never
      be moved;
they will be remembered forever.
Unafraid of evil tidings;
their heart is firm, secure in the Lord.

That person's heart is steady and will not
      be afraid.
One who has distributed freely, who has
      given to the poor,
their righteousness endures forever:
their name is exalted in honour.

Corinthians = kohr-IN-thee-uhnz

The energy of this reading relies on the accumulation of negatives—negative attributes as well as things Paul claims he did not do. And these accumulate right up to the concluding line of the reading, when the "power of God" bursts forth in a positive shower.

READING II   1 Corinthians 2.1–5

A reading from the first Letter of Saint Paul to the Corinthians.

When I **came** to you, **brothers** and **sisters**,
I **did not come proclaiming** the **mystery** of **God** to you
in **lofty** words or **wisdom**.
For I **decided** to know **nothing among** you
except **Jesus Christ,** and **him** crucified.
And I **came** to you in **weakness** and in **fear**
and in **much trembling**.
My **speech** and my **proclamation**
were **not** with **plausible words** of **wisdom**,
but with a **demonstration** of the **Spirit** and of **power**,
so that your **faith** might rest **not** on **human wisdom**
but on the **power** of **God**.

> **TO KEEP IN MIND**
> Pause to break up separate thoughts, set apart significant statements, or indicate major shifts. Never pause in the middle of a thought. Your primary guide for pauses is punctuation.

the Promised Land as a renewal of the covenant that summons the people to act as God has acted toward them.

READING II One of Paul's major reasons for writing to the Corinthians was to combat the influence of those who considered themselves spiritually sophisticated. Within the Corinthian church there were some who took on an air of elitism, believing that the way of Christ constituted the attainment of wisdom. Very similar to their gnostic counterparts among the pagans, these Christians believed that

wisdom separated them from the cares and concerns of the world.

Thus, Paul wants to be perfectly clear near the beginning of his letter that he does not align himself with this group of elitists. His wisdom alone is that of Christ crucified, which he has just called a "stumbling block" and "foolishness" to the Jews and the Gentiles (1 Corinthians 1.23). Paul goes so far as to suggest that this message was all that he could offer the Corinthians during his time among them. Thus, they should not expect his message to be any different now. He admits to them that

although he came to them "in weakness and in fear and in much trembling," his message proved to be powerful and true. It may not have been full of worldly wisdom, but it demonstrated the power and wisdom of God.

Paul's introduction of himself to the Corinthians in this passage is in keeping with a plan that appears in other letters written by him. In playing down his own power and authority, Paul seeks to win the listening ear of his audience for Christ alone. In speaking of himself as weak and fearful, his humility attracts the attention of the

GOSPEL Matthew 5.13–16

A reading from the holy Gospel according to Matthew.

Jesus said to his **disciples**:
"**You** are the **salt** of the **earth**;
but if **salt** has **lost** its **taste**,
how can its **saltiness** be **restored**?
It is **no longer good** for **anything**,
but is **thrown out** and **trampled** under **foot**.
You are the **light** of the **world**.
A city **built** on a **hill cannot** be **hidden**.
No one after **lighting** a **lamp** puts it **under** the **bushel basket**,
but on the **lampstand**,
and it gives **light** to **all** in the **house**.
In the **same way**,
let your **light shine** before **human beings**,
so that they may **see** your **good works**
and give **glory** to your **Father** in **heaven**."

This reading begins with a truly mysterious question. Slow your pace in these opening lines.

Express this characterization as sincerely as you can.

Give special emphasis to this line, with special emphasis on "light" and "shine."

Corinthians. Paul knows that it will not be an easy task to challenge the attitude of the spiritually elite in Corinth, and thus, he must make clear from the outset that God's grace prevails over human wisdom and action.

GOSPEL In hearing today's short Gospel reading, which continues Jesus' preaching that began last week in the Sermon on the Mount, we recall the theme of light which is present in today's first reading: when people act with justice for the oppressed, then their light shines in the darkness. In today's Gospel, Jesus refers to those who follow him as both salt and light.

While salt serves as a preservative and gives flavour to food, light illumines and allows clearer perception of the world. This passage immediately follows the beatitudes, in which Jesus calls "blessed" those who act with compassion and justice. Bringing these passages together forms a picture of discipleship: disciples of Jesus bring clarity into a darkened world by providing a vision revealed in selflessness. Furthermore, Jesus emphasizes that disciples will only be able to make a difference in the world if they use their gifts. Otherwise, they will be as useless as salt that has lost its taste and light that is hidden away.

The Gospel reading ends with Jesus cautioning his followers to avoid allowing their accomplishments to be a source of personal pride. Good deeds must always be done for the sake of others, and ultimately, all works of discipleship glorify God's name, not one's own. S.W.

SIXTH SUNDAY IN ORDINARY TIME

LECTIONARY #76

READING I   Sirach 15.15–20

A reading from the book of Sirach.

If you **choose**, you can **keep** the **commandments**,
and they will **save** you. If you **trust** in **God**, you **too** shall **live**,
and to act **faithfully** is a **matter** of your own **choice**.
The **Lord** has placed **before** you **fire** and **water**;
stretch out your **hand** for **whichever** you **choose**.
Before **each person** are **life** and death, **good** and **evil**
and **whichever** one **chooses**, **that** shall be **given**.
For **great** is the **wisdom** of the **Lord**;
he is mighty in **power** and **sees everything**;
his **eyes** are on **those** who **fear** him,
and he knows every **human action**.
He has not commanded **anyone** to be **wicked**,
and he has not given **anyone** permission to **sin**.

Sirach = SEER-ak

The tone of this reading is set by the "ifs" that begin it, placing it in the conditional. The claims it makes are somewhat harsh.

Emphasis on "anyone."

For meditation and context:

RESPONSORIAL PSALM   Psalm 119.1–2, 4–5, 17–18, 33–34 (R.1)

R. Blessed are those who walk in the law of the Lord!

Blessed are those whose way is blameless,
who walk in the law of the Lord.
Blessed are those who keep his decrees,
who seek him with their whole heart.

You have commanded your precepts
to be kept diligently.
O that my ways may be steadfast
in keeping your statutes!

Deal bountifully with your servant,
so that I may live and observe your word.
Open my eyes, so that I may behold
wondrous things out of your law.

Teach me, O Lord, the way of your statutes,
and I will observe it to the end.
Give me understanding, that I may keep
your law
and observe it with my whole heart.

TO KEEP IN MIND
The attention you bring to your proclaiming enables you to pray the Word of God with the assembly.

READING I The wisdom writing of Ben Sira comes from the early second century BC. This was a time of difficult choices for the descendants of Abraham. When the Babylonians destroyed the first Temple in 586 BC and forced the Israelites into exile, the chosen people wrestled with how to live the covenant with God without temple sacrifice. Their solution was to write down and to study the Torah, learning to inscribe the Law in their hearts. Upon their return to Jerusalem, with the second Temple reconstructed around the year 515 BC, the Israelites had to reconsider how to worship. Did keeping the covenant demand animal sacrifice or study of the Torah?

The words in today's first reading can help illuminate what the life of the faithful should look like. Life is to be found in the choice to keep the commandments and to pursue understanding the Lord's wisdom. For generations, the Hebrew people learned to trust in the sacrifices they made as a means of assuring God's blessing. However, Sirach reminds them of the choice between truly trusting in God or relying upon themselves. Placing one's confidence and hope in God's wisdom will be the path to life.

This reading helps us to better understand the gift of free will. One who chooses the path of life does so freely. The same is true with the one who chooses to follow the way of death. God does not lead a person to choose one path over the other. God is not responsible for our sin; sin comes from human choice alone. Human freedom is a part of God's will, and God wills not to rid the world of sin, because to do so would be to remove the gift of freedom. Following the commandments prevents one from

READING II   1 Corinthians 2.6–10

A reading from the first Letter of Saint Paul to the Corinthians.

Brothers and **sisters**:
Among the **mature** we do speak **wisdom**,
though it is not a **wisdom** of this **age**
or of the **rulers** of this age, who are **doomed** to perish.
But we speak **God's wisdom**, **secret** and **hidden**,
which **God decreed** before the **ages** for our **glory**.
None of the **rulers** of this **age understood** this;
for if they **had**, they would **not** have **crucified** the **Lord** of **glory**.
As it is **written**,
"What **no eye** has **seen**, nor **ear heard**,
nor the **human** heart **conceived**,
what **God** has **prepared** for **those** who love him."
These things God has **revealed** to us through the **Spirit**;
for the **Spirit** searches **everything**,
even the **depths** of **God**.

Corinthians = kohr-IN-thee-uhnz

Paul deftly shifts the source of wisdom from the human to the divine, which is "secret" and "hidden." His tone is authoritative but also awed.

Emphasis on "Spirit" and "depths."

GOSPEL   Matthew 5.17–37

A reading from the holy Gospel according to Matthew.

[**Jesus** said to his **disciples**:
"Do not **think** that I have **come**
to **abolish** the **Law** or the **Prophets**;
I have come **not** to **abolish** but to **fulfill**.]
For **truly I tell** you, until **heaven** and **earth** pass **away**,
not **one letter**, not one stroke of a **letter**,
will **pass** from the **Law** until all is **accomplished**.
Therefore, whoever breaks one of the **least**
       of these **commandments**,
and teaches **others** to do the **same**,
will be called **least** in the **kingdom** of **heaven**;

A lengthy reading extensively recording Jesus' instruction and advice to his disciples. Because of its legalistic quality, pacing yourself as you proclaim will be helpful, so its points can come through.

Emphasis on "not."

---

making the choice to sin; thus, how foolish one would be to choose sin over searching for the Lord's wisdom!

READING II It is not often in the Sunday lectionary that the first and second readings are closely connected thematically, but today's readings are a rare exception. Just as Ben Sira urges the pursuit of wisdom as a life-giving choice, so too does Paul call the Christians in Corinth to proclaim God's wisdom. Let us not forget that some within the Corinthian community believed themselves to be spiritually elite,

priding themselves over and above "weaker" members.

For Paul, wisdom is a gift provided by the Spirit that is meant to draw the community closer together. It is not to be a source of pride or a cause for division. Unlike the wisdom provided by this world, the wisdom of God is eternal and unknown by political forces or even those who claim to be religious (such as the type Paul suggests are responsible for the Lord's crucifixion). The wisdom of God is not something that human power can attain on its own, it belongs to those upon whom it is bestowed by God.

Thus, those who are wise ought to never be full of their own wisdom, since God is the source of this gift.

It is not by accident that wisdom, "secret and hidden," came into this world; rather, the revelation of wisdom is part of God's plan for salvation. If the "rulers of this age" (both the Jewish and Roman ones) had properly discerned this plan, they would not have put Jesus to death. According to God's plan, his wisdom rests on those who love him.

In establishing that the Spirit is the conduit through which God reveals himself,

This begins a long series of characterizations in which the word at the end of the line (for the most part) is emphasized. Let the emphasized words guide your proclamation.

but whoever **does** them and **teaches** them
will be called **great** in the **kingdom** of **heaven**.
[For I **tell** you, unless your **righteousness**
exceeds that of the **scribes** and **Pharisees**,
you will **never enter** the **kingdom** of **heaven**.
You have **heard** that it was **said** to those of **ancient times**,
'You **shall not murder**';
and 'whoever **murders** shall be liable to **judgment**.'
But **I** say to **you**
that the **one** who is **angry** with their **brother** or **sister**,
will be **liable** to **judgment**;
and whoever **insults** their **brother** or **sister**,
will be **liable** to the **council**;
and whoever says, 'You **fool**,'
will be **liable** to the **hell** of fire.
So when you are **offering** your **gift** at the **altar**,
if you **remember** that your **brother** or sister has **something**
        against you,
leave your **gift** there before the **altar** and **go**;
first be **reconciled** to your **brother** or **sister**,
and then **come** and offer your **gift**.]
Come to terms **quickly** with your **accuser**
while the **two** of you are on the **way** to **court**,
or your **accuser** may hand you **over** to the **judge**,
and the **judge** to the **guard**,
and you will be **thrown** into **prison**.
Truly I **tell** you, you will **never** get out
until you have **paid** the last **penny**.
[You have **heard** that it was **said**,
'You shall **not** commit **adultery**.'
But I **say** to you
that **everyone** who looks at a **woman** with **lust**
has **already** committed **adultery** with her in his **heart**.] »

This volatile and problematic topic demands that you move slowly through this passage.

Paul loosely quotes Isaiah 64.4, writing: "What no eye has seen, nor ear heard, nor the human heart conceived, what God has prepared for those who love him." Love of God is necessary for the gift of wisdom. Paul suggests that one who does not love God, and therefore neighbour, is incapable of understanding God's ways. God's plan may have been kept secret for many ages, but now it is revealed to those who believe. The one who knows a Christian's belief is the Spirit alone; the spiritually wise are incapable of this discernment without the searching of the Spirit.

GOSPEL In today's Gospel, Jesus continues the Sermon on the Mount with teaching his disciples a new way of observing the commandments. His way of approaching the ancient law is not to throw it out but rather to fulfill it, which is fully in keeping with Matthew's presentation of Jesus' ministry. Even though the Gospel of Matthew highlights many of the confrontational interactions between Jesus and the Pharisees, Jesus consistently takes a positive approach to the Jewish law.

In this time of waiting for the eschatological conclusion of the world as we know

it ("until heaven and earth pass away"), God's commands ought to continue to remain in force. With that said, Jesus probes the commandments more deeply than most scribes and scholars of the law. He is interested not only in the overt actions that the law either permits or prohibits, but he also wants to scrutinize intentions and the movement of the heart. For example, the first topic from the law that Jesus addresses is murder. Jesus examines the law and suggests that this commandment also calls for the elimination of the anger that would eventually cause someone to kill another.

Still slow.

If your **right** eye causes you to **sin**,
tear it **out** and throw it **away**;
it is **better** for you to lose **one** of your **members**
than for your **whole body** to be **thrown** into **hell**.
And if your **right** hand causes you to **sin**,
cut it **off** and throw it **away**;
it is **better** for you to lose **one** of your **members**
than for your **whole body** to **go** into **hell**.
It was **also said**, 'Whoever **divorces** his **wife**,
let him **give** her a certificate of **divorce**.'
But **I** say to **you**
that **anyone** who **divorces** his **wife**,
except on the **ground** of **unchastity**,
causes her to commit **adultery**;
and whoever marries a **divorced woman** commits **adultery**.
[**Again**, you have **heard**
that it was **said** to those of **ancient times**,
'You shall **not** swear **falsely**,
but **carry out** the **vows** you have **made** to the **Lord**.'
But **I** say to **you**:
Do not swear at **all**],
either by **heaven**, for it is the **throne** of **God**,
or by the **earth**, for it is his **footstool**,
or by **Jerusalem**, for it is the **city** of the **great King**.
And do not **swear** by your **head**,
for you **cannot make one** hair **white** or **black**.
[Let your **word** be 'Yes,' if 'Yes,' or 'No,' if 'No';
anything more than **this** comes from the **evil** one."]

[Shorter: Matthew 5.17, 20–24, 27–28, 33–34, 37++ (see brackets)]

Furthermore, anger within one's heart must not simply be overturned, it must also include proper reconciliation with the other. This teaching on the command "you shall not murder" shows that Jesus demands a deeper sense of ethical responsibility whereby a person does not simply refrain from an evil action but must identify and correct the root causes for the evil action in the first place.

Jesus continues his teaching to his followers by addressing the thorny issues of adultery, divorce, and lying. Adultery is clearly forbidden by the law of Moses (see Exodus 20.14). However, Jesus wants his disciples to scrutinize the underlying reason for adultery, namely lust. As a means to avoid this temptation, Jesus figuratively suggests tearing one's eye out or cutting off one's sinful hand. The point is to underscore the importance of maintaining right virtue, as to lose virtue would be more detrimental than losing a valuable body part. One exception to the law here that Jesus does make is in regard to divorce. The Mosaic law permitted divorce in certain situations (see Deuteronomy 24.1–4). However, Jesus looks at divorce differently, suggesting that it leads the abandoned woman to commit adultery. Jesus understands the importance of the permanent nature of marriage, but also sees it as an institution that provides for the woman's needs. In the society of his day, a divorced woman would have been without any means of support or security. Finally, Jesus expands the command to refrain from taking the name of the Lord in vain (see Leviticus 19.12) to apply to oath-taking in general. Because God witnesses all false speech, it is necessary to be truthful in all things. S.W.

SEVENTH SUNDAY IN ORDINARY TIME

LECTIONARY #79

READING I   Leviticus 19.1–2, 17–18

Leviticus = lih-VIT-ih-kuhs

A short and potent reading that compresses into it the core of the Abrahamic faith.

A reading from the book of Leviticus.

The **Lord** spoke to **Moses**:
"Speak to **all** the **congregation** of the **children** of **Israel**
and **say** to them:
'You shall be **holy**, for **I** the **Lord** your **God** am **holy**.
You shall not **hate** in your **heart** any**one** of your **kin**;
you shall **reprove** your **neighbour**,
or you will incur **guilt yourself**.
You shall not take **vengeance**
or bear a **grudge** against **any** of your **people**,
but you shall **love** your **neighbour** as **yourself**:
I am the **Lord**.'"

Slight pause between "guilt" and "yourself."

For meditation and context:

RESPONSORIAL PSALM   Psalm 103.1–2, 3–4, 8+10, 12–13 (R.8)

R. The Lord is merciful and gracious.

Bless the Lord, O my soul,
and all that is within me, bless his
    holy name.
Bless the Lord, O my soul,
and do not forget all his benefits.

It is the Lord who forgives all your iniquity,
who heals all your diseases,
who redeems your life from the Pit,
who crowns you with steadfast love
    and mercy.

The Lord is merciful and gracious,
slow to anger and abounding in
    steadfast love.
He does not deal with us according to
    our sins,
nor repay us according to our iniquities.

As far as the east is from the west,
so far he removes our transgressions from us.
As a father has compassion for his children,
so the Lord has compassion for those who
    fear him.

READING I The Book of Leviticus gives a legal framework for matters of ritual, society, and life. The law that undergirds the covenant between God and the people is based on an ethical understanding whereby the people are to act in a way that corresponds to God's actions. In today's passage from Leviticus, we hear of the call to holiness. Quite simply, because God is holy, all those bound to the covenant are called to be holy. The foundation of holiness for both God and the people is to give oneself for others. Such generative giving is demonstrated by God in Genesis in the very desire to create something out of nothing. Therefore, an attitude of "otherness" must always guide the outlook of God's people.

The law proceeds to provide examples of how an attitude toward "otherness" is to be lived. First, one is prohibited from harbouring any anger toward another. This flows into a second manifestation of "otherness," namely fraternal correction. Rather than harbouring a grudge against another (which is sinful), one must reach out to correct others who may have committed some wrongdoing. Third, vengeance is not to be tolerated, as it demonstrates a desire to hold a grudge against another. Finally, love is to be given to a neighbour according to the manner in which one wants to be loved. Besides the command to love God above all others, the instruction to love others is a capstone of the Israelite law. We can see this law of loving others as self as part of the foundation of what is called the "golden rule" in Christianity and other religious and ethical traditions.

65

READING II   1 Corinthians 3.16–23

A reading from the first Letter of Saint Paul to the Corinthians.

Corinthians = kohr-IN-thee-uhns

Paul's focus in this reading is wisdom: specifically, its transcendent power. Take a forceful tone with this reading.

Brothers and **sisters**:
Do you not **know** that you are **God's temple**
and that **God's Spirit** dwells in **you**?
If **anyone** destroys **God's temple**,
God will **destroy** that **person**.
For **God's temple** is **holy**, and **you** are that **temple**.
Do not deceive yourselves.
If you **think** that you are wise in this **age**,

Slight pause between "do not" and "deceive."

you should become fools so that you may become **wise**.
For the **wisdom** of this **world** is **foolishness** with **God**.
For it is **written**,
"He catches the **wise** in their **craftiness**,"
and again,
"The **Lord** knows the **thoughts** of the **wise**,
that **they** are **futile**."
So let **no one boast** about **human** beings.
For **all things** are **yours**—

Apollos = uh-POL-uhs
Cephas = SEE-fuhs

whether **Paul** or **Apollos** or **Cephas**,
or the **world** or **life** or **death**,
or the **present** or the **future**—
all belong to **you**,

The whole thrust of Paul's argument is felt in the shift from "you," to "Christ," to "God."

and **you** belong to **Christ**,
and **Christ** belongs to **God**.

READING II Three Pauline themes can be detected in today's reading from 1 Corinthians. The first is that the Christian community may be likened to "God's temple." The one who inhabits this temple is God's very Spirit, which is why this temple is to be called holy. Paul is not simply talking about a holiness that comes from participation in worship but a holiness that characterizes the very nature of the Christian community. Similar to Paul's reference to the Church as the Body of Christ (1 Corinthians 6.15–20), this building imagery emphasizes unity. All members of the community have a responsibility to maintain the temple's holiness through their actions.

This leads to a second Pauline theme, namely that such holiness is not to be found in human wisdom. Paul writes that "the wisdom of this world is foolishness," as he suggests that human wisdom leads individuals to self-reliance and therefore away from dependence upon God, who is the source of all wisdom. Paul tells the Corinthians that God is able to see how foolish the way of their human wisdom is, as he quotes Job 5.13 and Psalm 94.11—God sees both their behaviour and their thoughts.

Finally, a third Pauline theme appears at the end of today's pericope which provides for the proper ordering of the community, namely that all belong to Christ. Because all belong to Christ, every member of the community has personal responsibility for the other members. Belonging to Christ means that relationship with God is fortified and unbreakable. Proper order within the "temple of God" exhibits true "holiness": care and concern for all relationships from God right on down to the

GOSPEL   Matthew 5.38–48

A reading from the holy Gospel according to Matthew.

Jesus said to his **disciples**,
"You have **heard** that it was **said**,
'An **eye** for an **eye** and a **tooth** for a **tooth**.'
But **I** say to **you**,
Do not resist an **evildoer**.
But if anyone **strikes** you on the **right cheek**,
turn the other **also**;
and if anyone wants to **sue** you and take your **coat**,
give your cloak as **well**;
and if **anyone** forces you to go one **mile**,
go with them **also** the **second mile**.
Give to **everyone** who **begs** from you,
and **do not refuse anyone** who wants to **borrow** from you.
You have **heard** that it was **said**,
'You shall **love** your **neighbour** and **hate** your **enemy**.'
But **I** say to **you**,
Love your **enemies**
and **pray** for those who **persecute** you,
so that you may be **children** of your **Father** in **heaven**;
for he makes his **sun rise** on the **evil** and on the **good**,
and sends **rain** on the **righteous** and on the **unrighteous**.
For if you **love** those who **love** you,
what **reward** do you **have**?
Do not even the tax collectors do the **same**?
And if you greet only your **brothers** and **sisters**,
what **more** are you **doing** than **others**?
Do not even the Gentiles do the **same**?
Be **perfect**, therefore, as your **heavenly Father** is perfect."

A powerful reading filled with familiar but perennially challenging teachings to take to heart. Proclaim as though these things are being said for the first time.

At this point, Jesus intensifies his teachings. Proclaim sincerely, tingeing your voice with surprise.

The questions that conclude this reading are not merely rhetorical. Imagine posing these questions to the members of your assembly.

---

seemingly most insignificant member of the Church. Because all are one in Christ, there is no cause for boasting of one's own merits.

GOSPEL This week we continue to hear from the Sermon on the Mount, as Jesus focuses on two basic Christian attitudes: acting with selflessness and loving one's enemies. The taking of "an eye for an eye" is an often-quoted element of the Jewish law (for example, see Exodus 21.24), which was originally intended to keep the deliverance of retaliation in pro-

portion to the wrong committed. However, Jesus believes that a response in kind is not appropriate for the Christian disciple. Instead, the injured party must surrender pride and ego and take no retribution on the one who inflicts some sort of evil. This same selflessness is to guide Christian charity in general; one must go the extra mile in assisting those in need. By acting in such a way in all these circumstances, God's love prevails over sin.

The second teaching involves developing a love for one's enemies and not simply for one's neighbours. Once again, Jesus

instructs his disciples to grasp the spirit of the ancient law. Love is meant to break down barriers of every sort. Thus, extending love to one's neighbour ought to naturally lead a person to avoid the desire to judge others by turning them into enemies. In other words, friends and enemies must be treated alike. A disciple does not hold back love on account of human judgment; instead, each follower is to strive for divine perfection, a perfection which bears no discrimination. S.W.

ASH WEDNESDAY

LECTIONARY #219

READING I   Joel 2.12–18

A reading from the book of the Prophet Joel.

Even **now**, says the Lord,
return to me with **all** your **heart**,
with **fasting**, with **weeping**, and with **mourning**;
rend your **hearts** and not your **clothing**.
Return to the **Lord**, your **God**,
for he is **gracious** and **merciful**,
slow to anger, and **abounding** in steadfast love,
and **relents** from punishing.
Who knows whether the Lord will **not turn** and **relent**,
and leave a **blessing behind** him:
a **grain offering** and a **drink offering**
to be presented to the Lord, your God?
Blow the trumpet in **Zion**;
sanctify a fast;
call a solemn assembly;
gather the people.
Sanctify the congregation;
assemble the aged;
gather the children, even **infants** at the breast.
Let the **bridegroom** leave his **room**,
and the **bride** her **canopy**.
Between the **vestibule** and the **altar**
let the **priests**, the **ministers** of the Lord, **weep**.

Joel = JOH-*l
A reading in which Joel in his role as Prophet becomes the mouthpiece for the Lord; it is as if God is addressing the people directly in this reading. Proclaim this reading like Joel himself, with a sure and steady voice so that its vibrancy will come through.

rend = tear
This reading makes use of frequent parallels. Give the words in pairs emphasis: "hearts" and "clothing"; "gracious" and "merciful"; "slow" and "abounding"; "grain offering" and "drink offering."

The energy picks up with a series of imperative verb forms. These words are highly charged—God is telling the assembly directly what to do. "Blow," "sanctify," "call," "gather," "assemble," "let."

READING I The prophecy of Joel is directed toward a nation that is in the midst of a great crisis. Devastation of the land was brought on both by a drought as well as by a plague of locusts. The people believed that they had been abandoned by God because of a national sin. In today's reading from Joel, Joel has a message of repentance for the people: transformation of life will result in God's favour once more.

The reading that opens our Lenten season represents Joel's call to the people to assemble to hear God's redeeming word.

Joel's message is simple: "return to me [the Lord]." For the Prophet, this return entails individual and communal transformation of heart. For him, it is not enough to fast, to weep, to mourn, and to perform outward gestures of penance such as tearing one's clothes. Instead, the people must seek the mercy of God together.

The communal importance of seeking the gift of this mercy is demonstrated by Joel's command to "blow the trumpet" and to summon the people to a public fast. People of every age are invited to seek the way of God's mercy together. God can easily

peer into the hearts of each individual, but the community needs the participation of all its members if it is to display its fidelity to strive to live anew for God.

In addition to the communal acts that make visible a real willingness to return to the Lord, Joel calls the priests to a particular responsibility. They are to weep for the sins of the people and are to intercede on their behalf, asking God to withhold his punishment upon the nation. Joel suggests that if God bestows mercy instead of punishment upon the people, then other nations will see God's blessing. Otherwise,

Let them say, "**Spare** your **people**, O Lord,
and do **not** make your **heritage** a **mockery**,
a **byword** among the **nations**.
Why should it be **said** among the **peoples**,
'**Where** is their **God**?'"
Then the **Lord** became **jealous** for his **land**,
and had **pity** on his **people**.

Allow for a slight pause between the question and the final expression in the reading.

For meditation and context:

RESPONSORIAL PSALM   Psalm 51.1–2, 3–4a, 10–11, 12+15 (R.1a+4a)

R. Have mercy, O Lord, for we have sinned.

Have mercy on me, O God,
according to your steadfast love;
according to your abundant mercy
blot out my transgressions.
Wash me thoroughly from my iniquity,
and cleanse me from my sin.

For I know my transgressions,
and my sin is ever before me.
Against you, you alone, have I sinned,
and done what is evil in your sight.

Create in me a clean heart, O God,
and put a new and right spirit within me.
Do not cast me away from your presence,
and do not take your holy spirit from me.

Restore to me the joy of your salvation,
and sustain in me a willing spirit.
O Lord, open my lips,
and my mouth will declare your praise.

READING II   2 Corinthians 5.20—6.2

Corinthians = kohr-IN-thee-uhnz

A reading in which Paul seeks to impress upon the members of the early church at Corinth the importance of reconciliation with God in preparation to receive God.

The phrasing in this statement is a little peculiar. Practise it a few times and sound it out. The strangeness is in the phrase "God made Christ to be sin." It's not an expression we commonly use in relation to sin. "Be" is paralleled with "knew." Emphasize those two words to anchor your proclamation.

A reading from the second Letter of Saint Paul to the Corinthians.

Brothers and **sisters**:
We are **ambassadors** for **Christ**,
since **God** is making his appeal **through** us;
we **entreat** you on behalf of **Christ**,
be **reconciled** to God.
For **our** sake God made Christ to **be** sin who **knew no** sin,
so that in **Christ** we might become the **righteousness** of **God**.
As we work **together** with him,
we **urge** you also **not** to **accept** the grace of God in **vain**. ≫

---

other nations might look at Israel and accuse God of being weak for not giving them aid. The passage ends with God's recognition of the people's contrition. Once again, God takes notice of the people and has "pity on his people." True repentance involves more than individuals striving to better themselves before God; it demands individuals work together to form a people that is just.

READING II   Prior to the passage we read in today's second reading, Paul has been reminding the

Corinthians that they have been made a new creation by their membership in Christ. Furthermore, he explains that Christ is the way through which the world is reconciled with God. Being refashioned in Christ means that Christians have been called to take up Christ's ministry of reconciliation so that others may participate in this relationship between God and humanity (see 2 Corinthians 5.17–19). All of this leads him to the conclusion that Christians are called to be "ambassadors for Christ." An ambassador is not simply someone who represents another; he or she is someone who has

developed a relationship with the people to whom he or she has been sent. Because ambassadors know the life situation of the people with whom they live, they are better able to represent their needs.

Paul's point here is that Christians do not act alone in the mission of the Church. Instead, Christian ambassadors work together, satisfying the obligations of loving and serving God as well as creating a healthy community that is united in Christ. Notice Paul's use of the plural "we"—"we are ambassadors," "we entreat you," and "we urge you." As a spiritual leader in the

For the Lord **says**,
"At an acceptable time I have **listened** to you,
and on a day of salvation I have **helped** you."
See, **now** is the **acceptable time**;
see, **now** is the **day** of **salvation**!

The exhortation of the reading resolves in Paul's use of the word "acceptable." In its first appearance, you do not need to emphasize it. When it reappears, be sure to give it extra emphasis.

GOSPEL   Matthew 6.1–6, 16–18

A reading from the holy Gospel according to Matthew.

Jesus said to the disciples:
"**Beware** of **practising** your **piety** before people
in order to be **seen** by them;
for **then** you have **no** reward from your Father in heaven.
So whenever you give **alms**,
do **not** sound a **trumpet** before you,
as the **hypocrites** do in the **synagogues** and in the **streets**,
so that they may be **praised** by others.
Truly **I** tell you, they have **received** their **reward**.
But when **you** give alms,
do not let your **left** hand know what your **right** hand is doing,
so that your **alms** may be **done** in **secret**;
and your **Father** who sees in secret will **reward** you.
And whenever you **pray**,
do **not** be like the **hypocrites**;
for they **love** to **stand** and **pray**
in the **synagogues** and at the street corners,
so that they may be **seen** by **others**.
Truly **I** tell you, they have **received** their **reward**.
But whenever **you** pray,
go into your **room** and shut the door
and **pray** to your **Father** who is in **secret**;
and your **Father** who **sees** in secret will **reward** you.

A reading in which Jesus provides advice for how to approach the practices of almsgiving, prayer, and fasting. Each section of advice is constructed very similarly, creating parallel expressions. Don't let them become formulaic in your proclamation. Each of these practices is important to Jesus for bringing us closer to God.

Almsgiving comes first. Emphasis on "left," "right," "secret," "Father," and "reward."

Next comes prayer. The wording is very similar to that in the almsgiving section. Emphasis on "room," "secret," "Father," "secret," and "reward."

---

community and an ambassador of Christ's word, Paul does not stand above or apart from the people, but instead reminds all of their need to be open to the grace of God that reconciles people to himself.

In order to enact the ministry of reconciling the world to God, the Corinthians must make reconciliation among themselves a chief priority. To attain this "righteousness," the community must acknowledge the sacrifice of the cross and the grace that comes from it. The urgency for this reconciliation is great, as Paul contends that *"now"* is the time for conversion of heart. In our con-

temporary gathering today at the start of Lent, Paul challenges modern-day ambassadors of Christ to work together to discover the grace of God anew.

| GOSPEL | Today's reading from Matthew is essentially taken from the midpoint of Jesus' inaugural sermon to his disciples, known as the Sermon on the Mount (Matthew 5.1—7.29). In the previous chapter, Jesus instructed his disciples on what it means to be blessed in the kingdom of heaven (the beatitudes) and how to interpret the religious law in a new

way. In this passage, Jesus teaches his disciples about the proper attitude of prayer and approaches to self-discipline.

When it comes to the personal disciplines of fasting, praying, and the giving of alms, Jesus tells his disciples that actions are to be performed in such a way as to avoid gaining recognition. How easy it is to misuse these core practices as a means of measuring spiritual achievement and personal righteousness. Gaining "reward" from the Father takes place when the sacrifice of food, the attention to prayer, and the gift of charity are all done from an inward

And finally comes fasting. Once again, similar wording. This time, emphasis on "head," "face," "seen," "Father," "secret" and "reward."

And whenever you **fast**,
do not look **dismal**, like the **hypocrites**,
for they **disfigure** their **faces**
so as to **show others** that they are **fasting**.
Truly **I** tell you, they have **received** their **reward**.
But when **you** fast,
put oil on your **head** and wash your **face**,
so that your **fasting** may be **seen** not by **others**
but by your **Father** who is in **secret**;
and your **Father** who **sees** in secret will **reward** you."

attitude of selflessness. When almsgiving, fasting, and prayer are conducted in such a way as to lose the self for others, then they are rightly directed toward the fulfillment of God's kingdom. God knows the intentions of our hearts, and this is how we are to be repaid.

As we hear this Gospel passage proclaimed on the first day of Lent, it is important to return to the context of Joel's prophecy in the first reading. He calls the people to assemble. As a Christian assembly, we hear these cautionary words of Jesus to his disciples and are reminded that

our Lenten journey is meant to help us grow together as a community. While fasting, prayer, and almsgiving are certainly prescribed in order for individuals to grow in the image of Christ, they are also in place that we might understand better our dependence upon one another as brothers and sisters in the Lord. Hopefully, we are not like the hypocrites who simply want to be noticed but rather are like those Jesus calls "blessed" in the beatitudes, bearing poverty in spirit, acting with gentleness and compassion, striving for righteousness, showing mercy, exhibiting purity of heart,

working for peace, and accepting persecution for the sake of justice. The season of Lent is all about our growth together in the Paschal Mystery of Christ—learning more and more how to die to self in order to live anew for others. S.W.

FIRST SUNDAY OF LENT

LECTIONARY #22

READING I Genesis 2.7–9, 16–18, 25; 3.1–7++

A reading from the book of Genesis.

The **Lord God** formed **man** from the **dust** of the **ground**,
and **breathed** into his **nostrils** the **breath** of **life**;
and the **man** became a **living being**.
And the **Lord God** planted a **garden** in **Eden**, in the **east**;
and **there** he put the **man** whom he had **formed**.
Out of the **ground** the **Lord God** made to **grow**
every **tree** that is **pleasant** to the **sight** and **good** for **food**,
the tree of **life also** in the **midst** of the **garden**,
and the **tree** of the **knowledge** of **good** and **evil**.
And the **Lord God commanded** the **man**,
"You may **freely eat** of every **tree** of the **garden**;
but of the **tree** of the **knowledge** of **good** and **evil** you **shall
  not eat**,
for in the **day** that you **eat** of it **you shall die**."
Then the **Lord God said**,
"It is not **good** that the **man** should be **alone**;
I will **make** him a helper as his **partner**."
And the **man** and his **wife** were both **naked**,
  and were **not ashamed**.
Now the **serpent** was more **crafty** than any other **wild animal**
that the **Lord God** had **made**.
He **said** to the **woman**, "Did **God say**,
'You **shall not eat** from **any tree** in the **garden**'?"

Genesis = JEN-uh-sis

This is a very familiar reading of one of the foundational stories of the Abrahamic religions. Its tone is simultaneously austere, menacing, and playful.

Eden = EE-d*n

Slight pause between "life" and "also."

Slight pause between "God" and "commanded."

The serpent is the focal character in this narrative.

READING I Lent is a time of repentance and renewal, which makes today's first reading from the Book of Genesis particularly fitting. It comes from the second of two creation stories. This one gives particular attention to the creation of the first parents and the sin that causes them to be removed from the garden in Eden.

This highly symbolic story begins with God forming a man (Hebrew, *ha adam*) "from the dust of the ground" (Hebrew, *ha adamah*), and then he "breathed into his nostrils the breath of life." Of course, this is the breath of God. Thus, the first human being is both of the earth and of God. Then God, as provider for his creatures, plants a garden with trees that are not just good for food but beautiful to look at and places the man (*adam*) in the garden to tend and care for it.

Two trees in the middle of the garden represent attributes that do not belong to humans—only to God—and from which humans must be protected for their welfare. One is the tree of life, which probably represents immortality. The other is the tree of the knowledge of good and evil. In Hebrew, "to know" is experiential. The phrase "good and evil" is an example of a literary technique called a merism, in which two contrasting elements represent those and everything in between. Thus, eating the fruit of the tree of the knowledge of good and evil signifies the experience of everything on the spectrum of good and evil, which is dangerous and life-threatening for humans who do not have the wisdom and mastery that God has.

With this background in mind, we can better understand what the author of this creation account sought to convey about human sin and its consequences. Adam

Slight pause between "woman" and "said."

The **woman said** to the **serpent**,
"We may **eat** of the **fruit** of the **trees** in the **garden**;
but **God said**, 'You **shall not eat** of the **fruit** of the **tree**
that is in the **middle** of the **garden**,
nor shall you **touch** it, or **you shall die**.'"
But the **serpent said** to the **woman**,
"You **will not die**;
for **God knows** that when you **eat** of it your **eyes** will be **opened**,
and you will **be like God**, **knowing** good and evil."

The serpent's argument that God knows what eating the fruit will be like for Eve is what persuades her to eat. Don't overdo this, but keep in mind that the serpent's cunning is persuasiveness.

So when the **woman saw** that the **tree** was **good** for **food**,
and that it was a **delight** to the **eyes**,
and that the **tree** was to be **desired** to make one **wise**,
she **took** of its **fruit** and **ate**;
and she **also** gave some to her **husband**, who was **with** her,
and he **ate**.

The conclusion demonstrates the grim underside of the knowledge the serpent promised: self-awareness.

Then the **eyes** of **both** were **opened**,
and they **knew** that they were **naked**;
and they sewed **fig leaves together**
and made **loincloths** for **themselves**.

For meditation and context:

RESPONSORIAL PSALM   Psalm 51.1–2, 3–4a, 10–11, 12+15 (R.1a+4a)

R. Have mercy, O Lord, for we have sinned.

Have mercy on me, O God,
according to your steadfast love;
according to your abundant mercy
blot out my transgressions.
Wash me thoroughly from my iniquity,
and cleanse me from my sin.

For I know my transgressions,
and my sin is ever before me.
Against you, you alone, have I sinned,
and done what is evil in your sight.

Create in me a clean heart, O God,
and put a new and right spirit within me.
Do not cast me away from your presence,
and do not take your holy spirit from me.

Restore to me the joy of your salvation,
and sustain in me a willing spirit.
O Lord, open my lips,
and my mouth will declare your praise.

---

and Eve are living in the garden in perfect harmony with God and God's creation. Then, into the garden appears a serpent. Many of us assume that this serpent is Satan or the devil, but, in fact, the narrator describes it as the most cunning of God's creatures. The serpent poses a question to the woman concerning what God told Adam about the tree of the knowledge of good and evil, and she responds with an imperfect facsimile of what God said. Finally, when the serpent assures her that they—Adam was with her—would not die if they ate from the tree in the middle of the garden, but they would

"be like God, knowing good and evil," she ate of the tree and so did her partner. Like the word "knowing," eating is also a verb of experiencing. Why did they do it? The woman concluded, "the tree was to be desired to make one wise." In other words, they wanted to be like God, despite God's warning that it would bring death to them. Immediately, the humans began to experience the consequences of their action—alienation, shame, and blame. What about us? How do we try to play god with our lives and the lives of others, and what consequences come of it?

READING II Today's second reading from Paul's Letter to the Romans adds another interpretive layer to the Genesis story of Adam and Eve and the introduction of sin into the world. Paul employs a literary feature called a type. Generally speaking, a type is a pattern or blueprint. When used as a tool for biblical interpretation, a type is a person or event from the Old Testament that is used as a blueprint for a more perfect person or event in the New Testament.

In this reading, Paul uses the first human, Adam, as a type of the second

READING II   Romans 5.12–19

A reading from the Letter of Saint Paul to the Romans.

[**Brothers** and **sisters**:
Just as **sin** came into the **world** through **one man**,
and **death** came through **sin**,
so **death spread** to **all people**, because **all** have **sinned.**]
Sin was **indeed** in the **world before** the **law**,
but **sin** is not **reckoned** when there **is** no **law**.
Yet **death** exercised **dominion** from **Adam** to **Moses**,
even over **those** whose **sins** were **not** like the **transgression**
        of **Adam**,
who is a **type** of the **one** who was to **come**.
But the **free gift** is **not** like the **trespass.**
For if the **many died** through the **one man's trespass**,
much more surely have the **grace** of **God**
and the **free gift** in the **grace** of the **one man**, **Jesus Christ**,
abounded for the **many**.
And the **free gift** is **not like** the **effect** of the **one man's sin.**
For the **judgment following one trespass** brought **condemnation**,
but the **free** gift **following many trespasses** brings **justification.**
[**If**, **because** of the **one man's trespass**,
death exercised **dominion** through **that one**,
much more surely will **those** who receive the **abundance**
        of **grace**
and the **free gift** of **righteousness**
exercise dominion in **life** through the **one man**, **Jesus Christ.**
Therefore just as **one man's trespass**
led to **condemnation** for **all people**,
so **one man's act** of **righteousness**
leads to **justification** and **life** for **all people.**

The reading consists of Paul's discourse on sin, death, and redemption. Its tone is earnest.

Slight pause between "world" and "before."

Though unstressed, "But" signals an intensification of the earnest tone of the reading.

The second half of the reading really focuses on the word "gift."

Note the inversion and repetition Paul uses here: one man's trespass leading to condemnation for all; one man's righteousness to justification and life.

---

human, Jesus Christ, but this type is a bit out of the ordinary, because it describes an inverse relationship between the two. Through the first human, Adam, sin and death entered into the world, and all were affected by it. Paul then contrasts Adam's pitiful situation and the consequences that it had *for the many* with the overflowing abundance of grace that the second human, Jesus Christ, brought into the world *for the many*. He wants to make clear that the gift is not in proportion to the judgment and condemnation that one would expect

from one man's sin, as if God's mercy covered over only this one sin.

And what is this gift? Paul describes it as justification, the process of being set right with God, or acquittal, as in a court of law. The defendant is sinful humanity from the time of Adam and Eve to the present. Through the sacrifice of atonement that Jesus effected in his crucifixion, God, the judge, declares that humanity is acquitted and the case against it is dismissed, so that humanity is restored to right relationship with God. This is Paul's teaching on justifica-

tion by faith. But acquittal is not the same thing as innocence. Humanity did nothing to earn this gift of right relationship with God. Rather, it is given as a free gift to anyone who trusts in the graciousness of God as expressed through Jesus' sacrificial love.

Paul's Jewish background shines through when he writes about how sin was in the world even before the law was given to Moses and the Israelites. His logic is that people cannot be held responsible for transgressing the law if it has not been given to them. Still, it is important to notice how

For **just** as by the **one man's disobedience**
the **many** were made **sinners**,
so by the **one man's obedience**
the **many** will be made **righteous**.]

[Shorter: Romans 5.12, 17–19 (see brackets)]

GOSPEL   Matthew 4.1–11

A reading from the holy Gospel according to Matthew.

This reading relates a dramatic story in the life of Christ. Its tone is magical.

Jesus was led **up** by the **Spirit**
into the **wilderness** to be **tempted** by the **devil**.
He fasted **forty days** and **forty nights**,
and **afterwards** he was **famished**.

Slight pause between "tempter" and "came."

The **tempter came** and **said** to him,
"If **you** are the **Son** of **God**,
command these **stones** to become **loaves** of **bread**."

A familiar statement. Proclaim as if it is being spoken for the first time.

But he answered, "It is **written**,
'**Man** does not **live** by **bread alone**,
but by **every word** that **comes** from the **mouth** of **God**.'"
Then the **devil** took him to the **holy city**

pinnacle = PIN-uh-k*l

and **placed** him on the **pinnacle** of the **temple**, **saying** to him,
"If **you** are the **Son** of **God**, **throw** yourself **down**;
for it is **written**,
'He will **command** his **Angels concerning** you,'

The exchange between Jesus and the devil has a rabbinical character, in which they argue by quoting Scripture to each other.

and 'On their **hands** they will **bear you up**,
so that you **will not dash** your **foot** against a **stone**.'"
Jesus **said** to him, "**Again** it is **written**,
'**Do not** put the **Lord** your **God** to the **test**.'" »

Paul personifies sin as an evil force that is hostile to God and how he talks about death as not limited to physical death but as alienation from the relationship that God wishes for humanity.

GOSPEL Today's Gospel reading is the story of Jesus' temptation in the wilderness as told by the author of Matthew's Gospel. This story is also included in Luke and Mark.

Mark's version of the story is very brief, indicating only that Jesus was driven into the desert by the Spirit and spent forty days there, before beginning his public ministry. Mark's reference to forty days might evoke in your memory the forty years that the Israelites wandered in the desert during the Exodus. But Matthew's "forty days and forty nights" further suggests the time that Moses spent on Mount Sinai, when the covenant between God and the Israelites was ratified (Exodus 24.18) and the forty days and nights when he fasted on Mount Sinai in the presence of God and wrote the words of the covenant on two stone tablets

(Exodus 34.27–35). Forty is a symbolic number, representing transition from one state to another. In this case, it is a transition from Jesus' private life to his public ministry.

Mark's version of the story says that Jesus was tempted by Satan and ministered to by Angels (Mark 1.12–13). Matthew's version has these same basic elements, but can you also imagine a second generation of Jesus followers wondering what Jesus was doing out in the desert for such a long time? Perhaps that is why Matthew's version includes an extended dialogue or

"Away with you, Satan": As much an expression of exasperation as it is a command.

Again, the **devil** took him to a **very high mountain**
and **showed** him
all the **kingdoms** of the **world** and their **splendour**;
and he **said** to him,
"**All these** I will **give** you,
if you will **fall down** and **worship** me."
Jesus **said** to him, "**Away** with you, **Satan**!
for it is **written**,
'**Worship** the **Lord** your **God**,
and **serve only him**.'"
Then the devil **left** him,
and suddenly **Angels came** and **waited** on him.

debate between Jesus and Satan, who is also identified as the tempter and the devil. Matthew tells us that Jesus was fasting during that time, and fasting has traditionally been understood to be a way of moving more deeply into prayer and preparing oneself for significant life transitions.

The enhancements that the author of Matthew's Gospel made to Mark's version of this story are significant because they flesh out what it meant when Jesus was declared Son of God at his baptism. In particular, pay attention to the three tests that are placed before Jesus: (1) "If you are the

Son of God, command these stones to become loaves of bread," (2) "If you are the Son of God, throw yourself down" from the top of the Temple, and (3) "All these I will give you, if you will fall down and worship me." As a whole, these temptations are tests of Jesus' willingness, as Son of God, to rely on God alone for nourishment, protection, and safety. All three of Jesus' responses come from the Book of Deuteronomy, which consists mostly of a very long speech that Moses gives when recommitting the Israelites to the covenant that God made with them on Sinai, before they cross over

to the Promised Land. More precisely, they come from Deuteronomy 6—8, a section of text devoted to what the Israelites must do to faithfully live out the covenant in the Promised Land. Moreover, there is cause for rejoicing, because, unlike the dialogue between Eve and the serpent, Jesus wins this debate! C.C.

SECOND SUNDAY OF LENT

LECTIONARY #25

READING I   Genesis 12.1–4

Genesis = JEN-uh-sihs

Abram = AY-br*m

The tone of this reading is commanding. God is speaking to Abram as if to all his people.

Though not emphasized, the repetition of "I will" guides this reading. These are promises God is making for the future of his people.

A reading from the book of Genesis.

The **Lord** said to **Abram**,
"**Go** from your **country** and your **kindred**
    and your **father's house**
to the **land** that I will **show** you.
I will **make** of you a **great nation**,
and I will **bless** you, and **make** your **name great**,
so that you will **be a blessing**.
I will **bless those** who **bless** you,
and the one who **curses you** I will **curse**;
and **in you** all the **families** of the **earth** shall be **blessed**."
So Abram went, as the **Lord** had **told** him.

For meditation and context:

RESPONSORIAL PSALM   Psalm 33.4–5, 18–19, 20+22 (R.22)

R. Let your love be upon us, Lord, even as we hope in you.

The word of the Lord is upright,
and all his work is done in faithfulness.
He loves righteousness and justice;
the earth is full of the steadfast love of
    the Lord.

Truly the eye of the Lord is on those
    who fear him,
on those who hope in his steadfast love,
to deliver their soul from death,
and to keep them alive in famine.

Our soul waits for the Lord;
he is our help and shield.
Let your steadfast love, O Lord, be upon us,
even as we hope in you.

READING I | The readings for this Second Sunday of Lent focus on God's invitation to enter into relationship with God and humans' response of trust in the covenant.

Today's first reading is one of three accounts of the covenant that God made with Abram. The other two accounts are Genesis 15 and Genesis 17.1–21. Each is interesting in its own right, but together they paint a rich and vibrant picture of Abram's relationship with God. It is in the last of these three accounts that God changes Abram's name to Abraham, mean-

ing "father of nations." But in this first account we hear today, we learn of God's invitation to Abram to leave his family and homeland to migrate to Shechem in the land of Canaan, which is in the central part of the West Bank today. Later he would migrate to the Negev in southern Israel.

Tradition tells us that he was living in Haran (in modern southeastern Turkey) at the time, but his original homeland was Ur of the Chaldees (in southern Iraq today). These are extremely long distances to travel on foot and with all their flocks and other belongings, especially when the com-

mand from a God that he does not yet know is so vague: "Go . . . to the land that I will show you."

This same God bestows a series of blessings on Abram. Some biblical scholars argue, based on the Hebrew text, that there are seven, but the English translation makes it hard to enumerate them exactly. Why seven? Seven is a perfect number, representing wholeness or fullness. God also gives two promises: multitudes of descendants and possession of the land. Constructing altars to the God who appeared

---

READING II   2 Timothy 1.8b–10

A reading from the second Letter of Saint Paul to Timothy.

Brothers and **sisters:**
Join with **me** in **suffering** for the **Gospel**,
relying on the **power** of **God**,
who **saved** us and **called** us with a **holy calling**,
not according to our **works**
but **according** to his **own purpose** and **grace**.
This grace was **given** to us in **Christ Jesus**
before the ages **began**,
but it has **now** been **revealed**
through the **appearing** of our **Saviour Christ Jesus**,
who **abolished death**
and **brought life** and **immortality** to **light** through the **Gospel**.

The tone of this reading is intimate and tender.

Slight pause between "Saviour" and "Christ Jesus."

to Abram indicates that he acknowledges God as having authority in that land.

READING II Our second reading is from the Second Letter to Timothy. Timothy is presented as a companion of Paul in his missionary activity and later the pastor of a church in Ephesus. The letter is attributed to Paul, though biblical scholars mostly agree that it was written after Paul's death, perhaps as late as AD 100. While this might seem strange to us today, it was not unusual for disciples of a great teacher to write in the name of their honoured one in order to extend his message to another generation.

This reading picks up a theme that we find in Paul's authentic letters, namely, enduring suffering for the sake of the Gospel. The sentence that immediately precedes today's reading is "Do not be ashamed, then, of the testimony about our Lord or of me his prisoner" (2 Timothy 1.8; see also Romans 1.16). Using the phrase "the power of God," the author of this letter goes on to give a rationale for not being ashamed of suffering for Christ and trusting in God's power to protect oneself.

GOSPEL In today's Gospel reading, we hear the magnificent story of Jesus' transfiguration. The narrator describes Jesus as taking his inner circle of disciples—Peter, James, and John—and going up a mountain. These same disciples will be with Jesus in the Garden of Gethsemane on the Mount of Olives before he is arrested (Matthew 26.36–46).

Mountains were thought to be places of divine revelation. In Matthew's Gospel, this mountain is unnamed. Most biblical scholars think it is a symbol of Mount Sinai, because of the two figures who appear

GOSPEL　Matthew 17.1–9

A reading from the holy Gospel according to Matthew.

Jesus took with him **Peter** and **James** and his brother **John**
and **led** them **up** a **high mountain**, by **themselves**.
And he was **transfigured before** them,
and his **face shone** like the **sun**,
and his **clothes** became **dazzling white**.
Suddenly there **appeared** to them **Moses** and **Elijah**,
　　talking with him.
Then **Peter** said to **Jesus**,
"**Lord**, it is **good** for us to **be** here;
if you **wish**, I will make **three dwellings** here,
one for **you**, one for **Moses**, and one for **Elijah**."
While he was **still speaking**,
suddenly a **bright** cloud **overshadowed** them,
and from the **cloud** a **voice** said,
"**This** is my **Son**, the **Beloved**;
with **him** I am **well pleased**;
listen to him!"
When the disciples **heard** this,
they **fell** to the **ground** and were **overcome** by **fear**.
But **Jesus** came and **touched** them, **saying**,
"Get **up** and do **not** be **afraid**."
And when they **looked up**,
they saw **no one** except **Jesus himself alone**.
As they were **coming down** the **mountain**, Jesus **ordered** them,
"Tell **no one** about the **vision**
until **after** the **Son** of **Man** has been **raised** from the **dead**."

"Transfigured" focuses this reading, sets its tone. This is a celestial event.

Moses = MOH-zihz or MOH-zihs

Elijah = ee-Lī-juh

Initially, the appearance of Moses and Elijah intensifies the focus.

But then Peter humanizes things in his desire to set up a shrine.

At "suddenly," the focus shifts back to a heavenly perspective that overwhelms the earthly perspective.

The mystery of this final command of Jesus is worth lingering over as you conclude your proclamation.

---

with Jesus. When Moses ascended Mount Sinai to receive the words of God's covenant, Moses' face became radiant with light (Exodus 34.27–35). Here, too, Jesus' face shines like the sun and his clothes become brilliant white. Likewise, Elijah was given the privilege of experiencing God in "a sound of sheer silence" when he was on Mount Sinai, and he hides his face (1 Kings 19.9–13). Here, too, Jesus' disciples hide their faces. Peter's offer to build tents for Jesus, Elijah, and Moses suggests the Feast of Tabernacles, also called *Sukkot* or Booths, which is a reminder of the time that the

Israelites spent dwelling in tents during the Exodus.

What a marvellous experience for these three disciples. Suddenly, they see a shining cloud overhead. It is the *shekinah*, the glory of God's presence, which led the Israelites out of the wilderness in cloud and fire and which fills the Holy of Holies in the Jerusalem Temple. And they hear a voice from the heavens, "This is my Son, the Beloved; with him I am well pleased; listen to him!" A voice from the heavens had a similar message at Jesus' baptism, when God's Spirit descended upon him like a

dove (Matthew 3.13–17). They are so awe-struck by the heavenly voice that they prostrate themselves in reverence. Suddenly, the vision passes, and they see only Jesus standing before them. Although some biblical scholars interpret this scene to be a preview of the Resurrection, it is first and foremost a theophany, a manifestation of the divine Jesus, the Son of God. C.C.

THIRD SUNDAY
OF LENT

LECTIONARY #28

READING I   Exodus 17.3–7

A reading from the book of Exodus.

In the **wilderness** the people **thirsted** for water;
and the people **complained** against Moses and said,
"**Why** did you bring us out of **Egypt**,
to **kill** us and our children and livestock with **thirst**?"
So **Moses** cried out to the Lord,
"What shall **I do** with this **people**?
They are almost ready to **stone** me."
The Lord said to Moses,
"Go on **ahead** of the **people**,
and take some of the **elders** of **Israel** with you;
take in your **hand** the **staff** with which you **struck** the Nile,
    and **go**.
I will be **standing** there in front of you on the **rock** at Horeb.
Strike the **rock**, and **water** will come **out** of it,
so that the **people** may **drink**."
Moses did so, in the sight of the elders of Israel.
He called the place **Massah** and **Meribah**,
because the **children of Israel quarrelled** and **tested** the Lord,
saying, "Is the **Lord among** us or **not**?"

Exodus = EK-suh-duhs

A reading which is essentially a dialogue involving the Israelites, Moses, and the Lord. Its tone is dramatic; you need mainly emphasize when the different speakers begin to speak.

Moses is exasperated here.

The words of the Lord are meant to placate Moses' exasperation. But they are also instructions. Read them in this spirit.

Horeb = HOHR-eb

Massah = MAS-uh
Meribah = MAYR-ih-bah

The passage concludes with a naming of the place where this happened, but in the form of a question. The question does not shed the most generous light on the Israelites. Be sure to give emphasis to the word "not."

| READING I | The central image of this Sunday's lectionary readings is water. Depending on where we live, we might be tempted to take water for granted. But water is an essential element of life. Without water, plants dry up and forests burn. Without fresh water, animals and humans become sick and die. But when water is plentiful, all of creation flourishes. If we can say these things about water as an element of creation, how much more can we say about spiritual water, in all its forms, constantly flowing from God into our lives?

In today's first reading, we learn that the Israelites had escaped their slavery in Egypt and found themselves facing the harsh realities of life in the wilderness. These moments of challenge are described as tests that God imposed to see if their allegiance to God was strong and true. Two tests lead up to today's first reading. The first takes place at Marah in the wilderness of Shur. The people were thirsty, and there was water in that place, but they could not drink it because it was too bitter. (Marah means "bitter" in Hebrew.) Moses cried out to God and God provided him with a stick,

which, when thrown into the water, turned the bitter water into fresh water (Exodus 15.22–27). The second test was similar. Now in the wilderness of Sin (or Zin) between Elim and Sinai, the people were hungry for food. Again, the people complained against Moses. Again, God did not rebuke the people. Instead, God sent manna from the heavens and quail for the people to eat (Exodus 16).

The third test, which is conveyed in today's first reading, also takes place in the wilderness of Sin at a place called Rephidim. Finding no water in this place, the Israelites

For meditation and context:

RESPONSORIAL PSALM Psalm 95.1–2, 6–7ab, 7c–9 (R.7c+8a)

R. O that today you would listen to the voice of the Lord.
Do not harden your hearts!

O come, let us sing to the Lord;
let us make a joyful noise to the rock of
    our salvation!
Let us come into his presence with
    thanksgiving;
let us make a joyful noise to him with songs
    of praise!

O come, let us worship and bow down,
let us kneel before the Lord, our Maker!
For he is our God, and we are the people of
    his pasture,
and the sheep of his hand.

O that today you would listen to his voice!
Do not harden your hearts, as at Meribah,
as on the day at Massah in the wilderness,
when your ancestors tested me,
and put me to the proof,
though they had seen my work.

READING II Romans 5.1–2, 5–8

A reading from the Letter of Saint Paul to the Romans.

A reading in which Paul provides a clear sense of how faith progresses from the proof of God's love evident in Christ's death. As is often true in Paul's letters, he gets right to the point. You should allow yourself to read this passage in the same spirit.

Brothers and sisters:
Since we are **justified** by faith,
we have **peace** with God through our **Lord** Jesus Christ,
through whom we have obtained **access** to this **grace**
    in which we **stand**;
and we **boast** in our hope of sharing the **glory** of God.

The tone shifts slightly here, especially at "disappoint." Despite the difficulty of what Christ accomplished, his success means victory, giving us hope.

And **hope** does **not** disappoint us,
because God's **love** has been **poured** into our **hearts**
through the **Holy Spirit** that has been **given** to us.
For while we were still **weak**,
at the **right** time **Christ died** for the **ungodly**.
Indeed, **rarely** will anyone **die** for a **righteous** person—
though perhaps for a **good person** someone might actually
    dare to **die**.

The words in this line should have almost equal emphasis, especially "proves," "love," and "us."

But **God proves** his **love** for **us**
in that while we **still** were **sinners** Christ **died** for us.

---

quarrel with Moses and grumble against him, but Moses challenges them in return, after making it clear in the preceding verse that their problem is not with him but with God: "Why do you test the Lord?" (Exodus 17.2). Once again God does not rebuke the people but instead directs Moses to take the staff that he used in the execution of the ten plagues against the Egyptians and hit the rock in Horeb, making abundant water flow from the rock to quench the Israelites' thirst. The elders are there to witness God's work on behalf of the people.

The purpose of these three tests is now fully revealed in the closing sentence of this reading: "Is the Lord among us or not?" When we are angry with God and want to test whether God cares for us, can we also trust that God will not rebuke us and instead turn our hearts to witness God's benevolence on our behalf?

READING II Our second reading comes from Paul's Letter to the Romans. In the preceding chapters of this letter, Paul gives an intensive but somewhat abstract teaching on justification by

faith. Here he focuses on the gifts that justification brings to believers who trust in the power of God on their behalf.

But first, what does Paul mean when he talks about justification by faith? The words justification and righteousness are synonyms for the same Greek word, *dikaiosuné*. In the broadest sense, it means "the condition that is acceptable to God." But Paul gives this word a somewhat more precise meaning. When he refers to the righteousness of God, he means something like "God behaving as God is in God's self," and when Paul refers to human righteousness,

Samaria = suh-MAYR-ee-uh
Sychar = SĪ-kahr
Samaritan = suh-MAYR-uh-tuhn

A lengthy reading with a rich narrative progression. The focus of this reading is on the transformation of the Samaritan woman, who presents herself to Jesus as a skeptic but becomes a true believer by the end of the reading. Her conversion is presented in slight contrast to the work of Jesus' disciples, who themselves are skeptical of the Samaritan woman, mostly out of prejudice. Allow the rich social and spiritual realities of this passage to resonate in your proclamation.

At this point the dialogue between Jesus and the Samaritan woman begins. Distinguish between their words by slightly adjusting the pitch of your voice for each speaker.

The rhythm of this line is emphatic. Notice the stresses.

These words of Jesus are the core of his exchange with the Samaritan woman.

GOSPEL   John 4.5–42

A reading from the holy Gospel according to John.

[Jesus came to a **Samaritan** city called **Sychar**,
near the **plot** of ground that **Jacob** had given to his son **Joseph**.
Jacob's well was **there**,
and **Jesus**, tired out by his **journey**, was sitting by the **well**.
It was about **noon**.
A Samaritan **woman** came to draw **water**,
and Jesus said to her, "**Give me** a **drink**."
(His disciples had gone to the **city** to buy **food**.)
The Samaritan woman **said** to him,
"How is it that **you**, a **Jew**,
ask a **drink** of **me**, a **woman** of **Samaria**?"
(Jews **do not** share things in common with **Samaritans**.)
Jesus answered her,
"If you **knew** the **gift** of God,
and who it is that is **saying** to you, 'Give me a **drink**,'
you would have asked **him**,
and he would have **given** you **living water**."
The woman **said** to him,
"**Sir**, you have no **bucket**, and the well is **deep**.
Where do you **get** that **living** water?
Are you **greater** than our father **Jacob**, who **gave us** the well,
and with his **children** and his **flocks drank** from it?"
Jesus said to her,
"Everyone who **drinks** of **this** water will be **thirsty** again,
but the one who drinks of the water that **I** will give
will **never** be thirsty.
The water that **I** will give him will **become** in him a spring
     of water
gushing up to **eternal** life."

he means something like "having been put right with God." Why do humans need to be put right with God? Paul says it is because of the nature of the first sin that affected and continues to affect all humanity, namely, the refusal to acknowledge God as God and to worship God accordingly (see Romans 1.18–23). But justification is not something that humans can do for themselves. Rather, it is God's free gift effected through the atoning death and Resurrection of Jesus to all who will receive it in trust. Such is the graciousness of God.

Thus, in today's second reading, Paul says that all of us who are justified by *faith* can enjoy peace (Greek, *eiréné,* meaning "tranquility, harmony, concord, security, or safety") with God as a free gift; we are acquitted of our sin and are no longer estranged but are now reconciled with God. This gift gives us assurance even in the face of difficulties, because these struggles develop our endurance, which in turn manifests as hope. And what is the source of this hope? It is not our doing, Paul says, but it is the outpouring of the superabundance of God's love through the Holy Spirit. It is

Christ who died for us; even when we did not deserve his sacrifice of love, he freely offered this gift so that we could be put in right relationship with God. How amazing is this gift!

GOSPEL   This reading from the Gospel of John has as its central character an unnamed woman of Samaria, who appears nowhere else in the Gospels. Yet, when we dig deeply into her story, you will find this woman to be utterly unforgettable because of her journey of faith.

The woman **said** to him, "Sir, **give** me this **water**,
so that I may **never** be thirsty
or have to keep **coming** here to draw **water**."]
Jesus said to her, "Go, **call** your husband, and come back."
The woman answered him, "I **have** no husband."
Jesus said to her, "You are **right** in saying, 'I **have** no **husband**';
for you have had **five** husbands,
and the one you have **now** is **not** your husband.
What you have **said** is **true**!"
The woman said to him, ["**Sir**, I see that you are a **Prophet**.
Our **ancestors worshipped** on this mountain,
but you say that the **place** where people must **worship**
is in **Jerusalem**."
Jesus said to her,
"**Woman**, **believe** me, the **hour** is coming
when you will **worship** the Father
neither on this **mountain** nor in **Jerusalem**.
You **worship** what you do not **know**;
we **worship** what we know,
for **salvation** is from the **Jews**.
But the **hour** is coming, and is **now** here,
when the **true worshippers** will worship the Father
in **spirit** and **truth**,
for the Father **seeks** such as these to **worship** him.
God is **spirit**,
and those who **worship** him must **worship** in **spirit** and **truth**."
The woman said to him, "**I know** that the Messiah is **coming**"
(who is called the **Christ**).
"When he **comes**, he will proclaim **all things** to us."
Jesus said to her, "I am **he**,
the one who is **speaking** to you."] »

With these words, the Samaritan woman's skepticism shifts into belief.

And here, Jesus reveals himself as the Messiah. Emphasize "he" and "speaking" to express the revelation.

The setting for this story is Jacob's well in the city of Sychar. In biblical tradition, wells are described as places of first encounter between men and their soon-to-be spouses. Abraham's servant found a wife, Rebekah, for Isaac at a well (Genesis 24), Jacob met Rachel at a well (Genesis 29.1–20), and Moses met his wife Zipporah at a well (Exodus 2.15–22). But the well in today's Gospel is the setting for a different type of meeting.

The encounter between Jesus and the Samaritan woman is complicated. Both Jews and Samaritans tie their identity to Jacob, the son of Isaac, the ancestor of the twelve tribes of Israel. But Samaritans and Jews did not get along. In fact, they had been bitterly divided since after the Babylonian Exile in the sixth century BC. Things got so bad that the Samaritans built their own temple on Mount Gerizim in the fourth century BC rather than participate in the Temple activities in Jerusalem. Sadly, this animosity continues even today.

The narrator of this story identifies the time of this encounter as noon, the brightest point of the day. The Gospel of John is highly symbolic, and here we see the author's use of dualism. He uses polar opposites like light and darkness, truth and falsehood, from above and from below to signal belief versus unbelief. In John's Gospel, belief is not a mental activity that results in assent to a set of doctrines; it is trusting in and allying oneself with Jesus and the Father. Thus, this encounter between Jesus and the Samaritan woman is not about clock time but about coming into the full light of faith in Jesus Christ.

As this story unfolds, Jesus issues two commands to the woman: (1) "Give me a drink," and (2) "Go, call your husband, and

The return of the disciples reinforces the "problem" of Jesus interacting with a Samaritan woman (something Jewish custom ordinarily forbade); it also marks a slight excursion, because the disciples want Jesus to eat, while he has a lesson he wants to convey to them.

Just then his **disciples** came.
They were **astonished** that he was speaking with a **woman**,
but no one said, "What do you want?"
or, "Why are you speaking with her?"
Then the woman left her **water** jar and went back to the **city**.
She said to the **people**,
"Come and see a **man** who told me **everything** I have **ever done**!
He cannot be the **Messiah, can** he?"
They left the city and were **on their way** to him.
Meanwhile the disciples were urging him,
"**Rabbi, eat** something."
But he said to them,
"I have **food** to eat that you do not **know** about."
So the disciples said to one another,
"Surely **no one** has brought him something to **eat**?"
Jesus said to them,
"My **food** is to do the **will** of him who **sent** me
and to **complete** his **work**.
Do you not say, '**Four** months more, **then** comes the **harvest**'?
But I tell you, look **around** you,
and see how the **fields** are **ripe** for **harvesting**.
The **reaper** is already **receiving** wages
and is **gathering fruit** for eternal **life**,
so that **sower** and **reaper** may rejoice **together**.
For **here** the saying holds **true**, 'One sows and another **reaps**.'
I sent you to **reap** that for which you did not **labour**.
Others have **laboured**, and **you** have entered into **their** labour.
[Many **Samaritans** from that city **believed** in Jesus
because of the woman's **testimony**,
"He told me **everything** I have **ever** done."
So when the Samaritans **came** to him,
they asked him to **stay** with them;
and he **stayed** there two **days**.

The conclusion returns us to the Samaritan woman; not only does she believe in Jesus, she is able to convert the other Samaritans because of her conviction. The words of the assembled Samaritans are spoken directly to the congregation's own faith.

come back." After each command, Jesus and the Samaritan woman engage in dialogue. Concerning the first command, the woman knows that Jews would not accept anything that had been in the possession of a Samaritan, and she is not subtle about pointing out their prejudice: "How is it that you, *a Jew*, ask a drink of me, *a woman of Samaria*?" When Jesus offers to give her living water, she answers in retort: "Are you *greater than our father Jacob*?" But, of course, Jesus is greater than Jacob! She responds to his offer by saying, "*Sir*, give me this water, so that I may never be thirsty or

have to keep coming here to draw water." Notice how her tone and disposition toward Jesus is changing.

When Jesus delivers his second command, she responds that she has no husband, which Jesus confirms by detailing her history of having had five husbands and that the one she is currently with is not her husband. This bit of dialogue has led some to conclude that this woman is a sinner, but the text does not support this view. Jesus does not condemn her or tell her to stop sinning, and later the townspeople immediately listen to her testimony about Jesus

and show no signs of her having been shunned by her neighbours. Was she the victim of many divorces? Was she widowed and married off again many times over? Or are the five husbands a symbol of her Samaritan beliefs that only the five books of the Torah are sacred Scripture? Following this revelation of Jesus' knowledge, the woman's tone shifts again as she responds, "Sir, I see that you are *a Prophet*."

This woman, who is not afraid to speak her mind, even when her culture forbade it, is also theologically literate. She takes advantage of this opportunity to ask

And many more **believed** because of his **word**.
They said to the woman,
"It is no longer because of what **you said** that we believe,
for we have **heard** for **ourselves**,
and we know that this is **truly** the Saviour of the **world**."]

[Shorter: John 4.5–15, 19–26, 39a, 40–42 (see brackets)]

about the right place to worship: the Temple in Jerusalem or their temple on Mount Gerizim. When Jesus answers, saying that neither of these places of worship will matter in the end, because a time will come "when the true worshippers will worship the Father in spirit and truth," she concludes that Jesus is talking about the messianic age. Her response is in the form of a statement, "I know that *the Messiah* is coming," but listen carefully and you can hear the question in her heart: "Is he the one?" Jesus answers by saying, "*I am*." It is the same response that Moses received

when he asked God to reveal his name: "I AM WHO I AM" (Exodus 3.14).

Almost immediately, the Samaritan woman leaves her water jar behind and goes into the village to tell the townspeople about her encounter with Jesus. When the villagers meet Jesus and hear his words, they proclaim him to be "the Saviour of the world." Pay attention to the progression of titles given to Jesus as we follow the trajectory of this woman's faith journey. She is transformed from a water carrier to a proclaimer of the Good News and shares the message of that "spring of water gushing

up to eternal life." Consider what this woman can teach us about our own journey of faith. C.C.

FOURTH SUNDAY OF LENT

LECTIONARY #31

READING I   1 Samuel 16.1b, 6–7, 10–13

A reading from the first book of Samuel.

The Lord said to **Samuel**,
"Fill your **horn** with **oil** and **set out**;
I will **send** you to **Jesse** of **Bethlehem**,
for I have **provided** for myself a **king** among his **sons**."
When the **sons of Jesse** came,
Samuel looked on **Eliab** and thought,
"**Surely** the Lord's anointed is now **before** the **Lord**."
But the Lord said to Samuel,
"**Do not look** on his **appearance**
or on the height of his **stature**,
because I have **rejected** him;
for the **Lord** does not **see** as the **human sees**;
the **human** looks on the **outward** appearance,
but the **Lord** looks on the **heart**."
Jesse made **seven** of his sons pass before **Samuel**,
and Samuel said to Jesse,
"The **Lord** has not chosen **any** of these."
Samuel said to Jesse, "Are **all** your **sons** here?"
And he said, "There remains yet the **youngest**,
but he is **keeping** the **sheep**."
And Samuel said to Jesse,
"**Send** and **bring** him;
for we will not **sit down** until he comes **here**."

Samuel = SAM-yoo-uhl

Jesse = JES-ee

A reading with a dramatic conclusion, in which Samuel, sent by the Lord and endowed with power, is sent among the sons of Jesse to find and anoint a new king. Samuel's power is the ability to recognize this king, whose appearance, when he sees him at last, thrills him. The words themselves convey the drama of this reading compellingly.

Eliab = ee-Lī-uhb

Emphasize the parallel: not as people see does God see.

Samuel cannot see the chosen king among the sons. Subtle emphasis on "any."

READING I On this Fourth Sunday of Lent, the lectionary readings invite us to reflect on the nature of God's revelatory activity and our journey of faith.

The First Book of Samuel tells the story of Samuel's emergence as a Prophet and spokesperson for God in the period leading up to Israel's transition to leadership under a king. Early on, Israel depended on charismatic leaders, called judges, whom God would raise up in times of trouble to rescue the people. Samuel is the last of these judges. When the people push him

to give them a king like their neighbours had, Samuel delivers God's warning about what that could mean, and the picture is quite terrifying (see 1 Samuel 8.10–18). But on God's directive, Samuel relents and appoints Saul as the first king of Israel. However, almost immediately God rejects Saul, because he failed to obey God's word. Therefore, even as Saul continued to serve as king, God directs Samuel to anoint David as its second king, which he did secretly.

In today's first reading, we pick up with the story of David's anointing. God orders Samuel to fill his oil flask and ready

himself for his journey to Bethlehem. Samuel purportedly comes to this town to offer sacrifice to God, and he asks both the elders and Jesse and his sons to come to the sacrifice. In actuality, he wanted God to point out the next king and have witnesses to testify to the selection. Saul examines seven of Jesse's sons, one by one, hoping for a sign. But God says no. Finally, Samuel asks, "Are all your sons here?" When Jesse produces David, his youngest and presumably least valued son, immediately Samuel knows that he is God's anointed. It is noteworthy that David came from shepherding

ruddy = RUHD-ee =
having a reddish complexion

Samuel can see the chosen king at last. Equal
emphases on "anoint," "this," and "one."

Jesse **sent** and **brought David** in.
Now he was **ruddy**, and had beautiful **eyes**, and was **handsome**.
The Lord said,
"Rise and **anoint** him; for **this** is the **one**."
Then **Samuel** took the horn of **oil**,
and **anointed** him in the **presence** of his **brothers**;
and the **spirit** of the Lord came **mightily** upon David
from **that** day **forward**.

For meditation and context:

RESPONSORIAL PSALM   Psalm 23.1–3a, 3b–4, 5, 6 (R.1)

R. The Lord is my shepherd; I shall not want.

The Lord is my shepherd, I shall not want.
He makes me lie down in green pastures;
he leads me beside still waters;
he restores my soul.

He leads me in right paths for his
    name's sake.
Even though I walk through the darkest
    valley, I fear no evil;
for you are with me;
your rod and your staff—they comfort me.

You prepare a table before me
in the presence of my enemies;
you anoint my head with oil;
my cup overflows.

Surely goodness and mercy shall follow me
all the days of my life,
and I shall dwell in the house of the Lord
my whole life long.

READING II   Ephesians 5.8–14

Ephesians = ee-FEE-zhuhnz

A reading from the Letter of Saint Paul to the Ephesians.

A reading in which Paul tries to convince
the Ephesians to live as children of the light.

Brothers and sisters:
Once you were **darkness**, but **now** in the Lord you are **light**.
Live as **children** of **light**—
for the **fruit** of the light is found
in **all** that is **good** and **right** and **true**.
Try to **find out** what is **pleasing** to the **Lord**.
Take no **part** in the unfruitful works of **darkness**,
but instead **expose** them. »

---

his father's sheep, because shepherding was also symbolic of a king's pastoral leadership toward his subjects. The narrator ends the story by saying, "the spirit of the Lord came mightily upon David from that day forward." The Hebrew word for "spirit" is *ruach*, which also means "breath or wind." Thus, in his anointing, the breath of God guided David's leadership.

READING II Our second reading comes from the Letter to the Ephesians and is attributed to Paul but was probably written by one of his disciples.

Most biblical scholars assign a date of composition of approximately AD 90–100. Today's reading is part of the paraenesis of this letter, that is, the section of the letter dedicated to advice about how the members of the church at Ephesus ought to behave. In the verses immediately prior to this reading, the author is admonishing the community not to accept "empty words" or to pay attention to people who promote them (Ephesians 5.6). We can assume that "empty words" refers to a way of life that is suggested by the catalogue of vices found in Ephesians 5.3–5: behaviours like greed,

various forms of idolatry, and "obscene, silly and vulgar talk"—three words that are used nowhere else in the New Testament.

These are the unethical behaviours that the author of the Letter to the Ephesians is talking about when he reminds his readers that they once lived in darkness, before they became followers of Jesus. The word "darkness" is used by this author to describe the personification of all that was evil in the world and of evil spirits that were always battling against the light, threatening to overcome it. Further, the letter writer encourages the community by

Take note of the parallels and shifts in these lines: from "everything" to "visible," and then "everything" to "light."

"Awake," "rise," and "shine" are the focal points of these final lines. Don't rush through them.

For it is **shameful** even to **mention** what such people do **secretly**;
but **everything** exposed by the light becomes **visible**,
for **everything** that becomes visible is **light**.
Therefore it is said,
"Sleeper, **awake**!
Rise from the **dead**, and **Christ** will **shine** on you."

GOSPEL   John 9.1–41

A reading from the holy Gospel according to John.

Rabbi = RAB-ī

This is a complex narrative reading with many characters, each with different motivations, as well as several scene changes. In this reading, Jesus upturns traditional rabbinic understanding of blindness as a punishment for immorality. It also relies on a defiant tone to make its point. Keep this in mind as you proclaim.

This line has an anticipatory, prophetic quality, characteristic of John's Gospel.

These details of Jesus' healing powers are interesting; don't rush through them.

Siloam = sih-LOH-uhm

Any expression of "I am" in John's Gospel is freighted with authority.

[As Jesus walked along, he saw a man **blind** from **birth**.]
His disciples asked him,
"**Rabbi**, who **sinned**, this **man** or his **parents**,
that he was **born blind**?"
Jesus answered, "Neither **this** man nor his **parents** sinned;
he was **born blind** so that God's works might be **revealed**
        in him.
We must work the **works** of him who sent me while it is **day**;
night is coming when **no one** can **work**.
As long as I am in the **world**, I am the **light** of the **world**."
When he had **said** this, [he **spat** on the ground
and made **mud** with the **saliva** and **spread** the mud
        on the man's **eyes**,
saying to him, "**Go**, **wash** in the **pool** of **Siloam**"
(which means **Sent**).
Then the man who was blind **went** and **washed**,
        and came back **able** to see.
The neighbours and those who had seen him **before** as a **beggar**
began to ask, "Is this not the man who used to **sit** and **beg**?"
Some were saying, "It **is** he."
Others were saying, "**No**, but it is someone **like** him."
He kept saying, "I **am** the **man**."]
But they kept asking him, "Then how were your **eyes** opened?"

---

saying "in the Lord you are light" and therefore they should "live as children of light." And what does the light of God produce? "All that is good and right and true." Clearly, this author is convinced that good will triumph over evil, because only good things come from God. Moreover, light has the ability to expose the darkness and has the potential even to transform it. This beautiful piece of poetic text that concludes today's second reading is most likely part of an early Christian hymn, perhaps one that was used in the celebration of baptism.

GOSPEL   This reading from the Gospel of John has as its central character an unnamed blind man whom Jesus heals, even without the man asking to be healed. Although the other Gospels also include stories about Jesus healing a blind man or blind men, this is the only Gospel that includes a series of scenes in which the formerly blind man gives witness to Jesus when confronted by his neighbours and the scribes and Pharisees.

This reading consists of a miracle story and six follow-up scenes. The miracle story has the basic elements that we would

expect of any New Testament miracle story: (1) a description of need, in this case, a man who was blind from birth; (2) the miracle worker's word or deed, in this case, Jesus making and putting clay on the man's eyes; and (3) evidence that the miracle took place, in this case, the man washing and being able to see. But the way in which the miracle story is framed is most important. When Jesus' disciples notice the blind man, they ask about who is at fault. Today, theologians would not espouse this view that physical ailments are caused by human sinfulness. Yet, we still hear people in crisis

The (formerly) blind man's tone here is somewhat exasperated.

He answered, "The man called **Jesus** made **mud**,
    spread it on my **eyes**,
and said to me, 'Go to **Siloam** and **wash**.'
Then I **went** and washed and received my **sight**."
They said to him, "Where **is** he?"
He said, "I do not **know**."
[They brought to the **Pharisees** the man who had formerly
    been blind.
Now it was a **Sabbath** day when Jesus **made** the mud and **opened**
    his eyes.
Then the **Pharisees** also began to ask him
how he had received his **sight**.
He said to them, "He put **mud** on my eyes.
Then I **washed**, and now I **see**."
Some of the Pharisees said,
"This man is **not** from God, for he **does not observe**
    the **Sabbath**."
But others said, "How can a man who is a sinner perform
    such **signs**?"
And they were **divided**.
So they said again to the blind man,
"What do you **say** about him? It was **your** eyes he **opened**."

Once again, the man who had been blind has to explain his story, this time to the Pharisees. His exasperation mounts to defiance when he proclaims Jesus a Prophet.

He said, "He is a **Prophet**."]
They did not **believe** that he had been **blind**
and had received his **sight**
until they called the **parents** of the man who had **received**
    his sight
and asked them, "Is this your **son**, who you say was born **blind**?
How then does he now **see**?"
His parents answered, "We **know** that this is our son,
and that he was born **blind**;

Because the Pharisees don't believe the man who had been blind, they question his parents. Crucially, they repeat that he is of age and can speak for himself. Their tone is defiant. They believe their son.

but we do **not** know how it is that now he **sees**,
nor do we know who **opened** his eyes.
Ask him; he is of **age**.
He will **speak** for **himself**." »

ask, "What did I do to deserve this?" Jesus makes clear that physical illness is not a platform for assigning blame but an opportunity to do the works of God. But there is an urgency to this work because while Jesus is in the world, he tells us, he is the light of the world. When darkness comes, no one can work.

And what is the work of God? The man's blindness would have been viewed as an extremely serious condition. Ancients believed that a person was able to see because of the light that was within them. If this person was blind from birth, it meant

that he had no light in him, even from the moment that he was born. This is why the disciples ask about the parents' sin. At the end of the miracle story, we learn that the man did as Jesus directed; he went and washed in the pool of Siloam and was able to see. But in the symbolism of John's Gospel, seeing is believing, and believing is doing the work of God (John 6.26–29). Perhaps, then, the washing is an allusion to baptism, an action that Christ instituted as the way of salvation and a way of commissioning us for our taking up of his mission.

The first scene to follow this miracle story describes the formerly blind man's neighbours who observe him being able to see and wonder whether the man they see is the one they knew when he was still blind or someone else. When the man confirms his identity and tells them how he was healed, he describes the healer as "the man called *Jesus*." In the second scene, we learn that the neighbours brought the man to the Pharisees, scholars of the Law, because the healing took place on the Sabbath. Sabbath observance was one of the most important obligations of the Law,

His parents said this because they were **afraid**
     of the Jewish **authorities**,
who had already **agreed**
that anyone who **confessed** Jesus to be the **Messiah**
would be **put out** of the **synagogue**.
Therefore his parents said, "He is of **age**; **ask** him."
So for the second time they **called the man** who had been blind,
and they said to him, "Give **glory** to **God**!
We **know** that this man is a **sinner**."
He answered, "I do not **know** whether he is a **sinner**.
One thing I **do know**, that though I was **blind**, now I **see**."
They said to him, "What did he **do** to you?
How did he open your **eyes**?"
He answered them,
"**I** have told you already, and you would not **listen**.
Why do you want to hear it **again**?
Do you **also** want to become his **disciples**?"
Then they **reviled** him, saying,
"**You** are his disciple, but **we** are disciples of **Moses**.
We **know** that God has **spoken** to **Moses**,
but as for this man, we do not **know** where he **comes from**."
The man answered, "Here is an **astonishing** thing!
You do not **know** where he **comes from**,
     and yet he **opened** my **eyes**.
We know that **God** does **not** listen to sinners,
but he **does** listen to one who **worships** him and **obeys** his **will**.
Never since the world **began** has it been **heard**
that **anyone** opened the eyes of a person born **blind**.
If this man were **not** from God, he could do **nothing**."
[They **answered** him, "You were born **entirely** in sins,
and are **you** trying to teach **us**?"
And they **drove** him out.
Jesus heard that they had **driven him out**,
and when he found him, he said,
"Do you **believe** in the Son of **Man**?"

Exasperation and defiance.

The Pharisees cannot believe his temerity.
This disbelief intensifies to the point where
they throw him out because he has the gall
to try to teach them. Ridiculous as they are,
don't ridicule the Pharisees with your tone
of voice.

which could be broken only in life-or-death situations. But a man born blind could certainly wait another day for healing, and now the Pharisees are divided about Jesus and whether he was from God. When questioned further, the formerly blind man says of Jesus, "He is a *Prophet*."

In the third scene that follows this miracle story, the Pharisees summon the formerly blind man's parents to ask about their son's blindness. Sadly, the parents sacrifice their son to save themselves, because "the Jewish authorities" had decided that anyone who recognized Jesus

as *the Messiah* would be banned from the synagogue. Most likely, the parents are Jesus followers, though hidden ones, because they are not willing to endure the consequences of their belief.

In the fourth scene, the tone and direction of the story begin to change dramatically. The Jewish religious authorities call the man to stand before them again, as if in a court of law, and they announce their decision that Jesus is a sinner, presumably to get the man to denounce Jesus as well. But the formerly blind man turns the tables on them. They treat him as the accused in

earlier scenes of this story, but now he becomes the accuser, launching a fierce argument against them for their failure to recognize Jesus as coming *from God*. The consequence of the man's witness is immediate: "And they drove him out."

In the fifth scene, Jesus seeks out the formerly blind man to ask him whether he believed in the *Son of Man*. In the other Gospel accounts, this title is used only by Jesus and only to speak of himself, and that appears to be the case here, as well. Earlier in the Gospel of John, when Jesus is calling his disciples, he uses the story of Jacob's

Jesus validates the belief of the man who had been blind.

The reading concludes with a crucial inversion: blindness to sight, sight to blindness. The sin tradition indicated in the blind man has been shifted to the Pharisees. When we believe something blindly, are we believing or are we blind?

He answered, "And who **is** he, sir?
Tell me, so that I may **believe** in him."
Jesus said to him,
"You have **seen** him, and the one **speaking** with you is **he**."
He said, "**Lord**, I **believe**."
And he **worshipped** him.]
Jesus said, "I **came** into this world for **judgment**
so that **those** who do not **see** may **see**,
and **those** who do **see** may become **blind**."
Some of the Pharisees near him **heard** this and said to him,
"**Surely** we are not blind, **are** we?"
Jesus said to them,
"If you were **blind**, you would have no sin.
But now that you say, 'We **see**,' your **sin** remains."

[Shorter: John 9.1, 6–9, 13–17, 34–38 (see brackets)]

ladder to speak about the "greater things" that Nathanael will see because of his belief, and he likens the Son of Man to the ladder that bridges earthly and heavenly realities (see John 1.43–51).

In the final scene of this story, Jesus condemns the religious authorities for being blind, even as they have eyes to see. Recall the comments that Jesus made to the disciples in the first scene. As light of the world, Jesus' mission is one of judgment, not against people who are physically blind but against those who are spiritually blind and who refuse to recog-

nize Jesus' true identity. Moreover, Jesus has the authority to judge because he is the agent of God who bridges the earthly and heavenly realities by doing only what the Father tells him to do.

And what about us? With whom do you most identify? Let us approach Jesus, the light of the world, so that he can shed light on our blindness and enable us to do the works of God. C.C.

MARCH 20, 2023

SAINT JOSEPH, HUSBAND OF THE BLESSED VIRGIN MARY (PATRON OF CANADA)

LECTIONARY #543

READING I   2 Samuel 7.4–5a, 12–14a, 16

A reading from the second book of Samuel.

The word of the Lord came to **Nathan**:
"**Go** and **tell** my servant **David**:
'When your **days** are **fulfilled**
and you lie **down** with your ancestors,
I will **raise up** your **offspring after** you,
who shall come **forth** from your **body**,
and I will **establish** his **kingdom**.
He shall build a **house** for my **name**,
and I will **establish** the **throne** of his kingdom **forever**.
I will be a **father** to him,
and he shall be a **son** to me.
Your **house** and your **kingdom** shall be made **sure forever**
before me.'"

A reading in which Nathan prophesies about the house of King David and its longevity, anticipating both Joseph and Jesus himself. This is a short reading that makes bold claims. Read it with vigour.

Note the parallels between "down" and "up."

Almost even emphasis on the words in this line; slow the tempo of your reading ever so slightly.

There are options for today's readings. Contact your parish staff to learn which readings will be used.

READING I   Today's readings speak to the person of St. Joseph. The Gospels don't tell us much about this important father figure in the life of Jesus, but his qualities shine through his actions. The readings also help us to place Joseph in the context of God's plan of salvation history.

The first reading comes from the Second Book of Samuel, in which the Prophet Nathan delivers a message to King David, who wanted to build a house for God after he had built his palace in Jerusalem and after God had granted peace in the land of Israel (see 2 Samuel 7.13). At first, Nathan thought David's idea was a good one, but later he returned with a message from God that was quite radical. He tells David that God never asked for a house (i.e., a temple): not during the Israelites' wanderings in the wilderness or during the time of the tribal leaders who preceded David's reign, and not now (see 2 Samuel 7.57). Instead, Nathan says that God will establish a house (i.e., dynasty) for David, and David can be assured that God will raise up from his lineage a son who will build a house (i.e., temple) for God. This son is Solomon, who is credited with building the Jerusalem Temple. But then the language of this oracle broadens a bit. Nathan speaks God's words to David: "I will be a father to him, and he shall be a son to me. Your house and your kingdom shall be made sure forever before me." Thus, this oracle becomes a foundational teaching for both Jews and Christians about a royal messiah whose reign will last forever. Later,

92

For meditation and context:

RESPONSORIAL PSALM   Psalm 89.1–2, 3–4, 26+28 (R.36)

R. His line shall continue forever.

I will sing of your steadfast love,
    O Lord, forever;
with my mouth I will proclaim your
    faithfulness to all generations.
I declare that your steadfast love is
    established forever;
your faithfulness is as firm as the heavens.

You said, "I have made a covenant with
    my chosen one,
I have sworn to my servant David:
I will establish your descendants forever,
and build your throne for all generations."

He shall cry to me, "You are my Father,
my God, and the Rock of my salvation!"
Forever I will keep my steadfast love for him,
and my covenant with him will stand firm.

READING II   Romans 4.13, 16–18, 22

A reading from the Letter of Saint Paul to the Romans.

Brothers and sisters:
The **promise** that Abraham would **inherit** the world
did not **come** to Abraham or to his **descendants** through the **law**
but through the **righteousness** of faith.
For **this reason** the promise **depends** on faith,
in order that the **promise** may rest on **grace**
and be **guaranteed** to **all** his **descendants**,
not only to the **adherents** of the law,
but also to those who share the **faith** of **Abraham**.
He is the **father** of **all** of us,
as it is **written**,
"I have **made you** the **father** of many **nations**."
Abraham **believed** in the **presence** of the God
who **gives life** to the **dead**
and **calls** into existence the **things** that do **not** exist.
Hoping against hope, Abraham **believed**
that he would become "the **father** of many **nations**,"
according to **what** was **said**,
"So **numerous** shall your descendants **be**."
Therefore his faith "was **reckoned** to him as **righteousness**."

Paul's Letter to the Romans echoes the first reading from 2 Samuel. Principally, he is signalling the size and durability of Abraham's offspring, as well as the righteousness of faith that caused it. These are confident claims Paul is making.

Abraham's belief is a focus in this passage; let the words "believed" and "presence" ring out in your reading.

we will see that Joseph is also depicted as part of David's royal lineage.

READING II Our second reading comes from the Letter to the Romans, in which Paul comments on another promise that God made—this one to Abraham and Sarah concerning the descendants that she would provide for him (Genesis 17.1–22). The backdrop for this reading is Paul's teaching on justification by faith, in which he argues that God restored humanity's intended relationship with God as a free gift to those who trust in him.

As a starting point for this teaching, Paul quotes Genesis 15.6, "Abraham believed God, and it was reckoned to him as righteousness" (Romans 4.3), and he goes on to talk about how the promise was realized not because of any works that Abraham did—in Paul's context, he understands "works" to mean "obedience to Jewish law"—but as a free gift. Abraham is an apt example for this teaching on justification because there is no law until Moses comes onto the scene some 600 or more years later. And, when Paul talks about "grace" (Greek, *charis*, meaning "goodwill, loving-

kindness, or favour"), he is referring to the gift of justification by faith. Paul also quotes Genesis 17.5, "I have made you the father of many nations," which is what the name Abraham means. Thus, Paul can easily argue that this promise is not limited to our Jewish brothers and sisters but has been extended to all of humanity, because, as Paul has interpreted the quotation, "all nations" no longer refers to biological descendants of Abraham but to all people of faith, Jews and Gentiles.

GOSPEL   Matthew 1.16, 18–21, 24a

A reading from the holy Gospel according to Matthew.

Jacob was the father of **Joseph**, the **husband** of Mary,
of whom **Jesus** was born, who is **called** the **Christ**.
Now the **birth** of **Jesus** the Christ took place in this way.
When his **mother Mary** had been engaged to **Joseph**,
but **before** they lived together,
she was **found** to be with **child** from the Holy Spirit.
Her husband **Joseph**, being a **righteous man**
and unwilling to **expose** her to public **disgrace**,
planned to **dismiss** her **quietly**.
But just when he had **resolved** to do this,
an **Angel** of the Lord **appeared** to him in a **dream** and said,
"**Joseph**, son of **David**,
do not be afraid to take **Mary** as your wife,
for the **child conceived** in her is from the Holy **Spirit**.
She will **bear** a son,
and you are to **name** him **Jesus**,
for he will save **his** people from their **sins**."
When Joseph **awoke** from **sleep**,
he did as the **Angel** of the Lord **commanded** him;
he **took** her as his **wife**.

Or:

A well-known reading that invokes Joseph's righteousness in the light of his fear and anxiety about his engagement to Mary, resulting from her pregnancy. Joseph's fears are ours; his righteousness is God's.

Almost even emphases on these words, with slightly extra emphasis on "resolved."

Even emphasis on "do not be afraid," which should equal the emphasis on "Mary."

GOSPEL **Matthew.** This story about how Joseph became the foster father of Jesus is taken from the Gospel of Matthew. The opening sentence of this reading is actually part of the closing of Matthew's genealogy of Jesus, which establishes that Joseph belongs to the lineage of David, echoing the prophecy that Nathan made to David approximately one thousand years earlier, and it identifies Jesus as the Christ, the long-awaited Messiah.

Some of the traditions that we associate with Joseph (for example, that he was an old man at the time that he became Mary's husband) come from a non-canonical second-century document called the *Infancy Gospel of James*. However, today's reading from the Gospel of Matthew tells us only that his betrothed was pregnant and that he intended to divorce her quietly, so as not to bring shame on her or her family. This was his plan until an Angel told him to go ahead with their marriage, because the infant in Mary's womb was conceived by the Holy Spirit. What you might not know is that this was likely an arranged marriage. Fathers would arrange for their sons and daughters to be given in marriage perhaps as early as ten to twelve years of age in order to secure inheritance rights between the families. However, in early Judaism, this period of betrothal had the full power of marriage, except that the young girl continued to live in her father's house until she was old enough to bear children. The only way to break this contract was for the man to divorce her, but any blame for severing that relationship would fall on the woman. Yet, Joseph proves himself to be a righteous man, obedient to God's will as spoken through the Angel.

A well-known narrative about the childhood of Jesus and his preaching at the Temple. The story hinges on Jesus' parents anxiously looking for him, followed by his other-worldly answer to their fears, and finally his capitulation to be obedient. It's a dramatic tale packed into a small number of verses.

This phrase has mostly even emphases with a little extra on "behind" and "Jerusalem."

The drama and mystery of the tale intensify when Mary addresses Jesus. His response to her is honest but hard to understand. The sympathetic perspective here is that of Mary and Joseph. Their lack of understanding reflects our own.

GOSPEL   Luke 2.41–51a

A reading from the holy Gospel according to Luke.

Every year the parents of Jesus went to **Jerusalem**
for the **festival** of the **Passover**.
And when he was **twelve** years old,
they went up as **usual** for the **festival**.
When the festival was **ended** and they started to **return**,
the boy Jesus stayed **behind** in **Jerusalem**,
but his **parents** did not **know** it.
Assuming that he was in the group of **travellers**,
they went a **day's** journey.
Then they **started** to look for him among their **relatives**
and **friends**.
When they did not **find him**,
they returned to **Jerusalem** to **search** for him.
After **three days** they found him in the **temple**,
sitting among the **teachers**,
listening to them and **asking** them **questions**.
And all who **heard** him were **amazed**
at his **understanding** and his **answers**.
When his parents **saw** him they were **astonished**;
and his mother **said** to him,
"**Child**, why have you treated us like **this**?
Look, your father and I have been **searching** for you
     in great **anxiety**."
He said to them, "**Why** were you **searching** for me?
Did you not **know** that I must **be** in my Father's **house**?"
But they did **not** understand what he **said** to them.
Then he went **down** with them and came to **Nazareth**,
and was **obedient** to them.

Luke. This Gospel reading is Luke's account of the boy Jesus listening to the teachers in the Jerusalem Temple. Often, when we read this story, we focus on Jesus' superior wisdom and intelligence, but today let us turn our attention to what the story tells us about Joseph. He and Mary are presented as devout Jews, making the long trip from Nazareth to Jerusalem every year for Passover. The distance was approximately 100 kilometres on foot, and neighbours and extended families would have travelled as a caravan for safety. At twelve years of age, Jesus would have been considered nearly a man. Can you understand, then, how Mary and Joseph could have left Jesus behind in Jerusalem and not realized it for a full day? But imagine also their fright and concern when they realized Jesus was not among the caravan. They chose to walk back to Jerusalem alone, making themselves vulnerable to bandit attacks along the road. After three days of searching, they finally find Jesus in the Temple. If Jesus was your child, I suspect that you might have wanted to throttle him about now for causing so much worry. Luke presents Mary as chastising Jesus for his outwardly disrespectful behaviour, but Joseph is presented as the silent protector of his family who is ever obedient to God's calling for him. C.C.

THE ANNUNCIATION
OF THE LORD

LECTIONARY #545

READING I   Isaiah 7.10–14; 8.10d

A reading from the book of the Prophet Isaiah.

The Lord spoke to **Ahaz**, saying,
"**Ask** a sign of the **Lord** your God;
let it be **deep** as Sheol or **high** as heaven."
But Ahaz said, "I will **not ask**,
and I will **not put** the Lord to the **test**."
Then Isaiah said:
"**Hear** then, O house of David!
Is it **too little** for you to **weary** the people,
that you **weary** my God **also**?
Therefore the Lord himself will **give** you a **sign**.
Look, the young woman is with **child** and shall bear a **son**,
and shall name him **Emmanuel**,"
for **God** is **with** us.

A reading in which the Prophet Isaiah envisions the coming of a divine child to the house of David. The events of the reading are set in the future, but they are racing with authority to the present. Convey something of this reality in your proclamation.

While the pace of scriptural time quickens when Isaiah begins to speak, the pace of recitation should slow ever so slightly to savour the anticipation his words suggest.

READING I The solemnity of the Annunciation of the Lord, also known as Lady Day in some parts of the world, commemorates the event when the Angel Gabriel came to Mary to tell her that she would be the mother of Jesus. Church historians believe that this feast was celebrated as early as the fourth or fifth century and traditionally on March 25, which is nine months before Christmas on December 25. This date marked the spring equinox, when the hours of daylight begin to overtake the hours of darkness each day, so the early Christian church also associated it with the beginning of Christ's salvation of the world.

Today's first reading is from the Book of Isaiah, which is named after the Prophet who ministered in Jerusalem in the eighth century BC, during the time of the kings Ahaz and Hezekiah. Immediately preceding this reading, the narrator tells us that King Ahaz is in a difficult situation. The kings of Syria and the northern kingdom of Israel were trying to force him into an alliance against the Assyrians. Ahaz and the people of Judah were so terrified, Isaiah says, that their hearts "shook as the trees of the forest shake before the wind" (Isaiah 7.2).

This is the context for our first reading. Using Isaiah as his spokesperson, God tells King Ahaz to ask for a sign from God about what he should do, but Ahaz refuses. Even so, God's reply sounds something like this to our modern ears: "It's not enough to wear out the people around you, but do you need to wear out your God, too?" Doesn't that sound like a harried parent of a misbehaving child? Still, God continues, "Look, the young woman is with child and shall bear a son, and shall name him

For meditation and context:

RESPONSORIAL PSALM   Psalm 40.6, 7–8, 9, 10 (R.7–8)

R. Here I am, Lord; I come to do your will.

Sacrifice and offering you do not desire,
but you have given me an open ear.
Burnt offering and sin offering
you have not required.

Then I said, "Here I am;
in the scroll of the book it is written of me.
I delight to do your will, O my God;
your law is within my heart."

I have told the glad news of deliverance
in the great congregation;
see, I have not restrained my lips,
as you know, O Lord.

I have not hidden your saving help within
my heart,
I have spoken of your faithfulness and your
salvation;
I have not concealed your steadfast love and
your faithfulness
from the great congregation.

READING II   Hebrews 10.4–10

A reading from the Letter to the Hebrews.

It is **impossible** for the blood of **bulls** and **goats**
to take away **sins**.
Consequently, when **Christ** came into the **world**, he said,
"**Sacrifices** and **offerings** you have not **desired**,
but a **body** you have **prepared** for me;
in **burnt** offerings and **sin** offerings
you have **taken** no **pleasure**.
Then I said,
as it is **written** of me in the **scroll** of the book,
'See, God, I have **come** to do your **will**, O God.'"
When Christ said,
"You have **neither** desired nor taken **pleasure**
in **sacrifices** and **offerings**
and **burnt** offerings and **sin** offerings"
(**these** are offered according to the **law**),
then he added,
"**See**, I have **come** to do your **will**." »

A reading rich in metaphor and suggestion. The reading involves an almost complete repetition of the words that Jesus spoke, first to use them as an example, but second to use them to emphasize the conclusion the writer of Hebrews makes, in which the word "offerings" plays a crucial role. Focus your reading on the repetitions of this word.

At this point, when the words of Jesus are repeated almost verbatim, be sure to use the same tone you used when first proclaiming these words.

Emmanuel." As the Prophet would have understood the message, the young woman (Hebrew, *ha alma*, meaning "a newly married woman or a woman ready for conception") would have been a member of Ahaz's harem, and the son who will be born is probably Hezekiah, the next king of Judah. But Emmanuel means "with us is God," so it would have been easy for early Christians to interpret this oracle as being about Mary, who would become the mother of Jesus.

READING II The second reading is from the Letter to the Hebrews. This document is difficult to read and understand because of its Platonic worldview, and because it is preoccupied with aspects of Jewish religious practice, which is unfamiliar to most Christians today.

Here the author is talking about the Day of Atonement and the sacrifices that needed to be repeated every year, because they could not take away sin but only remind people of their sin. The author of this work asserts that Christ's atoning sacrifice abolishes the need for those annual

sacrificial offerings because this sacrifice of Christ's body takes away sin once and for all humanity. The quotation that begins with the words, "Sacrifices and offerings," appears to be derived from a Greek translation of Psalm 40.6–8, which focuses on the superiority of obedience to God's will over the offering of sacrifices to God. Did Jesus actually recite Psalm 40 when he was born? Certainly not, but the point is that Jesus' Incarnation is not random or accidental. Rather, it is part of God's will that will be accomplished in his crucifixion.

He **abolishes** the first in order to **establish** the second.
And it is by **God's will** that we have been **sanctified**
through the **offering** of the **body** of Jesus Christ
once for all.

GOSPEL   Luke 1.26–38

A reading from the holy Gospel according to Luke.

The **Angel** Gabriel was sent by God
to a town in Galilee called **Nazareth**,
to a **virgin** engaged to a man whose name was **Joseph**,
of the house of **David**.
The virgin's name was **Mary**.
And he **came** to her and **said**,
"**Hail, full** of grace! The **Lord** is **with** you."
But she was **much** perplexed by his **words**
and **pondered** what sort of greeting this might **be**.
The Angel said to her,
"**Do not** be **afraid**, Mary, for you have found **favour** with God.
And **now**, you will conceive in your **womb** and bear a **son**,
and you will name him **Jesus**.
He will be **great**,
and will be called the **Son** of the Most **High**,
and the **Lord God** will give to him the **throne**
    of his father **David**.
He will **reign over** the house of Jacob **forever**,
and of his **kingdom** there will be no **end**."
Mary said to the Angel,
"**How** can this be, since I am a **virgin**?"
The **Angel** said to her,
"The **Holy Spirit** will **come** upon you,
and the **power** of the Most **High** will **overshadow** you;
therefore the child to be born will be **holy**;

Here begins the didactic conclusion: pitch your proclamation accordingly. You are making a point.

Here is a scene of bottomless power and gravity. Despite our familiarity with them, some parts of Scripture are so burnished with imagination, they always seem novel. This is one of them.

Words of nearly unapproachable tenderness and glory.

Here, in words of simple authority, begins the whole mystery of redemption.

Read these words with almost even emphasis.

GOSPEL   Luke's Gospel is remarkable for its many beautiful stories that feature women as one of its central characters. The story of the Angel's visit to Mary to announce the conception and birth of Jesus appears only in this Gospel, so it is certainly appropriate for this feast. However, it is also told in the *Infancy Gospel of James*, a second-century document that is not in the Bible but that was widely read in the period of the early Church. It tells the story of Mary's birth and early childhood and how she became the mother of Jesus. English translations are available on the internet, if you are interested.

Luke's version of the story of the Annunciation begins with a reference to the "sixth month," which is the sixth month of Elizabeth's pregnancy with her son John, later known as John the Baptist. In terms of form or structure, the announcement of Jesus' birth closely parallels the announcement of John's birth. In both cases, the Angel Gabriel appears to announce the good news. In both cases, the women involved are not in a position to conceive a child.

Elizabeth was too old; Mary was still a virgin and not living with her intended spouse. In both cases, the Angel announces the child's mission in life. In both cases, the soon-to-be parent expresses concern and asks a question. Zechariah asks, "How will I know that this is so?" (Luke 1.18) and Mary asks, "How can this be . . . ?"

Biblical scholars note that Luke employs a theme of promise and fulfillment throughout this Gospel, and this is a good example. The sign that Zechariah is given is that he would be made speechless until the

With these words of Gabriel, the mystery of conception is undertaken. Gabriel's tone shifts when he begins to talk about Elizabeth. Your tone should shift as well. We're at the edges of mystery, moving back into the world.

"Here am I": proclaim these words without adornment. Let their power resonate.

he will be called **Son** of **God**.
And **now**,
your relative **Elizabeth** in her old age has also **conceived** a **son**;
and this is the **sixth month** for her who was said to be **barren**.
For **nothing** will be **impossible** with **God**."
Then Mary said,
"**Here am I**, the **servant** of the **Lord**;
let it be **done** to me **according** to your **word**."
Then the Angel **departed** from her.

child is named. Why? The author of Luke's Gospel describes Gabriel as saying, "But now, because you did not believe my words, which will be fulfilled in their time, you will become mute, unable to speak, until the day these things occur" (Luke 1.20). But when Mary asks, "How can this be?" Gabriel says, "The Holy Spirit will come upon you, and the power of the Most High will overshadow you; therefore the child to be born will be holy; he will be called Son of God." Mary's response is an essential element of this promise/fulfillment theme: "Here am I, the servant of the Lord; let it be done to me according to your word."

We recognize in this reading some of the words of the Hail Mary, the traditional Catholic prayer of intercession to Mary. The first evidence of a prayer like this one dates to the eleventh century, but it was widely popular by the fifteenth century. The first part of the prayer, "Hail Mary, full of grace, the Lord is with you," comes from Gabriel's words of greeting in this Gospel. The second part of the prayer, "blessed are you among women, and blessed is the fruit of your womb, Jesus," comes partly from the Angel's words to Mary and partly from Elizabeth's words of greeting to Mary, when she came to visit her cousin. The third part, the request that Mary pray on our behalf now and at the time of death, was officially recorded in the catechism of the Council of Trent, originally published in 1566. C.C.

FIFTH SUNDAY
OF LENT

LECTIONARY #34

READING I   Ezekiel 37.12–14

A reading from the book of the Prophet Ezekiel.

Thus says the Lord God:
"I am going to **open** your **graves**,
and **bring you up** from your graves, **O** my people;
and I will **bring you back** to the land of **Israel**.
And you shall **know** that I am the **Lord**,
when I **open** your graves,
and **bring you up** from your **graves**, O my people.
I will **put** my spirit **within** you, and you shall **live**,
and I will **place** you on your **own soil**;
then you shall **know** that I, the **Lord**,
have **spoken** and will **act**," says the **Lord**.

Ezekiel = ee-ZEE-kee-uhl

A reading in which a small number of promises are repeated and varied a few times to impressive effect. Focus on the phrase "O my people," which includes all the feelings of care and connection that motivate this reading.

This line rephrases the opening lines. Slow down very slightly to signal the repetition.

Emphasize "spoken" and "act" to conclude the exhortation.

READING I As we move into the final days of Lent, the readings for this Fifth Sunday of Lent invite us to reflect on the movement from death to life.

Today's first reading is from the Book of Ezekiel, which contains the visions and oracles of the Prophet Ezekiel as he ministered to the exiles of Judah during the Babylonian Exile. The Babylonian empire had already taken control of Judah in 605 BC, but Johoiakim, who was retained as its vassal king, made a mistake in considering Babylon's weakened state, after a failed invasion of Egypt, and refused to pay trib-

ute to King Nebuchadnezzar. Babylon's armies responded in 598/7 BC by sacking Jerusalem and exiling its leading citizens. Biblical scholars think that Ezekiel was taken to Babylon with this first round of exiles. Not long afterward, Johoiakim's brother, Zedekiah, was installed by Nebuchadnezzar to oversee Judah. He, too, attempted to rebel against the Babylonians, whose armies returned in 589 and by 586 BC they had decimated much of Judah, destroyed the Jerusalem Temple, and taken more of Judah's population into exile in Babylon.

Needless to say, this was a terrible time for the people of Judah, whether they were in exile in Babylon or left behind in devastated Judah and Jerusalem. Like Prophets before him, Ezekiel sees Judah's political troubles as God's punishment for their unfaithfulness to God's covenant, but he also holds out the possibility that the people will repent and that God would restore them, because God's covenant is eternal and because God will never abandon his people. This is the backdrop to the vision of the dry bones (Ezekiel 37.1–10) and

For meditation and context:

RESPONSORIAL PSALM   Psalm 130.1–2, 3–4, 5–6, 7b–8 (R.7b)

R. With the Lord there is steadfast love and great power to redeem.

Out of the depths I cry to you, O Lord.
Lord, hear my voice!
Let your ears be attentive
to the voice of my supplications!

If you, O Lord, should mark iniquities,
Lord, who could stand?
But there is forgiveness with you,
so that you may be revered.

I wait for the Lord,
my soul waits, and in his word I hope;
my soul waits for the Lord
more than watchmen for the morning.

For with the Lord there is steadfast love,
and with him is great power to redeem.
It is he who will redeem Israel
from all its iniquities.

READING II   Romans 8.8–11

A reading from the Letter of Saint Paul to the Romans.

Paul's reading contrasts the flesh and the spirit. In Paul's letters, the spirit is superior to the flesh, which desires, fades, and dies, while the spirit lives. This can make it challenging to read him to an assembly, each member of whom is in the flesh, in a body.

Brothers and sisters:
Those who are in the **flesh cannot** please God.
But you are **not** in the flesh;
you are in the **Spirit**,
since the **Spirit** of God dwells **in** you.
Anyone who does not **have** the Spirit of **Christ**
does not **belong** to him.
But if **Christ** is **in** you,
though the **body** is dead because of **sin**,
the **Spirit** is life because of **righteousness**.
If the **Spirit** of God who raised **Jesus** from the dead dwells
       in you,
he who raised **Christ** from the dead
will give **life** to your mortal bodies **also**
through his Spirit that dwells in **you**.

The sense of life is decidedly in the spirit, but it can enter the mortal body, too. Emphasize the phrase "give life."

---

the *interpretation* of the vision (Ezekiel 37.11–14), which is our first reading for today.

First, a word about the vision: Ezekiel tells us that he was led out by the spirit of the Lord into a broad valley filled with dry bones in every direction. When asked whether the bones could come back to life, Ezekiel answers, "O Lord God, you know" (Ezekiel 37.3). God responds by telling Ezekiel to prophesy over the bones, with these words: "I will cause breath to enter you, and you shall live" (Ezekiel 37.5). The Hebrew word for "breath" is *ruach*, also meaning "wind or spirit," but remember

that this is God's breath! Soon Ezekiel hears a loud clattering noise and the bones come together, muscles and tendons grow on them, and skin covers them. Then God tells Ezekiel to prophesy to the breath (Hebrew, *ruach*) with these words: "Come from the four winds, O breath, and breathe upon these slain, that they may live" (Ezekiel 37.9). Finally, Ezekiel is told that the dry bones now come to life are the people of Israel.

This is where our first reading begins. God tells Ezekiel to prophesy to the people in these words: "I am going to open your graves. . . . I will put my spirit [Hebrew,

ruach] within you, and you shall live, and I will place you on your own soil." Thus, to the exiles in Babylon, who feel as good as dead, the Prophet is saying that God has not abandoned them and that God will one day restore them to their land. And why will God do this? It is not because the people have earned forgiveness. No, it is so that the people will know that God is all-sovereign and that God's word can be trusted, because it is in the nature of God to care for God's people.

GOSPEL   John 11.1–45

A reading from the holy Gospel according to John.

Now a certain man, **Lazarus**, was **ill**.
He was from Bethany, the village of **Mary** and her sister **Martha**.
Mary was the one who **anointed** the Lord with **perfume**
and **wiped** his feet with her **hair**;
her brother **Lazarus** was **ill**.
So [the sisters sent a message to Jesus,
"**Lord**, he whom you **love** is **ill**."
But when Jesus **heard** this, he said,
"This **illness** does not **lead** to **death**;
rather it is for **God's glory**,
so that the **Son** of God may be glorified **through** it."
Accordingly, though Jesus loved **Martha** and her **sister**
    and **Lazarus**,
after having **heard** that Lazarus was **ill**,
he stayed **two days** longer in the place where he **was**.
Then **after** this he said to the disciples,
"Let us **go** to Judea **again**."]
The disciples said to him,
"**Rabbi**, the people there were just **now** trying to **stone** you,
and are you going there **again**?"
Jesus answered,
"Are there not **twelve hours** of daylight?
Those who **walk** during the **day** do not **stumble**,
    because they **see** the **light** of this **world**.
But those who **walk** at **night stumble**,
because the **light** is not **in** them."
After saying this, he told them,
"Our friend **Lazarus** has **fallen asleep**,
but I am going there to **awaken** him."
The disciples said to him,
"**Lord**, if he has fallen **asleep**, he will be **all right**."

Lazarus = LAZ-uh-ruhs
Bethany = BETH-uh-nee
A long and complex reading energized by the intense emotions of the figures in the story. The outcome of this story is well known. Its mysteries reside in the power over death that Jesus demonstrates, as well as his declarations about himself ("I am the resurrection and the life"). There are also the curious details that texture the imagination, such as the days Lazarus has been dead and the potential stench of his corpse. You can linger on these details in your proclamation.

These are the four main characters in the story.

Rabbi = RAB-ī

Emphasize the relationships between "walk" and "day," "walk" and "night," "the light" and "stumble."

READING II   Our second reading is taken from Paul's Letter to the Romans. The section from which today's second reading is excerpted begins with these words: "Therefore, since we are justified by faith, we have peace with God through our Lord Jesus Christ, through whom we have obtained access to this grace in which we stand" (Romans 5.1–2). With that introduction, Paul continues to talk about the life of the justified (i.e., the Christian believer) in today's reading. Although somewhat indirectly, Paul suggests that the goal of the Christian believer should be to please God, because the believer has done nothing to justify themselves, that is, to put themselves in right relationship with God. Only God can restore humanity to the relationship that it had with God before the fall, and God does so through the death and Resurrection of Jesus Christ as a free gift to all who trust in God, because it is in the nature of God to be righteous. This reading can be somewhat confusing, because Paul uses the titles and phrases "Spirit of God," "Spirit of Christ," and "Christ" interchangeably, but what is important to notice is that Paul is describing the Christian believer's participation in the divine life: we are in Christ and Christ is in us. We have been invited to share in the life of God!

Paul also talks about those who are in the flesh and those who are in the spirit. Sometimes people are tempted to interpret these phrases as referring to the body and the soul, but, in fact, Paul is talking about the way his readers lived before they became Jesus followers and how they live now in the Spirit of Christ. Like the Hebrew word *ruach*, the Greek word *pneuma* means "spirit, wind, or breath." Paul suggests that

Jesus, however, had been speaking about his **death**,
but they **thought** that he was referring merely to **sleep**.
Then Jesus told them plainly,
"**Lazarus** is **dead**.
For your sake I am **glad** I was not **there**,
so that you may **believe**.
But let us **go** to him."
Thomas, who was called the **Twin**,
said to his fellow disciples,
"Let us **also** go, that we may **die** with him."
[When Jesus **arrived**,
he found that **Lazarus** had already been in the **tomb** four days.]
Now Bethany was near **Jerusalem**,
some **two miles** away,
and many **Jews** had come to **Martha** and **Mary**
to **console** them about their **brother**.
[When **Martha** heard that **Jesus** was coming, she went
      and **met** him,
while **Mary** stayed at home.
Martha said to Jesus,
"**Lord**, if you had **been** here, my **brother** would not have **died**.
But even **now** I know that **God** will **give** you whatever you
      ask of him."
Jesus said to her, "Your **brother** will **rise** again."
Martha said to him,
"I **know** that he will rise again in the **resurrection**
      on the last **day**."
Jesus said to her, "**I** am the **resurrection** and the **life**.
Whoever **believes** in me,
even though they die, will **live**,
and **everyone** who lives and **believes** in me will **never** die.
Do **you** believe this?"
She said to him,
"**Yes**, Lord, I **believe** that you are the **Christ**,
the Son of God, the one **coming** into the world."] »

This exchange, concluding with "everyone who lives and believes in me will never die," expresses the core of this reading. Read it with care, allowing for Jesus' striking expression that he is the Resurrection and the life to arise directly, even irrefutably, from this exchange.

there was a time when humanity was not capable of pleasing God because its priorities were focused on turning upside down the relationship between creator and creature (see Romans 1.16–23). But that is no longer the case, Paul says, because now they are committed to living according to the Spirit. Yet, sin still has power over humanity; this is what Paul means when he says, "the body is dead because of sin." But the Spirit of God gives vitality to our dead bodies, as he did to Christ's dead body in the Resurrection. What a tremendous mystery.

GOSPEL   Today's Gospel is the story of the resuscitation of Jesus' friend Lazarus, which is strange and compelling in so many ways. We learn of this story only in John's Gospel, and, although there are two characters named Mary and Martha in Luke's Gospel (Luke 10.38–42), they are presented quite differently here, even if they are the same characters.

The story in full is very long, but, in its essence, it is a highly embellished miracle story, which would have at least three parts: the description of the problem, in this case, the report that Jesus' friend

Lazarus is ill; the miracle worker's healing word or deed, in this case, Jesus' words to his dead friend, "Lazarus, come out!"; and evidence that the miracle took place, in this case, the characters in the story who see Lazarus come out of the tomb, still wrapped in his burial bands. This is the seventh and last sign—the term that John's Gospel uses to refer to Jesus' miracles—which clearly points to Jesus' own impending death. Seven is a number symbolizing fullness or completion.

Within the framework of this miracle story, the author of John's Gospel includes

Even emphasis on the words in this line.

When she had **said** this, she went back and called
    her sister Mary,
and told her **privately**,
"The **Teacher** is here and is **calling** for you."
And when Mary **heard** it, she got up **quickly** and **went** to him.
Now Jesus had not yet come to the village,
but was **still** at the place where Martha had **met** him.
The **Jews** who were **with her** in the house, **consoling** her,
saw Mary get up **quickly** and go **out**.
They **followed** her because they thought
that she was going to the **tomb** to **weep** there.

Even emphasis here as well.

Mary repeats the same words as her sister Martha. Repeat them yourself plainly.

When Mary came where Jesus was and saw him,
she **knelt** at his feet and **said** to him,
"**Lord**, if you had **been** here, my **brother** would not have **died**."
When Jesus saw her **weeping**,
and the **Jews** who came with her **also** weeping,
[he was **greatly disturbed** in spirit and **deeply moved**.
He said, "**Where** have you **laid** him?"
They said to him, "Lord, **come** and **see**."
Jesus began to weep.
So the Jews said, "See how he **loved** him!"
But some of them said,
"Could **not** he who opened the **eyes** of the **blind** man
have kept **this** man from **dying**?"

Jesus weeping over Lazarus is a foretaste of his own Passion.

Then **Jesus**, again **greatly disturbed**, **came** to the tomb.
It was a **cave**, and a **stone** was lying against it.
Jesus said, "**Take away** the **stone**."
Martha, the sister of the dead man, said to him,
"**Lord**, already there is a **stench**
because he has been **dead four days**."
Jesus said to her,
"Did I not tell you that if you **believed**,
you would see the **glory** of God?"
So they **took away** the **stone**.

From here to the conclusion of the reading, Jesus is in complete command. He has an audience, to whom he relates his miracle. Take note of the rhythm of the words "Take away the stone."

Even emphasis on this line with a slight additional emphasis on "believed."

---

several other literary units. The first is a two-part dialogue between Jesus and his disciples. This is followed by two very similar units, which we will call the Martha cycle and the Mary cycle. Finally, when the miracle story is complete and in the verses that follow today's reading, the author of this Gospel includes a section that describes the people's reaction to Jesus and the high priest Caiaphas' prophecy about him (John 11.45–52). It concludes with a resolve on the part of the Pharisees and chief priests of Jerusalem to put Jesus to death (John 11.53).

These additional literary units are laden with emotion, confusion, and befuddlement, but they are essential to the rich fabric of this story. The two-part interaction that Jesus has with his disciples immediately after the problem is described is an example. Jesus tells his disciples that Lazarus' illness "is for God's glory, so that the Son of God may be glorified through it." What is he talking about? If you do a deep dive into John's Gospel, you will recognize that John uses "glorification" to refer to Jesus' death and Resurrection, his lifting up

on the cross and his lifting up to God in glory. But then Jesus waits for two days to begin the trip to Bethany in Judea. Why?

The sections of this story that we are calling the Martha and Mary cycles are remarkably similar to one another. First, we learn that Jesus is coming or calling to the women. Next, the narrator tells us that mourners are present. Third, we hear that the sister goes to meet Jesus and says to him, "Lord, if you had been here, my brother would not have died."

And Jesus looked upward and said,
"**Father**, I thank you for having **heard** me.
I knew that you **always** hear me,
but I have **said** this for the sake of the **crowd** standing here,
so that they may **believe** that you **sent** me."
When he had **said** this, he cried with a **loud voice**,
"**Lazarus**, come **out**!"
The dead man came **out**,
his **hands** and **feet** bound with **strips** of **cloth**,
and his **face wrapped** in a cloth.
Jesus said to them, "**Unbind** him, and let him **go**."
Many of the Jews therefore, who had come with **Mary**
and had seen what Jesus **did**, **believed** in him.]

[Shorter: John 11.3–7, 17, 20–27, 33b–45 (see brackets)]

Both cycles contain some dialogue. In the Martha cycle, Jesus consoles her by reminding her that her brother will rise, and Martha assumes that he is referring to the end-time resurrection of the dead. But Jesus tells her, "I am the resurrection and the life," and she responds with a beautiful and powerful profession of faith of who Jesus is. These three attributes—"the Christ, the Son of God, the one coming into the world"—are central to the way the Johannine community understood Jesus and his mission.

In the Mary cycle, Jesus dialogues with others, while Mary weeps in grief and pain. Jesus, likewise, is filled with emotion. The author describes him as "greatly disturbed in spirit" (i.e., emotionally) and "deeply moved" in his body (i.e., agitated). Finally, shedding tears, Jesus went to Lazarus' tomb and ordered that it be opened. Why did Jesus wait so long to come to Bethany? He could have avoided this tragedy by coming as soon as Martha and Mary called for him! Or is that the point of the story: to show that Jesus could raise the dead, even as the act of resuscitating Lazarus will lead directly to his own death? C.C.

PALM SUNDAY OF THE LORD'S PASSION

LECTIONARY #37

GOSPEL AT THE PROCESSION WITH PALMS
Matthew 21.1–11

A reading from the holy Gospel according to Matthew.

When they had come **near** Jerusalem
and had **reached Bethphage**, at the **Mount** of Olives,
Jesus sent **two** disciples, **saying** to them,
"**Go** into the village **ahead** of you,
and **immediately** you will find a donkey **tied**,
and a colt **with** her;
untie them and bring them to **me**.
If **anyone** says **anything** to you, just **say this**,
'The **Lord** needs them.'
And he will **send** them **immediately**."
This took place
to fulfill what had been **spoken** through the **Prophet**, saying,
"**Tell** the daughter of **Zion**,
Look, your **king** is **coming** to you,
humble, and **mounted** on a **donkey**,
and on a **colt**, the **foal** of a **donkey**."
The **disciples** went and **did** as **Jesus** had **directed** them;
they **brought** the **donkey** and the **colt**,
and put their **cloaks** on them, and he **sat** on them.
A **very large** crowd spread their cloaks on the road,
and **others** cut **branches** from the trees
and **spread** them on the road.

This Gospel reading is full of mysterious commands and a sense of destiny fulfilled.
Bethphage = BETH-fuh-jee

Slight pause between "colt" and "with."

Zion = Zī-uhn or Zī-ahn

foal = fohl
Note the repetition of words from the Scriptural quotation in the narrative itself.

GOSPEL | *Gospel at the procession.* The reading that accompanies the procession with palms on this Palm Sunday comes to us from the Gospel of Matthew. A version of this story is found in all four Gospels. However, Matthew's version more closely follows Mark's version than the others (cf. Mark 11.1–11; Luke 19.28–38; John 12.12–19). The story is designed to suggest a joyful procession into the holiest city of early Judaism, not unlike a great king coming to visit an important city in his kingdom. However, as the story unfolds, one can discern in it a sense of dark times ahead.

The setting for this story is a small village called Bethphage. The village opposite it is probably Bethany. Both were on the eastern slope of the Mount of Olives and 2 to 3 kilometres from the gates of Jerusalem. Jesus tells two of his disciples to go into Bethany and locate a female donkey and her colt waiting for them. Donkeys were beasts of burden and symbols of domestic life, whereas horses were more often associated with the military and warrior kings. As Matthew tells the story, the disciples appear to be unphased by the strangeness of this request, and they simply do as Jesus

commanded them to do. This kind of foreknowledge might be surprising to us, but people likely saw this as a measure of Jesus' prophetic powers. At the conclusion of this reading, when people of Jerusalem ask, "Who is this?" who is able to shake up an entire city, the crowds respond, "This is the Prophet Jesus from Nazareth in Galilee."

If you read the text carefully, perhaps you wondered how Jesus could ride two donkeys at once. The author of Matthew's Gospel regularly uses quotations from the Old Testament to shed light on events in

The **crowds** that went **ahead** of him
and that **followed** were **shouting**,
"**Hosanna** to the **Son** of **David**!
Blessed is the **one** who **comes** in the **name** of the **Lord**!
Hosanna in the **highest heaven**!"
When **Jesus** entered **Jerusalem**,
the **whole city** was in **turmoil**, asking, "Who is this?"
The **crowds** were **saying**,
"**This** is the **Prophet Jesus** from **Nazareth** in **Galilee**."

LECTIONARY #38

READING I   Isaiah 50.4–7

A reading from the book of the Prophet Isaiah.

The **servant** of the Lord said:
"The **Lord God** has **given** me the **tongue** of a **teacher**,
that I may **know** how to **sustain** the **weary** with a **word**.
Morning by **morning** he wakens—
wakens my **ear** to **listen** as those who are **taught**.
The Lord **God** has **opened** my ear,
and I was not **rebellious**,
I did not turn **backward**.
I **gave** my back to **those** who **struck** me,
and my **cheeks** to those who **pulled out** the **beard**;
I **did** not **hide** my **face**
from **insult** and **spitting**.
The Lord God **helps** me;
therefore I have not been **disgraced**;
therefore I have **set** my **face** like **flint**,
and I **know** that I shall **not** be put to **shame**."

Words very familiar to the assembly from the Sanctus (Holy, Holy, Holy) in the Mass. Proclaim them as if they are being spoken for the first time.

Isaiah = ī-ZAY-uh

A short and powerful reading in which Isaiah asserts his trust in God.

Note the poetic rhythm that begins with the phrase "Morning by morning."

Give "not" and "shame" equal emphasis. These last lines can be read with conviction.

Jesus' life. Biblical scholars have engaged in much debate over the years about the sources of Matthew's quotations, whether from a Hebrew text or a Greek translation of the Old Testament, but a likely reason why the author of this Gospel describes Jesus as riding two donkeys at once is that he was reading from a Hebrew text that read "riding on a donkey, even on a colt" and he interpreted it to read "riding on a donkey, and on a colt" in Greek. These things happen, and they should not be a concern for us, except for us to recognize how important it was for Matthew to show that Jesus was exactly what the Prophets of old said the messiah would be. Thus, he also presents the crowds as crying out in the words of Psalm 118.25–26, a psalm of thanksgiving and possibly a liturgical prayer of welcome as God's people entered into the Jerusalem Temple, though here it is applied to Jesus. "Hosanna!" can be translated as "Please save us!"

The words that Matthew quotes from the Old Testament add richness to his Gospel, and often the context from which these quotes were taken can add even more meaning to the text. For example, the words of the Prophet Matthew quotes is actually a conflation or mashing together of a quotation from Isaiah and another from Zechariah. The line that Matthew borrows from Isaiah reads, "Say to daughter Zion, / 'See, your salvation comes'" (Isaiah 62.11) and is taken from the part of the book that is associated with the period after the Babylonian Exile, when those who returned from exile were trying to rebuild the Temple and the city of Jerusalem. It is a message of hope in the midst of hard times. The quote from Zechariah reads, "Rejoice greatly, O daughter Zion! / Shout aloud, O daughter

For meditation and context:

RESPONSORIAL PSALM   Psalm 22.7–8, 16–17, 18–19, 22–23 (R.1)

R. My God, my God, why have you forsaken me?

All who see me mock at me;
they make mouths at me, they shake
    their heads;
"Commit your cause to the Lord; let
    him deliver;
let him rescue the one in whom
    he delights!"

For dogs are all around me;
a company of evildoers encircles me.
My hands and feet have shrivelled;
I can count all my bones.

They divide my clothes among themselves,
and for my clothing they cast lots.
But you, O Lord, do not be far away!
O my help, come quickly to my aid!

I will tell of your name to my brothers
    and sisters;
in the midst of the congregation I will
    praise you:
You who fear the Lord, praise him!
All you offspring of Jacob, glorify him;
stand in awe of him, all you offspring
    of Israel!

Philippians = fih-LIP-ee-uhnz

An exhortation in which Paul seems to quote to the members of the early Church at Philippi an early Christian hymn, whose focus is the *kenosis*, or emptying, mentioned in the third line of the reading. It's an utterly mysterious presentation of the power of Jesus' Incarnation. When you get to "emptied," give the word extra emphasis.

Give emphasis and rhythm to the words "human," "human," and "humbled."

READING II   Philippians 2.6–11

A reading from the Letter of Saint Paul to the Philippians.

Christ **Jesus**, though he was in the **form** of God,
did not regard **equality** with God as something to be **exploited**,
but **emptied** himself, taking the form of a **slave**,
being born in **human** likeness.
And being found in **human** form,
he **humbled** himself
and became **obedient** to the point of death—
even **death** on a cross.
Therefore God **highly** exalted him
and **gave** him the name that is above **every** name,
so that at the **name** of **Jesus** every **knee** should **bend**,
in **heaven** and on **earth** and **under** the earth,
and every **tongue** should **confess** that Jesus **Christ** is **Lord**,
to the **glory** of God the **Father**.

Even emphasis on these four words: "Jesus Christ is Lord."

Jerusalem! / Lo, your king comes to you; / triumphant and victorious is he, / humble and riding on a donkey, / on a colt, the foal of a donkey" (Zechariah 9.9). The oracle from which this quotation is taken proclaims the arrival of an earthly king who would bring peace to the land.

READING I   Our first reading for the Eucharistic celebration is taken from the third of four "servant poems" found in the Book of Isaiah. The others are Isaiah 42.1–7, Isaiah 49.1–7 and Isaiah 52.13—53.12. These four poems are

similar insofar as they reflect messianic hopes of the time in which they were written. They differ in the clues they offer about the identity of the servant. He is variously described as God's chosen one, a king who will bring peace, a Prophet like Jeremiah, or a representative of suffering Israel whom God will raise up. In today's reading, the servant is described as a disciple, part of an inner circle of learned ones, whose teacher is God and who is given the ability to speak to the weary and faint of heart. Remember that this text was written in the time of the Babylonian Exile.

Whether left behind or exiled abroad in Babylon, the people of Judah were in a very dark place.

The servant first describes how he was given the authority to speak this word. Every morning, day after day, God awakens him and opens his ears to hear God's word and teach him as a disciple is taught, without any resistance on his part. Implied in this statement is the strong conviction that, when the disciple speaks, it is God's word and not his own. Second, in order to speak God's word of consolation with integrity, this disciple would have had to

PASSION Matthew 26.14—27.66

The Passion of our Lord Jesus Christ according to Matthew.

One of the **twelve**, who was called **Judas Iscariot**,
went to the **chief priests** and **said**,
"What will you **give** me if I **betray** him to you?"
They **paid** him **thirty pieces** of silver.
And from **that moment**
he **began** to look for an **opportunity** to **betray** him.
On the **first day** of **Unleavened Bread**
the **disciples** came to **Jesus**, saying,
"Where do you **want** us to make the **preparations**
for you to **eat** the **Passover**?"
He said, "**Go** into the **city** to a **certain man**, and **say** to him,
'The **Teacher** says, My **time** is **near**;
I will **keep** the **Passover** at your **house** with my **disciples**.'"
So the **disciples** did as **Jesus** had **directed** them,
and they **prepared** the **Passover** meal.
When it was **evening**,
he took his **place** with the **twelve**;
and while they were **eating**, he said,
"**Truly** I **tell** you, **one** of you will **betray** me."
And they became **greatly distressed**
and began to **say** to him **one** after **another**,
"**Surely** not I, Lord?"
He **answered**,
"The **one** who has **dipped** his **hand** into the **bowl** with me
will **betray** me.
The **Son** of **Man goes** as it is **written** of him,
but **woe** to **that man** by **whom** the **Son** of **Man** is **betrayed**!
It would have been **better** for **that man not** to have been **born**."
Judas, who **betrayed** him, said,
"**Surely** not I, **Rabbi**?"
He **replied**, "You have **said** so." »

Iscariot = ih-SKAYR-ee-uht

An intensely powerful reading of the story at the core of our faith. This is also the longest reading that most congregants experience during the annual cycle. It is as dramatic as a novel, told with unusual economy and speed. But it also lingers on vivid scenes, vivid moments. Although the reading is dramatic, its drama is inherent in the language and the pacing of the story. Allow the language itself to dictate the drama. You will need to remain focused during this lengthy reading.

Note the mystery nested in words within words.

It is commonplace for lectors to be involved in the proclamation of this Gospel. Whether passages in the Gospel are divided up among a group of readers, including the celebrant, the deacon, and some lectors, or it's portioned out in something more dramatic (where there is a narrator and then readers for each of the speakers), avoid theatricality. You may have an instinct to intensify the drama by "acting out" some of the voices and scenes, but this can give the Passion narrative a community theatre vibe. It is better to avoid that in favour of proclaiming boldly, clearly, and slowly.

The early portion of this reading focuses on betrayal.

Don't overplay Judas' words. He's conflicted about the betrayal he is committing.

experience what the people were experiencing. Thus, the servant explains how he was beaten and humiliated, like Prophets before him. For ancient peoples, to have one's beard torn away was the epitome of insult. Likewise, spitting on someone is considered very disrespectful in most cultures, even today, and a sign of extreme hatred. But the servant stands strong in his trust in God's power to save and to take away his shame. The phrase to "set my face like flint" is also associated with other Prophets like Jeremiah and Ezekiel, as flint is

a metaphor for something that is extremely hard or firm, as in a firm resolve.

But this servant poem prompts a question for us today. Will we also be like the servant, a steadfast disciple of God and one who will speak words of consolation, even in the face of our attackers?

READING II Our second reading comes from Paul's Letter to the Philippians. Paul established this Christian community in Philippi. Acts of the Apostles tells us that Paul was prompted in a vision to go to the region of Macedonia and to the

city of Philippi, an important Roman city that was likely populated by retired Roman military personnel (Acts 16.6–40). It was also an important trade city, located on the Egnatian Way, which traversed the countries we now know as Albania, Macedonia, Greece, and Bulgaria to northern Turkey. Biblical scholars think that Paul might have visited Philippi as early as AD 50. Identified as one of Paul's prison letters, this letter might have been written in around AD 54–56, while he was in prison in Ephesus, some 650 kilometres from Philippi. This letter is a particularly tender one, because Paul sees

The words of institution. Though extremely familiar, proclaim them as if they are being spoken for the first time.

While they were **eating**, **Jesus** took a **loaf** of **bread**,
and after **blessing** it he **broke** it,
gave it to the **disciples**, and **said**,
"**Take**, **eat**; **this** is my **Body**."
Then he **took** a **cup**,
and after **giving thanks** he **gave** it to them, **saying**,
"**Drink** from it, **all** of you;
for **this** is my **Blood** of the **covenant**,
which is **poured out** for **many** for the **forgiveness** of **sins**.
I **tell** you,
I will **never again drink** of this **fruit** of the **vine**
until that **day** when I **drink** it **new** with you
        in my **Father's kingdom**."
When they had **sung** the **hymn**,
they went **out** to the **Mount** of **Olives**.
Then **Jesus said** to them,

Slight pause between "deserters" and "because."

"You will **all** become **deserters because** of me **this night**;
for it is **written**,
'I will **strike** the **shepherd**,
and the **sheep** of the **flock** will be **scattered**.'
But after I am **raised up**,
I will go **ahead** of you to **Galilee**."
Peter **said** to him,
"Though **all** become **deserters because** of you,
I will **never desert** you."
Jesus **said** to him,
"**Truly I tell** you, this **very night**, before the **cock crows**,

Emphasize "three times."

you will **deny** me **three times**."
Peter **said** to him,
"**Even though** I must **die** with you, I will **not deny** you."
And so said **all** the **disciples**.
Then **Jesus went** with them to a **place** called **Gethsemane**;

Gethsemane = gehth-SEM-uh-nee

and he **said** to his **disciples**,
"**Sit here** while I go **over there** and **pray**."

---

the community as suffering for the faith just as he suffers for the faith.

Today's reading is perhaps the most well-known section of this Letter to the Philippians. It is written in the form of a poem; theologians point to it as the clearest and most definitive statement of what Paul believed about Jesus as the Christ. But the situation is complicated. Biblical scholars believe that this poem was already in use as a liturgical hymn in Paul's day and that Paul adapted it for his purposes, but it is not clear how much he changed it—perhaps

adding only "even death on a cross" to the statement about Jesus being obedient to death—or how he interpreted the parts that he did not change. Did he understand Jesus to be a new Adam, who was made in the image and likeness of God, but, unlike the first Adam, "did not regard equality with God as something to be exploited," and instead was humbly obedient to God even to death? Alternatively, did Paul understand Jesus to be a divine being, who was equal to God but who chose not to exploit his divinity and instead humbled

himself to become like us, even to the point of death?

Unfortunately, we may never know with full certainty what Paul intended to say about Jesus as the Christ. What we can say, however, is that Paul's Christology centres on the death and Resurrection of Jesus. He seems to know very little about Jesus' teachings and nothing about his miracle working, but he knows deeply in his body the transformative power of Jesus' death and Resurrection, as it relates to his own suffering and his hope for exaltation,

Zebedee = ZEB-uh-dee

These words of Christ are very sad; let the words themselves convey the sadness.

Slight pause between "cup" and "pass." Christ's prayer to his Father is filled with pathos. Again, let the words convey the deep feeling and sadness.

Christ's tone is exasperated.

He **took** with him **Peter** and the **two sons** of **Zebedee**,
and **began** to be **grieved** and **agitated**.
Then he **said** to them,
"I am **deeply grieved**, **even** to **death**;
remain here, and **stay awake** with me."
And going a **little farther**,
he **threw** himself on the **ground** and **prayed**,
"My **Father**, if it is **possible**, let this **cup pass** from **me**;
yet **not** what I **want**, but what **you** want."
Then he **came** to the **disciples** and found them **sleeping**;
and he said to **Peter**,
"So, could you **not** stay **awake** with me **one hour**?
Stay awake and **pray**
that you **may not come** into the **time** of **temptation**;
for the **spirit indeed** is **willing**, but the flesh is **weak**."
Again he went **away** for the **second time** and **prayed**,
"My **Father**, if this **cannot pass** unless I **drink** it,
your **will** be **done**."
Again he **came** and found them **sleeping**,
for their **eyes** were **heavy**.
So **leaving** them **again**,
he went **away** and **prayed** for the **third time**,
saying the **same words**.
Then he **came** to the **disciples** and **said** to them,
"Are you **still sleeping** and **taking** your **rest**?
See, the **hour** is at **hand**,
and the **Son** of **Man** is **betrayed** into the **hands** of **sinners**.
Get **up**, let us be **going**.
See, my **betrayer** is at **hand**."
While he was **still speaking**,
Judas, one of the **twelve**, **arrived**;
with him was a **large crowd** with **swords** and **clubs**,
from the **chief priests** and the **elders** of the **people**. ≫

and he wants this community at Philippi to experience it, too. Therefore, he exhorts them to "let the same mind be in you that was in Christ Jesus" (Philippians 2.5). What might this exhortation mean for the way we live our lives as Christians today?

GOSPEL Today's Gospel reading is the entire narrative of Jesus' arrest, suffering, and death as told in the Gospel of Matthew. Its length can be a bit overwhelming, but it is important for helping us to grasp the enormity of the events that we commemorate during this Holy Week, from the time of the triumphant entry into Jerusalem on Palm Sunday to the last meal that Jesus shares with his disciples to the terrible death that he endures on Golgotha to his internment in a tomb that was not his own and a plan by the religious leaders to cover up news of an empty tomb, should the problem arise. Next year, on Palm Sunday, we will hear Mark's version of the story, and the following year we will hear Luke's version of the Passion narrative. These three stories are similar in many ways, but each contains details that make the story both unique and compelling.

The Passion narrative according to Matthew begins with a plot in which Judas, one of the twelve Apostles, agrees to hand Jesus over to the chief priests of the Temple for thirty pieces of silver, which they pay immediately. Only Matthew provides this detail, which appears to be an allusion to Zechariah 11.12–13. The Prophet is instructed to perform a symbolic action for which he is paid thirty pieces of silver. Coincidentally, this was the penalty imposed

The focus in this passage is on the kiss.

Now the **betrayer** had given them a **sign**, saying,
"The **one** I will **kiss** is the **man**; **arrest** him."
At **once** he came up to **Jesus** and **said**,
"**Greetings**, **Rabbi!**" and **kissed** him.
Jesus **said** to him,
"**Friend**, **do** what you are **here** to **do**."
Then they **came** and laid **hands** on **Jesus** and **arrested** him.
Suddenly, one of those with **Jesus** put his **hand** on his **sword**,
drew it, and **struck** the **slave** of the **high priest**,
cutting off his **ear**.
Then **Jesus said** to him,
"Put your **sword back** into its **place**;
for **all** who **take** the **sword** will **perish** by the **sword**.
Do you **think** that I cannot **appeal** to my **Father**,
and he will at **once** send me **more** than **twelve legions** of **Angels**?
But **how then** would the **Scriptures** be **fulfilled**,
which say it must **happen** in this **way**?"

Even emphasis on "At that hour."

At that hour Jesus **said** to the **crowds**,
"Have you come **out** with **swords** and **clubs** to **arrest** me
as though I were a **bandit**?

Slight pause between "temple" and "teaching."

Day after **day** I **sat** in the **temple teaching**,
and you did **not arrest** me.
But **all this** has **taken place**
so that the **Scriptures** of the **Prophets** may be **fulfilled**."
Then **all** the disciples **deserted** him and **fled**.
Those who had arrested **Jesus**

Caiaphas = KAY-uh-fuhs or Kī-uh-fuhs

took him to **Caiaphas** the **high priest**,
in whose **house** the **scribes** and the **elders** had **gathered**.
But **Peter** was following him at a **distance**,
as far as the **courtyard** of the **high priest**;
and going **inside**, he **sat** with the **guards**
in order to see **how** this would **end**.

on someone who allowed his ox to gore another person's slave (see Exodus 21.32). Zechariah is then told to throw the money into the Temple treasury, perhaps as a judgment against the Temple priests. Thus, Matthew seems to suggest that Judas' betrayal of Jesus is part of God's plan.

Next, we hear about preparations for Passover, one of three great pilgrimage feasts of early Judaism. Matthew's version of the story follows Mark's Gospel quite closely, but he strips away many of the unnecessary details, making the story appear stark in its brevity. In Matthew's description of the Passover meal itself, we see how Jesus transforms the meaning of the Passover elements of bread and wine into the sacrifice of his own body and blood. Immediately before this intimate sharing with his disciples, Jesus prophesies Judas' betrayal and points him out as "the one who has dipped his hand into the bowl with me," which suggests that Jesus' betrayer is reclining close enough to Jesus that they can eat from the same bowl. How disquieting! After singing a hymn to bring their Passover meal to a close and departing for the Mount of Olives, Jesus makes a general statement about the disciples abandoning him, this time citing Zechariah 13.7, followed by a more specific prophecy about Peter's denial of Jesus. Peter is fierce in his protest, even swearing that he would die for Jesus, but later we see how quickly he gives in and denies him.

Here the outrage of the priests is introduced; it will intensify.

As Jesus replies to the high priest, he alludes to Scripture.

Slight pause between "high priest" and "tore."
blasphemed = blas-FEEMD
"Blasphemed!" The spite of the high priest.

prophesy (verb) = PROF-uh-sī

Now the **chief priests** and the **whole council**
were looking for **false testimony** against **Jesus**
so that they might **put** him to **death**,
but they **found none**, though many **false witnesses**
    came **forward**.
At last **two** came **forward** and **said**,
"**This fellow said**,
'I am **able** to **destroy** the temple of **God**
and to **build** it in **three days**.'"
The **high priest** stood up and **said**,
"**Have** you no **answer**?
What **is** it that they **testify against** you?"
But **Jesus** was **silent**.
Then the **high priest** said to him,
"I **put** you **under oath** before the **living God**,
tell us if you are the **Christ**, the **Son** of **God**."
Jesus **said** to him,
"You have **said** so.
But I **tell** you,
from **now on** you will **see** the **Son** of **Man**
seated at the **right hand** of **Power**
and **coming** on the **clouds** of **heaven**."
Then the **high priest tore** his **clothes** and **said**,
"He has **blasphemed**!
Why do we **still need witnesses**?
You have **now** heard his **blasphemy**.
What is your **verdict**?"
They **answered**, "**He** deserves **death**."
Then they **spat** in his **face** and **struck** him;
and some **slapped** him,
saying, "**Prophesy** to us, **Christ**!
Who **is** it that **struck** you?" »

Matthew continues to follow Mark's version of the Gethsemane scene in which Jesus takes aside three of his disciples—Peter and the two sons of Zebedee, James and John—and tells them that he is filled with sorrow and grief, "even to death." Before he goes off to pray, he tells them that they should watch with him. He prays that "this cup," meaning his death, will pass him by, but only by God's will, not his. And each time Jesus returns, he finds the disciples asleep. Finally, he tells them that "the

hour is at hand," meaning the time of his death, and he mentions his betrayer, which moves us into the next scene of the Passion narrative, in which Judas betrays Jesus to the crowd who come to arrest him.

The scene of Judas' betrayal is thick with irony and emotional distress. The kiss was understood as a sign of friendship among men in the first-century world, but Judas betrays Jesus with a kiss, turning him over to those who want to destroy him! And then he greets Jesus with the words

"Greetings, Rabbi!" Judas is feigning respect, but his words and action are disparaging in every way. Jesus responds by calling Judas "friend" and tells him to do what he came to do. Can you feel the tension?

Suddenly, someone from Jesus' company takes a sword and cuts off the ear of the high priest's servant. This is no ordinary servant and no accident; an assistant to the high priest who has a deformity such as this would not be allowed to serve in the Temple (see Leviticus 21.17–22). Thus, this

Here the focus shifts to Peter and his denial.

Galilean = gal-ih-LEE-uhn

"Do not know": These words will be repeated with the same emphasis two more times.

Slight pause between "girl" and "saw."

Slight pause between "also" and "one."

Pilate = PĪ-luht
Here the focus shifts to Pilate.

Slight pause between "betraying" and "innocent."

Slow your pace slightly at this point to allow the grim fate of Judas to register with your assembly.

Now **Peter** was **sitting outside** in the **courtyard**.
A **servant girl came** to him and **said**,
"**You also** were with **Jesus** the **Galilean**."
But he **denied** it before **all** of them, **saying**,
"I **do not know** what you are **talking** about."
When he went **out** to the **porch**,
another **servant girl saw** him,
and she **said** to the **bystanders**,
"**This man** was with **Jesus** of **Nazareth**."
Again he **denied** it with an **oath**,
"I **do not know** the **man**."
After a **little while** the **bystanders** came **up** and said to **Peter**,
"**Certainly** you are **also one** of them,
for your **accent betrays** you."
Then he began to **curse**, and he swore an **oath**,
"I **do not know** the **man!**"
At **that moment** the **cock crowed**.
Then Peter **remembered** what Jesus had **said**:
"Before the **cock crows**, you will **deny** me **three times**."
And he **went** out and **wept bitterly**.

When **morning came**,
all the **chief priests** and the **elders** of the **people**
conferred together against **Jesus**
in order to **bring** about his **death**.
They **bound** him, led him **away**,
and handed him **over** to **Pilate** the **governor**.
When **Judas**, his **betrayer**, saw that **Jesus** was **condemned**,
he **repented** and brought **back** the **thirty pieces** of **silver**
to the **chief priests** and the **elders**.
He said, "I have **sinned** by **betraying innocent blood**."
But they said, "What is **that** to **us**?
See to it **yourself**."
Throwing down the **pieces** of **silver** in the **temple**, he **departed**;
and he **went** and **hanged** himself.

act is an attack on the high priest and his Temple ministry. Only Matthew's Gospel has the saying "all who take the sword will perish by the sword" and the saying about the Father's ability to protect Jesus with twelve legions of Angels, if he chose to ask. Although the number of foot soldiers in a legion differed at different periods of history, biblical scholars think it numbered about 6,100 at this time. If so, twelve legions would amount to 73,200 Angels. What an army of heavenly beings!

All three synoptic Gospels have this accusatory question addressed to the crowd: "Have you come out with swords and clubs to arrest me as though I were a bandit?" The Greek word for "robber" or "bandit" might be better translated as "plunderer." Today, we might think of rioters or violent protesters. Thus, the synoptic Gospels present Jesus' arrest as a further sign of disrespect. The saying about the Scriptures being fulfilled is the Gospel writers' way of asserting that Jesus' crucifixion

is part of God's plan, but the next statement is the most devastating of all: "Then all the disciples deserted him and fled." A literal translation of this sentence might read like this: "Then the disciples, all of them, went away from that place and ran for safety." Thus, Jesus is left utterly alone to face the crowd that wants him dead.

The next scene in the narrative is Jesus' appearance before the high priest and the Sanhedrin. The Sanhedrin consisted of an assembly of Jewish elders

Slight pause between "Blood" and "to."

Jeremiah = jayr-uh-Mī-uh

But the **chief priests**, taking the **pieces** of **silver**, **said**,
"It is not lawful to **put** them into the **treasury**,
since they are **blood** money."
After **conferring together**,
they **used** them to buy the **potter's field**
as a **place** to bury **foreigners**.
For t**his reason** that **field** has been called the **Field** of **Blood**
      to this day.
Then was **fulfilled**
what had been **spoken** through the **Prophet Jeremiah**,
"And they **took** the **thirty pieces** of **silver**,
the **price** of the **one** on whom a **price** had been **set**,
on whom **some** of the **people** of **Israel** had **set** a **price**,
and they **gave** them for the **potter's field**,
as the **Lord commanded** me."

The word "Now" signals another shift in focus, this time back to Pilate.

[Now **Jesus** stood before the **governor**;
and the **governor asked** him,
"Are **you** the **King** of the **Jews**?"
Jesus said, "You **say** so."
But when he was **accused** by the **chief priests** and **elders**,
he **did not answer.**
Then **Pilate said** to him,
"Do you not **hear** how many **accusations** they make
      against you?"
But he gave him **no answer**, not even to a **single charge**,
so that the **governor** was **greatly amazed**.
Now at the **festival**
the governor was **accustomed** to **release** a **prisoner** for the **crowd**,
anyone they **wanted**. ❯❯

Another "Now," another shift, this time to the negotiation between Pilate and the people for Christ's possible release.

which might have functioned somewhat like a grand jury today. Although all four Gospels have a similar account of this scene, Matthew's and John's Gospels are the only ones that name Caiaphas as the high priest at that time (see John 18.13). Matthew again follows Mark's version of the story, more or less, but with a few exceptions. For example, Matthew describes Peter as coming into the high priest's courtyard "to see how this would end," suggesting a formal trial, whereas Mark describes Peter as warming himself by the fire (Mark 14.54).

Both Gospels describe the high priest and the Sanhedrin as seeking witnesses against Jesus without much success, until Jesus breaks his silence and says, "You will see the Son of Man seated at the right hand of Power and coming on the clouds of heaven." Thus, Jesus is charged with blasphemy, a crime punishable by death. But we can expect that the initial readers of this account caught the irony of the situation: Jesus' statement is not blasphemy, but rather the truth about his identity!

The next two scenes in this Passion narrative share a similar structure and some common themes. In terms of structure, the story of Peter's denial of Jesus is so closely intertwined with the story of Jesus' hearing before the Sanhedrin that they appear to be happening at the same time. Likewise, the story of Judas' suicide is intertwined with the story of Jesus' appearance before Pontius Pilate, the governor of the region including Jerusalem, as if they are happening at the same time. The themes that hold these two sets of stories

Barabbas = buh-RAB-uhs

At that time they had a **notorious prisone**r, called **Barabbas**.
So **after** they had **gathered**, Pilate **said** to them,
"**Whom** do you want me to **release** for you,
Barabbas or **Jesus** who is **called** the **Christ**?"
For he **realized** that it was out of **jealousy**
that they had handed him **over**.
While he was **sitting** on the **judgment seat**,
his **wife** sent **word** to him,
"Have **nothing** to **do** with that **innocent man**,
for **today** I have **suffered** a **great deal**
because of a **dream about** him."
Now the **chief priests** and the **elders**
persuaded the **crowds** to ask for **Barabbas**
and to have **Jesus killed**.
The **governor** again **said** to them,
"**Which** of the **two** do you want me to **release** for you?"
And they said, "**Barabbas**."
Pilate **said** to them,
"Then **what** should I **do** with **Jesus** who is called the **Christ**?"
All of them said, "Let him be **crucified**!"
Then he asked, "**Why**, what **evil** has he **done**?"
But they **shouted** all the **more**,
"**Let** him be **crucified**!"
So when **Pilate** saw that he could **do nothing**,
but **rather** that a riot was **beginning**,
he took some **water** and washed his **hands**
        before the **crowd**, saying,
"I am innocent of **this man's blood**;
see to it **yourselves**."
Then the **people** as a **whole answered**,
"His **blood** be on us and on our **children**!"

Don't overplay these words. They are already powerful enough.

together are judgment and the ancient Mediterranean values of honour and shame. The theme of judgment is easy to see. In the first set of stories, Jesus is forced to appear before the high priest, and charges are made. In the second, he is brought before Pontius Pilate for judgment and execution.

The significance of an honour-shame culture is much harder for those of us who have been raised in the Western world to appreciate. Honour has to do with one's status in the community and the public recognition of that status. Losing honour is a very serious thing that requires a response designed to restore one's honour. The story of Peter's denial of Jesus is an example of honour lost. Notice how quickly the tension escalates as Peter is confronted three times about his association with Jesus. The first confrontation is from a female servant who speaks to Peter alone, though he responds to everyone, "I do not know what you are talking about." Notice how he is being evasive so as not to lose honour. The second is from another woman who says to those around her that Peter had been seen with Jesus, and he swears with an oath, "I do not know the man." The third encounter is with a group of bystanders who insist that Peter had been with Jesus. Now he curses and swears, "I do not know the man!" It was only a few hours earlier that evening that Jesus prophesied that Peter would deny him three times before the cockcrow, the name given to the period just before dawn. Remember how Peter vowed that he would die for Jesus before he would deny him? Peter clearly recognizes his failure to retain honour, as we are told that "he went out

Another grim word, "flogging." Allow its
menace to linger.

Another shift in focus, this time to the
soldiers crucifying Jesus.

cohort = KOH-hohrt

The tone of this passage is mocking. But
don't overdo the mockery. It will come
through by way of a forceful proclamation
focused on the words themselves.

Cyrene = sī-REEN or sī-REE-nee

Golgotha = GAWL-guh-thuh

gall = gawl

So he released **Barabbas** for them;
and after **flogging Jesus**,
he handed him **over** to be **crucified**.
Then the **soldiers** of the **governor**
took **Jesus** into the **governor's headquarters**,
and they **gathered** the **whole** cohort **around** him.
They **stripped** him and put a **scarlet robe** on him,
and after **twisting** some **thorns** into a **crown**,
they **put** it on his **head**.
They put a **reed** in his **right hand** and **knelt before** him
and **mocked** him, **saying**,
"**Hail**, **King** of the **Jews!**"
They **spat** on him,
and took the **reed** and **struck** him on the **head**.
After **mocking** him, they **stripped** him of the **robe**
and put his **own clothes on** him.
Then they **led** him **away** to **crucify** him.
As they **went out**,
they came upon a **man** from **Cyrene** named **Simon**;
they **compelled** this man to **carry** his **Cross**.
And when they **came** to a **place** called **Golgotha**
(which means **Place** of a **Skull**),
they **offered** him **wine** to **drink**, **mixed** with **gall**;
but when he **tasted** it, he **would not drink** it.
And when they had **crucified** him,
they divided his clothes among **themselves** by **casting lots**;
then they **sat down** there and kept **watch** over him.
Over his **head** they put the charge **against** him, which **read**,
"**This** is **Jesus**, the **King** of the **Jews**."
Then **two bandits** were **crucified** with him,
one on his **right** and **one** on his **left**. »

and wept bitterly." Peter's weeping is a sign of pain and grief. Leaving the scene and going out into the darkness is another sign of Peter's loss of honour. This is the last time that Peter is mentioned by name in this Gospel.

By contrast, the story of Judas' suicide is an example of an attempt to restore honour. This story is told only in Matthew's Gospel, though there is a reference to the violence of his death in Acts 1.18–19. Here we learn that Judas responds with regret or self-repentance, when he realizes that Jesus is condemned to death because of his action, and he does what he can to restore honour. He returns the thirty pieces of silver to the chief priests and elders, but they refuse to take back the money, thereby not allowing Judas to undo the terrible thing he had done. This is when he decides to end his life, not so much out of despair but as a way of restoring honour in a situation that is about to result in the death of another. A word of caution is needed concerning this story: suicide is never a solution to remedy a bad situation—all life is precious, regardless of our moral failures—but this story is an example of the depth of Judas' remorse, making forgiveness possible if he had chosen another path in this moment.

Next, we hear the story of Jesus' appearance before Pontius Pilate. Again, Matthew makes a few changes to Mark's version of the story. For example, when Pilate is about to sentence Jesus to death, his wife sends a message to him, urging him not to be involved in this case because of what she had suffered in a dream. This

Once again, mockery dominates the tone.

Those who passed **by derided** him,
shaking their **heads** and **saying**,
"**You** who would **destroy** the **temple** and **build** it in **three days**,
save yourself!
If **you** are the **Son** of **God**, come **down** from the **Cross**."
In the **same way** the **chief priests also**,
along with the **scribes** and **elders**,
were **mocking** him, **saying**,
"He **saved others**; he **cannot** save **himself**.
He is the **King** of **Israel**;
let him **come down** from the **Cross now**,
and we will **believe** in him.
He **trusts** in **God**;
let **God deliver** him **now**, if he **wants** to;
for he **said**, 'I am **God's Son**.'"
The **bandits** who were **crucified** with him
also **taunted** him in the **same way**.
From **noon on**, **darkness** came **over** the **whole land**
until **three** in the **afternoon**.
And about **three o'clock Jesus cried** with a **loud voice**,
"**Eli**, **Eli**, **lema sabachthani**?"
that is, "My **God**, my **God**, **why** have you **forsaken** me?"
When **some** of the bystanders **heard** it, they **said**,
"**This man** is calling for **Elijah**."
At **once one** of them **ran** and got a **sponge**,
filled it with **sour wine**, **put** it on a **stick**,
and **gave** it to him to **drink**.
But the **others said**,
"**Wait**, let us see whether **Elijah** will **come** to **save** him."
Then **Jesus cried again** with a **loud voice**
and **breathed** his **last**.

These authentic words of Christ are as wrenching as they are solemn.
Eli, Eli, lema sabachthani =
ay-LEE, ay-LEE, luh-MAH sah-bahk-TAH-nee

Elijah = ee-LĪ-juh
Slight pause between "once" and "one."

addition provides a fitting transition to the next scene, where Pilate attempts to release Jesus by offering a prisoner release in celebration of the Passover feast. He offers the crowd two choices: Jesus or Barabbas, whose name ironically means "son of the father." Luke's Gospel describes the latter as an insurrectionist and a murderer (Luke 23.19). The author of Matthew's Gospel changes the title given to Jesus from "king of the Jews" to "the Christ," further suggesting that Jesus is not guilty of a crime deserving death. Matthew reinforces this

point by adding the scene in which Pilate publicly washes his hands and declares himself innocent in the anticipated execution of Jesus. The narrator tells us that Pilate finally released Jesus to the crowd because he feared a riot would break out, but we should not assume that he is an innocent victim in all this. Pontius Pilate was a very complex historical character, and even today historians are divided about how we should view him.

But we cannot leave this scene without commenting on Matthew's addition of

the famous or infamous quotation that he attributes to the chief priests, the elders and the crowd: "His blood be on us and on our children!" Regrettably, the historical context for this quotation was quickly lost—Matthew's community of Jews together with some Gentiles who believed in Jesus as the Christ were battling with other Jews who refused to recognize Jesus as the Christ—but it soon became a rallying cry for fear and hatred of the Jewish people. They were seen as Christ-killers, who must pay the price for their crime of deicide!

Here, another shift in tone, this time to wonder mixed with awe—it's even a little frightening.

centurion = sen-TOOR-ee-uhn

Magdalene = MAG-duh-luhn or MAG-duh-leen

Zebedee = ZEB-uh-dee

Arimathea = ayr-ih-muh-THEE-uh

hewn = hyoon

At **that moment** the **curtain** of the **temple** was **torn** in **two**,
from **top** to **bottom**.
The **earth shook**, and the **rocks** were **split**.
The **tombs also** were **opened**,
and **many bodies** of the saints who had **fallen asleep**
    were **raised**.
After his **resurrection** they came **out** of the **tombs**
and **entered** the **holy city** and **appeared** to **many**.
Now when the **centurion** and **those with** him,
who were **keeping watch** over **Jesus**,
saw the **earthquake** and **what took place**,
they were **terrified** and **said**,
"**Truly** this **man** was **God's Son!**"]
Many women were **also there**, looking **on** from a **distance**;
they had followed **Jesus** from **Galilee** and had **provided** for him.
Among them were **Mary Magdalene**,
and **Mary** the **mother** of **James** and **Joseph**,
and the **mother** of the **sons** of **Zebedee**.
When it was **evening**,
there came a **rich man** from **Arimathea**, named **Joseph**,
who was **also** a **disciple** of **Jesus**.
He went to **Pilate** and **asked** for the **body** of **Jesus**;
then **Pilate ordered** it to be **given** to **him**.
So **Joseph** took the **body**
and **wrapped** it in a **clean linen cloth**
and **laid** it in his **own new tomb**,
which he had **hewn** in the **rock**.
He then **rolled** a **great stone** to the **door** of the **tomb**
    and **went away**.
Mary Magdalene and the **other Mary** were **there**,
sitting **opposite** the **tomb**. »

While antisemitism persists even in our time, it is not representative of Catholic theology, nor is it supported by the Gospels, which indicate clearly that Jesus' death was part of God's plan of salvation for the whole human race. The Second Vatican Council asserts that "neither all Jews indiscriminately at that time, nor Jews today, can be charged with the crimes committed during his [Christ's] passion" and that the Church "deplores all hatreds, persecutions, displays of antisemitism levelled at any time or from any source against the Jews" (*Nostra aetate*, 4).

Following Mark's Gospel, Matthew goes on to tell the story of the Roman soldiers mocking Jesus in the praetorium, Pilate's residence in Jerusalem. However, he changes the colour of the robe that the soldiers placed on Jesus from purple in Mark's Gospel, a colour of royalty, to red, the colour that the soldiers wore, and he describes the soldiers as placing a reed sceptre in Jesus' right hand, the hand of power. This act, along with stripping Jesus of his clothing and spitting on him, should be seen as efforts to destroy Jesus' honour status as Messiah and Son of God. Likewise, the inscription placed on the cross, "This is Jesus, the King of the Jews" and the passersby who were hurling abuse at Jesus were attempts to strip Jesus of his honour. Yet, when all seems lost and Jesus gives up his spirit in death, the Gospel writer adds that the barrier that separated the Holy of Holies from the rest of the Temple was torn open—remember that the Holy of Holies was where God would reside when visiting

Pharisees = FAYR-uh-seez
Slight pause between "Pharisees" and "gathered."

The **next day**, that is, **after** the day of **Preparation**,
the **chief priests** and the **Pharisees gathered** before **Pilate**
        and **said**,
"**Sir**, we **remember** what that **impostor** said
        while he was **still alive**,
'After **three days** I will **rise again**.'
Therefore command the **tomb** to be made **secure**

Slight pause between "Therefore" and "command."

        until the **third day**;
otherwise his **disciples** may **go** and **steal** him **away**,
and tell the **people**, 'He has been **raised** from the **dead**,'
and the **last deception** would be **worse** than the **first**."
Pilate **said** to them,

It's worth noting the anxious conclusion of this reading.

"You have a **guard** of **soldiers**;
go, make it as **secure** as you **can**."
So they **went** with the **guard**
and made the **tomb secure** by **sealing** the **stone**.

[Shorter: Matthew 27.11–54 (see brackets)]

God's people—the earth was trembling from earthquakes, and dead people were walking around. These signs prompt the centurion and some of his soldiers to proclaim, "Truly this man was God's Son!" and thus Jesus' honour is restored.

Matthew's Passion narrative ends rather quickly with an abbreviated version of Mark's story of Jesus' burial. Joseph of Arimathea is now described as a rich disciple of Jesus, though there is no mention of him being a member of the Sanhedrin. Further, Matthew describes the shroud, in

which Jesus' body is wrapped, as clean, and the tomb, in which he was laid, as new. Thus, Matthew portrays Joseph as attempting to give Jesus a burial that restores his honour in the world. Finally, the Gospel writer adds a scene in which the chief priests and the Pharisees request and are granted guards to secure the tomb so that Jesus' disciples cannot commit fraud by stealing the body and claiming that Jesus had risen from the dead. By suggesting that Jesus is a deceiver and arguing that Jesus' disciples might create an even greater

deception, these religious leaders make one final effort to attack Jesus' honour. What they do not know is that God's efforts to restore Jesus' honour will win out in the end. All we need to do now is wait. C.C.

THE MASS OF THE LORD'S SUPPER (HOLY THURSDAY)

LECTIONARY #39

READING I   Exodus 12.1–8, 11–14

A reading from the book of Exodus.

The **Lord** said to **Moses** and **Aaron** in the land of **Egypt**:
This month shall **mark** for you the beginning of **months**;
it shall be the **first** month of the **year** for you.
Tell the **whole** congregation of **Israel**
that on the **tenth** of this month
they are to take a **lamb** for **each** family,
a **lamb** for each **household**.
If a household is too **small** for a **whole** lamb,
it shall **join** its closest neighbour in **obtaining** one;
the **lamb** shall be **divided**
in **proportion** to the number of **people** who **eat** of it.
Your lamb shall be without **blemish**, a **year-old male**;
you may take it from the **sheep** or from the **goats**.
You shall **keep** it until the fourteenth day of this **month**;
then the **whole** assembled congregation of Israel
shall **slaughter** it at **twilight**.
They shall take **some** of the blood
and put it on the **two doorposts** and the **lintel**
of the **houses** in which they **eat** it.
They shall **eat** the lamb that **same night**;
they shall eat it **roasted** over the **fire**
with **unleavened bread** and bitter **herbs**. »

Exodus = EK-suh-duhs

A reading that includes detailed instructions from God to Moses and Aaron to convey to the Israelites so that they will be prepared for the events now commemorated as Passover. The instructions have ritual power anticipating one of the most spectacular narratives in the Old Testament. Read these instructions with some reverence.

These details are part of the appeal of this reading. Don't rush through them.

Emphasis on "slaughter."

Again, important details.

| READING I | Holy Thursday, also called Maundy Thursday, is a commemoration of the synoptic Gospels' story of the Passover meal that Jesus shared with his disciples before his death and a celebration of the institution of the Eucharist. Today's readings speak well to the robust, multilayered meanings attached to this feast.

In the first reading, we hear an account of the Passover ritual as explained in the Book of Exodus. It appears immediately after the announcement of the tenth plague, the death of the firstborn of Egypt (Exodus 11), and immediately before the execution of this tenth plague (Exodus 12.29–30). However, the ritual itself probably reflects a later period of development—in this case, a time when two separate rituals had been joined into one. The first is the ritual of the Passover lamb (Exodus 12.1–13), and the second is the ritual of the unleavened bread (Exodus 12.14–20). Here God is speaking to Moses, who will later describe the rituals to the Israelite peoples (see Exodus 12.21–27).

The ritual of the Passover lamb always occurred in the springtime and was con-nected to the tenth plague by the directive to the Israelites to put the blood of the lamb on the doorposts and lintels of the homes where they were eating the sacrificial meal, so that God would know to pass over those places and protect them from the destruction that would come upon Egypt, when God killed all of the firstborn. Although it is troubling for us to think about God doing such a terrible thing, we need to remember that the plagues were God's "weapons" in the battle with the hard-hearted pharaoh, who claimed divinity but was not really a god. Thus, Passover is a

girded = gerded = belted

This line announces the purpose of this reading; it is followed by the grim details of God's judgment. Give them the emphasis they deserve.

This is how you shall **eat** it:
your **loins girded**, your **sandals** on your **feet**,
and your **staff** in your hand;
and you shall **eat** it **hurriedly**.
It is the **Passover** of the **Lord**.
For I will **pass** through the land of **Egypt that night**,
and I will **strike** down **every firstborn** in the land of Egypt,
both **human beings** and **animals**;
on **all** the gods of **Egypt** I will **execute judgments**:
I am the **Lord**.
The **blood** shall be a **sign** for you on the **houses** where you **live**:
when I **see** the **blood**, I will **pass over** you,
and **no plague** shall **destroy** you
when I **strike** the land of **Egypt**.
This **day** shall be a day of **remembrance** for you.
You shall **celebrate** it as a **festival** to the **Lord**;
throughout your **generations**
you shall **observe** it as a **perpetual** ordinance.

For meditation and context:

RESPONSORIAL PSALM   Psalm 116.12–13, 15+16bc, 17–18 (R. 1 Cor 10.16)

R. The cup of blessing that we bless is a sharing in the Blood of Christ.

What shall I return to the Lord
for all his bounty to me?
I will lift up the cup of salvation
and call on the name of the Lord.

Precious in the sight of the Lord
is the death of his faithful ones.
I am your servant, the son of your
    serving girl.
You have loosed my bonds.

I will offer to you a thanksgiving sacrifice
and call on the name of the Lord.
I will pay my vows to the Lord
in the presence of all his people.

TO KEEP IN MIND
Recognize how important your proclamation of the Word of God is. Prepare well and take joy in your ministry.

---

joyous, anticipatory celebration of freedom from slavery, which God will surely and immediately win for the Israelites.

READING II Our second reading, from Paul's First Letter to the Corinthians, is part of a longer teaching on how to share the Eucharist with integrity and attention to the welfare of the entire community. In the early centuries of Christianity, the Eucharist took place as part of a common meal in the homes of wealthy patrons. But someone, perhaps Chloe's people (see 1 Corinthians 1.11), told

Paul about the community's bad behaviour when they gathered to eat the Lord's supper. Apparently, the wealthy arrived early and were eating and drinking to excess, so that when the poor arrived, the food was gone. Not only were the lower-class members of the community hungry, but they were shamed by the fact that the wealthy had no regard for their need.

Paul is being extremely radical here. When the Christian community gathered for Eucharist, they were doing exactly what everyone else was doing at banquets, in keeping with cultural practices in the first-

century Mediterranean world. But Paul is fierce in his condemnation of the community's behaviour, arguing that "all who eat and drink without discerning the body, eat and drink judgment against themselves" (1 Corinthians 11.29). Why? Paul recites the words of the institution of the Eucharist that was already in use in Christian communities, tracing them back to the authority of Jesus. Biblical scholars think that Paul might have altered the original wording by adding, "Do this, as often as you drink it, in remembrance of me" to the statement "This cup is the new covenant

Corinthians = kohr-IN-thee-uhnz

A commemoration of the words at the heart of the Mass. These words of Paul's to the Corinthians are a Scriptural echo of the words in the reading from Exodus.

Here begin the words of institution, always spoken by a priest, but here, most likely, spoken by a lector. These words can take on a freshness in your proclamation.

In a slow, commemorative rhythm.

A reading that provides the basis for one of the most powerful of Christian rituals, the washing of feet. Its power resides in the directness of its depiction of the ritual itself but also the ways the act anticipates Christ's Passion.

Iscariot = ih-SKAYR-ee-uht

READING II   1 Corinthians 11.23–26

A reading from the first Letter of Saint Paul to the Corinthians.

Brothers and sisters:
I **received** from the Lord what I also **handed** on to you,
that the **Lord** Jesus on the **night** when he was betrayed
took a loaf of **bread**,
and when he had given **thanks**,
he **broke** it and said,
"**This** is my **Body** that is for **you**.
Do this in remembrance of **me**."
In the **same way** he took the **cup** also, after **supper**, saying,
"**This cup** is the **new covenant** in my **Blood**.
Do this, as **often** as you **drink it**, in **remembrance** of me."
For as **often** as you eat this **bread** and drink the **cup**,
you **proclaim** the Lord's **death** until he **comes**.

GOSPEL   John 13.1–15

A reading from the holy Gospel according to John.

Before the festival of the **Passover**,
Jesus **knew** that his **hour** had **come**
to **depart** from this world and **go** to the **Father**.
Having **loved** his **own** who were in the **world**,
he **loved** them to the **end**.
The **devil** had **already** put it into the **heart** of **Judas**,
    son of Simon **Iscariot**,
to **betray** him.
And during **supper**
Jesus, **knowing** that the **Father** had given **all** things into
    his **hands**, »

in my Blood," thereby highlighting the Eucharist as a commemoration of a supreme act of love, Jesus' death on a cross. The community should do likewise, no matter how radical it might seem. They should love even those who were different from themselves.

GOSPEL At first glance, today's reading from the Gospel of John might seem like a strange choice for Holy Thursday. John's story of Jesus' last meal with his disciples is not a Passover meal. Rather, it takes place several days before Passover because, in John's Gospel,

Jesus is sentenced to death and crucified on the preparation day for Passover, when the Passover lambs were being sacrificed in the Temple. Also, the story begins on an ominous note by explaining that Jesus' "hour," that is, the time of his death and return to the Father, had come and that he had loved his own to the end or to the fullest. These verbs are aorist tense, which denotes a past action completed. The narrator also notes that Judas had already plotted to hand Jesus over to his enemies.

Today's reading describes a ritual of hospitality, the washing of feet, that would

have preceded any banquet in the first-century Mediterranean world. This was a fitting way to indicate to your guests a sense of welcome. However, this work would have been done not by the master of the household or the host of a dinner but by the master's slaves. Hence, we can sense Peter's horror as he watches Jesus remove his outer garment in preparation for work and engage in a slave's task to provide hospitality to his guests.

But this foot washing is so much more than an act of hospitality. When Peter protests that he wants no part in Jesus'

The details here are important.

and that he had **come** from God and was **going** to God,
got **up** from the table,
took **off** his outer robe,
and tied a **towel** around **himself**.
Then he **poured water** into a **basin**
and **began** to wash the disciples' **feet**
and to **wipe them** with the **towel** that was tied around him.
He came to Simon **Peter**, who **said** to him,
"**Lord**, are you going to **wash** my **feet**?"
Jesus answered,
"You do not **know now** what I am doing,
but **later** you **will understand**."
Peter said to him, "You will **never** wash my **feet**."
Jesus answered,
"Unless I **wash** you, you have no **share** with me."
Simon Peter said to him,
"**Lord**, not my **feet** only but also my **hands** and my **head**!"
Jesus said to him,
"One who has **bathed** does not **need** to wash,
except for the **feet**, but is **entirely clean**.
And **you** are **clean**, though not **all** of you."
For he **knew** who was to **betray** him;
for **this** reason he said,
"Not **all** of you are **clean**."
After he had **washed** their feet, **put on** his **robe**,
and **returned** to the **table**,
Jesus said to them,
"Do you **know** what I have **done** to you?
You call me **Teacher** and **Lord**—
and you are **right**, for **that** is what I **am**.
So if **I**, your **Lord** and **Teacher**,
have **washed** your feet,
you **also** ought to **wash** one another's feet.
For I have **set** you an **example**,
that **you** also should **do** as **I** have done to **you**."

Peter's inability to understand what Jesus is doing reflects the congregation's. Though Peter is a bit thick, Jesus is gentle but authoritative in his responses.

These lines to the end of the reading are firm and mysterious.

self-shaming act, Jesus tells Peter that, if he refuses, he can have no part in what Jesus has in store for the disciples. Peter's response is somewhat humorous, because he takes Jesus' words literally and requests a full bath! John frequently uses this literary technique of having characters understand only the plain meaning of Jesus' words so that Jesus can go on to explain the deeper meaning. Thus, Jesus responds, "One who has bathed does not need to wash, except for the feet, but is entirely clean. And you are clean, though not all of you." The phrase "though not all of you" refers to Judas.

Biblical scholars have debated whether bathing is a reference to baptism. The Greek word is *louó*, meaning "to bathe or to wash," which can be applied in a variety of settings, but, at the very least, we can say that bathing is a symbol of abiding or remaining with Jesus. Abiding is the way this Gospel refers to discipleship. Now only the feet need to be washed. Why? The foot washing is an action and symbol of the extent to which the disciples must go to be servants of one another. They must follow Jesus' example of servanthood in loving others to the end.

And what about us? Are we willing to follow Jesus' example? For the author of John's Gospel, responding to the call of discipleship is more than pious thoughts. It requires that we be humble servants of all God's children. C.C.

CELEBRATION OF THE LORD'S PASSION (GOOD FRIDAY)

LECTIONARY #40

READING I   Isaiah 52.13—53.12

A reading from the book of the Prophet Isaiah.

See, my servant shall **prosper**;
he shall be **exalted** and lifted **up**,
and shall be **very** high.
Just as there were **many** who were **astonished** at him
—so **marred** was his appearance, beyond **human semblance**,
and his **form beyond** that of the sons of **man**—
so he shall startle many nations;
kings shall **shut** their **mouths** because of him;
for that which had not been **told** them they shall **see**,
and that which they had not **heard** they shall **contemplate**.
Who has **believed** what we have **heard**?
And to **whom** has the **arm** of the Lord been **revealed**?
For he grew **up** before the Lord like a **young plant**,
and like a **root** out of **dry ground**;
he had no **form** or **majesty** that we should **look** at him,
nothing in his appearance that we should **desire** him.
He was **despised** and **rejected** by men;
a man of **suffering** and acquainted with **infirmity**;
and as **one** from whom others hide their **faces**
he was **despised**,
and we **held him** of no **account**. »

Isaiah = ī-ZAY-uh

A reading whose power arises from bold claims and compelling rhythms. Allow these elements to ring out in your proclamation. Isaiah's prophecy speaks directly to the congregation and the mystery into which it is immersed.

Even emphasis on the words in this line.

The questions Isaiah asks set the tone for the lines to follow.

READING I   The first reading for today's liturgy is commonly known as the Suffering Servant song. The tone is mournful at times—some have compared it to a dirge—but hopeful, too. Altogether, there are four servant songs, all of which are found in Second Isaiah (Isaiah 40–55). The time and place of this writing is the sixth century BC, while the Jews were in exile in Babylon.

In the opening sentence of this reading, God is the speaker, and God refers to the subject of this oracle as "my servant," but the text gives us few clues about the servant's identity. The Hebrew word translated here as "many" has the connotation of a number too big to count, and the word translated as "astonished" also means "appalled, stunned, or desolated," like a desert is desolate. The servant is presented as so disfigured that he could hardly be recognized as human. Further, we are told that the kings and nations were startled by him. The word translated as "to startle" is most often understood to mean "to spurt or splatter." The connection here might be that the servant's disfigurement is so terrible that it causes the observers to spurt, metaphorically, or leap into a response of horror at what they see.

Suddenly and without transition, God is no longer speaking. Instead, a group identified only as "we" speaks. Their message is one of amazement at what is happening before their eyes. The "arm of the Lord" is a phrase designed to evoke the idea of God's intervention in history, usually in victory, though not always in a military sense. The servant is compared to a tender

125

Note the rhythms in the lines in this section, many of which place an emphasis on two of the words in the line: "borne" and "infirmities"; "carried" and "diseases"; and so forth. Let these rhythms carry your proclamation.

The story of the Suffering Servant is of course anticipatory of the Passion in John's Gospel.

The rhythms that prevail in the previous section continue in this one, often with an emphasis on two words in the line. Once again, let these rhythms carry your proclamation.

Words like "slaughter," "perversion," and "wicked" are loaded with significance. Recite them clearly and that significance will be evident to the assembly. No need to overdramatize the words when you proclaim them.

As the reading concludes, the mood lifts. There is a sense of promise and redemption. Don't, however, overdo it. The hope will come through when you proclaim these words straightforwardly.

Surely he has **borne** our **infirmities** and **carried** our **diseases**;
yet we **accounted** him **stricken**,
struck down by God, and **afflicted**.
But he was **wounded** for our transgressions,
crushed for our iniquities;
upon **him** was the **punishment** that made us **whole**,
and by his **bruises** we are **healed**.
All **we** like **sheep** have gone **astray**;
each has turned to their **own** way
and the **Lord** has laid on him
the **iniquity** of us **all**.
He was **oppressed**, and he was **afflicted**,
yet he did not **open** his **mouth**;
like a **lamb** that is **led** to the **slaughter**,
and like a **sheep** that before its **shearers** is **silent**,
so he did not **open** his **mouth**.
By a **perversion** of **justice** he was taken **away**.
Who could have **imagined** his **future**?
For he was cut **off** from the land of the **living**,
stricken for the **transgression** of my **people**.
They made his **grave** with the **wicked**
and his **tomb** with the **rich**,
although he had **done** no **violence**,
and there was no **deceit** in his mouth.
Yet it was the **will** of the **Lord** to **crush** him with **pain**.
When you make his life an **offering** for **sin**,
he shall **see** his **offspring**, and shall **prolong** his days;
through him the **will of the Lord** shall **prosper**.
Out of his **anguish** he shall see **light**;
he shall find **satisfaction** through his **knowledge**.
The **righteous** one, my servant, shall make **many righteous**,
and he shall **bear** their **iniquities**.

plant or a shoot emerging out of the dry desert soil, evoking the wonder that we experience on an early spring day in a climate that is somewhat hostile to new life (see also Isaiah 11.1), but the group notes that the servant, at his arrival, is nothing much to look at and is even rejected or forsaken by those around him. Notice also the use of the phrase "one from whom others hide their faces," which was used to describe a person's response to seeing a leper in the ancient world.

This same unidentified group goes on to talk about the suffering that the servant

endured, not because of his own wrongdoing but on behalf of those who rejected him, because they thought his sorry state was due to his own misdeeds. The language used to describe the servant's suffering is extremely weighty and graphic. The word translated here as "wounded" is also translated as "thrust through," and the word translated here as "crushed" can mean "broken into pieces" or "shattered." Similarly, the word translated here as "bruises" can be translated as "scourging or beatings." Thus, although the group's amazement is proportional to the horror

that they are witnessing, it is even more striking because they say, "the Lord has laid on him the iniquity of us all." This kind of suffering for the sake of another is unheard of and is almost too much for our small minds to comprehend. How could God love humanity this much?

This Suffering Servant song uses the sheep metaphor in two separate instances. First, the group identifies itself as sheep: "each has turned to their own way." Second, the sheep metaphor is applied to the servant who belongs to the flock and now is chosen to be a sacrificial offering for the

Therefore I will allot him a **portion** with the **great**,
and he shall **divide** the spoil with the **strong**;
because he **poured out** himself to **death**,
and was **numbered** with the **transgressors**;
yet he bore the **sin** of many,
and made **intercession** for the transgressors.

For meditation and context:

RESPONSORIAL PSALM   Psalm 31.1+5, 11–12, 14–15, 16+24 (R. Lk 23.46)

R. Father, into your hands I commend my spirit.

In you, O Lord, I seek refuge;
do not let me ever be put to shame;
in your righteousness deliver me.
Into your hand I commit my spirit;
you have redeemed me,
O Lord, faithful God.

I am the scorn of all my adversaries,
a horror to my neighbours,
an object of dread to my acquaintances.
Those who see me in the street flee from me.
I have passed out of mind like one who
    is dead;
I have become like a broken vessel.

But I trust in you, O Lord;
I say, "You are my God."
My times are in your hand;
deliver me from the hand of my enemies
    and persecutors.

Let your face shine upon your servant;
save me in your steadfast love.
Be strong, and let your heart take courage,
all you who wait for the Lord.

READING II   Hebrews 4.14–16; 5.7–9

A reading that prepares the assembly to understand the sacrifice of Jesus portrayed in the Passion to follow. The theology suggested in this reading is as mysterious as it is natural. Christ is our model, our exemplar. As a man, he felt things just as we feel them. And yet his suffering, as God, is inconceivable.

Though framed in a negative construction ("we do not have"), this statement expresses the crucial sympathy that Christ has for us and that we should have for him. Proclaim this sentence with care.

A reading from the Letter to the Hebrews.

Brothers and sisters:
Since we have a **great high priest**
who has passed **through** the heavens,
Jesus, the Son of **God**,
let us **hold fast** to our **confession**.
For we do not have a **high priest**
who is unable to **sympathize** with our **weaknesses**,
but we have one who in **every respect** has been **tested** as we are,
yet **without** sin. **»**

rest. The onlookers mistakenly think that he is a lamb made ready for slaughter and cut off from life. But the Prophet reminds us that this is not the end of the story. He tells us that God willed for the servant to be a reparation or guilt offering to seek purification from sin or to repair an offense. Thus, the servant, being one with the people of Israel, suffers for the sins of the people in fulfillment of God's plan of salvation.

You might recall that this oracle began with a declaration of the servant's eventual exaltation. Now, finally, the details of his victory are described. Having fulfilled God's

will to give himself over and shed his blood as a guilt offering for a sinful people, he will see the light and have length of days. Further, God says, "The righteous one, my servant, shall make many righteous." To make righteous means to be put in right relationship with God. Although the author of the Suffering Servant song could not have anticipated the crucifixion and exaltation of Jesus some 550 years later, it is easy to see how early Christians would latch on to this oracle to make sense of their experience of the living Christ who now stands before the throne of God.

READING II   Just as Isaiah's Suffering Servant song portrays the servant as both one with the sheep and set apart to be the sacrificial lamb in the guilt offering made on behalf of the people of God, the Letter to the Hebrews portrays Jesus as the great high priest who is without sin but who is one with God's people, even insofar as he could experience temptation and suffer pain. The Greek verb *sumpatheo*, translated here as "to sympathize," can also mean "to feel for or have compassion on another." Therefore, the author says, we can approach Jesus freely and

To intensify the sympathy, "In the days of his flesh."

Let us **therefore** approach the **throne** of **grace** with **boldness**,
so that we may receive **mercy**
and find **grace** to **help** in time of need.
In the **days** of his **flesh**,
Jesus offered up **prayers** and **supplications**,
with loud **cries** and **tears**,
to the **one** who was able to **save him** from **death**,
and he was **heard** because of his **reverent submission**.
Although he was a **Son**,
he learned **obedience** through what he **suffered**;
and having been made **perfect**,
he became the **source** of eternal **salvation** for all who **obey** him.

Even stresses on "source," "salvation," and "obey."

PASSION   John 18.1—19.42

The Passion of our Lord Jesus Christ according to John.

The Passion narrative in John's Gospel depicts Jesus foreknowing all that will happen to him, giving him an appearance of calm in a storm. John's Passion, like those in the synoptic Gospels, is full of drama, with scenes as vivid as those in any novel or film, but whose focus, Jesus, is defined by quiet intensity. Let that guide your recitation and let the drama inherent in the narrative express itself through you.

It is not uncommon, because of the length of this reading, for it to be shared among a group of lectors as well as a deacon and priest. While there are several characters in this narrative, including different speakers, avoid the tendency to do voices or to add drama by raising your voice unnecessarily. Let this narrative speak for itself through you.

Don't overdo these expressions of "I am."

After they had eaten the **supper**,
Jesus went out with his **disciples** across the Kidron **valley**
to a place where there was a **garden**,
which **he** and his disciples **entered**.
Now **Judas**, who betrayed him, also **knew** the place,
because **Jesus** often **met** there with his **disciples**.
So **Judas** brought a detachment of **soldiers**
together with **police** from the **chief priests** and the **Pharisees**,
and they came there with **lanterns** and **torches** and **weapons**.
Then **Jesus**, knowing **all** that was to **happen** to him,
came forward and asked them,
"**Whom** are you **looking** for?"
They answered, "**Jesus** of **Nazareth**."
Jesus replied, "**I am he**."
Judas, who betrayed him, was **standing** with them.
When Jesus said to them, "**I am he**,"
they stepped **back** and **fell** to the ground.

---

with great confidence to receive mercy and grace in troubled times.

When the author refers to the days when Jesus was "in the days of his flesh," he might have had in mind Jesus' forty days in the wilderness, when he was tempted by Satan, or the agony in the garden of Gethsemane before his arrest, or he might have been referring, more generally, to the human experience of fear in the face of suffering and death. Notice also that the author describes God as having heard Jesus' pleas "because of his reverent submission." This word can also be translated

as "Godly fear or piety." Jesus is further described as having learned obedience from what he suffered. The Greek word for obedience also means "compliance or submission." In other words, although Jesus was Son of God, he perfected his humanity in filial piety, perfectly honouring his Father by freely submitting to the will of God even unto death, whereby he was consecrated as the eternal high priest, who could convey salvation to the rest of humanity.

| GOSPEL | John's story of the Passion, death, and burial of Jesus, |

which is read every Good Friday, follows the general storyline of the synoptic Gospels, but it differs in several important ways, because John understood Jesus' death not as a discrete moment of despair but simply as a necessary part of his "lifting up" or his "glorification." Thus, John's version of the story of Jesus' suffering and death is part of a larger story of victory over the world's hate. In John's Gospel, the world is a symbol for all that is opposed to Jesus.

Even stresses on "let these men go."

Even stresses on "struck the high priest's slave."

John's Gospel tends to heap scorn upon the Jews (in contrast, for instance, to Mark's Gospel, where scorn is heaped upon the Romans). Because this has contributed to an ugly tendency toward anti-Semitism in Christianity, mindfulness of this history can empower your proclamation. This element comes through especially in the dialogue among Pilate, Jesus, and the assembled Jews below.

The story of Peter's denial provides a sympathetic note in an often harsh narrative. Peter's weakness is the assembly's; his denials ("I am not") speak directly to our spiritual struggles.

Even emphasis on the words in this line.

Again he asked them, "**Whom** are you looking for?"
And they said, "**Jesus** of **Nazareth**."
Jesus answered, "I **told** you that **I am he**.
So if you are **looking** for me, **let these men go**."
This was to fulfill the word that he had **spoken**,
"I did not **lose** a single **one** of those whom you **gave** me."
Then Simon **Peter**, who had a **sword**,
drew it, **struck the high priest's slave**,
and cut off his right **ear**.
The slave's name was **Malchus**.
Jesus said to Peter,
"Put your **sword** back into its **sheath**.
Am I **not** to **drink** the **cup** that the **Father** has **given** me?"
So the **soldiers**, their **officer**, and the Jewish **police**
arrested Jesus and **bound** him.
First they took him to **Annas**,
who was the **father-in-law** of Caiaphas,
the **high priest** that year.
Caiaphas was the one who had **advised** the **Jews**
that it was **better** to have one person die for the **people**.
Simon **Peter** and another disciple followed **Jesus**.
Since **that** disciple was known to the high **priest**,
he **went** with **Jesus** into the **courtyard** of the high priest,
but **Peter** was standing **outside** at the **gate**.
So the **other** disciple, who was **known** to the high priest,
went out, **spoke** to the woman who guarded the gate,
and brought Peter **in**.
The woman said to Peter,
"You are **not** also one of this man's **disciples**, **are you**?"
He said, "I am **not**."
Now the **slaves** and the **police** had made a **charcoal** fire
because it was **cold**,
and they were standing **around** it and **warming** themselves.
Peter also was **standing** with them and **warming** himself. »

This Passion narrative begins and ends in a garden. Because the garden is unnamed, some scholars of John's Gospel have suggested that the garden symbolizes the primeval garden of Eden in the Book of Genesis. Much of what we see in this Gospel is overlaid with symbolism, so this connection with the garden of Eden is certainly possible, though of course, we cannot know fully what was in John's mind.

Almost immediately, the narrator tells us that Judas knew this place where Jesus and the other disciples were gathered. We have also been told repeatedly that Judas is the one who will betray Jesus, so the reader knows what will happen in this garden scene. And now Judas appears with a large contingency of Roman soldiers and Jewish Temple guards. They come with lanterns and torches, indicating that this is the hour of darkness, which in John's Gospel represents the absence of belief (see John 8.12; 9.4). Likewise, Judas' betrayal of Jesus with a kiss is extremely dishonouring.

When Judas and the crowd of soldiers and Temple guards arrive on the scene, Jesus initiates a dialogue by saying, "Whom are you looking for?" Elsewhere in John's Gospel, this question is an invitation to discipleship (see John 1.35–51 and John 20.11–18). But those who come to arrest Jesus understand only the plain meaning of his words. Thus, the crowd answers, "Jesus of Nazareth," clearly missing the irony of his call to discipleship. In response, Jesus says, "I am he," which is reminiscent of Moses' encounter with God in the Burning Bush, when he asks God to reveal the divine name and God says, "I AM" (Exodus 3.14).

Even emphasis on the words in this line.

Jesus' response suggests the core of his resolve to face the suffering and sacrifice to come.

Again, a return to the story of Peter. Don't overly dramatize the denial. Peter's shame will come through clearly when you proclaim this passage deliberately and clearly.

Here begins a long passage of exceptional vividness and power, contrasting the conversation between Pilate and Jesus in the praetorium with the more aggressive exchanges between Pilate and the crowd of assembled Jews outside. The power of this scene arises, in part, from its being told from Pilate's point of view; this allows us (as readers, as members of the congregation) to begin to sympathize with Pilate, who makes the decision to put Jesus to death. It's a truly remarkable passage (continuing to the point where Jesus is handed over to be crucified), whose drama need not be exaggerated. Pace your reading to allow its potent drama to come through on its own.

Then the **high priest** questioned **Jesus**
about his **disciples** and about his **teaching**.
Jesus **answered**, "I have spoken **openly** to the **world**;
I have **always taught** in **synagogues** and in the **temple**,
where all the **Jews** come **together**.
I have said **nothing** in **secret**.
Why do you **ask me**?
Ask **those** who **heard** what I **said** to them;
they **know** what I **said**."
When he had **said** this,
one of the police standing nearby struck Jesus
    on the face, saying,
"Is **that** how you **answer** the high **priest**?"
Jesus answered, "If I have spoken **wrongly**,
testify to the wrong.
But if I have spoken **rightly**,
why do you **strike** me?"
Then **Annas** sent him bound to **Caiaphas** the high **priest**.
Now **Simon Peter** was standing and **warming** himself.
They **asked** him,
"You are not also one of his **disciples**, **are you**?"
He **denied** it and said, "I am **not**."
One of the **slaves** of the high **priest**,
a **relative** of the man whose **ear Peter** had cut **off**,
asked, "Did I not **see** you in the **garden** with him?"
Again Peter **denied** it,
and **at that moment** the cock **crowed**.
Then they **took Jesus** from Caiaphas to **Pilate's headquarters**.
It was **early** in the **morning**.
They themselves did not **enter** the headquarters,
so as to avoid **ritual defilement**
and to be able to **eat** the **Passover**.
So **Pilate** went out to them and said,
"**What accusation** do you bring **against** this **man**?"

Three times in this brief scene, Jesus is identified as "I AM." In Greek, it is *ego eime*.

Peter, likewise, does not understand the significance of this moment because, with a single sword, he attempts to defend Jesus from the well-armed crowd that seeks to arrest him. But the crowd of soldiers quickly grab Jesus and take him, bound, to Annas, the father-in-law of the high priest Caiaphas, who questions Jesus about his disciples and his teaching. The narrator reminds the reader that Caiaphas was the one who prophesied about Jesus'

death after the Jewish religious authorities became fearful about the tumult that would arise when people started to learn about the raising of Lazarus (John 11.45–53).

Meanwhile, interspersed among the presentation of Jesus before Caiaphas and the trial before Pontius Pilate, we learn that Peter and another disciple, possibly the Beloved Disciple, who is first mentioned in the story of Jesus' last supper with his disciples (John 13.21–30), follow Jesus to the gate of the high priest's courtyard. The other disciple is allowed into the courtyard,

but Peter was made to stay outside until the other disciple summoned for him to be allowed inside. This detail is significant because while Peter is in the high priest's courtyard and Jesus is inside the high priest's home, Peter is confronted three times: first by the woman who guarded the gate, next by the slaves and guards gathered around the fire, and finally by a slave who was related to the person whose ear was cut off by Peter. Each time they ask whether he is one of Jesus' disciples, Peter denies it. Twice he says, *ouk eimi*, that is,

Pilate is dismissive here, but don't exaggerate his dismissiveness.

The crucial question. Again, don't exaggerate it. Pilate, a government official, is asking an earnest question.

Even emphasis on the words in this question.

Jesus' answer is completely mysterious but supercharged with confidence. Read these words clearly and plainly.

Again, mysterious and confident.

Almost even emphasis on the words in this line, with extra added to "case."

They **answered**, "If this man were **not** a criminal,
we would **not** have handed him **over** to you."
Pilate said to them,
"**Take him yourselves** and **judge** him according to **your** law."
They replied, "We are not **permitted** to put **anyone** to **death**."
(This was to **fulfill** what **Jesus** had said
when he **indicated** the kind of **death** he was to **die**.)
Then **Pilate** entered the **headquarters** again,
summoned Jesus, and **asked** him,
"**Are you** the **King** of the **Jews**?"
Jesus answered, "Do you **ask this** on your **own**,
or did others **tell** you **about** me?"
Pilate replied, "I am not a **Jew**, **am** I?
Your own **nation** and the chief **priests** have handed you
        over to me.
What have you done?"
Jesus answered, "My kingdom is not from this **world**.
If my kingdom **were** from this world,
my **followers** would be **fighting**
to **keep** me from being **handed** over to the **Jews**.
But as it **is**, my **kingdom** is not from **here**."
Pilate asked him, "So you **are** a king?"
Jesus answered, "You **say** that I am a king.
For **this** I was born,
and for **this** I came into the world,
to **testify** to the **truth**.
Everyone who **belongs** to the truth **listens** to my **voice**."
Pilate asked him, "What is **truth**?"
After he had **said** this,
Pilate went out to the Jews **again** and **told** them,
"I find no **case against** him.
But you have a **custom** that I **release** someone for you
at the **Passover**.
Do you want me to **release** for you the **King** of the **Jews**?" »

"*not* I am!" The sentence in Greek places the emphasis on "not," which calls our attention to the "I am" sayings attributed to Jesus earlier in the Gospel. It also signals to the reader the irony of Peter's denial of Jesus. Is the Gospel writer trying to present Peter as one who *should* be able to speak openly or publicly on Jesus' behalf but who cannot muster the courage to do so?

Next, John tells the story of Jesus' trial before Pontius Pilate, and he does it in seven scenes. In the first scene, we learn that it is early in the morning, shortly before dawn, on the preparation day for Passover. Jesus had already been brought to Pilate's headquarters, the Roman governor's residence in Jerusalem. Those who came from Caiaphas' stayed outside. The narrator of the story says that it is to avoid being made ritually unclean and unable to celebrate the Passover meal, though we do not know whether there was such a rule in place at the time. But their action prompted Pilate to come *outside* into the predawn darkness to ask about the formal charges being brought against Jesus. Because of their ambiguous response, Pilate first chooses not to get involved. But the exchange between the crowd and Pilate reveals that they want Jesus executed. The narrator adds that this scene is a fulfillment of Jesus' words that he would die by being "lifted up" in crucifixion (John 12.32–33).

The crowd is now identified as the *judaioi*, which is here translated as "the Jews." However, many scholars of John's Gospel would caution against the use of this term, because it can be misinterpreted as an antisemitic trope. To better understand this term, it is helpful to know that the community for whom John is writing is also Jewish. Thus, these negative statements

Avoid the tendency to shout this line.

"Flogged" is a wicked word. Read it slowly, one elongated syllable.

No need to shout this line. It's all too clear what is happening.
Even stresses on the words in this line.

Pilate is at a loss, but he's also a dutiful Roman bureaucrat who has just ordered Christ's torture. There is little to sympathize with, despite Pilate's seeming desire to be exonerated from guilt.
Lower your voice here. Don't exclaim.

Don't shout.

This question has a note of astonishment to it.

They shouted in reply,
"Not **this** man, but **Barabbas**!"
Now **Barabbas** was a **bandit**.
Then **Pilate** took Jesus and had him **flogged**.
And the **soldiers** wove a **crown** of **thorns**
and **put** it on his **head**,
and they **dressed** him in a **purple robe**.
They kept **coming up** to him, saying,
  "**Hail**, **King** of the **Jews**!"
and they **struck** him on the face.
Pilate went out again and said to them,
"**Look**, I am **bringing** him out to you
to let you **know** that I find **no case** against him."
So **Jesus** came out,
wearing the **crown** of **thorns** and the **purple robe**.
Pilate **said** to them,
"**Here** is the **man**!"
When the **chief priests** and the **police** saw him, they **shouted**,
"**Crucify** him! **Crucify** him!"
Pilate **said** to them,
"**Take** him **yourselves** and crucify him;
I **find no case** against him."
They answered him, "We have a **law**,
and according to that **law** he ought to **die**
because he has **claimed** to be the Son of **God**."
Now when **Pilate** heard **this**, he was more **afraid** than ever.
He entered his **headquarters again** and asked Jesus,
"**Where** are you **from**?"
But Jesus gave him **no answer**.
Pilate therefore **said** to him,
"Do you refuse to **speak** to me?
Do you not **know** that I have **power** to **release** you,
and **power** to **crucify** you?"

about the *judaioi* are more likely the effects of an intra-family fight: a minority community of Jewish Christians struggling against a larger community of Jews who refuse to believe that Jesus is the Christ. To avoid this problem, biblical scholars suggest that we translate *judaioi* as "Judeans" or that we substitute "Jewish religious authorities" in place of "the Jews."

In the second scene of this trial, Pilate goes *inside* the praetorium to question Jesus. He asks, "Are you the King of the Jews?" Perhaps he had heard rumors about Jesus being called the Messiah, meaning

"anointed one." But Jesus refuses to answer Pilate's question about whether he is a king. Instead, he talks about a kingdom that is not of this world, which prompts Pilate to ask his question again. Jesus continues with statements about how he "came into the world, to testify to the truth" and how those who believe respond to the truth. The truth is the revelation of God, and Jesus is God's revealer (John 1.17–18). But Pilate remains totally clueless about Jesus and his identity. Hence, his sardonic question, "What is truth?"

In the third scene, Pilate again goes *outside*, this time to tell the crowd that he does not find Jesus guilty and that he wants to make a deal. He would release Jesus, whom he calls "King of the Jews," as a Passover prison release. But the crowd refuses and wants Barabbas instead. The narrator tells us that Barabbas was a robber and revolutionary, but we should not miss the irony. His name means "son of the father."

In the fourth scene, Pilate goes back *inside* to have Jesus flogged. His soldiers mock Jesus by dressing him in a purple

Jesus' answer to Pilate's question once again is mysterious and confident.

Don't shout.

This line of the chief priests is dismissive; don't overdo the dismissiveness.

In two short lines the act of Jesus' crucifixion, to which this whole Passion has been building, is expressed. Read these lines plainly and slowly.

Jesus **answered** him,
"You would have **no powe**r over **me**
unless it had been **given** you from **above**;
therefore the one who handed me **over** to you
is **guilty** of a greater **sin**."
From then on Pilate tried to **release** him,
but the Jews cried out,
"If you **release** this man, you are no **friend** of the **emperor**.
Everyone who claims to be a **king**
sets **himself** against the **emperor**."
When Pilate **heard these words**,
he brought Jesus **outside** and **sat** on the **judge's bench**
at a **place** called "The Stone **Pavement**,"
or in Hebrew "**Gabbatha**."
Now it was the **day** of **Preparation** for the **Passover**;
and it was about **noon**.
Pilate said to the **Jews**,
"**Here** is your **King**!"
They cried out,
"**Away with him**! **Away with him**! **Crucify** him!"
Pilate **asked** them, "Shall I **crucify** your **King**?"
The chief priests answered,
"We have **no king** but the **emperor**."
Then Pilate handed Jesus **over** to them to be **crucified**.
So they took **Jesus**;
and carrying the **Cross** by himself,
he went out to what is called The **Place** of the **Skull**,
which in Hebrew is called **Golgotha**.
There they **crucified** him,
and **with** him two **others**, **one** on either **side**,
with **Jesus between** them.
Pilate also had an **inscription** written and put on the **Cross**.
It read, "**Jesus** of **Nazareth**, the **King** of the **Jews**." ➤➤

robe and placing a crown of thorns on his head. As they strike him repeatedly and shout, "Hail, King of the Jews!" the irony of their actions weighs heavily on the scene. Jesus really is the king of the Jews.

In the fifth scene, once again Pilate goes *outside*. He attempts to demonstrate to the crowd that he views Jesus as innocent of any crime. As Jesus stands before the crowd, beaten and bloodied but still wearing the regalia of a bemocked king, Pilate announces, "Here is the man!" Is this yet another insult hurled at Jesus, so as to say, "Look at this puny and powerless crea-

ture!" or is Pilate unwittingly setting the stage for the crowd to reveal the real reason for wanting Jesus to be put to death? They explain, Jesus "claimed to be the Son of God."

In the sixth scene, Pilate goes *inside* to question Jesus once more. He asks Jesus, "Where are you from?" Jesus refuses to answer, but the Christian community for whom this Gospel was written can quickly say, "Jesus is from God. He is the Son of God!" Pilate persists, even threatening Jesus with his power to put someone to death, but Jesus responds, saying "You

would have no power over me unless it had been given you from above." But Pilate knows that he is quickly losing control of the situation, as the crowd's spokespeople charge him with acting against the emperor if he fails to put Jesus to death.

In the final scene, Pilate goes *outside* again, bringing Jesus before the crowd. Taking his place on the judgment seat, Pilate makes one last attempt to release Jesus as he declares, "Here is your King!" but again, here is the irony: Jesus really is the king of the Jews. The crowd screams for Jesus to be crucified. However, rather

These are Pilate's final, ominous words in this Passion. Pause slightly after proclaiming them.

Many of the people **read** this inscription,
because the **place** where Jesus was crucified was near the **city**;
and it was written in **Hebrew**, in **Latin**, and in **Greek**.
Then the **chief priests** of the Jews said to **Pilate**,
"Do not write, 'The **King** of the **Jews**,'
but, 'This man said, I **am** King of the Jews.'"
Pilate answered, "What I have **written** I have **written**."
When the **soldiers** had crucified **Jesus**,
they took his **clothes** and divided them into **four parts**,
one for each **soldier**.
They also took his **tunic**;
now the **tunic** was **seamless**, **woven** in one piece from the **top**.
So they said to one **another**,
"Let us not **tear** it,
but cast **lots** for it to see who will **get** it."
This was to fulfill what the **Scripture** says,
"They **divided** my clothes among themselves,
and for my **clothing** they cast **lots**."
And **that** is what the soldiers **did**.
Meanwhile, standing near the Cross of **Jesus** were his **mother**,
and his mother's **sister**, **Mary** the wife of **Clopas**,
and Mary **Magdalene**.
When Jesus saw his **mother**
and the disciple whom he **loved** standing **beside** her,
he said to his **mother**,
"**Woman**, **here** is your **son**."
Then he said to the **disciple**,
"**Here** is your **mother**."
And from **that hour** the **disciple** took her into his **own home**.
After **this**, when Jesus **knew** that all was now **finished**,
he said (in order to **fulfill** the **Scripture**),
"**I am thirsty**."
A **jar** full of **sour wine** was standing there.

Be sure to read the names of these women clearly.

Almost even stresses on the words in this line.

This expression "I am thirsty" concentrates the agony of the crucifixion. Say it simply and clearly.

than issue the order, Pilate turns Jesus over to the crowd for sentencing. The narrator notes that this scene takes place at noon on the preparation day for Passover. Why is this detail important? Jesus, the Lamb of God (John 1.29, 36), is sentenced to death at the same time that the Passover lambs were being sacrificed in the Temple not far away.

These seven scenes of Jesus' trial before Pilate are organized to create a chiasm. In a chiasm, the first scene of this story matches the last scene, the second matches the second-to-last scene and so on. Since this chiasm has an odd number of scenes, the main theme and focus of the chiasm can be found in scene four, in which the soldiers mock Jesus as a king, but Jesus is not a victim. He truly is the king of the Jews.

Turning now to the crucifixion scene, the Gospel writer continues this theme of Jesus as the victor. The narrator tells us that Pilate placed an inscription at the head of Jesus' cross. The chief priests of the Temple expressed their opposition, saying, "Do not write, 'The King of the Jews,' but, 'This man said, I am King of the Jews.'" The difference is significant, since the first is a proclama-

tion of faith, whereas the chief priests' attempted rewording is a statement of the charges made against Jesus. But Pilate insisted on his own wording, and the inscription was posted in three languages—Latin, Greek, and Hebrew—for the whole world to see. The Latin reads *Iesus Nazarenus Rex Iudaeorum*; this produces the acronym INRI, which we often see on crucifixes or in artistic renditions of the crucifixion.

Also noteworthy is the detail about Jesus' seamless garment, which is not found in the synoptic Gospels. Some have speculated that this is an allusion to Jesus'

The words "It is finished" culminate the drama of the Passion. Give each word even stress, pausing ever so slightly between them, almost: "It. Is. Finished."

So they put a **sponge** full of the wine on a branch of **hyssop**
and held it to his **mouth**.
When **Jesus** had received the wine, he said,
"**It is finished**."
Then he **bowed** his head and **gave up** his **spirit**.

[Here all kneel and pause for a short time.]

The details in the passage that concludes John's Passion are of interest because they speak to the awful economy of torture and execution (on the part of the Roman soldiers) as well as the requirements of the burial of a corpse according to Jewish custom. It's effective to read these words with scrutiny and with openness.

Since it was the **day** of **Preparation**,
the Jews did not want the bodies left on the **cross**
        during the **Sabbath**,
especially because **that Sabbath** was a day of great **solemnity**.
So they asked **Pilate** to have the **legs** of the crucified men **broken**
and the bodies **removed**.
Then the **soldiers** came and broke the **legs** of the first
        and of the other
who had been **crucified** with him.
But when they came to **Jesus**
and saw that he was already **dead**,
they did **not** break his **legs**.
Instead, one of the soldiers **pierced** his **side** with a **spear**,
and at **once blood** and **water** came out.
(**He who saw** this has testified so that **you also** may **believe**.
His **testimony** is true, and he **knows** that he tells the **truth**.)
These things **occurred** so that the **Scripture** might be **fulfilled**,
"None of his **bones** shall be **broken**."
And again another passage of Scripture says,
"They will **look** on the **one** whom they have **pierced**."
After **these things**, Joseph of **Arimathea**,
who was a **disciple** of Jesus,
though a **secret** one because of his **fear** of the **Jews**,
asked **Pilate** to let him **take away** the body of **Jesus**.
Pilate **gave** him **permission**;
so he **came** and removed his **body**. »

John is speaking directly to his audience in these words; through you, directly to the assembly.

---

priestly role, because the first-century Jewish historian Josephus writes about the high priest wearing a seamless garment under his outer robes. Others have suggested that it is a symbol of unity, a theme that Jesus addresses in his lengthy farewell discourse before his arrest. The Gospel writer tells us only that it was to fulfill Scripture, namely Psalm 22.18: "They divide my clothes among themselves, / and for my clothing they cast lots."

Another detail that is only in John's Gospel is the scene in which we see Mary Magdalene; Mary, the mother of Jesus; her sister; and the Beloved Disciple at the cross. Jesus asks his mother to take the Beloved Disciple as her son, and likewise, the Beloved Disciple is asked to take Mary as his mother. The narrator tells us that the Beloved Disciple took Mary into his home "from that hour." Although the Gospel writer is not explicit about this connection, one can surmise that this scene reflects the notion that the Johannine community understood the Beloved Disciple to be their leader and spiritual guide.

Finally, Jesus is offered wine from a sponge that is attached to a branch of hys-

sop. Hyssop is associated with the first Passover (Exodus 12.22–23), and the narrator also notes Jesus' unbroken legs, which alludes to the unblemished lambs offered in sacrifice. This is in keeping with John the Baptist's introduction of Jesus as the Lamb of God (John 1.29, 36). We also have the detail about the piercing of Jesus' side and the blood and water pouring out. This detail might simply indicate that Jesus was dead. However, in John's Gospel, water is associated with baptism and new life, and blood reminds us of Jesus' statements about drinking the cup that the Father gave him

Nicodemus, who had at **first come** to Jesus by **night**,
also came, bringing a mixture of **myrrh** and **aloes**,
weighing about a **hundredweight**.
They took the body of **Jesus**
and wrapped it with the **spices** in **linen cloths**,
according to the **burial custom** of the **Jews**.
Now there was a **garden** in the **place** where he was **crucified**,
and in the **garden** there was a new **tomb**
in which **no one** had ever been **buried**.
And **so**, because it was the Jewish day of **Preparation**,
and the **tomb** was **nearby**,
they laid Jesus there.

Read this concluding phrase, "they laid Jesus there," slowly.

to drink (John 18.11) and about consuming his blood in the "Bread of Life" discourse (John 6.53–56), which Johannine scholars associate with the Eucharist.

John's story of the burial of Jesus also has some unique details. We learn that Joseph of Arimathea was a disciple of Jesus, but a secret one for fear of being ostracized by his Jewish comrades for believing that Jesus was the Messiah. And then there is Nicodemus, whom we hear about earlier in John (see John 3.1–21) and who never seems to make the leap to full faith in Jesus. As they lay Jesus' body to rest, do they believe he will be raised from the dead? What is the purpose of this closing scene of the Passion narrative? What does it mean to you? C.C.

THE RESURRECTION OF THE LORD (EASTER VIGIL)

LECTIONARY #41

READING I Genesis 1.1—2.2

A reading from the book of Genesis.

[In the **beginning**
when God created the **heavens** and the **earth**,]
the **earth** was a **formless** void
and **darkness** covered the **face** of the **deep**,
while the **spirit** of God swept **over** the **face** of the **waters**.
Then God said,
"Let there be **light**";
and there was **light**.
And God saw that the light was **good**;
and God **separated** the **light** from the **darkness**.
God called the light "**Day**,"
and the darkness he called "**Night**."
And there was **evening** and there was **morning**, the **first** day.
And God said,
"Let there be a **dome** in the **midst** of the **waters**,
and let it **separate** the **waters** from the **waters**."
So God made the **dome**
and separated the waters that were **under** the dome
from the waters that were **above** the dome.
And it was **so**.
God called the dome "**Sky**."
And there was **evening** and there was **morning**,
        the **second** day. »

Genesis = JEN-uh-sihs

A reading of one of the most familiar passages in all of Scripture. Because the language in this reading is so grand, you will be tempted perhaps to dramatize your proclamation. No need: the language is so finely wrought, if you read at a measured pace, its glories will come through in your recitation.

The word "and" appears repeatedly in this reading. It's one of the main sources of its power. It functions almost like a verb. Let the word do the work for you as you proclaim.

Pause ever so slightly after "first day." You will repeat this slight pause five more times.

Pause slightly after "second day."

There are options for today's readings. Contact your parish staff to learn which readings will be used.

The vigil of Easter Sunday is a time for us to meditate on God's gracious deeds on behalf of humanity and the rest of the created order throughout the story of salvation from the beginning of time to the death and Resurrection of Jesus, who is the Christ. Seven readings are taken from the Old Testament books of the Law and the Prophets. Seven is a perfect number repre-senting fullness or wholeness. The eighth reading is taken from Paul's Letter to the Romans and the Gospel is taken from Matthew's story of the Resurrection of Jesus.

READING I The first reading, taken from the Book of Genesis, is not intended to be a science or history lesson about the creation of the world. Rather, it is a theological narrative about the nature of God and God's relationship to humans. In contrast to the origin stories of the Israelites' neighbours, which were often violent and chaotic, this story celebrates the sovereignty of God almighty, who creates everything by the power of his word and declares all God's creation as good. As the scene opens, we are told that the earth was uninhabitable—"a formless void" is the translation of the Hebrew *tohu wabohu*—covered in water and enveloped in darkness. Ancients might have thought of this as a frightening and chaotic scene, except for the next phrase, which some translate as "a mighty wind" but which also can be translated as "the spirit of God," hovering

Almost even stresses on the words in this line, with "good" receiving a little extra emphasis.

Pause slightly after "third day."

The passage that follows, describing the fourth day of creation, includes a series of oppositions to emphasize the separation of night from day. Stress the words that indicate these oppositions.

And God said,
"Let the **waters** under the **sky** be gathered together
        into **one place**,
and let the **dry land** appear."
And it was **so**.
God called the dry land "**Earth**,"
and the waters that were gathered together he called "**Seas**."
And God saw that it was **good**.
Then God said,
"Let the **earth** put **forth** vegetation:
plants yielding **seed**,
and **fruit** trees of every **kind** on earth
that bear fruit with the seed **in** it."
And it was **so**.
The **earth** brought **forth** vegetation:
plants yielding **seed** of every kind,
and **trees** of **every** kind bearing **fruit** with the seed **in** it.
And God saw that it was **good**.
And there was **evening** and there was **morning**, the **third** day.
And God said,
"Let there be **lights** in the **dome** of the **sky**
to separate the **day** from the **night**;
and let them be for **signs** and for **seasons**
and for **days** and **years**,
and let them be lights in the **dome** of the **sky**
to give **light** upon the **earth**."
And it was **so**.
God **made** the two great **lights**—
the **greater** light to rule the **day**
and the **lesser** light to rule the **night**—
and the **stars**.

over the water. Even from the very beginning, God is in charge!

The dramatic imagery of this opening sentence, along with its poetic wordplay, should alert us to the literary quality of the rest of the account. The narrator marks out each day of creation with the phrase "there was evening and there was morning," and each day follows the structure of "Then God said. . ." and "God saw that it was good." This is the power of God's word; it is a power only for good. Notice also that God names

the various elements of creation. In the ancient world, to name something was to have authority over it.

The first three days of creation are focused on separation: On the first day, God separated light from darkness. On the second day, God separated the waters above from the waters below. On the third day, God separated the waters below from the earth.

The latter three days of creation are focused on populating creation: On the

fourth day, God created the sun, moon, and stars to illuminate the earth. Notice the parallel with day one. On the fifth day, God populated the water below, the seas, with sea creatures, and the dome that held up the water above, the sky, with birds. These God blessed and told them to be fertile and multiply. Notice the parallel with day two. On the sixth day, God populated the earth with every kind of creature, wild and tame, big and small. Also on the sixth day, God created human beings in God's image

God set them in the **dome** of the **sky**
to give **light** upon the **earth**,
to rule over the **day** and over the **night**,
and to separate the **light** from the **darkness**.
And God saw that it was **good**.
And there was **evening** and there was **morning**, the **fourth** day.

Pause slightly after "fourth day."

And God said,
"Let the **waters** bring forth **swarms** of **living creatures**,
and let **birds** fly **above** the earth **across** the **dome** of the **sky**."
So God created the great **sea monsters**
and every living **creature** that **moves**, of every kind,
with which the **waters swarm**,
and every **winged bird** of every kind.
And God saw that it was **good**.
God blessed them, saying,
"Be **fruitful** and **multiply** and **fill** the waters in the **seas**,
and let **birds** multiply on the **earth**."
And there was **evening** and there was **morning**, the **fifth** day.

Pause slightly after "fifth day."

And God said,
"Let the **earth** bring **forth** living **creatures** of **every** kind:

Even pace through this line.

cattle and **creeping** things
and **wild animals** of the earth of every **kind**."
And it was **so**.
God made the **wild animals** of the **earth** of every kind,
and the cattle of every kind,
and everything that **creeps** upon the **ground** of every kind.
And God saw that it was **good**.

This passage repeats the word "kind" three times. These kinds anticipate the image of humankind shortly to come.

[Then God said,
"Let us make **man** in our image, **according** to our **likeness**;
and let them have **dominion** over the **fish** of the **sea**,
and over the **birds** of the **air**,
and over the **cattle**,
and over **all** the wild **animals** of the **earth**,
and over every **creeping** thing that **creeps** upon the **earth**." »

Don't treat the appearance of humankind at this point as a break, as something separate; rather, treat it as part of a continuum. The tone and pitch of your proclamation do not need to change here.

(Hebrew, *tselem*, also meaning "likeness or resemblance") and told them to be fruitful and multiply and have dominion over the rest of the created world. Notice the parallel with day three.

Thus, human beings are depicted as the crowning event of God's creation. But what does it mean to be created in God's likeness? Perhaps it lies in the phrase "have dominion over or master." This is God's role in creation—to bring everything out of chaos and make it ordered and fruitful—

and now this role is extended to humans to maintain into the future. Notice that God makes no allowance for killing, even for food. Then God rested on the seventh day, creating the foundation for the Jewish practice of Sabbath rest.

READING II The second reading in this series of seven Old Testament readings focuses on Abraham, often called the father of Judaism, and God's request that he sacrifice his only son.

Knowing some background to the story will help us to understand how significant it is for both Jews and Christians. The account of the interaction between God and Abraham, then called Abram, begins in Genesis 12, where he is told by this God whom he does not yet know to go to the land that God would show him. He is also told that God would make him a great nation and a blessing and that in him "all the families of the earth shall be blessed" (Genesis 12.2–3). This promise is reiterated

Pause slightly after "sixth day."

For these concluding lines of this reading, which describe the Sabbath, you can allow your proclamation to relax a little without overdoing it.

So God created **man** in his **image**,
in the **image** of **God** he created **him**;
male and **female** he created **them**.
God **blessed** them, and God **said** to them,
"Be **fruitful** and **multiply**, and **fill** the earth and **subdue** it;
and have **dominion** over the **fish** of the **sea**
and over the **birds** of the **air**
and over **every** living thing that **moves** upon the **earth**."
God said,
"**See**, I have given you every plant **yielding** seed
that is upon the face of all the **earth**,
and every **tree** with seed in its **fruit**;
you shall **have** them for **food**.
And to every **beast** of the earth, and to every **bird** of the air,
and to everything that **creeps** on the earth,
everything that has the **breath** of **life**,
I have given **every green plant** for food."
And it was **so**.
God saw **everything** that he had made,
and **indeed**, it was **very good**.
And there was **evening** and there was **morning**, the **sixth** day.]
Thus the **heavens** and the **earth** were **finished**,
and all their **multitude**.
And on the **seventh** day God **finished** the **work** that he had done,
and he **rested** on the seventh day from **all** the work
that he had **done**.

[Shorter: Genesis 1.1, 26–31a (see brackets)]

two more times, at least in part: first in Genesis 15.2–7 and again in Genesis 17.3–10, even as Abraham faces numerous challenges and setbacks along the way, many of his own making.

At the beginning of Genesis 22, the phrase "After these things" (Genesis 22.1a) is used to transition to the story we hear in this second reading. It is referring to the period of time after Abraham had settled a dispute over a well that he dug at Beer-sheba and after he made a covenant of mutual support with the Philistine King Abimelech (Genesis 21.25–32). This is the beginning of Abraham's claim on the Promised Land. The story that precedes this reading, the birth of Isaac, is the beginning of the fulfillment of the promise that Abraham would have "offspring as numerous as the stars of heaven and as the sand that is on the seashore." Therefore, as we enter this second reading, Abraham and Sarah are safe and secure and are settled in the land. But this is where the story gets very complicated, and we see a true threat to the fulfillment of the promise that God made to Abraham that he would have numerous descendants. To make matters worse, it was not Abraham who was interfering with the fulfillment of the promise, as he had done so many times before, but now it appeared that God himself is standing in the way!

The narrator of this story describes the sacrifice of Isaac as a test instigated by God, who tells Abraham to take his son,

For meditation and context:

RESPONSORIAL PSALM   Psalm 104.1–2a, 5–6, 10+12, 13–14, 24+35c (R.30)

R. Lord, send forth your Spirit, and renew the face of the earth.

Bless the Lord, O my soul.
O Lord my God, you are very great.
You are clothed with honour and majesty,
wrapped in light as with a garment.

You set the earth on its foundations,
so that it shall never be shaken.
You cover it with the deep as with a garment;
the waters stood above the mountains.

You make springs gush forth in the valleys;
they flow between the hills.
By the streams the birds of the air have
     their habitation;
they sing among the branches.

From your lofty abode you water
     the mountains;
the earth is satisfied with the fruit of
     your work.
You cause the grass to grow for the cattle,
and plants for people to use, to bring forth
     food from the earth.

O Lord, how manifold are your works!
In wisdom you have made them all;
the earth is full of your creatures.
Bless the Lord, O my soul.

Or:

For meditation and context:

RESPONSORIAL PSALM   Psalm 33.4–5, 6–7, 12–13, 20+22 (R.5b)

R. The earth is full of the steadfast love of the Lord.

The word of the Lord is upright,
and all his work is done in faithfulness.
He loves righteousness and justice;
the earth is full of the steadfast love of
     the Lord.

By the word of the Lord the heavens
     were made,
and all their host by the breath of his mouth.
He gathered the waters of the sea as in
     a bottle;
he put the deeps in storehouses.

Blessed is the nation whose God is the Lord,
the people whom he has chosen as
     his heritage.
The Lord looks down from heaven;
he sees all human beings.

Our soul waits for the Lord;
he is our help and shield.
Let your steadfast love, O Lord, be upon us,
even as we hope in you.

Isaac, and go to Moriah and sacrifice him on the mountain. Pay careful attention to how Abraham is portrayed in this scene. Clearly, he understands what God is asking him to do, and the narrator is keen to tell us about Abraham's affection for Isaac, but Abraham is unflinching in his resolve to obey God's word. Even as he and his son climb the mountain together and Isaac asks about the animal to be sacrificed, the only thing he says is "God himself will provide." Notice also the several times in which

Abraham is described as saying, "Here I am." This is a phrase indicating openness and availability to respond to the speaker. Having arrived at the mountain, Abraham goes so far as to bind Isaac, place him on the wood that was set upon the altar, and raise his knife to slaughter him, before God's Angel intervenes and tells him not to harm his son, adding, "Now I know that you fear God." The Hebrew word translated here as "fear" has the connotation of reverence or respect for God's authority. Abraham's

devotion to God is confirmed, and God's Angel appears again to renew the promises of land, descendants, and a blessing because Abraham obeyed God's command.

One of the ways that early Christians made sense of stories like this one was to see them as a *type* or pattern or example of something greater to come. Abraham's willingness and resolve to sacrifice his son, who is described as his only one and the one whom he loves, is a type of God who offers up his beloved Son, Jesus, for the

Genesis = JEN-uh-sihs
Moriah = moh-RĪ-uh

A reading of another very familiar story from Scripture. Its elements, including its conclusion, are universally known, something that in no way diminishes its power. A passage such as this one is already so inherently dramatic, your task is to proclaim as clearly as you can. Even though there are several exclamations in this passage, you will not need to raise your voice any more than you normally do when proclaiming.

First exclamation: No need to shout. There is an aura of otherworldly silence around Abraham's name.

The great literary critic Erich Auerbach describes this passage as "fraught with background," a delicious phrase. He means to point out that while the action is spare, the scene itself is filling with tension. When you proclaim, "On the third day," you are skipping over two full days of travelling.

Second exclamation: Don't shout.

"walked on together": This phrase is "fraught with background."

READING II   Genesis 22.1–18

A reading from the book of Genesis.

[God **tested Abraham**.
He said to him, "**Abraham**!"
And Abraham said, "**Here** I am."
God said,
"Take your **son**, your **only** son **Isaac**, whom you **love**,
and **go** to the land of **Moriah**,
and **offer** him there as a **burnt offering**
on one of the **mountains** that I shall **show** you."]
So Abraham rose **early** in the morning, **saddled** his **donkey**,
and took **two** of his **young** men **with** him, and his son **Isaac**;
he cut the **wood** for the burnt offering,
and set **out** and went to the **place** in the **distance**
that **God** had **shown** him.
On the third day **Abraham** looked up and saw the place
        far away.
Then Abraham **said** to his young men,
"Stay **here** with the **donkey**;
the **boy** and I will go over **there**;
we will **worship**, and then we will come **back** to you."
Abraham took the **wood** of the **burnt offering**
and **laid** it on his **son** Isaac,
and he himself carried the **fire** and the **knife**.
So the two of them walked on **together**.
Isaac said to his father **Abraham**, "**Father**!"
And Abraham said,
"Here I **am**, my son."
Isaac said, "The **fire** and the **wood** are here,
but **where** is the **lamb** for a burnt **offering**?"
Abraham said,
"God **himself** will provide the **lamb** for a **burnt offering**,
my son."
So the two of them **walked** on **together**.

salvation of humanity. Similarly, the ram caught in the thicket, a dense group of bushes or trees, is a type of Jesus on the wood of the cross. Finally, this story contains an etiology, which in this case is a story that explains why the place of sacrifice was called "Yahweh-yireh" in some translations. It means "It will be provided of God" or "God will see to it." This is what Abraham said to Isaac, when Isaac asked about the animal to be sacrificed. Some biblical scholars suggest that Moriah is not a historical place name but another reference to the idea that God will provide, because it contains the same Hebrew root *ra'ah*, which means "to provide." In other words, this is a story of total and steadfast trust in a God who provides.

READING III   Tonight's third reading is the story of Moses parting the Red Sea and the Israelites' exodus into the wilderness. This, too, is a story about trust in a God who provides. The chapters of Exodus that precede this story recount the ten plagues, an extended contest between the God of Abraham, Isaac, and Jacob and the Egyptian pharaoh, who thought himself to be a god on earth, but clearly was not, because he lost every single bout of the contest and ended up with nothing but a hardened heart (Exodus 7.8—11.10).

After celebrating what came to be known as the first Passover, and after the pharaoh finally let Moses and the Israelites

Take note of the details. Abraham is preparing an altar for sacrifice.

[When Abraham and Isaac **came** to the place
    that **God** had **shown** him,
Abraham built an **altar** there and laid the **wood** in order.
He **bound** his son Isaac,
and **laid** him on the altar, on **top** of the **wood**.
Then Abraham **reached out** his hand
and took the **knife** to **kill** his son.
But the Angel of the Lord **called** to him from **heaven**, and said,
"**Abraham**, **Abraham**!"
And he said, "**Here** I am."

Third exclamation: Don't shout.

The Angel said,
"Do **not** lay your **hand** on the **boy** or do **anything** to him;
for now I **know** that you **fear God**,
since you have not **withheld** your son, your **only son**, from me."
And Abraham looked **up** and saw a **ram**,
caught in a **thicket** by its **horns**.
Abraham **went** and took the **ram**
and offered it **up** as a **burnt offering** instead of his **son**.]
So Abraham called that place "**The Lord will provide**";
as it is said to this day,
"On the **mount** of the Lord it shall be **provided**."
[The **Angel** of the Lord called to Abraham a **second** time
    from heaven,

Though an Angel of God is relaying these words, it's God himself who speaks here. Set off the phrase "says the Lord" in such a way to make it clear that God is speaking.

and said, "By **myself** I have **sworn**, says the Lord:
Because you have **done** this,
and have **not withheld** your **son**, your **only** son,
I **will indeed bless** you,
and I will make your **offspring** as **numerous** as the **stars**
    of heaven
and as the **sand** that is on the **seashore**.
And your **offspring** shall **possess** the **gate** of their **enemies**,
and **by** your **offspring**
shall all the **nations** of the **earth** gain **blessing** for themselves,
because you have **obeyed** my voice."]

[Shorter: Genesis 22.1–2, 9–13, 15–18 (see brackets)]

leave Egypt, they wandered in the wilderness for a bit until God directed them toward the Red Sea by means of a column of cloud during the day and a column of fire at night, but they were fearful, because they could see the Egyptian armies coming after them. These terrified refugees complained to Moses about being brought out into the desert to die. What a disaster! But, to paraphrase God's word in today's vernacular, God tells Moses to stop whining and get his act together. This is where today's reading begins. Moses is told to ready the people to move out, and God tells Moses to lift his staff and raise his hand to divide the sea.

About now, people of a certain generation might be imagining Charlton Heston's portrayal of Moses parting the sea in the 1956 movie *The Ten Commandments*. Tall and handsome, almost god-like in appearance, he commands everyone's attention and makes the water do his bidding. But in the Book of Exodus, God is clearly the hero. Moses does what he is told, but God controls the sea and even the hearts of the pharaoh and his armies, eventually drowning every one of the Egyptians. Why? "And the Egyptians shall know that I am the Lord, when I have gained glory for myself over Pharaoh, his chariots, and his chariot drivers." In other words, this God of Abraham, Isaac, and Jacob establishes with full certainty that he is sovereign and that no forces of evil will defeat him. It also reveals that God is the faithful and steadfast benefactor

For meditation and context:

RESPONSORIAL PSALM   Psalm 16.5+8, 9–10, 11 (R.1)

R. Protect me, O God, for in you I take refuge.

The Lord is my chosen portion and my cup;
you hold my lot.
I keep the Lord always before me;
because he is at my right hand, I shall not
        be moved.

Therefore my heart is glad, and my
        soul rejoices;
my body also rests secure.
For you do not give me up to Sheol,
or let your faithful one see the Pit.

You show me the path of life.
In your presence there is fullness of joy;
in your right hand are pleasures
forevermore.

Exodus = EK-suh-duhs

Another very familiar story to many, in no small part because it is the centrepiece of a famous Hollywood film. This reading is full of action, with occasional instruction by God himself. But mostly action. And its drama will come through your proclamation if you allow the details of the action to be voiced. You don't need to dramatize any excitement in your proclamation. Let the words of the reading speak for themselves.

Here, God instructs Moses on how to perform a miraculous act. He's a little impatient, but he's also providing the details of a carefully considered plan.

The passage that follows includes many vivid details.

READING III   Exodus 14.15–31; 15.20, 1++

A reading from the book of Exodus.

The Lord said to Moses, "**Why** do you cry **out** to me?
Tell the **children of Israel** to go **forward**.
But **you**, lift up your **staff**,
and stretch out your **hand** over the **sea** and **divide** it,
that the **children of Israel** may go into the sea on **dry ground**.
Then I will **harden** the **hearts** of the **Egyptians**
so that they will go in **after** them;
and so I will **gain glory** for myself over **Pharaoh** and all
        his **army**,
his **chariots**, and his **chariot drivers**.
And the **Egyptians** shall know that I am the **Lord**,
when I have gained **glory** for myself over **Pharaoh**,
his **chariots**, and his **chariot drivers**."
The **Angel** of God who was going **before** the Israelite **army**
moved and went **behind** them;
and the pillar of cloud **moved** from in **front** of them
and took its place **behind** them.
It came **between** the army of **Egypt** and the army of **Israel**.

---

and protector of God's people. In concluding the story, the narrator expresses how the people now viewed God: that they revered God and trusted in the one who provides. After such a dramatic scene, an acknowledgement of God's graciousness is warranted and, thus, we hear how all the Israelites began to sing an ancient song of thanksgiving with these words: "I will sing to the Lord, for he has triumphed gloriously; / horse and rider he has thrown into the sea" (see the following Responsorial Psalm).

As you reflect on this reading and try to follow the plot of the story, you might find yourself a bit confused. For example, how exactly was the Egyptian army destroyed? Did they get scared when their chariots got stuck in the bottom of the sea and run away, or did the walls of water crash down on them, swamp their chariots, and drown the soldiers? We see these oddities in the text elsewhere in the Old Testament, but this example is worth noting. Biblical scholars have determined that bits and pieces of several versions of this

story have been woven together to create the version that we are reading today. While the final result might appear somewhat choppy, it speaks to how pivotal this event was in Israel's identity formation: that communities in different locations and time periods had their own versions of the story and that the final redactor decided that none of the details should be lost.

And so the **cloud** was there with the **darkness**,
and it **lit up** the **night**;
one did not come **near** the **other** all night.
Then **Moses** stretched out his **hand** over the **sea**.
The **Lord** drove the sea **back** by a **strong east wind** all night,
and **turned** the sea into **dry land**;
and the **waters** were **divided**.
The **children of Israel** went into the **sea** on **dry ground**,
the **waters** forming a wall for them on their **right**
        and on their **left**.

Again, vivid details. Give your voice to them.

The **Egyptians** pursued, and **went** into the sea **after** them,
all of Pharaoh's **horses**, **chariots**, and **chariot drivers**.
At the **morning watch**,
the **Lord** in the **pillar** of **fire** and **cloud**
looked **down** upon the Egyptian army,
and **threw** the Egyptian army into **panic**.
He **clogged** their chariot wheels so that they turned
        with **difficulty**.
The **Egyptians** said,
"Let us **flee** from the **children of Israel**,
for the **Lord** is fighting for them against **Egypt**."
Then the Lord said to Moses,

God speaks, once again instructing Moses on how to perform another miraculous act, one that parallels the earlier act.

"**Stretch** out your hand over the **sea**,
so that the **water** may come **back** upon the **Egyptians**,
upon their **chariots** and **chariot drivers**."
So Moses stretched **out** his hand over the **sea**,
and at dawn the **sea returned** to its normal **depth**.
As the Egyptians fled **before** it,
the Lord **tossed** the **Egyptians** into the **sea**. »

READING IV Our fourth reading is part of an oracle from Second Isaiah (chapters 40–55) that dates to the period of the Babylonian Exile, when Judea and the Jerusalem Temple were destroyed and the people taken away to exile in Babylon. In the verses preceding this passage, we hear the Prophet telling the people that they will be able to sing a joyous song, because Zion or Jerusalem will once again be filled with her children. Jerusalem is personified as God's wife through much of this oracle, but this is not to be taken literally. Rather, it is a metaphor for the quality of God's covenant love for the people of Israel.

The reading begins with an intimate and tender statement about God's relationship to Jerusalem: "Your Maker is your husband." Notice how God—metaphorically, the husband of Jerusalem—is given four additional attributes or titles: the Lord of hosts, Zion's redeemer, the Holy One of Israel, and God of the whole earth. The fact that this God chose battered and insignificant Israel to be his bride is amazing! Also remarkable is the hint of regret that the Prophet attributes to God, after seeing how grief-stricken Jerusalem and the exiled people of Judea are in their current state of abandonment. The Prophet asserts that God had a right to be angry with his chosen people, who, like an adulterous wife, broke covenant with God, but he also acknowledges that God's love is so steadfast and that the tenderness God feels for his beloved is so great that God quickly overcomes his

The **waters** returned
and covered the **chariots** and the **chariot drivers**,
the **entire army** of Pharaoh that had **followed** them into the **sea**;
not **one** of them **remained**.
But the **children of Israel** walked on **dry ground** through the **sea**,
the **waters** forming a **wall** for them on their **right**
      and on their **left**.
Thus the Lord saved **Israel** that day from the **Egyptians**;
and Israel saw the Egyptians **dead** on the **seashore**.
Israel saw the **great work** that the Lord **did**
      against the **Egyptians**.
So the people **feared** the Lord and **believed** in the Lord
and in his servant **Moses**.
The Prophet **Miriam**, Aaron's **sister**,
took a **tambourine** in her hand;
and **all** the **women** went out **after** her with **tambourines**
and with **dancing**.
Moses and the **children of Israel** sang this **song** to the **Lord**.

RESPONSORIAL PSALM   Exodus 15.1–2, 3–5, 6–7, 17–18 (R.1)

R. Let us sing to the Lord; he has covered himself in glory.

I will sing to the Lord, for he has
      triumphed gloriously;
horse and rider he has thrown into the sea.
The Lord is my strength and my might,
and he has become my salvation;
this is my God, and I will praise him,
my father's God, and I will exalt him.

The Lord is a warrior;
the Lord is his name.
Pharaoh's chariots and his army he cast
      into the sea;
his picked officers were sunk in the Red Sea.
The floods covered them;
they went down into the depths like a stone.

Your right hand, O Lord, glorious in power;
your right hand, O Lord, shattered
      the enemy.
In the greatness of your majesty
you overthrew your adversaries;
you sent out your fury,
it consumed them like stubble.

You brought your people in
and planted them
on the mountain of your own possession,
the place, O Lord, that you made your abode,
the sanctuary, O Lord, that your hands
      have established.
The Lord will reign forever and ever.

Don't overly dramatize the doom that comes to Pharaoh and his army—let the grim details speak for themselves.

"Great work": its manifestation defines this reading.

The reading leads into the Responsorial Psalm, which in this case is the continuation of the reading. The song is triumphant, but its contents are a little grim.

For meditation and context:

"overflowing wrath" and calls Israel back into covenant relationship in mercy and without rebuke.

The Prophet utilizes a second metaphor to describe God's change of heart toward Zion, namely, the story of Noah and the flood, which opens with the narrator telling us that God observed all of the evil in the world that was brought upon by humans, and "the LORD was sorry that he had made humankind on the earth, and it grieved him to his heart" (Genesis 6.6). This

is the reason given for the flood that was intended to wipe away all evil from the earth and return everything to the way it was before creation, without form or shape, and covered with water (Genesis 1.1). "But Noah found favour in the sight of the LORD" (Genesis 6.8). Thus, when the rains stopped and the waters receded, Noah and his family were permitted to leave the ark, along with the other creatures Noah had rescued. When God received Noah's offering, he made this vow that we hear about in this

passage from Isaiah: "I will never again curse the ground because of humankind, for the inclination of the human heart is evil from youth; nor will I ever again destroy every living creature as I have done" (Genesis 8.21). Thus, despite knowing what God knows about the failings of the human heart, he recreates the world as an act of love.

The final metaphor that the Prophet brings into this oracle of salvation is that of a beautifully adorned and securely walled

READING IV   Isaiah 54.5–14

A reading from the book of the Prophet Isaiah.

Thus says the **Lord**, the **God** of hosts.
Your **Maker** is your **husband**,
the **Lord** of **hosts** is his **name**;
the **Holy One of Israel** is your **Redeemer**,
the **God of the whole earth** he is called.
For the **Lord** has **called** you
like a **wife** forsaken and **grieved** in spirit,
like the wife of a man's **youth** when she is **cast off**,
says your God.
For a **brief moment** I **abandoned** you,
but with **great compassion** I will **gather** you.
In **overflowing wrath** for a moment
I **hid** my **face** from you,
but with **everlasting love** I will have **compassion** on you,
says the Lord, your **Redeemer**.
This is like the **days** of Noah to me:
Just as I **swore** that the waters of Noah
would **never again** go over the **earth**,
so I have **sworn** that I will not be **angry** with you
and will not **rebuke** you.
For the **mountains** may **depart**
and the **hills** be removed,
but my **steadfast love** shall not **depart** from you,
and my **covenant** of **peace** shall not be **removed**,
says the Lord, who has **compassion** on you.
O **afflicted** one, **storm**-tossed, and **not comforted**,
I am about to **set** your **stones** in **antimony**,
and **lay** your **foundations** with **sapphires**. »

Isaiah = ī-ZAY-uh

A reading in which the Prophet speaks on behalf of God to the people, seeking to intensify the intimacy between them.

The core of the reading is this simile comparing the people ("you") to a forsaken wife whom God, as the husband, wants back. The conflict described and the strife implied in this passage should be familiar to many in the assembly. Don't get too dramatic with your proclamation, but don't shy away from its implications.

God promises peace, despite previously turbulent times.

Many jewels. The names of jewels are appealing to say and hear.

antimony = AN-tih-moh-nee = a silvery metallic element

city, the new Jerusalem. The Prophet does not tell us the significance of the various jewels that adorn the city, its streets, and its gates, but we can say, at least, that they signify a place that is worthy of God's presence (see also Revelation 4.1–6 and 21.9–21). The learning that takes place in this city will be divinely inspired, and the city will be established in God's justice (Hebrew, *tsedaqah*, meaning "righteousness"). When applied to God, "justice" describes how God acts in keeping with God's nature as

goodness itself and as being in eternal covenant with God's people. Thus, Israel has no need to fear for its well-being.

READING V   Our fifth reading is the culmination of Second Isaiah, which began with chapter 40, and which contains a number of the themes that we find repeated here, such as the invitation to come and eat, the call to covenant relationship with God, the efficacy of God's word, and the new exodus, which appears in the

section immediately following this reading. Second Isaiah was written during the Babylonian Exile in the sixth century BC. Thus, many of its oracles are oracles of consolation.

This reading begins with a number of imperatives directed at the poor and needy, inviting them to attend God's banquet, which is a theme commonly used in the Bible's wisdom literature to describe God's desire to care for humanity. For example, the language is very similar to Proverbs

I will make your **pinnacles** of **rubies**,
your **gates** of jewels,
and all your **walls** of **precious** stones.
All your **children** shall be **taught** by the Lord,
and **great** shall be the **prosperity** of your **children**.
In **righteousness** you shall be **established**;
you shall be **far** from **oppression**, for you shall **not fear**;
and from **terror**, for it shall not come **near** you.

The peace God promises is like the jewels: enduring, precious, and consoling.

For meditation and context:

RESPONSORIAL PSALM   Psalm 30.1+3, 4–5, 10+11a+12b (R.1a)

R. I will extol you, Lord, for you have raised me up.

I will extol you, O Lord, for you have
    drawn me up,
and did not let my foes rejoice over me.
O Lord, you brought up my soul from Sheol,
restored me to life from among those
    gone down to the Pit.

Sing praises to the Lord, O you his
    faithful ones,
and give thanks to his holy name.
For his anger is but for a moment;
his favour is for a lifetime.
Weeping may linger for the night,
but joy comes with the morning.

Hear, O Lord, and be gracious to me!
O Lord, be my helper!
You have turned my mourning into dancing.
O Lord my God, I will give thanks to
    you forever.

READING V   Isaiah 55.1–11

A reading from the book of the Prophet Isaiah.

Thus says the **Lord**:
"**Everyone** who **thirsts**,
come to the **waters**;
and **you** that have no **money**,
come, buy and **eat**!
Come, buy **wine** and **milk**
without **money** and without **price**.
Why do you spend your **money** for that which is not **bread**,

Isaiah = ī-ZAY-uh

A reading in which God through the voice of the Prophet Isaiah promises forgiveness. The message of this reading is direct and should be relatable to many in your assembly.

"You that have no money": even in affluent parishes, there are people who have felt this pinch. God is speaking directly to these people.

9.1–5 and Sirach 24.18–24, in which Lady Wisdom invites those who wish to be wise to come to her banquet. Wisdom is not a deity separate from God but rather a power or attribute of God. Notice that there are no social or ethical restrictions on who can come to the banquet. One needs only to be thirsty for God and willing to listen to God's voice. Notice also that the covenant agreement made with David has now been extended to this wider audience: to be "a

witness to the peoples, a leader and commander for the peoples." This is an everlasting covenant, meaning that it extends backward and forward in time without end. Moreover, God's steadfast loyalty promised to David now encompasses all peoples. The "nations that you do not know, and nations that do not know you" is most likely the Persian empire under King Cyrus the Great (reigned 559–530 BC). He is the one who released the Judeans from their exile (see

Isaiah 45.1, 13–14). Here, it is generalized to emphasize Israel's leadership role in the world.

The second half of this reading issues a similar imperative to the people of Israel using a type of Hebrew poetry called synonymous parallelism, in which the second line of text repeats, but in different words, the content of the first line. The imperative is to "Seek the Lord . . . call upon him" to find mercy and forgiveness, which is followed

and your **labour** for that which does not **satisfy**?
Listen carefully to me, and **eat** what is good,
and **delight** yourselves in **rich food**.
Incline your **ear**, and **come** to me;
listen, so that you may **live**.
I will **make** with you an everlasting **covenant**,
my **steadfast**, sure **love** for **David**.
See, I **made** him a **witness** to the **peoples**,
a **leader** and commander for the **peoples**.
See, **you** shall **call** nations that you do **not know**,
and **nations** that do not **know** you shall **run** to you,
because of the **Lord** your **God**, the **Holy One of Israel**,
for he has **glorified** you.
Seek the **Lord** while he may be **found**,
call upon him while he is **near**;
let the **wicked** person forsake their **way**,
and the **unrighteous** person their **thoughts**;
let **that** person **return** to the Lord that he may have **mercy**
      on them,
and to our **God**, for he will abundantly **pardon**.
For my **thoughts** are not **your** thoughts,
nor are your ways **my** ways, says the Lord.
For as the **heavens** are **higher** than the **earth**,
so are **my** ways **higher** than your **ways**
and my **thoughts** than your **thoughts**.
For **as** the **rain** and the **snow** come **down** from **heaven**,
and do not **return** there until they have watered the earth,
making it **bring forth** and **sprout**,
giving **seed** to the **sower** and **bread** to the one who **eats**,
so shall my **word** be that goes **out** from my **mouth**;
it shall **not return** to me **empty**,
but it shall **accomplish** that which I **purpose**,
and **succeed** in the thing for which I **sent** it."

"Seek the Lord while he may be found": this command speaks to the hope inherent in this reading. We hope it's true, that God may be found, especially when we call him.

Forgiveness. This is the heart of this reading.

Even stresses on the words in this line.

purpose = per-POSE

by two arguments for why God's people should act on this command. The first argument is an assertion that God is utterly transcendent such that God's thoughts are not our thoughts, but yet God is so near to us as to be touched by our sinfulness and wants to heal us. The second argument is about the efficacy of God's word. It comes upon us like a gentle rain or unexpected snow to water the thirsty soil and make it produce fruit for those who have need.

God's word does not dissipate in the wind, but rather it accomplishes everything that God wants it to accomplish. We can count on this because God is ever faithful.

READING VI | The sixth reading of this Easter Vigil celebration is part of a longer poem in praise of personified Wisdom taken from the Book of Baruch. According to the first-century AD Jewish historian Josephus, Baruch was a scribe for the Prophet Jeremiah from the sixth century BC (see Josephus' *Antiquities of the Jews* 10.9.1). However, this book that bears his name is generally thought to be an edited collection of smaller works by various unknown authors written in the style of the Prophets and dating to the second century BC. After a brief introduction from the narrator of this book (Baruch 1.1–14), we find a confession of sin attributed to the exiles in Babylon and addressed to

For meditation and context:

RESPONSORIAL PSALM   Isaiah 12.2–3, 4bcd, 5–6 (R.3)

R. With joy you will draw water from the wells of salvation.

Surely God is my salvation;
I will trust, and will not be afraid,
for the Lord God is my strength and
   my might;
he has become my salvation.
With joy you will draw water
from the wells of salvation.

Give thanks to the Lord,
call on his name;
make known his deeds among the nations;
proclaim that his name is exalted.

Sing praises to the Lord,
for he has done gloriously;
let this be known in all the earth.
Shout aloud and sing for joy, O royal Zion,
for great in your midst
is the Holy One of Israel.

READING VI   Baruch 3.9–15, 32—4.4

A reading from the book of the Prophet Baruch.

Hear the **commandments** of life, O Israel;
give ear, and learn **wisdom**!
Why **is** it, O Israel,
why **is** it that you are in the **land** of your **enemies**,
that you are growing **old** in a foreign **country**,
that you are **defiled** with the **dead**,
that you are **counted** among those in **Hades**?
You have **forsaken** the fountain of **wisdom**.
If you had **walked** in the way of **God**,
you would be **living** in **peace** forever.
Learn where there is **wisdom**,
where there is **strength**,
where there is **understanding**,
so that you may at the **same time discern**
where there is length of **days**, and **life**,
where there is **light** for the eyes, and **peace**.
Who has found her **place**?
And **who** has entered her **storehouses**?
But the one who knows all things **knows** her,
he **found** her by his **understanding**.

Baruch = buh-ROOK

An exhortation on wisdom, personified in this reading in her ancient feminine principle. A powerful reminder.

The reading makes use of rhetorical questions. Use these questions—this first one stretches over several lines—to organize the pace of your proclamation.

Take note of the questions here.

"Her" refers to Wisdom, *Hokhmah* in Hebrew, *Sophia* in Greek, always personified in feminine form in the ancient imagination.

---

those who were left behind in Jerusalem and Judah (Baruch 1.15—2.10), in which they attribute their sorry situation to their refusal to listen to God and their failure to follow God's precepts (Baruch 1.18, 2.10). This confession is followed by a prayer to God that Israel might have a change of heart during the time of its exile and return to a life lived in obedience to God's law (Baruch 2.11—3.8).

This reading, a poem in praise of Wisdom, is addressed to Israel. It continues the theme of obedience to God's law. It begins with a call to heed the command-

ments of life and know prudence. The Greek *phronesis*, translated here as "wisdom," has a range of meanings, including intelligence, good judgment, and practical advice or action. Thus, wisdom is equated with the law. This invitation is followed by a rhetorical question, which could be restated like this: "How did you get into such a mess?" The poet's answer: "You have forsaken the fountain of wisdom!" If Jewish law is equated with wisdom, then the fount of wisdom is God. The exiles in Babylon were "defiled with the dead" insofar as they lived in the diaspora, among

Gentiles who were destined for death because they did not follow Jewish law. Had Israel not abandoned the fountain of wisdom, the nation would be experiencing long life, peace, and "light for the eyes" (perhaps meaning insight; ancients believed that people could see because of the light that dwelt within them).

The next section of this poem (see Baruch 3.15–23), which is not fully included in the lectionary reading, begins with another rhetorical question: "Who has found her place?" The answer is clear. No human can find wisdom through their own

The one who prepared the **earth** for all time
filled it with four-footed creatures;
the one who **sends forth** the light, and it **goes**;
he **called** it, and it **obeyed** him, **trembling**;
the **stars shone** in their watches, and were **glad**;
he **called** them, and they **said**, "**Here** we are!"
They **shone** with **gladness** for **him** who **made** them.
This is our **God**;
no **other** can be **compared** to him.
He **found** the whole way to **knowledge**,
and **gave** her to his servant **Jacob**
and to **Israel**, whom he **loved**.
Afterward she **appeared** on **earth**
and **lived** with humanity.
She is the **book** of the commandments of **God**,
the **law** that endures **forever**.
All who **hold** her **fast** will **live**,
and those who **forsake** her will **die**.
Turn, O Jacob, and **take** her;
walk toward the **shining** of her **light**.
Do not give your **glory** to another,
or your **advantages** to an alien **people**.
Happy are **we**, O Israel,
for we **know** what is **pleasing** to God.

Wisdom's divinity—the part she plays in God's creative imagination—is implied in this closing passage.

For meditation and context:

RESPONSORIAL PSALM   Psalm 19.7, 8, 9, 10 (R. Jn 6.68)

R. Lord, you have the words of eternal life.

The law of the Lord is perfect,
reviving the soul;
the decrees of the Lord are sure,
making wise the simple.

The precepts of the Lord are right,
rejoicing the heart;
the commandment of the Lord is clear,
enlightening the eyes.

The fear of the Lord is pure,
enduring forever;
the ordinances of the Lord are true
and righteous altogether.

More to be desired are they than gold,
even much fine gold;
sweeter also than honey,
and drippings of the honeycomb.

abilities. The poet notes that not even kings with great powers over the created world can find wisdom, nor can those who amass great wealth or scheme to acquire it. And later generations are no better off. Whatever else they achieve in their lifetimes, they have not discerned the path to wisdom or found her. The poet notes that even the ancient seats of human knowledge—Phoenicia (here called Canaan) and Edom (including Teman)—did not know wisdom. Likewise, the descendants of Hagar—the tribes that trace themselves back to Ishmael, son of Abraham—did not find wisdom.

Why can no human find wisdom? The poet expounds on this question next, beginning with a statement about vastness of God's dwelling and the scope of God's authority. Only the one who knows all things (i.e., God) knows wisdom, because "she is the book of the commandments of God" and "the law that endures forever." The poem concludes with an admonition to walk by wisdom's light and a somewhat veiled threat that God will give Israel's glory and privilege to another nation, if it refuses. Finally, at the end, there is a blessing! Although no one can secure wisdom on

their own, God is pleased to make her known to God's people through the giving of the law.

READING VII   The last in the series of seven readings for meditation on this Easter vigil comes from the Book of Ezekiel. Ezekiel was a Prophet of the sixth century bc who ministered to the exiled Judeans in Babylon. In this section of the Prophet's writing, Ezekiel uses the Babylonian Exile as the historical reference for his theology of God's plan of salvation. It is written in the form of an oracle delivered

Ezekiel = ee-ZEE-kee-uhl

A challenging reading. Challenging because the tone of this passage is largely wrathful and accusatory. The language in this reading is so charged, the wrath will come through. It consists almost entirely of the words of God spoken to Ezekiel

Here the tone is clear: the words *wrath*, *defiled*, and *profaned* set that tone.

God is so worked up, he begins quoting himself!

Note the shift into the future tense. The tone doesn't change significantly, but from here to the conclusion of the reading, God is speaking about the future.

READING VII   Ezekiel 36.16–17a, 18–28

A reading from the book of the Prophet Ezekiel.

The **word** of the Lord **came** to me:
Son of man, when the **house** of Israel lived on their own **soil**,
they **defiled** it with their **ways** and their **deeds**;
their **conduct** in my sight was **unclean**.
So I **poured out** my **wrath** upon them
for the **blood** that they had **shed** upon the **land**,
and for the **idols** with which they had **defiled** it.
I **scattered** them among the **nations**,
and they were **dispersed** through the **countries**;
in accordance with their **conduct** and their **deeds** I **judged** them.
But when they came to the **nations**,
wherever they **came**, they **profaned** my holy **name**,
in that it was **said** of them,
"**These** are the **people** of the **Lord**,
and yet they had to **go out of** his land."
But I had **concern** for my holy **name**,
which the **house** of Israel had **profaned**
among the **nations** to which they **came**.
Therefore say to the house of Israel,
Thus says the Lord God:
It is not for **your sake**, O house of Israel, that I am about to act,
but for the **sake** of my holy **name**,
which you have **profaned** among the **nations** to which you **came**.
I will **sanctify** my great **name**,
which has been **profaned** among the **nations**,
and which **you** have **profaned** among them;
and the **nations** shall know that **I** am the Lord,
says the Lord God,
when through **you** I display my **holiness** before their **eyes**.
I will **take** you from the **nations**,
and **gather** you from **all** the countries,
and **bring** you into your **own land**.

to Ezekiel, who is addressed as "son of man," meaning "a human being," most likely to contrast with the utter transcendence of God. God is the speaker.

The oracle opens with a condemnation of the house of Israel for defiling the land with their behaviours and actions that are contrary to the covenant God had made with them. God charges them with idol worship and offering sacrifices to idols, which, in the Prophet's mind, would be considered an extreme act of dishonour toward God. Therefore, God is justified in responding to their actions by scattering the people across the lands. Israel's dispersion (scattering) further dishonours God because the nations to which Israel was scattered question the power of a God who cannot maintain the people in their own land. Therefore, God decides to show his holiness by withdrawing the punishment on Israel and promising to regather Israel and bring them back to their own land. But God states clearly, "It is not for your sake, O house of Israel, that I am about to act, but for the sake of my holy name, which you have profaned among the nations to which you came."

Further, God says that he intends to perform a ritual cleansing for Israel in order to remove the impurities of their idolatry. From this point on, the vocabulary is highly covenantal, but this covenant is new and different. God says that he will give Israel a new heart and a new spirit. Ancient people understood the heart to be the seat of thinking and loving. The Prophet says that God will remove their hearts of stone and give them a fleshly or human heart. The new spirit that God will give is described further in the next oracle, the vision of the dry bones, where God's spirit or breath

God wants to cleanse the future of its impurities.

And give people a new heart.

I will **sprinkle** clean water **upon** you,
and you shall be **clean** from all your **uncleanness**,
and from **all** your idols I will **cleanse** you.
A new **heart** I will give you,
and a new spirit I will put **within** you;
and I will **remove** from your body the **heart** of **stone**
and **give** you a **heart** of **flesh**.
I will put my **spirit** within you,
and make you **follow** my statutes
and be **careful** to observe my **ordinances**.
Then you shall **live** in the land that I **gave** to your ancestors;

God's hope: this is his covenant.

and you shall be my **people**, and I will be your **God**.

For meditation and context:

RESPONSORIAL PSALM   Psalm 42.2, 4bcd; 43.3, 4 (R.42.1)

R. As a deer longs for flowing streams, my soul longs for you, O God.

My soul thirsts for God, for the living God.
When shall I come and behold the face
    of God?

I went with the throng,
and led them in procession to the
    house of God,
with glad shouts and songs of thanksgiving,
a multitude keeping festival.

O send out your light and your truth;
let them lead me;
let them bring me to your holy mountain
and to your dwelling.

Then I will go to the altar of God,
to God my exceeding joy;
and I will praise you with the harp,
O God, my God.

Or:

For meditation and context:

RESPONSORIAL PSALM   Psalm 51.10–11, 12–13, 16–17 (R.10)

R. Create in me a clean heart, O God.

Create in me a clean heart, O God,
and put a new and right spirit within me.
Do not cast me away from your presence,
and do not take your holy spirit from me.

Restore to me the joy of your salvation,
and sustain in me a willing spirit.
Then I will teach transgressors your ways,
and sinners will return to you.

For you have no delight in sacrifice;
if I were to give a burnt offering,
    you would not be pleased.
The sacrifice acceptable to God
is a broken spirit;
a broken and contrite heart, O God,
you will not despise.

gives new life to the community of Israel. Thus, God restores God's honour by returning the people to their land and reaffirming that he will be their God and they will be God's people. What can we say in response? God's faithfulness endures, even in spite of our sin.

EPISTLE The structure of the Easter Vigil liturgy is different from our normal Masses, as evidenced by the number of readings we have. Another unique element of it is that the Gloria is sung before the Epistle reading, rather than

before the first reading. This joyful hymn leads us into this reading from Paul's Letter to the Romans, where we are reminded of the meaning of Baptism, the foundation of our faith, and the reason for our joyful songs and celebrations. Hearing Paul's theology of baptism is extremely significant for this Easter feast because it grounds our participation in the sacrament of Baptism in the Paschal Mystery, the mystery of Jesus' death and Resurrection for our salvation. Prior to this reading, Paul had been writing about the efficacy of God's justification of sinful humanity. The word "justifica-

tion," also translated as "righteousness," has legal overtones and involves acquittal of the charges brought against humanity, where God is the judge and humanity is the accused. Be aware that acquittal in a court of law is not the same as being declared innocent. Humanity cannot earn justification. It is purely and in every way grace, that is, a gift from God. But, of course, someone will ask, "Should we continue in sin in order that grace may abound?" to which Paul says, "By no means!" (Romans 6.1–2).

Paul then likens a Christian's Baptism to being baptized into Christ's death. The

A short reading focused on baptism. Because the Easter Vigil often includes the baptism of the elect, you should imagine you are speaking directly to those about to be baptized.

Paul begins by making a connection between Baptism, life and death, and resurrection. These are the terms that define this passage from his Letter to the Romans.

EPISTLE   Romans 6.3–11

A reading from the Letter of Saint Paul to the Romans.

Brothers and **sisters**:
Do you **not know**
that **all** of us who have been **baptized** into Christ **Jesus**
were **baptized** into his **death**?
Therefore we have been **buried** with him by **baptism** into **death**,
so that, **just** as Christ was **raised** from the dead
by the **glory** of the Father,
so we **too** might walk in **newness** of life.
For if we have been **united** with him in a **death** like his,
we will certainly be **united** with him in a **resurrection** like his.
We know that our **old self** was **crucified** with him
so that the body of **sin** might be **destroyed**,
and we might no longer be **enslaved** to **sin**.
For whoever has **died** is **freed** from sin.
But if we have **died** with Christ,
we **believe** that we will also **live** with him.
We know that **Christ**, being **raised** from the **dead**,
will **never die again**;
death no longer has **dominion** over him.
The **death** he died, he **died** to **sin**, **once** for **all**;
but the **life** he lives, he **lives** to **God**.
So **you also** must consider yourselves **dead** to sin
and **alive** to God in Christ **Jesus**.

To die with Christ is also to live with him, to be resurrected with him. Baptism is like rebirth.

Paul re-emphasizes this point about resurrection in these concluding words.

Greek verb *baptizó* means "to dip, immerse, or submerge" into Christ, which means that the Christian is also buried with Christ. And because baptized Christians are immersed into Christ, they can also hope to be raised from the dead "as Christ was raised from the dead by the glory of the Father." This word "glory" is important. In the Exodus stories, miracles are attributed to God's glory (see Exodus 15.7, 11; 16.7, 10). Likewise, Paul attributes the miracle of Jesus' Resurrection to God's glory, which invests the risen Christ with life-giving power (Romans 1.4; see also 1 Corinthians 15.44).

But Paul has not forgotten that question about whether Christians can keep on sinning because God's grace abounds. Beginning with the notion that the Christian is united with Christ through baptism, he notes that it is our old self that dies when we die with Christ. Our old self, which was under the power of sin since the fall, is freed from its slavery to sin. Moreover, when Christ was raised from the dead, he would not die again because "death no longer has dominion over him." Rather, now Christ lives for God. So, too, those of us who are united with Christ in his death are

no longer under the power of sin. Our new selves are "alive to God in Christ Jesus."

GOSPEL   The Gospel reading for the vigil of the celebration of Christ's Resurrection is from Matthew's Gospel. The synoptic Gospels' versions of the empty tomb story share a basic plot, but they differ quite a bit in the details. In Matthew's version, two women come to the tomb after the Sabbath but before the dawn on the first day of the week, which would be a Sunday. The women are identified as Mary Magdalene and the other Mary,

For meditation and context:

RESPONSORIAL PSALM – SOLEMN ALLELUIA   Psalm 118.1–2, 16–17, 22–23

R. Alleluia! Alleluia! Alleluia!

O give thanks to the Lord, for he is good;
his steadfast love endures forever.
Let Israel say,
"His steadfast love endures forever."

"The right hand of the Lord is exalted;
the right hand of the Lord does valiantly."
I shall not die, but I shall live,
and recount the deeds of the Lord.

The stone that the builders rejected
has become the chief cornerstone.
This is the Lord's doing;
it is marvellous in our eyes.

GOSPEL   Matthew 28.1–10

A reading from the holy Gospel according to Matthew.

After the **Sabbath**,
as the **first day** of the **week** was **dawning**,
Mary Magdalene and the **other Mary** went to **see** the **tomb**.
And **suddenly** there was a **great earthquake**;
for an **Angel** of the **Lord**, **descending** from **heaven**,
came and **rolled back** the **stone** and **sat** on it.
His **appearance** was like **lightning**,
and his **clothing white** as **snow**.
For **fear** of him the **guards shook** and **became** like **dead men**.
But the **Angel** said to the **women**,
"**Do not** be **afraid**;
I **know** that you are **looking** for Jesus who was **crucified**.
He is **not** here;
for he has been **raised**, as he **said**.
Come, see the **place** where he **lay**.
Then go **quickly** and tell his **disciples**,
'He has been **raised** from the **dead**,
and **indeed** he is going **ahead** of you to **Galilee**;
there you will **see** him.' »

The tone of this reading, which comes from the last chapter of Matthew, is conclusive. Its focus is on vision. The witnesses of this vision are women. State their names clearly.

who is likely the woman mentioned in Matthew 27.55–56 and 61. These two are listed as witnesses to Jesus' death, the place of his burial, and also the empty tomb, but under Jewish law, women were not considered to be reliable witnesses. The fact that they are mentioned here in all three places is significant, but the Gospel writer does not explain. What do you think? What meaning might you attach to this detail?

A consistent feature of first-century burial sites in Israel was the large stone used to cover the entrance to the tomb so that animals could not enter the tomb and devour parts of the body or so that it would be harder for grave robbers to steal the body and any items of value that were placed in the tomb. Matthew's Gospel notes that the Jewish religious authorities requested and were granted permission to have Roman soldiers placed at the tomb to prevent Jesus' disciples from stealing his body and claiming that he had been raised from death (Matthew 27.62–66). The period of their assignment was three days, because after that time it was believed that resuscitation was not possible.

We are also told that the women "went to see the tomb," but there is no mention of them coming to wash and anoint the body, as women would have done in a normal burial. Was it because they expected that the soldiers would not have allowed it? Certainly, they would have known that they could not open the tomb by themselves. Were they simply coming to mourn in a ritual way, as in later Jewish traditions such as *shiva*?

Imagine the women's surprise and terror when they arrive at the tomb and see an Angel come down from heaven in a

The tone of this reading overall is characterized by this line: "with fear and great joy."

The reading concludes on a note of vision/seeing.

This is my **message** for **you**."
So they **left** the tomb **quickly** with **fear** and **great joy**,
and **ran** to tell his **disciples**.
Suddenly Jesus met them and **said**, "**Greetings!**"
And they **came** to him,
took **hold** of his **feet**, and **worshipped** him.
Then **Jesus said** to them,
"**Do not** be **afraid**;
go and tell my **brothers** to go to **Galilee**;
there they will **see** me."

mighty earthquake to remove the stone and sit on it. But we might also imagine their curiosity at witnessing such a sight! The earthquake, the Angel's lightning-like appearance, and his radiant clothing are all signs of divine presence. The soldiers, likewise, are terrified, so much so that they become "like dead men." But now the Angel's mission becomes clear. He comforts the women by telling them not to be afraid and showing them the empty tomb as proof of the Resurrection. He also sends them on a mission: "go quickly and tell his disciples, 'He has been raised from the dead, and indeed he is going ahead of you to Galilee; there you will see him.'" They leave immediately, we are told, "with fear and great joy."

But here is another interesting detail in Matthew's story of the empty tomb. Jesus' disciples are not present at the tomb—this is not their finest day—and they will need to wait to see Jesus until they receive the message from the women to meet him in Galilee. But Mary Magdalene and the other Mary, who have no status as witnesses to the Resurrection, will have a chance to greet the risen Jesus now! The women prostrate themselves and kiss Jesus' feet, indicating that they recognize his divinity but also that they are not just seeing a ghost. Jesus has a real, resurrected body and he is truly raised from the dead. Alleluia! C.C.

THE RESURRECTION OF THE LORD: EASTER SUNDAY

LECTIONARY #42

READING I Acts 10.34a, 37–43

A reading from the Acts of the Apostles.

Peter began to **speak**:
"You **know** the **message** that spread throughout **Judea**,
beginning in **Galilee** after the **baptism** that **John** announced:
how **God** anointed **Jesus** of **Nazareth**
with the Holy **Spirit** and with **power**;
how he went **about** doing **good**
and healing all who were **oppressed** by the **devil**,
for **God** was **with** him.
We are **witnesses** to all that he **did**
both in **Judea** and in **Jerusalem**.
They put him to **death** by hanging him on a **tree**;
but God **raised** him on the third day
and **allowed** him to appear,
not to all the people
but to **us** who were **chosen** by God as **witnesses**,
and who **ate** and drank with him **after**
he **rose** from the dead.
He **commanded** us to preach to the **people**
and to **testify** that he is the one **ordained** by God
as **judge** of the **living** and the **dead**.
All the **Prophets testify** about him
that everyone who **believes** in him
receives **forgiveness** of sins through his **name**."

Judea = joo-DEE-uh
In this reading, Peter is telling an assembled crowd the story of Jesus' life and the important lessons learned from his instructions.

Here is the first point: Jesus went about doing good.

Here is the second point: He was crucified.

Here is the third point: He was resurrected. Mostly even stresses on the words in this line.

Here is the fourth point: He commanded Peter and the other disciples to preach.

And finally, the fifth point: If you believe in Jesus, your sins will be forgiven. This point speaks directly to the assembly.

There are options for today's readings. Contact your parish staff to learn which readings will be used.

READING I Our first reading is a speech attributed to Peter on the occasion of his visit to the household of Cornelius, a Roman centurion who was posted in Caesarea and who was a generous supporter of the Jewish community there. One day, in a vision, Cornelius is told to call for Peter to come to his home. The next day, Peter receives a vision that he does not understand at first but that appears to cancel certain food prohibitions that kept Jews separate from Gentiles at meals and from entering each other's homes. Therefore, when Cornelius' men arrived at his home, Peter knew that he could go with them (see Acts 10.1–23).

When Peter enters Cornelius' home, he discovers that his entire household, along with relatives and friends, were gathered there. The first thing Peter does is acknowledge publicly that Jews were not supposed to associate with Gentiles, but that God showed him that no human person is to be considered "profane or unclean" (Acts 10.28). This is a radical break with tradition.

After Cornelius explains to Peter why he was summoned, Luke presents Peter as delivering a testimony to his audience about the central mystery of Christian faith: that Jesus was crucified, that God raised him, and that he appeared to the apostolic witnesses. Peter also testifies to Jesus' baptism by John, in which the Holy Spirit descends on Jesus in the form of a dove and a heavenly voice declares Christ's sonship, and to Jesus' ministry of good deeds, which shows that God was with him. Peter

For meditation and context:

RESPONSORIAL PSALM   Psalm 118.1–2, 16–17, 22–23 (R.24)

R. This is the day the Lord has made; let us rejoice and be glad.
or:
Alleluia! Alleluia! Alleluia!

O give thanks to the Lord, for he is good;
his steadfast love endures forever.
Let Israel say,
"His steadfast love endures forever."

"The right hand of the Lord is exalted;
the right hand of the Lord does valiantly."
I shall not die, but I shall live,
and recount the deeds of the Lord.

The stone that the builders rejected
has become the chief cornerstone.
This is the Lord's doing;
it is marvellous in our eyes.

READING II   Colossians 3.1–4

Colossians = kuh-LOSH-uhnz

An exhortatory reading, compressed in its length but powerful in its message. The focal word in this reading is "above."

A reading from the Letter of Saint Paul to the Colossians.

Brothers and **sisters**:
If **you** have been **raised** with **Christ**,
seek the things that are **above**,
where **Christ** is, seated at the **right hand** of God.
Set your **minds** on things that are **above**,
not on things that are on **earth**,
for you have **died**,
and your **life** is hidden with **Christ** in God.
When **Christ** who is your **life** is **revealed**,
then **you also** will be revealed with him in glory.

The syntax here is strange. Be sure to practise.

Or:

---

also notes that he and the other Apostles ate and drank with him after the Resurrection, presumably to say that Jesus' Resurrection was real. Finally, calling on the witness of the Prophets, Peter says, "everyone who believes in him receives forgiveness of sins through [Jesus'] name."

As if to testify to the quality of faith found among his Gentile audience, we hear in the verses following today's reading that the Holy Spirit comes down upon everyone gathered at Cornelius' home and they begin speaking in tongues. What else could Peter conclude from this glorious event but that

everyone should be baptized in Jesus' name (Acts 10.47–48)!

READING II   **Colossians.** Our second reading, from the Letter to the Colossians, marks the beginning of a section of paraenetic material that extends almost to the end of the letter. The word *paraenesis* means "advice, instruction, or counsel." Before going into specific and practical advice about how Christians ought to live their lives, the letter writer exhorts the community to "seek the things that are above," that is, to seek the resur-

rected Christ, who is "seated at the right hand of God." Most likely, this is the snippet of a credal statement based on Psalm 110.1. In this context, it affirms the summation of the Paschal Mystery: once crucified and buried, Jesus Christ was raised from the dead and now is exalted in glory.

But the key to fully understanding this text is a theology of baptism that appears to be similar to what Paul describes in Romans 6.1–11. Christian believers are baptized into Christ's death, and their old self is now dead to sin. This is what the author of the Letter to the Colossians means when

Corinthians = kohr-IN-thee-uhnz

A reading in which Paul makes use of an ingenious metaphor.

Yeast is Paul's metaphor for Christ's sacrifice. Just as there would be no feast without bread, so there is no spiritual life without leaven.

READING II 1 Corinthians 5.6b–8

A reading from the first Letter of Saint Paul to the Corinthians.

Do you not **know** that a little **yeast**
leavens the whole batch of **dough**?
Clean **out** the **old** yeast so that you may be a **new batch**,
as you really are **unleavened**.
For our **paschal lamb**, Christ, has been **sacrificed**.
Therefore, let us **celebrate** the **festival**,
not with the **old yeast**, the yeast of **malice** and **evil**,
but with the **unleavened** bread of **sincerity** and **truth**.

SEQUENCE

On this day the following sequence is sung.
It may also be used during the Easter Octave.

Christians, praise the paschal victim!
Offer thankful sacrifice!

Christ the Lamb has saved the sheep,
Christ the just one paid the price,
Reconciling sinners to the Father.

Death and life fought bitterly
For this wondrous victory;
The Lord of life who died reigns glorified!

"O Mary, come and say
what you saw at break of day."

"The empty tomb of my living Lord!
I saw Christ Jesus risen and adored!

"Bright Angels testified,
Shroud and grave clothes side by side!

"Yes, Christ my hope rose gloriously.
He goes before you into Galilee."

Share the Good News, sing joyfully:
His death is victory!
Lord Jesus, Victor King, show us mercy.

TO KEEP IN MIND

Sequences originated as extensions of the sung Alleluia before the proclamation of the Gospel, although they precede the Alleluia now. The Easter Sequence is an ancient liturgical hymn that praises Christ, the paschal victim, for his victory over death. Mary Magdalene recounts her experience at Christ's tomb, proclaiming, "Christ my hope rose gloriously."

he says, "for you have died." And just as, in Baptism, Christian believers are united with Christ in his death, they are united in his Resurrection and emerge to newness of life. This is what the author of this letter means at the beginning of this reading when he writes, "If you have been raised with Christ." But for now, Christian believers live in the "between times," after Jesus' salvific death and Resurrection but before he returns at the end time. This is what the letter writer means when he says, "your life is hidden with Christ in God."

1 Corinthians. Paul knew the Christian community at Corinth well, perhaps because he stayed with them for an extended period when he first established the community there (see Acts 18.1–11). When he writes to them a few years later, he takes them to task for their bad behaviour and for their boastful attitude.

The situation described in today's reading concerns a report that Paul received about a member of the Christian community who has been sleeping with his mother or stepmother. Of course, Paul is not

happy! He is equally displeased with the rest of the community, because they seem not to consider the harm that this does to everyone else.

To explain his position regarding what should happen to this man, Paul appeals to the metaphor of Passover preparation, for which every form of leavening must be removed from the house before Passover can begin, as a way of indicating one's commitment to a new beginning for a people no longer in slavery. Although the Christian community at Corinth consisted mostly of

GOSPEL   John 20.1–18++

A reading from the holy Gospel according to John.

Early on the **first day** of the week,
while it was still **dark**,
Mary Magdalene came to the **tomb**
and saw that the **stone** had been **removed** from the tomb.
So she **ran** and went to Simon **Peter** and the other **disciple**,
the one whom Jesus **loved**, and said to them,
"They have **taken** the Lord **out** of the **tomb**,
and we do not **know** where they have **laid** him."
Then **Peter** and the other **disciple** set out
and went toward the **tomb**.
The two were running **together**,
but the **other** disciple outran **Peter**
and **reached** the tomb **first**.
He bent **down** to look in
and saw the **linen wrappings** lying there,
but he did **not** go in.
Then Simon **Peter** came, following him, and went into the **tomb**.
He saw the linen **wrappings** lying there,
and the **cloth** that had been on Jesus' **head**,
not lying with the linen wrappings
but rolled **up** in a place by **itself**.

A reading relating a scene of enduring power and strangeness.

Magdalene = MAG-duh-len or MAG-duh-leen

The detail of the burial cloth is important. When Peter recognizes that the head cloth has been rolled up, he understands that the body of Jesus was not stolen (since thieves wouldn't take the time to fold up the linens).

Gentiles, they would have known about this practice, because many would have already been attending synagogue or because they were introduced to the message of Jesus Christ by Paul, who was himself a Jew. Paul likens this man to the yeast that must be removed from the house before Passover. Further, he likens the crucified Jesus to the Passover lamb that was sacrificed in the Temple on the day before Passover, and he wants the Corinthian community to be the new "unleavened bread of sincerity and truth."

GOSPEL Today's Gospel reading, taken from John's account of the empty tomb, is constructed as an intercalation, a story within a story. In the shorter reading, we first hear the outer story of Mary's arrival at the tomb, and then the text shifts to the inner story, focusing on Peter and the Beloved Disciple at the tomb. The long version of the reading includes the remainder of the outer story of this intercalation, refocusing on Mary, who stays at the tomb after the other disciples leave.

In the first half of the outer story, Mary of Magdala arrives at the tomb very early in the morning, when it is still dark outside, which would have been an extremely dangerous time for a woman to be out and about, especially alone. Only John's Gospel describes the tomb as being in a garden, perhaps an allusion to the paradisal garden of the first chapters of Genesis (John 19.41). But imagine her fright and alarm when she sees that the tomb is open. She immediately assumes the worst! Her fright is evidenced in the detail about her running to

Seeing is believing: belief dawns on them here.

Believing and understanding are two separate things. Understanding can take more time than belief.

Then the **other** disciple, who reached the tomb **first**,
    also went in,
and he **saw** and **believed**;
for as **yet** they did not **understand** the Scripture,
that he must **rise** from the **dead**.
Then the **disciples** returned to their **homes**.
But Mary **Magdalene** stood **weeping** outside the **tomb**.
As she **wept**, she bent over to **look** into the **tomb**;
and she saw two **Angels** in white,
    sitting where the body of **Jesus** had been **lying**,
one at the **head** and the other at the **feet**.
They said to her,
"**Woman**, why are you **weeping**?"
She said to them,
"They have **taken** away my **Lord**,
and I do not **know** where they have **laid** him."
When she had said this,
she turned around and saw Jesus **standing** there,
but she did not **know** that it was **Jesus**.
Jesus said to her,
"**Woman**, why are you **weeping**?
Whom are you **looking** for?"
Supposing him to be the **gardener**, she said to him,
"**Sir**, if you have **carried** him away,
tell me **where** you have **laid** him,
and I will **take** him away."
Jesus said to her, "**Mary**!"
She turned and **said** to him in Hebrew,
"**Rabbouni**!" which means **Teacher**. »

This is Jesus' first appearance after the Resurrection in the Gospel of John.

Don't overdo these exclamations. Say the name "Mary" emphatically but not with any excitement. Say "Rabbouni" in the same way.

find Peter and the Beloved Disciple to tell them the horrifying news that Jesus' body had been taken from the tomb and "we do not know where they have laid him." To whom does "we" refer? Is the Gospel writer using Mary to speak for the entire Johannine community? They must have struggled, at first, to understand the significance of Jesus' exaltation and return to the Father. Or perhaps there were other women with her, as in the other Gospel accounts.

The inner story begins with the narrator indicating that Peter and another disciple, presumably the Beloved Disciple, went to the tomb. They run to the tomb and the Beloved Disciple arrives first, but he waits for Peter to enter into the tomb. This is an indication of the community's acknowledgement of Peter's authority in church leadership. But, while the Beloved Disciple is waiting, he looks in and sees the burial cloths. Likewise, when Peter arrives, he looks in and sees the burial cloths as well

as the head covering, which is rolled up and set away from the other cloths. Why such detail? Some of the vocabulary in this story reminds us of the Lazarus story, in which Jesus orders Lazarus to come forth from his tomb (John 11.44). When he emerges, he is still bound by the burial cloths and the head covering, but Jesus' situation is different. How was Jesus freed from the burial cloths? Was this God's doing? And what does it mean that the head covering was rolled or folded up by itself? Certainly, we

Jesus said to her,
"Do not hold **on** to me,
because I have not yet **ascended** to the **Father**.
But go to my brothers and **say** to them,
'I am **ascending** to **my** Father and **your** Father,
to **my** God and **your** God.'"
Mary **Magdalene** went and **announced** to the disciples,
"I have **seen** the Lord,"
and she **told** them that he had **said** these things to **her**.

[Shorter: John 20.1–9 (see brackets)]

AFTERNOON GOSPEL   Luke 24.13–35

A reading from the holy Gospel according to Luke.

On the **first** day of the **week**,
two of the **disciples** were going to a **village** called **Emmaus**,
about eleven kilometres from Jerusalem,
and **talking** with each **other** about all these things
        that had **happened**.
While they were **talking** and **discussing**,
Jesus **himself** came **near** and went **with** them,
but their **eyes** were kept from **recognizing** him.
And he said to them,
"What are you **discussing** with each other
        while you walk **along**?"
They stood **still**, looking sad.
Then **one** of them, whose name was **Cleopas**, answered him,
"Are you the **only stranger** in Jerusalem
who does not **know** the things
that have taken **place there** in these days?"

A reading with great drama built into it. You can easily imagine it being filmed. The focus on the reading is recognition, specifically the time it takes Jesus' two disciples to recognize that he has been raised from the dead. The build-up of the narrative intensifies the excitement and joy of their recognition.

This phrase introduces the motif of recognition that guides the passage. Recognition is connected initially to seeing. You can note, even emphasize slightly, verbs and phrases that indicate seeing, for instance, "looking sad," a few lines below.

It's interesting that only one of these two disciples is named.

can assume that Jesus' body was not stolen. After all, grave robbers who are in such a hurry as to steal a body are not going to take the time to undress the corpse and neatly fold up the face covering!

In this inner story, we are also told that Peter saw the burial cloths, but the Beloved Disciple "saw *and believed*." The narrator adds, "for as yet they did not understand the Scripture, that he must rise from the dead." We do not know which Old Testament texts the Johannine author might have had in

mind, if any, but at a minimum, we can say that Jesus' Resurrection was part of God's plan from the start.

This passage in John continues with the note that the disciples went home. What a strange ending! This inner story reminds us that Mary Magdalene, Peter, and the Beloved Disciple are all persons of limited faith at this point. This is important for us to acknowledge because they are us. We, too, find ourselves to be of limited faith more often than we would like to admit.

In the second half of the outer story, we learn that Mary remained at the tomb weeping. When she looks inside, she sees two Angels to whom she expresses a second lament: "They have taken away my Lord, and I do not know where they have laid him." She turns and encounters someone whom she assumes to be the gardener, and she makes a third lament, but when he calls her by name, she recognizes him to be the risen Christ. Sent off by Jesus with a message to deliver to the disciples,

Note that "they" are speaking, both of them, even though it's one unified speech. The purpose of this description of Jesus' deeds and words is to build toward recognition.

He asked them, "**What** things?"
They replied, "The **things** about **Jesus** of Nazareth,
who was a **Prophet** mighty in **deed** and **word**
before **God** and all the **people**,
and how our **chief priests** and leaders **handed** him **over**
to be **condemned** to **death** and **crucified** him.
But we had **hoped** that he was the **one** to redeem Israel.
Yes, and **besides** all this,
it is now the **third day** since these things took **place**.
Moreover, some **women** of our group **astounded** us.
They were at the tomb **early** this morning,
and when they did not find his **body** there,
they came **back**
and **told** us that they had **indeed seen** a vision of **Angels**
who said that he was **alive**.

Note "a vision of Angels." Recognition and seeing are still urgently connected.

Some of those who were with us went to the **tomb**
and found it **just as** the women had **said**;
but they did **not** see him."
Then he said to them,
"**Oh**, how **foolish** you are,
and how **slow** of heart to believe
all that the Prophets have **declared**!
Was it not **necessary** that the Christ should **suffer** these things
and **then** enter into his **glory**?"
Then beginning with **Moses** and all the **Prophets**,
he **interpreted** to them
the things about **himself** in all the **Scriptures**.
As they came **near** the village to which they were **going**,
he walked **ahead** as if he were going **on**.
But they **urged** him **strongly**, saying,
"**Stay** with us, because it is **almost evening**
and the day is now nearly **over**." »

After spending time with Jesus (whom they still don't recognize), these disciples have a desire for further fellowship with him. They are beginning to sense something—different than seeing something.

she is able to proclaim, "I have seen the Lord," making her the first Apostle of the Resurrection. But seeing is believing in John's Gospel. Mary's journey to full faith is now complete!

AFTERNOON GOSPEL This Gospel reading is the story of the disciples on the road to Emmaus. As Luke tells the story, this encounter with the risen Christ takes place on the same day that Jesus was raised from the dead. We learn that two of Jesus' disciples are deep in conversation as they make their way to Emmaus, which is approximately 11 kilometres from Jerusalem. The narrator notes that they appear sad or downcast and, when the risen Jesus joins them on the road, they do not recognize him.

As Jesus engages these two disciples in conversation, he prompts them to tell the story of what happened to him in Jerusalem. Their response reads like a credal formula, but noticeably absent is any mention of the Resurrection. This is at odds with what they reveal next, that news of the Resurrection had been proclaimed to them earlier that day. Thus, the risen Jesus confronts them, calling them foolish and slow of heart and scolding them about not understanding the Scriptures that describe the necessity of Jesus' suffering and glorification. We do not know what texts Luke had in mind, but more important is the message that Jesus' death and Resurrection were all part of God's plan from the start.

In the breaking of the bread—the ritual that repeats the Passover when they last were in Jesus' company—there is recognition. Ritual and presence.

Confirmation of their recognition, repeated in the phrase "the breaking of the bread," the message of this reading.

So he went in to stay with them.
When he was at the **table** with them,
he took **bread**, **blessed** and **broke** it,
and **gave** it to them.
Then their eyes were **opened**, and they **recognized** him;
and he **vanished** from their **sight**.
They **said** to each other,
"Were not our **hearts** burning **within** us
while he was **talking** to us on the **road**,
while he was opening the **Scriptures** to us?"
That **same** hour they got **up** and **returned** to Jerusalem;
and they **found** the **eleven** and their companions
    gathered together.
These were saying,
"The **Lord** has risen **indeed**, and he has **appeared** to Simon!"
Then **they** told what had happened on the **road**,
and how he had been made **known** to them
in the **breaking** of the **bread**.

The last scene in this story explains how and why the eyes and hearts of these two disciples were finally opened. Having arrived at Emmaus, they invite Jesus to stay with them. At their evening meal, Jesus blessed, broke, and shared the bread in much the same way he did at his last meal before his death. They remembered and were able to recognize Jesus for who he was. They also remembered how they felt when he was teaching them on their journey and how their hearts were set afire.

Finally, then, in the breaking of the bread, they complete their journey from unbelief to full faith. Certainly, this is cause for great joy. C.C.

SECOND SUNDAY OF EASTER (OR OF DIVINE MERCY)

LECTIONARY #43

READING I   Acts 2.42–47

A reading from the Acts of the Apostles.

They **devoted themselves** to the **Apostles' teaching**
    and **fellowship**,
to the **breaking** of **bread** and the **prayers**.
Awe came upon **everyone**,
because **many wonders** and **signs** were being **done**
    by the **Apostles**.
All who **believed** were **together** and had **all things** in **common**;
they would **sell** their **possessions** and **goods**
and **distribute** the **proceeds** to **all**, as **any** had **need**.
Day by **day**, as they spent **much time together** in the **temple**,
they **broke bread** in various **houses**
and **ate** their **food** with **glad** and generous **hearts**,
praising **God** and having the **goodwill** of **all** the **people**.
And **day** by **day** the **Lord added** to their **number**
those who were being **saved**.

The tone of this reading, from early in Acts, is one of awe at the vocation of the Apostles, as well as purpose, as the work of that vocation reveals itself.

Slight pause between "time" and "together."

Slight pause between "Lord" and "added."

READING I In today's first reading, from Acts of the Apostles, Luke describes his vision for the life of the early Church community, which he places immediately after Peter's speech to the Jews who had come to Jerusalem from many parts of the world for the feast of Pentecost and the subsequent baptism of some three thousand people that day (Acts 2.14–41). It will be followed by a story in which Peter heals a crippled man who used to beg at the Beautiful Gate of the Temple (Acts 3.1–10), perhaps intended as an example of the "wonders and signs [that] were being done by the Apostles."

The defining elements of this ideal Christian community are that they hold fast to the teachings of the Apostles and to the common life of Christian fellowship and that they share in the breaking of the bread (i.e., Eucharist) and the prayers. The Greek word translated here as "fellowship" is *koinonia*, meaning "partnership or communion." Although this is the only place it appears in Acts, Paul uses *koinonia* multiple times in his letters to refer to the notion of church. Further, we are told that they were together in one place and that they shared everything in common (Greek, *koinos*) and distributed things to those who had a need. What might it look like today for our parishes and families to be inspired by this life of common care, fellowship, and faith?

READING II Biblical scholars have wrestled with several questions related to the First Letter of Peter, including authorship and date of composition. Because the document contains hints that

For meditation and context:

RESPONSORIAL PSALM   Psalm 118.2–4, 13–15, 22–24 (R.1)

R. Give thanks to the Lord, for he is good; his steadfast love endures forever.
or:
Alleluia!

Let Israel say,
"His steadfast love endures forever."
Let the house of Aaron say,
"His steadfast love endures forever."
Let those who fear the Lord say,
"His steadfast love endures forever."

I was pushed hard, so that I was falling,
but the Lord helped me.
The Lord is my strength and my might;
he has become my salvation.
There are glad songs of victory
in the tents of the righteous.

The stone that the builders rejected
has become the chief cornerstone.
This is the Lord's doing;
it is marvellous in our eyes.
This is the day that the Lord has made;
let us rejoice and be glad in it.

READING II   1 Peter 1.3–9

A reading from the first Letter of Saint Peter.

Blessed be the **God** and **Father** of our **Lord** Jesus **Christ**!
By his **great mercy** he has **given** us a **new birth** into a **living hope**
through the **resurrection** of **Jesus Christ** from the **dead**:
a **birth** into an **inheritance**
that is **imperishable**, **undefiled**, and **unfading**,
kept in **heaven** for **you**,
who are being **protected** by the **power** of **God** through **faith**
for a **salvation ready** to be **revealed** in the **last time**.
In **this** you **rejoice**,
even if **now** for a **little while**
you have had to **suffer** various **trials**,
so that the **genuineness** of your **faith**
—being more **precious** than **gold** that,
though **perishable**, is **tested** by **fire**—
may be **found** to **result** in **praise** and **glory** and **honour**
when **Jesus Christ** is **revealed**.

Blessed = BLES-uhd

This reading begins a series of readings during Easter Time from the First Letter of St. Peter, the tone of which is thoughtful, joyful, hopeful, and gentle.

Slight pause between "salvation" and "ready."

Faith is Peter's watchword. Give it a little added emphasis here and at the end of the reading.

---

it was written after Peter's martyrdom, perhaps between AD 70 and 90, most biblical scholars believe that it is a pseudonymous work intended to preserve Peter's memory and extend his influence into the next generation of Christians. Additionally, biblical scholars have entertained questions about whether this document is a letter or some other literary genre. It has an opening and closing like a letter, but, instead of a thanksgiving, it has a blessing. The rest of the document reads more like a homily or an exhortation on baptism and Christian living.

Today's reading begins with the words "Blessed be the God," which is similar to other blessings that we find in Jewish prayers (e.g., Genesis 9.26; Psalms 66.20; 68.19; 72.18), and it goes on to describe how the recipients of this document are God's chosen ones. By the great mercy of God, they are begotten again to a life of hope in and through Jesus' Resurrection. To what else are they born anew? To an imperishable inheritance that is reserved in heaven for those who have been kept secure by God's power and the gift of faith. And for

what end? For the salvation that will be revealed at the end time. But we are not yet in the end time. The author tells his readers that they will have to endure suffering in order to test the genuineness of their faith. The imagery is that of the refiner's fire. One of the ways that Scripture explains suffering is to say that God is like the refiner who heats metal to separate gold from the impurities in order to create a more beautiful piece of handiwork (e.g., Malachi 3.2–4). Thus, suffering is not punishment, but rather it is purifying and educative in

Although you have not **seen** him, you **love** him;
and even though you do not **see** him **now**, you **believe** in him
and **rejoice** with an **indescribable** and **glorious** joy,
for you are **receiving** the **outcome** of your **faith**,
the **salvation** of your **souls**.

GOSPEL   John 20.19–31

A reading from the holy Gospel according to John.

It was **evening** on the day Jesus **rose** from the dead,
the **first** day of the week,
and the **doors** of the house where the **disciples** had met
were **locked** for fear of the **Jews**.
Jesus came and stood **among** them and said,
"**Peace** be with you."
After he **said** this, he **showed** them his hands and his **side**.
Then the disciples **rejoiced** when they saw the **Lord**.
Jesus said to them again,
"**Peace** be with you.
As the **Father** has sent me, so **I** send **you**."
When he had **said** this, he **breathed** on them and **said** to them,
"**Receive** the Holy Spirit.
If you **forgive** the sins of **any**, they are **forgiven** them;
if you **retain** the sins of any, they are **retained**."
But **Thomas**, who was called the **Twin**, one of the **twelve**,
was not **with** them when Jesus **came**.
So the other disciples told him,
"We have **seen** the Lord." »

A passage containing a great deal of inherent and relatable mystery. Thomas not only stands for the person who needs to see in order to believe; he is also a stand-in for the reluctant believer or for anyone struggling with belief, giving his recognition of Jesus and his expression of faith even greater resonance.

Jesus announces his presence with the word "peace" in this passage. The word is focal.

Repetition of "peace."

order to prepare the sufferer for a more beautiful reality, in this case, the salvation of their souls.

GOSPEL   Today's Gospel is taken from the post-Resurrection story in the Gospel of John. Mary Magdalene, who encountered the risen Jesus in the garden tomb in Jerusalem, is sent to tell the disciples that Jesus has been raised from the dead. She does so, beginning with the words "I have seen the Lord" (John 20.18). In John's Gospel, seeing is closely connected to belief or full faith in Jesus.

As this reading opens, we find that Jesus' disciples are in hiding "for fear of the Jews." Since these disciples are also Jews, we should not interpret statements like this one in John's Gospel as encouraging fear or hatred of Jewish people. Instead, most Johannine scholars suggest that the author is writing out of a context in which Jewish Jesus followers, including the author of this Gospel, are being persecuted by their fellow Jews over the idea that Jesus was the long-awaited Messiah. In most cases, "the Jews" is used interchangeably with references to the religious authorities in Jerusalem, so we can safely assume that they are the target of the author's ire.

The first part of this scene bears some similarities to Luke 24.36–40, in which the risen Jesus appears suddenly and displays his hands and feet to the disciples to allay their fears and show that he is truly alive. However, John's version of the story includes a greeting, "Peace be with you," along with a conferral of the Holy Spirit for

Thomas' expressions of doubt in this passage should be treated with care.

But he said to them,
"Unless I see the **mark** of the nails in his **hands**,
and put my **finger** in the mark of the nails
and my **hand** in his side,
I will **not** believe."
After **eight days** his disciples were **again** in the house,
and **Thomas** was with them.
Although the doors were **shut**,
Jesus came and stood **among** them and said,

Another repetition of "peace."

"**Peace** be with you."
Then he said to Thomas,

Jesus' words to Thomas are spoken with gentleness.

"Put your finger **here** and see my **hands**.
Reach out your **hand** and put it in my **side**.
Do not **doubt** but **believe**."
Thomas answered him,

Thomas' recognition is joyful—its expression conveys the joy. No need to overemphasize it.

"My **Lord** and my **God**!"
Jesus said to him,
"Have you **believed** because you have **seen** me?
Blessed are those who **have not seen**
and yet have **come** to **believe**."

The conclusion of this Gospel reading speaks directly to the assembly, using the second-person pronoun. Even though the word isn't rhythmically emphasized, it is thematically focal.

Now Jesus did many other signs in the presence of his **disciples**,
which are not **written** in this **book**.
But these are **written** so that you may come to **believe**
that **Jesus** is the **Christ**, the Son of **God**,
and that through **believing** you may have **life** in his **name**.

the forgiveness of sin. The greeting of peace is a reminder of Jesus' words to the disciples during the farewell discourse, when he says "Peace I leave with you; my peace I give to you. . . . Do not let your hearts be troubled" (John 14.27). The conferral of the Holy Spirit here, when Jesus breathes upon the disciples, should bring to mind the second creation story of Genesis where God creates a man, Adam, and breathes into him the breath of life (Genesis 2.7). The disciples are made "new" insofar as they have a new mission, which is to continue the work that

God had given Jesus to do—to be the light that casts out darkness (John 8.12).

The second part of this scene is about the Apostle Thomas. It is a reminder that not all of us come to faith in the same way and at the same time. The narrator of the story provides no new setting, suggesting that the disciples are still in hiding on this first day of the week, when Thomas arrives. When the disciples tell him, "We have seen the Lord," he adamantly refuses to believe. But when the risen Jesus appears again after eight days to respond to Thomas'

demand to see the risen Jesus' wounds, Thomas makes a profound expression of faith: "My Lord and my God." The blessing directed toward those who have not seen but believe is intended for the Johannine community and by extension to us. Such is the mercy of God! C.C.

THIRD SUNDAY OF EASTER

LECTIONARY #46

READING I Acts 2.14, 22b–28

A reading from the Acts of the Apostles.

When the **day** of **Pentecost** had **come**,
Peter, **standing** with the **eleven**,
raised his **voice** and **addressed** the **crowd**,
"**Men** of **Judea** and **all** who **live** in **Jerusalem**,
let **this** be **known** to **you**, and **listen** to **what** I **say**.
Jesus of **Nazareth**,
a **man attested** to you by **God** with **deeds** of **power**, **wonders**,
        and **signs**
that **God did** through **him among** you, as **you yourselves know**—
this **man**, handed over to **you**
according to the **definite plan** and **foreknowledge** of **God**,
you **crucified** and **killed** by the **hands** of **those outside** the **law**.
But **God** raised him **up**, having **freed** him from **death**,
because it was **impossible** for him to be **held** in its power.
For **David** says **concerning** him,
'I **saw** the Lord **always before** me,
for he is at my **right hand** so that I will **not** be **shaken**;
therefore my **heart** was glad, and my **tongue rejoiced**;
moreover my **flesh** will **live** in **hope**.
For you will **not** abandon my **soul** to **Hades**,
or let your **Holy** One **experience corruption**.
You have made **known** to me the **ways** of **life**;
you will make me **full** of **gladness** with your **presence**.'"

This reading consists of a rich and spirited proclamation by Peter to his fellow Apostles. It's filled with his enthusiasm for the meaning of the work they are beginning to do.

In quoting from King David, Peter lets David speak for himself and, therefore, for us.

READING I Our first reading for this third Sunday of Easter is part of a much longer speech attributed to Peter in the Acts of the Apostles. The setting is Jerusalem on the Jewish feast of Pentecost, also known as *Shavuot*, which occurs fifty days after the second day of Passover. Originally, this was a harvest festival, but by the first century, it included a commemoration of the giving of the Law on Sinai. Pentecost was one of three pilgrimage feasts in early Judaism, the other two being Passover and Tabernacles.

Luke, the author of the Acts of the Apostles, notes that the city was filled with "devout Jews from every nation" (Acts 2.5) and, when they heard the noise of the descent of the Holy Spirit upon Jesus' disciples, they all gathered round, wanting to know what was going on. The wind and fire from heaven certainly would have attracted attention, but even more confusing was the fact that members of the crowd were able to understand the disciples in their own tongue. But others in the crowd mocked them, saying that they were drunk.

Therefore, in the first part of his speech, Peter is presented as defending his companions, arguing that they are not drunk at this early hour of the day. Rather, he explains that their condition should be understood in terms of an oracle of the Prophet Joel, which he quotes somewhat differently: "I will pour out my Spirit; and they shall prophesy. And I will show portents in the heaven above and signs on the earth below. . . . Then everyone who calls on the name of the Lord shall be saved" (Acts 2.18–19, 21; see Joel 3.1–5).

For meditation and context:

RESPONSORIAL PSALM   Psalm 16.1–2+5, 7–8, 9–10, 11 (R.11)

R. Lord, you will show me the path of life.
or:
Alleluia!

Protect me, O God, for in you I take refuge.
I say to the Lord, "You are my Lord;
I have no good apart from you."
The Lord is my chosen portion and my cup;
    you hold my lot.

I bless the Lord who gives me counsel;
in the night also my heart instructs me.
I keep the Lord always before me;
because he is at my right hand, I shall not
    be moved.

Therefore my heart is glad, and my
    soul rejoices;
my body also rests secure.
For you do not give me up to Sheol,
or let your faithful one see the Pit.

You show me the path of life.
In your presence there is fullness of joy;
in your right hand are pleasures forevermore.

READING II   1 Peter 1.17–21

A reading from the first Letter of Saint Peter.

Beloved:
If you **invoke** as **Father**
the **one** who judges **each person impartially**
according to **each one's deeds**,
live in **reverent** fear during the **time** of your **exile**.
You **know** that you were **ransomed**
from the **futile ways inherited** from your **ancestors**,
not with **perishable things** like **silver** or **gold**,
but with the **precious blood** of **Christ**,
like that of a **lamb** without **defect** or **blemish**.
Christ was **destined** before the **foundation** of the **world**,
but was **revealed** at the **end** of the **ages** for your **sake**.
Through him you have **come** to **trust** in **God**,
who **raised** him from the **dead** and **gave** him **glory**,
so that your **faith** and **hope** are **set** on **God**.

"Reverent fear": These are the focal words in this passage. Reverence is foremost a form of care; Peter wants to endow the recipients of his letter with care.

Slight pause between "ways" and "inherited."

Note the rhythm that concludes this reading, where a stressed element near the beginning of the phrase leads to stressed elements toward the end of the phrase.

TO KEEP IN MIND
Pause to break up separate thoughts, set apart significant statements, or indicate major shifts. Never pause in the middle of a thought. Your primary guide for pauses is punctuation.

But today's reading focuses on the second part of Peter's speech. It begins with one of several kerygmatic statements, that is, brief initial proclamations of the good news about Jesus Christ, that are found throughout Acts of the Apostles (e.g., Acts 3.12–26; 4.8–12; 5.29–32; 10.34–43; 13.16–41). They often begin with a statement about Jesus' words and deeds followed by a proclamation of his death and Resurrection. The kerygmatic statements in Acts of the Apostles are typically directed toward Jewish audiences, and they often include an exhortation to forgiveness of sin. They have a somewhat accusatory tone, but the primary thing to notice is that the events described in this kerygmatic statement amount to a declaration that everything is under the power of God and in keeping with God's plan of salvation.

In the closing sections of this speech, Luke focuses on David, because he believed him to be the author of the Psalms and of this psalm in particular. However, today we would attribute a much more complex history of composition to the Psalms. Luke identifies David as a Prophet who spoke in Jesus' name, when he composed Psalm 16.8–10, and he sees these verses as testimony to Jesus' Resurrection, in fulfillment of a promise made to David that God would make one of his descendants the king of the Jewish people to reign forever (see 2 Samuel 7.12–17). Thus, Peter also quotes Psalm 110.1 to say that Jesus, who was crucified, is this Messiah-king, who now sits exalted on God's throne.

A reading with great drama built into it. You can easily imagine it being filmed. The focus on the reading is recognition, specifically the time it takes Jesus' two disciples to recognize that he has been raised from the dead. The build-up of the narrative intensifies the excitement and joy of their recognition.

This phrase introduces the motif of recognition that guides the passage. Recognition is connected initially to seeing. You can note, even emphasize slightly, verbs and phrases that indicate seeing, for instance, "looking sad," a few lines below.

It's interesting that only one of these two disciples is named.

Note that "they" are speaking, both of them, even though it's one unified speech. The purpose of this description of Jesus' deeds and words is to build toward recognition.

GOSPEL   Luke 24.13–35

A reading from the holy Gospel according to Luke.

On the **first** day of the **week**,
two of the **disciples** were going to a **village** called **Emmaus**,
about eleven kilometres from Jerusalem,
and **talking** with each **other** about all these things
    that had **happened**.
While they were **talking** and **discussing**,
Jesus **himself** came **near** and went **with** them,
but their **eyes** were kept from **recognizing** him.
And he said to them,
"What are you **discussing** with each other
    while you walk **along**?"
They stood **still**, looking sad.
Then **one** of them, whose name was **Cleopas**, answered him,
"Are you the **only stranger** in Jerusalem
who does not **know** the things
that have taken **place there** in these days?"
He asked them, "**What** things?"
They replied, "The **things** about **Jesus** of Nazareth,
who was a **Prophet** mighty in **deed** and **word**
before **God** and all the **people**,
and how our **chief priests** and leaders **handed** him **over**
to be **condemned** to **death** and **crucified** him.
But we had **hoped** that he was the **one** to redeem Israel.
Yes, and **besides** all this,
it is now the **third day** since these things took **place**.
Moreover, some **women** of our group **astounded** us.

READING II Our second reading is taken from the First Letter of Peter, which was most likely not written by Peter but by a pseudonymous author in AD 79–90 who wanted to extend Peter's memory and his teachings to future generations. Although we call this document a letter, it reads more like a homily on baptism and Christian living or as an exhortation to holiness.

This reading is preceded by statements about how believing Christians enjoy a new life that is lived in the hope of Christ's Resurrection and how God protects them, sustaining them in faith for the time of their salvation. The author of this letter goes on to speak directly to his audience, acknowledging that they will suffer as their faith is tested but will find joy in knowing Christ as their saviour.

Now, at the beginning of our reading, we are reminded of the intimate relationship that we have as children of our God, who is called Father in the best and purest sense of the word. This is a God who judges justly and with mercy, and therefore is deserving of our reverence. The Greek word *phobos*, translated here as "reverent fear," can also mean "fear or dread." But "fear of God" is not a concept that resonates well with modern readers. Instead, "awe" might be a better word to use. Reread that part of this reading with "awe of God" replacing "reverent fear." We are to act out of awe for our God who is so intimately tied to our lives as to treat us as his own dear children.

To expand on the notion of the awe or reverence that is due to God, the author of 1 Peter wants us to know that we are ransomed by the "precious blood of Christ" from our old way of life that goes back generations. A ransom is something that is

Note "a vision of Angels." Recognition and seeing are still urgently connected.

They were at the tomb **early** this morning,
and when they did not find his **body** there,
they came **back**
and **told** us that they had **indeed seen** a vision of **Angels**
who said that he was **alive**.
Some of those who were with us went to the **tomb**
and found it **just as** the women had **said**;
but they did **not** see him."
Then he said to them,
"**Oh**, how **foolish** you are,
and how **slow** of heart to believe
all that the Prophets have **declared**!
Was it not **necessary** that the Christ should **suffer** these things
and **then** enter into his **glory**?"
Then beginning with **Moses** and all the **Prophets**,
he **interpreted** to them
the things about **himself** in all the **Scriptures**.
As they came **near** the village to which they were **going**,
he walked **ahead** as if he were going **on**.
But they **urged** him **strongly**, saying,
"**Stay** with us, because it is **almost evening**
and the day is now nearly **over**."
So he went in to **stay** with them.
When he was at the **table** with them,
he took **bread**, **blessed** and **broke** it,
and **gave** it to them.

After spending time with Jesus (whom they still don't recognize), these disciples have a desire for further fellowship with him. They are beginning to sense something—different than seeing something.

In the breaking of the bread—the ritual that repeats the Passover when they last were in Jesus' company—there is recognition. Ritual and presence.

paid or agreed upon for the release of someone living in captivity. The Greek word *timios*, translated here as "precious," also means "held in honour, esteemed, or especially dear." Jesus' blood is especially dear, because it is the blood of the Passover lamb, poured out for our salvation. Coupled with the ancient belief that blood was the life force of all living beings, it is no small matter that it is given up for us. Moreover, this was part of God's plan from the begin-

ning of time so that our "faith and hope are set on God." We stand in awe!

GOSPEL　This Gospel reading is the story of the disciples on the road to Emmaus. As Luke tells the story, this encounter with the risen Christ takes place on the same day that Jesus was raised from the dead. We learn that two of Jesus' disciples are deep in conversation as they make their way to Emmaus, which is approximately 11 kilometres from Jerusalem.

The narrator notes that they appear sad or downcast and, when the risen Jesus joins them on the road, they do not recognize him.

As Jesus engages these two disciples in conversation, he prompts them to tell the story of what happened to him in Jerusalem. Their response reads like a credal formula, but noticeably absent is any mention of the Resurrection. This is at odds with what they reveal next, that news of the Resurrection had been proclaimed to

Then their eyes were **opened**, and they **recognized** him;
and he **vanished** from their **sight**.
They **said** to each other,
"Were not our **hearts** burning **within** us
while he was **talking** to us on the **road**,
while he was opening the **Scriptures** to us?"
That **same** hour they got **up** and **returned** to Jerusalem;
and they **found** the **eleven** and their companions
        gathered together.
These were saying,
"The **Lord** has risen **indeed**, and he has **appeared** to Simon!"
Then **they** told what had happened on the **road**,
and how he had been made **known** to them
in the **breaking** of the **bread**.

Confirmation of their recognition, repeated in the phrase "the breaking of the bread," the message of this reading.

them earlier that day. Thus, the risen Jesus confronts them, calling them foolish and slow of heart and scolding them about not understanding the Scriptures that describe the necessity of Jesus' suffering and glorification. We do not know what texts Luke had in mind, but more important is the message that Jesus' death and Resurrection were all part of God's plan from the start.

The last scene in this story explains how and why the eyes and hearts of these two disciples were finally opened. Having arrived at Emmaus, they invite Jesus to stay with them. At their evening meal, Jesus blessed, broke and shared the bread in much the same way he did at his last meal before his death. They remembered and were able to recognize Jesus for who he was. They also remembered how they felt when he was teaching them on their journey and how their hearts were set afire. Finally, then, in the breaking of the bread, they complete their journey from unbelief to full faith. Certainly, this is cause for great joy. C.C.

FOURTH SUNDAY OF EASTER

LECTIONARY #49

READING I   Acts 2.14a, 36b–41

A reading from the Acts of the Apostles.

When the **day** of **Pentecost** had **come**,
Peter, **standing** with the **eleven**,
raised his **voice** and **addressed** the **crowd**.
"Let the **entire house** of **Israel** know with **certainty**
that **God** has made him both **Lord** and **Christ**,
this **Jesus** whom you **crucified**."
Now when the **people heard this**, they were **cut** to the **heart**
and said to **Peter** and to the **other Apostles**,
"**Brothers, what** should we **do**?"
Peter **said** to them,
"**Repent**, and be **baptized every one** of you
in the **name** of Jesus Christ
so that your **sins** may be **forgiven**;
and you will **receive** the **gift** of the **Holy Spirit**.
For the **promise** is for **you**, for your **children**,
and for **all** who are **far away**,
everyone whom the **Lord** our **God calls** to him."
And he **testified** with **many other arguments**
and **exhorted** them, saying,
"**Save yourselves** from this **corrupt generation**."
So **those** who **welcomed** his **message** were **baptized**,
and **that day** were **added** about **three thousand souls**.

There is an urgent tone to this reading, with the sense especially of getting busy to fulfill the work of the Lord.

This statement expresses Peter's focus: repentance and baptism. Slight pause between "baptized" and "every."

There's an emphasis here on the numbers, suggesting a sense of the Apostles' initial success.

READING I   Peter's speech takes place in the context of the Jewish feast of Pentecost. Acts reports that "devout Jews from every nation under heaven living in Jerusalem" (2.5) had assembled to celebrate this agricultural feast of the first fruits. In order to underscore the fact that Peter's speech is in complete continuity with historic roots in Judaism, Acts notes that the eleven Apostles were with Peter, thereby fully representing the twelve tribes of Israel. Peter addresses "the entire house of Israel," upon whom he places the guilt of Jesus' crucifixion. In the context of this speech, Peter uses this accusation to point to the sovereignty of God and a call to conversion. To underscore the seriousness of the matter, Peter emphasizes that God has transformed this perceived criminal into "both Lord and Christ."

The reading suggests that the crowd is deeply wounded by Peter's accusation and questions how they could possibly repent for such a sin. Peter's solution is baptism. Some in the crowd would surely recall the baptism of John as they heard Peter's summons to "repent, and be baptized." However, unlike the baptism of John, this is not a baptism undertaken in preparation for the eschatological future; this is a baptism that imparts the gift of the Holy Spirit.

Peter concludes his exhortation with the assurance that the call to conversion goes out not only to the Jewish community but to the Gentiles (those who are "far away"). Unlike the Jewish understanding of the covenant, in which God carves out a special people destined for salvation, this message is given to whomever God wishes. Thus, God is not limited in whom he can elect for salvation. Acts suggests the far-reaching power of God's call when it reports

For meditation and context:

RESPONSORIAL PSALM   Psalm 23.1–3a, 3b–4, 5, 6 (R.1)

R. The Lord is my shepherd; I shall not want.
or:
Alleluia!

The Lord is my shepherd, I shall not want.
He makes me lie down in green pastures;
he leads me beside still waters;
he restores my soul.

He leads me in right paths for his
        name's sake.
Even though I walk through the darkest
        valley, I fear no evil;
for you are with me;
your rod and your staff—they comfort me.

You prepare a table before me
in the presence of my enemies;
you anoint my head with oil;
my cup overflows.

Surely goodness and mercy shall follow me
all the days of my life,
and I shall dwell in the house of the Lord
my whole life long.

READING II   1 Peter 2.20b–25

A reading from the first Letter of Saint Peter.

Peter is urging patience to this letter's
recipients; imagine you are offering the
same advice to the assembly.

Beloved:
If you **endure** when you do **right** and **suffer** for it,
you have **God's approval**.
For to **this** you have been **called**,
because **Christ** also **suffered** for **you**,
leaving you an **example**,
so that you should follow in his **steps**.
"He **committed** no **sin**, and **no deceit** was found in his **mouth**."

At "When," Peter shifts directly into the
lesson he wants to give, about patience in
the face of insult.

When he was **abused**, he **did not return** abuse;
when he **suffered**, he **did not threaten**;
but he **entrusted** himself to the **one** who judges **justly**.

Even emphasis on "Christ himself bore."

Christ himself bore our sins in his **body** on the **Cross**,
so that, **free** from **sins**, we might **live** for **righteousness**;
by his **wounds** you have been **healed**.

The reading concludes with the image of
Jesus as shepherd, which will reappear
immediately in the reading from the Gospel
of John. Allow the words "sheep,"
"shepherd," and "guardian" to resonate.

For you were going **astray** like **sheep**,
but **now** you have **returned**
to the **shepherd** and **guardian** of your **souls**.

---

that around three thousand people believed Peter's message and were baptized.

READING II This reading from this epistle attributed to St. Peter is thought to be part of an early Christian hymn based on the fifty-third chapter of Isaiah (Isaiah 53.4–12) that describes the lot of a "suffering servant" sent by God to heal the world. The author names Christ as this servant, who undergoes suffering without returning any sort of retribution. Christ is depicted here as the perfect model of suffering. The author's point is to remind Christians that while Christ's suffering was undertaken in their name, they must be willing to patiently endure similar suffering in their present-day reality. The ability to suffer along with Christ is both a grace and something Christians are called to by God.

What are the practical ways in which a Christian must patiently endure suffering? The author provides several answers: commit no sin, speak no words of deception, offer no insult when insulted, and make no threat when threatened. The proper response to all things that will test the patience of a Christian is to surrender the self just as Christ freely gave himself over to "the one who judges justly." This just judge is his own Father, and thus, suffering is to be seen as an offering of love.

The reading ends with a call to "live for righteousness," which is made possible because Christians have been healed by Christ's suffering. The Suffering Servant is now likened to a shepherd who is faithful in watching over his flock. The author accuses his readers of having once wandered from the flock but have now returned to the fold. The Greek word here for "guardian" is *episkopos*, the word used for "bishop." Thus,

GOSPEL   John 10.1–10

A reading from the holy Gospel according to John.

Jesus said:
"**Very truly**, I **tell** you,
anyone who does not **enter** the **sheepfold** by the **gate**
but **climbs in** by **another way** is a **thief** and a **bandit**.
The one who **enters** by the **gate** is the **shepherd** of the **sheep**.
The **gatekeeper opens** the **gate** for **him**,
and the **sheep** hear his voice.
He calls his **own sheep** by **name** and **leads** them **out**.
When he has **brought out all** his **own**,
he goes **ahead** of them,
and the **sheep follow** him because they **know** his **voice**.
They **will not follow** a **stranger**,
but they will **run** from him
because they **do not know** the **voice of strangers**."
Jesus used this **figure** of **speech** with them,
but they **did** not **understand** what he was **saying** to them.
So again Jesus **said** to them,
"**Very truly**, I **tell** you, I am the **gate** for the **sheep**.
All who came **before** me are **thieves** and **bandits**;
but the **sheep** did not **listen** to them.
I am the **gate**.
Whoever **enters** by **me** will be **saved**,
and will come **in** and go **out** and find **pasture**.
The thief comes **only** to **steal** and **kill** and **destroy**.
I **came** that they may have **life**, and have it **abundantly**."

An allegorical reading from John's Gospel with the potent, forceful quality repeated in its two parts. In the first part, John presents his allegory. In the second part, John explains the allegory. Don't let the repetition trip you up. John is extending his example with his explanation.

Slight pause between "gatekeeper" and "opens."

Here begins the explanation of the allegory.

Emphasis on "I."

---

this early Christian hymn can be understood to be a profession of belonging both to Christ and to the authority of the Church.

> GOSPEL The beginning of the tenth chapter of John introduces us to the theme of the "Good Shepherd." Here Jesus employs two different shepherding images to illustrate his care for all those who follow him. The first reference to a shepherd emphasizes the legitimacy of his authority. The legitimate shepherd is the one whose voice is known by the sheep and who in turn knows each of the sheep

by name. This shepherd does not lead them astray or take advantage of them by stealing. Instead, this shepherd has a genuine relationship of trust with his sheep. The Pharisees fail to recognize that Jesus is likening them to these false shepherds.

The second image Jesus uses at the outset of the "Good Shepherd" discourse is that of a "gate." He refers to himself as a gate that protects the sheep; it will keep the "thieves and bandits" (the false shepherds) away from the sheep. This reference also applies to salvation, as those who pass through the gate, namely those who come

to believe in Jesus and hear his voice, will have access to the Father. False shepherds seek to destroy the sheep (here we can read "Church"), whereas Jesus is the "Good Shepherd" who wishes to give life in abundance. Jesus is the one reliable "gate" that leads to God, and thus, he is the way to true salvation. S.W.

FIFTH SUNDAY OF EASTER

LECTIONARY #52

READING I Acts 6.1–7

A reading from the Acts of the Apostles.

Now **during** those **days**,
when the **disciples** were **increasing** in **number**,
the **Hellenists** complained against the **Hebrews**
because their **widows** were being **neglected**
in the **daily distribution** of **food**.
And the **twelve** called **together**
the **whole community** of the **disciples** and **said**,
"It **is not right** that we should **neglect** the word of **God**
in order to **wait** on **tables**.
Therefore, brothers,
select from **among yourselves seven men** of **good standing**,
full of the **Spirit** and of **wisdom**,
whom we may **appoint** to this **task**,
while **we**, for our **part**,
will **devote** ourselves to **prayer** and to **serving** the **word**."
What they **said** pleased the **whole community**,
and they chose **Stephen**, a **man** full of **faith** and the **Holy Spirit**,
together with **Philip**, **Prochorus**, **Nicanor**,
Timon, **Parmenas**, and **Nicolaus**, a **convert** of **Antioch**. »

Hellenists = HEL-uh-nists

This reading hinges on a dispute between the Hellenists and the Hebrews. The Hellenists were presumably Greek-speaking Jewish Christians, where the Hebrews were Aramaic-speaking Jewish Christians. The Hellenists are feeling short-changed at the communal meals.

Slight pause between "yourselves" and "seven."

Emphasis on "we." The Apostles want to give over management of meals to community members so that they can devote themselves to the ministry of the word.

Prochorus = PRAH-kuh-ruhs
Nicanor = nī-KAY-nuhr
Timon = TĪ-muhn
Parmenas = PAHR-muh-nuhs
Antioch = AN-tee-ahk

Names. No need to overdo it but add some reverence to your voice as you speak the names of these early members of the Church.

READING I Acts of the Apostles provides the account of the calling and the "ordaining" of the first deacons in the Church. Revealed in this short passage is an infant Church that is struggling with growing pains. Acts wishes to portray the early Church as striving to persevere in unity in community life, in worship, and in charitable outreach (see Acts 2.42–47). However, here we see unrest in the community as some members are complaining that their needs are being ignored while others are receiving special treatment. In particular, it is the Greek-speaking members of the community who are arguing that their widows are being neglected "in the daily distribution." The growing pains experienced here are those of growing diversity within the church; the Hellenists represent both a different culture and a different language. This accusation of bias serves as a bridge between the early Church centred in Jerusalem and the expansion of the Church into missionary territory.

It is significant to note that the seven men chosen for the task of diaconal service all have Greek names. Because they are Hellenists, they remain subordinate to the Apostles, who maintain the tradition of handing a portion of their authority through prayer and the laying on of hands. Acts is very clear to list the responsibilities of the Apostles: theirs is the ministry of prayer and preaching the word. The specific role of the seven men chosen for service is not specified, but we may assume that it is attending to the needs of those who are often overlooked, namely the widows whom God promised to sustain (see Jeremiah 49.11). Luke tells us that this decision to expand apostolic leadership had great success, as the Apostles were able to spread the word

The reading concludes on a note of the success of the Apostles' intervention.

They had these men **stand** before the **Apostles**,
who **prayed** and laid their **hands** on them.
The **word** of **God continued** to **spread**;
the **number** of the **disciples increased greatly** in **Jerusalem**,
and a **great many** of the **priests** became **obedient** to the **faith**.

For meditation and context:

RESPONSORIAL PSALM   Psalm 33.1–2, 4–5, 18–19 (R.22)

R. Let your love be upon us, Lord, even as we hope in you.
or:
Alleluia!

Rejoice in the Lord, O you righteous.
Praise befits the upright.
Praise the Lord with the lyre;
make melody to him with the harp of
    ten strings.

For the word of the Lord is upright,
and all his work is done in faithfulness.
He loves righteousness and justice;
the earth is full of the steadfast love of
    the Lord.

Truly the eye of the Lord is on those who
    fear him,
on those who hope in his steadfast love,
to deliver their soul from death,
and to keep them alive in famine.

READING II   1 Peter 2.4–9

A reading from the first Letter of Saint Peter.

Beloved:
Come to the Lord, a **living stone**,
though **rejected** by human **beings**
yet **chosen** and **precious** in **God's sight**.
Like **living stones**,
let yourselves be **built** into a **spiritual house**,
to be a **holy priesthood**,
to offer spiritual **sacrifices acceptable** to **God**
through **Jesus Christ**.

This section of Peter's letter is built on the unusually powerful metaphor of "living stone." Something both foundational and animated.

---

of God, and the Church continued to grow in numbers. This internal conflict allows Luke to show the need to broaden various ministries as the Church continues to grow and mature.

READING II The First Letter of St. Peter addresses a group of persecuted Christians in Asia Minor around the time of Nero and the burning of the city of Rome in AD 64. As one of the seven "catholic epistles," or universal letters, it employs the authorship of Peter as a means of encouraging Christians to persevere in the hope of

salvation through Christ, despite harsh rejection from the world.

Vivid language is used in this passage to express both the strength of individual and communal faith of those who come to Christ. Christians are portrayed here as stones that are being "built up into a spiritual house," with Christ as the foundation stone. Even though he has been rejected by humans, God has chosen him. With this "living stone," the temple of the Church surely cannot be destroyed. Referring to Isaiah 28.16, the author describes the cor-

nerstone of the church, which is Christ, as "chosen and precious."

Therefore, faith in Christ is seen as a valuable gift for those who believe. For people without faith, it makes sense that they choose to reject the gift, since they do not have the means of perceiving its value. Again, employing the writing of the Prophet Isaiah, this rejected stone becomes a problem for his own people; Christ is called "a stone that makes them stumble" for those who do not believe (see Isaiah 8.14). The failure to believe is blamed on the people's disobedience.

Peter uses Scripture to draw out his metaphor.

Zion = Zī-uhn or Zī-ahn

Slight pause between "cornerstone" and "chosen."

Peter is quoting here from Psalm 118.22. Even though it is very familiar, proclaim it afresh.

The tone of the reading's conclusion is rousing.

For it **stands** in **Scripture**:
"**See**, I am **laying** in **Zion** a stone,
a **cornerstone chosen** and **precious**;
and **whoever believes** in him will **not** be **put** to **shame**."
To **you then** who **believe**, he is **precious**;
but for **those** who do **not believe**,
"The **stone** that the builders **rejected**
has **become** the **very head** of the **corner**," and
"A **stone** that makes them **stumble**,
and a **rock** that makes them **fall**."
They **stumble** because they **disobey** the **word**,
as they were **destined** to **do**.
But **you** are a chosen race, a **royal priesthood**,
a **holy nation**, **God's own people**,
in **order** that you may **proclaim**
the **mighty acts** of **him** who **called** you out of **darkness**
into his **marvellous light**.

GOSPEL   John 14.1–12

A reading from the holy Gospel according to John.

A declarative tone pervades this reading. When Jesus speaks, he is doing so forcefully.

Jesus said to his **disciples**:
"Do not let your **hearts** be **troubled**.
Believe in **God**, believe **also** in **me**.
In my **Father's house** there are **many dwelling places**.
If it **were not so**, would I have **told** you
that I go to prepare a **place** for you?
And if I **go** and prepare a **place** for you,
I will come **again** and will **take** you to **myself**,
so that where I am, **there you** may be **also**. »

The passage concludes with a description of the value of being built up together as living stones. Christians enjoy chosen status because of their faith in Christ. However, just as in the Book of Exodus, which the author of 1 Peter references, when God chose the Israelites as "God's own people," calling them "a royal priesthood, a holy nation" (see Exodus 19.6), this designation comes with responsibility. Even in persecution, Christians are not meant to hide away in secret, but rather, they must proclaim God's praises. Coming to Christ involves rejecting the darkness of igno-

rance and sin and basking in "his marvellous light."

GOSPEL   Chapter 14 of the Gospel of John is part of Jesus' farewell discourse to his disciples at the Last Supper. John depicts Jesus as fully aware of his disciples' fragile faith, as they will struggle to know what direction to take when he is no longer with them to guide them. As Jesus commands his disciples to have no fear, he alludes to his death and Resurrection and even of his return. By the time John writes his Gospel, the understanding of the

parousia had changed significantly from an ushering in of a royal and mighty power to the belief that Christ would return to gather together all who had believed in him in this life. For this reason, Jesus speaks of preparing "many dwelling places" ahead of time for all who wait expectantly for his return.

In response to this talk about Jesus' leave-taking, Thomas utters the basic concern of all the disciples: "we do not know where you are going." The answer that Jesus gives is that he is "the way, and the truth, and the life." In the Acts of the Apostles, Christian life is called "the Way" (Acts 9.2).

And you **know** the way to the **place** where I am **going**."
Thomas **said** to him,
"**Lord**, we do not **know** where you are **going**.
How can we know the **way**?"
Jesus **said** to him,
"I am the **way**, and the **truth**, and the **life**.
No one comes to the **Father except** through **me**.
If you **know** me, you will **know** my Father **also**.
From **now on** you **do** know him and have **seen** him."
Philip **said** to him,
"**Lord, show** us the **Father**, and we will be **satisfied**."
Jesus **said** to him,
"Have I **been** with you **all this time, Philip**,
and you **still** do not **know** me?
Whoever has **seen** me has **seen** the **Father**.
How can you **say**, '**Show** us the **Father**'?
Do you not **believe**
that **I** am in the **Father** and the **Father** is in **me**?
The **words** that I **say** to you I do not **speak** on my **own**;
but the **Father** who dwells in me does his **works**.
Believe me that I am in the **Father** and the **Father** is in **me**;
but if you **do not,**
then **believe** me because of the **works themselves**.
Very truly, I **tell** you,
the one who **believes** in **me**
will also do the **works** that **I** do and, in **fact**,
will do **greater works** than **these**,
because I am **going** to the **Father**."

Familiar though this declaration is, proclaim it as though it is being said for the first time.

The pervasive tone of the conclusion of this Gospel reading is mysterious. But don't discount Jesus' slight irritation at Philip. You can colour your proclamation in very slight irritation.

The words "truth" and "life" are means of explaining the way. Very simply, in the Gospel of John, having faith is the source of truth and life. Writing at a time when many Christians were beginning to leave the faith because Jesus had not yet returned, Jesus' self-description here is meant to bolster the confidence of Christians to remain in the faith.

Jesus contends that adherence to him is the only way that one finds access to God. And yet this continues to be a concern for his disciples; they will not be satisfied until they have "seen" God. In addressing this issue put on the lips of Philip, Jesus chastises his followers for not being able to see and understand the intimate connection between himself and his Father. This intimacy is prevalent throughout John's Gospel, beginning with the prologue, in which the author's high Christology describes Jesus as the Word who was with God before the world began (see John 1.1). For readers of John's Gospel, who are unable to see Jesus in the flesh, trusting in their faith and accomplishing great works in his name ought to be signs enough that the Son and the Father are one. Those who see with the eyes of faith see the way, the truth, and the life; this sight is far greater than anything perceived by human sight alone. S.W.

SIXTH SUNDAY OF EASTER

LECTIONARY #55

READING I   Acts 8.5–8, 14–17

A reading from the Acts of the Apostles.

In **those** days:
Philip went down to the **city** of **Samaria**
and **proclaimed** the **Christ** to them.
The crowds with **one accord** listened **eagerly**
to what was **said** by **Philip**,
hearing and **seeing** the **signs** that he **did**,
for **unclean spirits**, **crying** with **loud shriek**s,
came out of **many** who were **possessed**;
and **many others** who were **paralysed** or **lame** were **cured**.
So there was **great joy** in that city.
Now when the **Apostles** at **Jerusalem** heard
that **Samaria** had accepted the **word** of **God**,
they sent **Peter** and **John** to them.
The two went **down** and **prayed** for them
that they might **receive** the **Holy** Spirit;
(for as yet the **Spirit** had not come upon **any** of them;
they had **only** been baptized in the **name** of the **Lord Jesus**).
Then **Peter** and **John** laid their **hands** on them,
and they received the **Holy Spirit**.

This reading describes what it was like for the Holy Spirit to work through the early Apostles of the Church, in this case, Philip, who is the focal figure of this reading.
Samaria = suh-MAYR-ee-uh

Emphasis on "unclean spirits." Their negative energy is exorcised by Philip's work.

The conclusion of this reading emphasizes the work of the Holy Spirit. Emphasis here and at the end of the reading on "Holy Spirit."

READING I In hearing of the success of Philip's preaching of the Gospel in the land of Samaria, we note a shift in the long-standing rift between the Samaritans and the Jews. We hear in Luke's Gospel of Jesus' healing of the ten lepers, with one being a Samaritan (Luke 17.11–19), and the telling of the parable of the Good Samaritan (Luke 10.25–37). These accounts, and the historical witness of the time, inform us about the discord between the Jews and the Samaritans. Yet here in the Acts of the Apostles, we see Philip going to Samaria to preach to them about Christ.

Philip was one of the seven chosen to assist the twelve Apostles in their ministry after the dispute broke out between the Hebrews and the Hellenists (Acts 6.1–7). Additionally, after the martyrdom of Stephen (who was one of the seven) and the persecution of the Church in Jerusalem, Philip and the other men were scattered but continued to preach the Good News (Acts 7.54—8.4).

Arriving at the passage we hear in today's first reading, Philip goes to Samaria and God makes good use of these circumstances in which he finds himself. The crowds were mesmerized by what Philip was both saying and doing. They heard the Gospel and they were moved by the signs Philip performed, such as freeing people who were possessed and curing those who were paralyzed. The author of Acts notes that "there was great joy in that city."

The discovery of Philip's success by the Apostles in Jerusalem affirms the growth of the Church even more. They send Peter and John to impart the gift of the Holy Spirit to those newly baptized. While these people had been baptized in the Lord's name, Acts suggests that apostolic

For meditation and context:

RESPONSORIAL PSALM   Psalm 66.1–3a, 4–5, 6–7a, 16+20 (R.1)

R. Make a joyful noise to God, all the earth!
or:
Alleluia!

Make a joyful noise to God, all the earth!
sing the glory of his name;
give to him glorious praise.
Say to God, "How awesome are your deeds!"

"All the earth worships you;
they sing praises to you, sing praises to
    your name."
Come and see what God has done:
he is awesome in his deeds among the
    children of Adam.

He turned the sea into dry land;
they passed through the river on foot.
There we rejoiced in him,
who rules by his might forever.

Come and hear, all you who fear God,
and I will tell what he has done for me.
Blessed be God, because he has not rejected
    my prayer
or removed his steadfast love from me.

READING II   1 Peter 3.15–18

A reading from the first Letter of Saint Peter.

Beloved:
In your **hearts sanctify Christ** as **Lord**.
Always be **ready** to **make** your **defence**
to **anyone** who **demands** from you an **accounting**
for the **hope** that is **in** you;
yet **do** it with **gentleness** and **reverence**.
Keep your **conscience clea**r,
so that, when you are **maligned**,
those who **abuse** you for your **good conduct** in **Christ**
may be **put** to **shame**.
For it is **better** to **suffer** for **doing good**,
if **suffering** should be **God's** will,
than to **suffer** for doing **evil**.
For Christ **also suffered** for **sins once** for **all**,
the **righteous** for the **unrighteous**,
in order to **bring** you to **God**.
He was put to **death** in the **flesh**,
but made **alive** in the **spirit**.

Slight pause between "hearts" and "sanctify." This selection from Peter's letter is in the imperative voice. He is deliberately offering advice to the recipients of this letter.

Note the power here of using Christ as an example for suffering. Your assembly is meant to identify emphatically and empathetically with Jesus.

authority is necessary for the completion of baptism through the conferral of the Holy Spirit. Receiving the giving of the Holy Spirit from the Apostles underscores the importance of the Spirit's role in unifying the universal Church. For Luke, the authority of the Apostles and the unity of the church are inseparable.

READING II   The first of two epistles attributed to St. Peter is addressed to the Christians of several Roman provinces in Asia Minor. A primary purpose of the letter is to encourage

Christians to maintain their belief and continue acting in a way that reflects their faith. The short excerpt that we read today is part of the author's encouragement to endure persecution for the sake of Christ. It opens with the command: "In your hearts sanctify Christ as Lord." This provides a solid foundation upon which Christians can make a defense of their faith in light of persecution. A Christian's response to the challenge of a non-believer must be the profession of Christ's name in a gentle and reverent manner.

The author continues by suggesting that a Christian's "good conduct" will not only serve to reveal loyalty to Christ, but it will eventually "shame" the one who scoffs at it. Just as the innocence of Christ led him to suffer for the guilty, so too are those who live virtuously in Christ to consider themselves as suffering for the sake of the unrighteous. In the same way that suffering led to Christ's glorification, so will persecuted Christians be raised up in the power of the Spirit. By putting to death the things "in the flesh" (things that are the opposite of gentleness, reverence, and a clear con-

GOSPEL   John 14.15–21

A reading from the holy Gospel according to John.

Jesus said to his **disciples**:
"If you **love** me, you will **keep** my **commandments**.
And I will **ask** the **Father**,
and he will **give** you **another Advocate**,
to **be** with you **forever**.
This is the **Spirit** of **truth**,
whom the **world** cannot **receive**,
because it neither sees him nor **knows** him.
You **know** him, because he **abides** with **you**,
and he will be **in** you.
I will **not** leave you **orphaned**;
I am **coming** to **you**.
In a **little while** the **world** will no longer see me,
but **you** will see me;
because I **live**, you **also** will **live**.
On **that day** you will **know** that I am **in** my **Father**,
and **you** in **me**, and **I** in **you**.
The **one** who has my **commandments** and **keeps** them
is the one who **loves** me;
and the one who loves me will be **loved** by my **Father**,
and I will **love** them and **reveal myself** to **them**."

Emphasis, from the beginning, on "love" and "keep."

In somewhat oblique terms, Jesus is speaking of the Holy Spirit.

Jesus in John's Gospel makes mysterious and complex statements that your slow and steady proclamation rewards.

TO KEEP IN MIND
When you proclaim the Word, you participate in catechizing the faithful and those coming to faith. Understand what you proclaim so those hearing you may also understand.

---

science), the Christian will experience newness of life "in the spirit." Suffering for the sake of Christ is not based on pacifism but on an ethical mandate to embody the virtues of the Lord.

GOSPEL Today's reading continues Jesus' farewell discourse given to his friends. Jesus has just finished telling them that he is the way that leads to the Father and to life eternal. The inheritance of a room in God's eternal dwelling place depends upon believing that Jesus and the Father are one. Now Jesus instructs them that the keeping of his commandments is an expression of their love for him and their ongoing relationship with him. Observing the commandments that Jesus leaves is real proof that God dwells with them.

The major point that we are called to focus on today is the sending of a second Advocate, with Jesus understood as the first. This Advocate's role will be to animate a "seeing" of the Lord's presence; believers will see what the world fails to see. Recognition of the Son's ongoing presence through the work of the Spirit will also reassure disciples of the intimate relationship that exists between the Father and the Son. Ongoing divine revelation is made known by keeping the commands and persevering in love of the Lord. Doing these things also expresses the theological theme of remaining in the Lord as a description of Christian life, which John will articulate in the following chapter when Jesus employs the image of a vine and branches to express the need to cling to him (John 15.1–17). Although Jesus must die and return to the Father, his followers should not feel abandoned. S.W.

THE ASCENSION OF THE LORD

LECTIONARY #58

READING I Acts 1.1–11

Theophilus = thee-AWF-uh-luhs

A narrative reading that recounts the Ascension of Jesus, along with some of Jesus' last words to the disciples before he departs for heaven. The reading is dramatic and visionary. You will only need to proclaim it with care for its power to come through.

"The day when he was taken up": the Ascension. The vertical direction is important.

A reading from the Acts of the Apostles.

In the **first** book, Theophilus,
I wrote about **all** that Jesus **did** and **taught** from the beginning
until the **day** when he was taken **up** to **heaven**,
after giving **instructions** through the Holy **Spirit**
to the **Apostles** whom he had **chosen**.
After his **suffering** he presented himself **alive** to them
by many convincing **proofs**,
appearing to them during forty **days**
and **speaking** about the **kingdom** of God.
While **staying** with them, he **ordered** them not to
    leave Jerusalem,
but to **wait** there for the **promise** of the **Father**.
"**This**," he said, "is what you have **heard** from me;
for **John** baptized with **water**,
but **you** will be **baptized** with the Holy **Spirit**
not many days from now."
So when they had come **together**, they asked him,
"**Lord**, is this the time when you will **restore** the **kingdom**
to Israel?"
He replied, "It is not for **you** to know the **times** or **periods**
that the **Father** has set by his own **authority**.

This question allows Jesus to provide the disciples with specific details of their task as well as advice before he departs.

READING I Acts opens with the announcement that this book is intended to be a sequel to the first correspondence addressed to Theophilus, which was the Gospel of Luke (see Luke 1.1–4). While the Gospel of Luke was designed to tell the story of Jesus' life and ministry during his time on earth, Acts turns to the mission bestowed upon the Apostles to witness to Jesus' Resurrection and to make believers of all the nations. Luke's Gospel ends with an extremely brief depiction of Jesus' Ascension. Now in Acts,

Luke provides a much more detailed account of what took place between the time of Jesus' death and Resurrection and his Ascension into heaven.

Acts tells us that the Apostles were instructed to remain together in Jerusalem for several days before they would be "baptized with the Holy Spirit." The risen Lord diligently prepares his followers for the work of continuing his mission. He offers them "many convincing proofs" during the forty days following his Resurrection, enlightening them about the kingdom of

God. Yet, Acts portrays the Apostles as failing to truly understand the Lord's teaching, as they question him on the possibility of restoring the kingdom of Israel rather than God's kingdom. Jesus gently corrects them and refocuses their vision on the kingdom, which the arrival of the Spirit will enable them to help build up. Through the instructions of the resurrected Jesus, Luke tells us that the mission will be rooted in Jerusalem and Judea, will go out to the partially Jewish region of Samaria, and will extend even beyond, "to the ends of the earth."

Emphasize "witnesses." Witnessing is essential to discipleship.

Judea = joo-DEE-uh

Samaria = suh-MAYR-ee-uh

But you will **receive** power
when the Holy **Spirit** has come **upon** you;
and you will be my **witnesses** in Jerusalem,
in all **Judea** and **Samaria**, and to the **ends** of the **earth**."
When he had **said** this, as they were **watching**,
he was lifted **up**, and a **cloud** took him out of their **sight**.
While he was **going** and they were **gazing** up toward **heaven**,
suddenly **two men** in **white robes** stood by them.
They said, "Men of **Galilee**,
why do you stand **looking** up toward **heaven**?
This **Jesus**, who has been taken **up** from you into **heaven**,
will **come** in the same way as you **saw** him go into **heaven**."

The reading concludes with a vision of two angelic beings. Give their speech emphasis by slowing your pace ever so slightly.

For meditation and context:

RESPONSORIAL PSALM   Psalm 47.1–2, 5–6, 7–8 (R.5a)

R. God has gone up with a shout, the Lord with the sound of a trumpet.
or:
Alleluia!

Clap your hands, all you peoples;
shout to God with loud songs of joy.
For the Lord, the Most High, is awesome,
a great king over all the earth.

God has gone up with a shout,
the Lord with the sound of a trumpet.
Sing praises to God, sing praises;
sing praises to our King, sing praises.

For God is the king of all the earth;
sing praises with a Psalm.
God is king over the nations;
God sits on his holy throne.

This order guides the growth and mission of the Church in the overall scheme of Acts.

The account of Jesus' Ascension in Acts concludes with his being "lifted up" in the midst of a cloud with the Apostles looking on. The dramatic portrayal is meant to bring to an end the earthly work of Jesus so that the ministry may begin anew under the guidance of the Holy Spirit and through the work of the disciples. Luke includes "two men in white robes" who observe the Apostles' reaction and provide a commentary on Jesus' ascent into heaven. Keeping the movement of Jesus into heaven at the Ascension in the context of his larger mission, they inform the Apostles that Jesus will someday return just as he departed (the parousia). It is a call to action for the Apostles, and there is an urgency with which they are to testify to the glorified Lord.

READING II The Letter to the Ephesians is an encouragement to Christian communities to understand themselves as united with Christ and in Christ so that they might continue his work.

In the passage we hear today, the author offers a prayer for the community for their further enlightenment in Christ. First, he asks that the Ephesians may be given the wisdom to come to know the mystery of God. Next, the prayer asks that this knowledge include an understanding of the "hope" of what it means to belong to Christ, namely, to be counted among the "saints," and those destined to inherit the "riches of his glorious inheritance."

The prayer for the church in Ephesus continues by describing the mighty power

READING II   Ephesians 1.17–23

A reading from the Letter of Saint Paul to the Ephesians.

Brothers and **sisters**:
I pray that the **God** of our Lord Jesus **Christ**, the Father of **glory**,
may give you a spirit of **wisdom** and **revelation**
as you come to **know** him,
so that, with **the** eyes of your heart **enlightened**,
you may **know** what is the **hope** to which he has **called** you,
what are the **riches** of his **glorious inheritance** among the **saints**,
and what is the immeasurable **greatness** of his **power**
for **us** who **believe**, according to the **working** of his **great power**.
God put this **power** to work in **Christ**
when he **raised** him from the **dead**
and **seated** him at his right **hand** in the heavenly **places**,
far above all **rule** and **authority** and **power** and **dominion**,
and above **every** name that is **named**,
not only in **this** age but also in the **age** to **come**.
And he has put **all things** under his **feet**
and has made him the **head** over all things for the **Church**,
which is his **body**,
the **fullness** of him who fills **all** in **all**.

Ephesians = ee-FEE-zhuhnz

An exhortatory reading, filled with high-hearted blessings.

The first blessing comes from God to the people of Ephesus.

The second blessing comes from Paul to the people of Ephesus, including knowledge, hope, and the riches of glory. Give each aspect of this blessing its due by emphasizing it slightly.

These are the traditional names of some of the angelic powers.

Paul concludes by invoking the power of Jesus himself.

of God. Not only did God raise Jesus from the dead, but he also seated him "at his right hand" to glorify him, allowing him to reign over every imaginable power. Far mightier than "all rule and authority and power and dominion," all things will be subjected to the power of Christ for all eternity. Christ's authority is complete and universal.

The prayer concludes with a further mention that God subjects "all things" to the reign of Christ, including, and perhaps most especially, the Church. In keeping

with other Pauline epistles, the Church is described as a body, with Christ as its head (see Colossians 1.18 and Romans 12.4–8). The head is understood as giving direction to the body. Because the body enacts the command of the head, the reign of Christ is handed on to the Church to be exercised in the world. With the church filled with "a spirit of wisdom and revelation" and with Christ as its head, the Christian community is meant to reveal the authority of the glorified Lord, cooperating with his work.

GOSPEL   The setting for Jesus' Ascension in Matthew is very similar to the one found in the evangelist's rendering of the Transfiguration in chapter 17. There Jesus leads Peter, James, and John up a mountain where he is transfigured, glorified by the voice of God, and then proceeds to tell the disciples about his Resurrection from the dead. Now, in the final verses of Matthew's Gospel, Jesus orders the eleven to a mountain in Galilee, where he reminds them of his divine

GOSPEL   Matthew 28.16–20

A reading from the holy Gospel according to Matthew.

The **eleven disciples** went to **Galilee**,
to the **mountain** to which **Jesus** had **directed** them.
When they **saw** him, they **worshipped** him;
but **some** doubted.
And **Jesus came** and **said** to them,
"All **authority** in heaven and on **earth** has been **given** to me.
Go therefore and make **disciples** of all **nations**,
baptizing them in the name of the **Father**
and of the **Son** and of the **Holy Spirit**,
and **teaching** them to obey **everything** that I have
      commanded you.
And remember, I am **with** you **always**,
to the **end** of the **age**."

This reading comes from the concluding words of Matthew's Gospel. Therefore, they have a valedictory quality to them.

Matthew's Gospel concludes with these words of Jesus, which function as a concise and moving summation of his teachings. He is encouraging his disciples while also saying farewell to them.

This last statement in light of Jesus' imminent departure is especially poignant.

authority and commissions them to go "make disciples of all nations."

An important detail of this short passage is the reaction of the disciples when they discover Jesus on this mountain. Matthew states that "they worshipped him; but some doubted." Unlike Mark's account of the Gospel, in which there are several appearances of the risen Lord prior to his Ascension (see Mark 16.9–14), the resurrected Lord in Matthew appears only to the women at the tomb before he meets the eleven in Galilee. Thus, the doubt they experience should not surprise us, as this is their first encounter with the risen Jesus. Their act of worship is meant to override their doubt.

After the Lord reveals the authority given to him from above, his commissioning of the Apostles contains two components that go into the making of disciples. First, they are commanded to baptize in the name of the triune God—Father, Son, and Holy Spirit. No longer is baptism simply about immersion into the kingdom and repentance (as John the Baptist's baptism was; see Matthew 3.11), but now it is to unite the recipient with God. The second important aspect of the Apostles' mission to "all nations" is that they are to teach all that Jesus has handed on to them. Thus, baptism is inseparable from the preaching of the Gospel. In word and sacrament, Jesus remains with the Church "to the end of the age." S.W.

VIGIL OF PENTECOST

LECTIONARY #62

READING I   Genesis 11.1–9

A reading from the book of Genesis.

Now the whole **earth** had one **language** and the same **words**.
And as **people** migrated from the east,
they came upon a **plain** in the land of **Shinar** and settled there.
And they said to one another,
"**Come**, let us make **bricks**, and **burn** them thoroughly."
And they had **brick** for stone,
and **bitumen** for mortar.
Then they said,
"**Come**, let us **build** ourselves a **city**,
and a **tower** with its top in the **heavens**,
and let us make a **name** for ourselves;
otherwise we shall be **scattered abroad**
upon the face of the **whole earth**."
The **Lord** came down to see the **city** and the **tower**,
which the **children of Adam** had built.
And the Lord said, "**Look**, they are one **people**,
and they have all one **language**;
and this is only the **beginning** of what they will do;
nothing that they propose to do will now be **impossible**
for them.
Come, let us go **down**, and **confuse** their language there,
so that they will not **understand** one another's **speech**."

A reading of a story absorbed in mysterious power. As much a parable as it is a demonstration of the incomprehensible mind of God, it can seem almost like science fiction. It's probably best to treat it that way in terms of proclaiming it: read what's in the text, straightforwardly and clearly.

The two repetitions of "Come" stand for the aspirations—or arrogance—of the people. Give a little edge to the word when you speak it.

God's use of "let us" repeats the use of the builders of the tower. Here, God's intention is unhelpful, destructive even. "Confuse" is the loaded word.

There are options for today's readings. Contact your parish staff to learn which readings will be used.

READING I | **Genesis.** The first eleven chapters of Genesis contain the primeval history of the world's creation and its need for salvation. While the world is deemed "good" by God, with all things manifesting perfect order and complementarity, and with humanity made in God's image, sin quickly enters the world through the human desire to possess the knowledge that belongs to God alone (Genesis 1–3). God's frustration with humanity comes to a high point in Genesis in the story of Noah, when God decides to destroy creation with a flood but then relents and establishes a new order of creation with Noah in the giving of a covenant that renews the face of the earth (Genesis 6.5—9.17). However, as the descendants of Noah begin to repopulate the earth, with everyone speaking the same language, the story unfolds in yet another rupture in the relationship with God. Once again, humanity forgets the providence of God and chooses to strive to become as great as God.

The story of the tower of Babel opens with the image that the whole world is united by the ability to communicate without difficulty. Nevertheless, the unity experienced by the human family is cause for the development of a fear. They come to believe that they must make a great name for themselves, or they will become separated from one another. Thus, they decide to build a tower that rises high into the sky in order to demonstrate their greatness on the face of the earth and to preserve their unity.

However, the Lord observes that the people have abused their gift of unity and

So the Lord **scattered** them **abroad** from there
over the face of **all** the **earth**,
and they **left off** building the city.
Therefore it was called **Babel**,
because **there** the Lord **confused** the language of **all** the earth;
and from **there** the Lord scattered **them** abroad
over the face of all the **earth**.

Or:

___

READING I   Exodus 19.3–8a, 16–20b

A reading from the book of Exodus.

Moses went up to **God**;
the Lord called to **him** from the mountain, saying,
"**Thus** you shall **say** to the house of **Jacob**,
and tell the **children of Israel**:
'You have **seen** what I **did** to the Egyptians,
and how I **bore** you on **eagles'** **wings** and **brought** you to **myself**.
Now **therefore**, if you **obey** my voice and **keep** my covenant,
you shall be my **treasured** possession out of **all** the peoples.
Indeed, the **whole** earth is **mine**,
but **you** shall be for me a **priestly** kingdom and a **holy** nation.'
These are the **words** that you **shall** speak to the **children**
          of Israel."
So **Moses** came, summoned the **elders** of the people,
and set **before** them all these **words**
that the Lord had **commanded** him.
The people all answered as one:
"**Everything** that the Lord has **spoken** we will **do**."
On the **morning** of the third **day** there was **thunder**
          and **lightning**,
as well as a thick **cloud** on the mountain,
and a **blast** of a trumpet so loud
that all the **people** who were in the camp **trembled**. »

Note the repetition of "confuse" in "confused." The word suggests something of the power of God.

Exodus = EK-suh-duhs

A reading of the sealing of the covenant between God and humankind, attended by powerful natural phenomena. The scene of this reading is especially vivid.

"Therefore" initiates the terms of the covenant. With authority.

"Everything that the Lord has spoken we will do": with these words, the covenant is sealed. Emphasis on "do."

Natural forces express themselves vividly in response.

Even stresses on the words in this line.

---

are moving along a path where they they no longer need God. Thus, God's punishment is to inflict upon the people precisely what they feared from the outset: they will forever be separated from one another. The primeval account of creation thus ends with an explanation as to why there is a diversity of languages in the world; confusion of speech prevents the human family from pursuing the destructive path of trying to be God's equal.

Exodus. This passage from the Book of Exodus is in two parts. The first half of the passage details the Lord's choice of Israel as his own possession and the promise of the covenant. The second portion focuses on the great theophany at Mount Sinai, when God makes the mountain come alive with his awesome presence. First God speaks, and then God manifests his power using the tangible means of natural wonders.

At the beginning of this passage we witness Moses climbing the mountain in order to meet privately with God. This takes place three months after the Israelites began their journey of freedom out of Egypt. The Lord calls Moses and commands him to speak to the Israelites, reminding them of God's action in their exodus from Egypt. Furthermore, God tells Moses that this newfound freedom comes with an important responsibility. The people are to respond to God's voice, keep his covenant, and display before all the world what it means to be his "treasured possession." Israel is to take on a priestly identity, suggesting that they are set apart from every other nation. Their holiness is to be a sign of God's power and fidelity, and as the Book of Exodus will show, of God's great mercy. When Moses speaks to the people,

Moses brought the people **out** of the camp to meet **God**.
They **took** their **stand** at the foot of the **mountain**.
Now Mount **Sinai** was wrapped in **smoke**,
because the **Lord** had **descended** upon it in **fire**;
the smoke went **up** like the smoke of a **kiln**,
while the whole **mountain** shook **violently**.
As the **blast** of the trumpet grew **louder** and **louder**,
Moses would **speak** and God would **answer** him in **thunder**.
When the Lord **descended** upon Mount **Sinai**,
to the **top** of the mountain,
the Lord summoned **Moses** to the top of the **mountain**,
and Moses went **up**.

Or:

_____

READING I　Ezekiel 37.1–14

A reading from the book of the Prophet Ezekiel.

The **hand** of the Lord came **upon** me,
and he brought me **out** by the **spirit** of the **Lord**
and set me down in the **middle** of a **valley**;
it was **full** of bones.
He **led** me all **around** them;
there were very **many** lying in the valley,
and they were **very** dry.
He said to me, "Son of **man**, can these bones **live**?"
I answered, "O Lord God, **you** know."
Then he said to me,
"**Prophesy** to these **bones**, and **say** to them:
O dry bones, **hear** the **word** of the **Lord**.
Thus says the Lord God to these bones:
I will cause **breath** to enter you, and you shall **live**.
I will lay **sinews** on you,
and will cause **flesh** to come **upon** you,

The vision of smoke and fire signals the power of God. These words paint a potent picture. No need, however, to raise your voice. Keep it steady.

A reading with visionary passages of exquisite strangeness and power. God speaks to and through Ezekiel throughout this reading. Because the punctuation isn't entirely clear, it's useful to have markers for yourself for when God is speaking and when Ezekiel is speaking for himself. Also, this reading makes use of the verb "prophesy" as well as its past tense, "prophesied." Pronunciation is important. Prophesy = PROF-uh-sī (not PROF-uh-see); Prophesied = PROF-uh-sīd (not PROF-uh-seed). Be sure to practise!

The vision, which is frightening, begins here with the valley of dry bones. The life of this vision relies on these dry bones coming to life.

God begins to speak here.

---

represented by a group of leaders, the people answer in unison that they will do all that the Lord has commanded.

Verses 9 through 15 of this chapter, which are omitted in our hearing of Exodus today, contains the preparations the Israelites make to ready themselves for God's formal giving of the law. Thus we hear the second portion of this reading, the theophany at Sinai. As the people look on, Moses and God carry on an intense conversation, which is made visibly present in fire and smoke, trumpet and thunder. Made ready for the deepening of his personal

encounter with God, Moses leaves the people and ascends the mountain, where he will receive instruction on the covenant from the mouth of God. This magnificent theophany reveals in a very physical way that God's power and might is beyond compare. Yet God will later come to demonstrate that his greatest strength of all is the ability to show mercy and compassion to his sinful people (for example, Exodus 34.6–7).

Ezekiel. The context for Ezekiel's prophecy is the utter desolation of Israel. The Temple in Jerusalem has been levelled, the people

have been banished to the land of Babylon, and the entire nation begins to doubt that God no longer wishes to be in relationship with them anymore. The Israelites had to ask themselves this basic question: How can we consider ourselves to be God's chosen people when our life situation only speaks of doom and gloom, despair and death?

Ezekiel uses this bleak outlook to provide the people with a new sense of hope. His vision of dry bones being put back together again with life and vitality not only forecasts the future of Israel as a new and vibrant nation, but it can also be seen as an

Emphasis on "know."

Ezekiel himself is speaking here.

sinews = SIN-yooz

God begins to speak again here.

Ezekiel himself is speaking again here.

From here to the end of the reading, God is speaking, even as he quotes the house of Israel.

and **cover** you with **skin**, and **put** breath in you,
and you shall **live**;
and you shall **know** that I am the **Lord**."
So I **prophesied** as I had been **commanded**;
and as I **prophesied**, suddenly there was a **noise**, a **rattling**,
and the bones came together, **bone** to its **bone**.
I looked, and there were **sinews** on them,
and **flesh** had come **upon** them, and skin had **covered** them;
but there was no **breath** in them.
Then he said to me,
"**Prophesy** to the **breath**, **prophesy**, son of man,
and **say** to the breath: **Thus** says the Lord God:
Come from the **four winds**,
and **breathe** upon these **slain**, that they may **live**."
I **prophesied** as he commanded me,
and the breath came **into** them,
and they **lived**, and **stood** on their feet, a vast **multitude**.
Then he said to me,
"Son of **man**, these bones are the **whole house** of Israel.
They say, 'Our **bones** are dried up, and our **hope** is lost;
we are cut off **completely**.'
Therefore **prophesy**, and say to them,
Thus says the Lord God:
I am going to **open** your **graves**,
and bring you **up** from your graves, O my **people**;
and I will bring you **back** to the land of **Israel**.
And you shall **know** that I am the **Lord**,
when I open your **graves**,
and bring you **up** from your graves, O my **people**.
I will put my **spirit** within you, and you shall **live**,
and I will **place** you on your own **soil**;
then you shall know that I, the Lord,
have **spoken** and will **act**," says the Lord.

Or:

image of resurrection in general. In the recreation of the human body, it is the Spirit who is hard at work providing the gift of new life.

The reading begins with Ezekiel testifying to the Lord's inspiration and to the Spirit's guidance in the vision that has been given to him. The dry bones indicate even greater lifelessness than can be seen from the outside. God commands Ezekiel to prophesy over the dry bones; they are to "hear the word of the Lord." The word God speaks is also to communicate the giving of

spirit that will make new life spring up in the seemingly worthless bones.

When Ezekiel follows the Lord's command and prophesies over the field of bones, they begin to take human form again, but they lack the invigorating life of the spirit. Thus, God commands Ezekiel to call upon the Spirit directly. When he does so, Ezekiel witnesses a "vast multitude" before him full of energy and life. God then interprets the scene to Ezekiel, stating that the dry bones represent the nation of Israel that cries out for new life fearing that they have nothing to hope for in their return to

the land God provided. Yet the Lord promises the gift of new life. Even more, God promises to provide them with the enduring power of his spirit, who will ensure their prosperity in the land. In the context of Pentecost, this reading from Ezekiel may renew in us the frequent utterance of the simple prayer "Come, Holy Spirit," seeking to find new life in what might appear as hopeless, death-dealing situations in our own lives.

Joel. The Book of Joel is a two-part prophecy. The first part of the book, chapters 1

READING I   Joel 2.28–32

A reading from the book of the Prophet Joel.

Thus says the Lord:
I will **pour out** my spirit on all **flesh**;
your **sons** and your **daughters** shall **prophesy**,
your **elders** shall dream **dreams**,
and your **young** people shall see **visions**.
Even on the male and female **slaves**,
in those days, I will pour out my **spirit**.
I will show **portents** in the **heavens** and on the **earth**,
blood and **fire** and **columns** of **smoke**.
The **sun** shall be turned to **darkness**,
and the **moon** to **blood**,
before the **great** and terrible **day of the Lord** comes.
Then **everyone** who **calls** on the name of the **Lord**
shall be **saved**;
for in Mount **Zion** and in **Jerusalem**
there shall be those who **escape**, as the **Lord** has said,
and among the **survivors** shall be **those** whom the **Lord calls**.

A reading of a prophetic vision of a cataclysmic event. Scripture often shifts into this visionary mode—which can be exciting to proclaim because the language is so vivid.

"The great and terrible day": with these words, Joel concludes his vision.

It is immediately followed by the promise of rescue from God, which continues to the end of the reading. Don't overdo your reading, but you can shift to a slightly more optimistic tone.

and 2, tell the story of a plague of locusts that serves to provoke the lamentation of the people of Israel. Joel calls the nation to repentance and prayer and is given the vision of a restored land that produces fruit in abundance. The second part of the book, chapters 3 and 4, issues forth God's judgment upon all the nations, with the assurance that God will spare "everyone who calls on the name of the Lord."

Our reading today is the opening of the book's second half. It begins with the outpouring of the spirit of God on all people. In other words, there is a universality in God's giving of the Spirit—all people on earth are recipients of this gift and therefore have the opportunity to respond to God's initiative. The reading continues by outlining those who will attempt to awaken all people to God's power; the young and the old, men and women, servants and handmaids will all be charged with the responsibility to prophesy in God's name.

Joel's vision proceeds to describe the wonders that God will perform in announcing his judgment upon earth. Blood, fire, and smoke will cover the land, the sun will not shine, the moon will be darkened. Joel refers to the dawning of this day as "great and terrible." Nevertheless, Joel assures the people that those who remain faithful to the Lord and call upon his name will be preserved in the new world that is to come. Those who recognize God's great power and authority and respond to the promptings of the spirit by making God's greatness known will survive any peril that may come as a part of God's vindication.

READING II   Living in a time when there were eyewitnesses to Christ himself, many early Christians were eager

For meditation and context:

RESPONSORIAL PSALM   Psalm 104.1–2a, 24+25c, 27–28, 29b–30 (R.30)

R. **Lord, send forth your Spirit, and renew the face of the earth.**
or: Alleluia!

Bless the Lord, O my soul.
O Lord my God, you are very great.
You are clothed with honour and majesty,
wrapped in light as with a garment.

O Lord, how manifold are your works!
In wisdom you have made them all;
the earth is full of your creatures,
living things both small and great.

These all look to you
to give them their food in due season;
when you give to them, they gather it up;
when you open your hand, they are filled
with good things.

When you take away their breath,
they die and return to their dust.
When you send forth your spirit, they
are created;
and you renew the face of the earth.

READING II   Romans 8.22–27

A reading from the Letter of Saint Paul to the Romans.

Brothers and **sisters**:
we **know** that the whole creation
has been **groaning** in labour pains until **now**;
and not only the **creation**,
but we **ourselves**, who have the **first fruits** of the **Spirit**,
groan **inwardly** while we wait for **adoption** to **sonship**,
the **redemption** of our **bodies**.
For in **hope** we were **saved**.
Now hope that is **seen** is not **hope**.
For who **hopes** for what is **seen**?
But if we **hope** for what we do not **see**,
we wait for it with **patience**.
Likewise the Spirit **helps** us in our **weakness**;
for we do not **know** how to pray as we **ought**,
but that very Spirit **intercedes** with **sighs** too deep for **words**.
And **God**, who searches the **heart**,
knows what is the **mind** of the Spirit,
because the **Spirit intercedes** for the **saints**
according to the **will** of **God**.

A reading that contains a potent and not easily digested message: That life is challenging—Paul compares it to childbirth—and its pain does not abate, even as we hope for its end. Nevertheless, we hope

The first lines are the core of Paul's message. Emphasize "know," "groaning," and "now."

Slight extra emphasis on "patience."

"Likewise": Paul intends to compare our life to the work of the Holy Spirit, who comes to our aid. In the Spirit lies our hope.

---

for Christ to return as he had promised. However, as time went on, some of these early Christians began to lose hope. The Spirit assists in guiding and directing the hope that looks forward to the day of final salvation. Paul provides an important reminder as to the true nature of hope. Hope looks to what has not been attained, and it is the Spirit who provides the hope necessary to endure the unknown. This applies also to the action of our prayer. By one's own power, prayer lacks confidence, but with the aid of the Spirit, one discovers how to pray and be heard by God.

Echoing his first imagery of creation groaning and labouring, Paul notes that in our prayer the "Spirit intercedes with sighs too deep for words." The Christian's effort must be attuned to cooperating with the movement of the Holy Spirit. Through this intercession of the Spirit, the Christian is guided along the path of holiness. When left to themselves, humans will always fall short of comprehending the will of God. However, with the power of the Spirit at work within them and in the world, disciples can hope that all of creation is moving toward God.

GOSPEL Today's passage from the Gospel of John takes place at the conclusion of the eight-day feast of Tabernacles. The feast of Tabernacles was one of the three great pilgrimage festivals—*Pesach* (Passover), *Shavuot* (Pentecost), and *Sukkot* (Tabernacles)—all of which required an annual journey to the Temple in Jerusalem in order to offer a sacrifice. The late summer/early autumn feast of Tabernacles celebrates the harvest and asks God for the blessing of plentiful rain for the fruition of next year's crops. It also commemorates the Israelites' freedom from slavery in

GOSPEL   John 7.37–39

A reading from the holy Gospel according to John.

On the **last** day of the festival, the **great** day,
while Jesus was standing in the temple, he **cried out**,
"Let anyone who is **thirsty** come to me and **drink**.
As the Scripture has said,
'Out of the **heart** of the one who **believes** in me
shall flow **rivers** of **living water**.'"
Now he said this about the **Spirit**,
which **believers** in him were to **receive**;
for **as yet** there was no **Spirit**,
because **Jesus** was not yet **glorified**.

A brief reading with an extraordinary exhortation embedded in it.

"Rivers of living water" is an especially evocative phrase, especially as a sign of belief.

The reading concludes with an anticipatory claim about Jesus' eventual glorification.

Egypt and God's protection of his people. Building on the theme of abundant rain, Jesus speaks within this context and invites people to come to him for "living water." In a not-so-subtle way, Jesus is using this traditional Jewish feast to reveal himself as the one who has the ability to bestow life in abundance. These words of Jesus cause the crowds to discuss anew how it is that he could be the Christ, the anointed one of God (in the verses following today's reading; see John 7.40–52).

This short passage moves from Jesus' proclamation about the true source of life to John's interpretation that Jesus' words serve as a foreshadowing of the giving of the Holy Spirit. John notes that it is the Spirit himself who is the "living water" that flows from the source of the glorified Lord. These explanatory comments from John are consistent with Johannine theology that reserves the giving of the Spirit to the Church after the Lord's Resurrection (for example, John 20.22). While Jesus provides

the invitation to the people around him to come to him to quench their thirst, he is also looking toward the time of the Church, when the Spirit will guide and support his followers after he has returned to the Father. S.W.

PENTECOST SUNDAY

LECTIONARY #63

READING I   Acts 2.1–11

A reading from the Acts of the Apostles.

When the **day** of **Pentecost** had come,
they were all **together** in one place.
And suddenly from **heaven** there came a **sound**
like the **rush** of a violent **wind**,
and it filled the entire **house** where they were **sitting**.
Divided **tongues**, as of **fire**, appeared among them,
and a **tongue rested** on each of them.
All of them were **filled** with the Holy **Spirit**
and began to **speak** in other **languages**,
as the Spirit **gave** them **ability**.
Now there were devout **Jews** from every **nation** under **heaven**
living in **Jerusalem**.
And at this **sound** the crowd **gathered** and was **bewildered**,
because each one heard them **speaking** in their own **language**.
Amazed and **astonished**, they asked,
"Are not all **these** who are speaking **Galileans**?
And how is it that we **hear**, each of us,
in our own **language**?
Parthians, Medes, Elamites, and residents of **Mesopotamia**,
Judea and **Cappadocia**, **Pontus** and **Asia**,
Phrygia and **Pamphylia**,

[handwritten annotations: pardiane; meedz; ilemites; mesopotay nia; Phrygia; cappadoshia; Pontue ("yu"); Pamphylia]

A narrative reading that directly inverts the Tower of Babel passage from Genesis. (See the first reading for the Pentecost Vigil.) This kind of inverted symmetry is one of the enduring pleasures of reading Scripture. Babel doesn't need to be mentioned in order for your assembly to sense its presence.

Air and fire are the two elements associated with the Holy Spirit. Here, it's air in the form of wind.

And here in the form of tongues of fire.

Read all of these names with care. Be sure to practise their pronunciation.

Parthians = PAHR-thee-uhnz
Medes = meedz
Elamites = EE-luh-mīts
Mesopotamia = mes-uh-poh-TAY-mee-uh
Judea = joo-DEE-uh
Cappadocia = cap-uh-DOH-shee-uh
Pontus = PON-tuhs
Phrygia = FRIJ-ee-uh
Pamphylia = Pam-FIL-ee-uh
Libya = LIB-ee-uh
Cyrene = sī-REE-nee
Cretans = KREE-tuhnz

READING I On this feast of Pentecost, our first reading is taken from the Acts of the Apostles. The setting is the Jewish feast of Pentecost, also known as *Shavuot*. As Luke tells the story, Jesus' disciples and followers remained in the Jerusalem area after Jesus' Ascension into heaven. Because it was a pilgrimage feast, Jews from other parts of the world had also come to Jerusalem. On this particular day, Jesus' followers were gathered together in a house. Suddenly, they receive the Holy Spirit in the forms of a strong wind from the sky and tongues of fire that come down upon each of them. Wind and fire are signs of a theophany, a manifestation of the divine.

The New Testament associates a wide variety of gifts and abilities with the Holy Spirit, including speaking in tongues. When Jesus' followers in this story begin to speak to the crowd, the crowd is aware that each hear them in their own language. Notice the crowd's reaction first to the sound coming from the house and later to the followers of Jesus speaking in tongues, but try not to get caught up in the drama. It is most important to observe that the Spirit moves Jesus' followers and uses them as his agents to preach "God's deeds of power," and they do so with great gusto!

READING II Today's second reading also focuses on the gifts of the Holy Spirit. Paul begins by making the point that a person cannot proclaim faith in Jesus Christ without the Holy Spirit. Apparently, some members of the Christian community at Corinth were "puffed up" over their ability to go into ecstatic trance in prayer and prophecy and to speak in tongues. Paul asserts that there are not

Cretans a

Egypt and the parts of **Libya** belonging to **Cyrene**,
and **visitors** from **Rome**, both **Jews** and **converts**,
Cretans and **Arabs**—
in our own **languages** we hear them **speaking**
about God's **deeds** of **power**."

For meditation and context:

RESPONSORIAL PSALM   Psalm 104.1ab+24ac, 29b–30, 31+34 (R.30)

**R. Lord, send forth your Spirit, and renew the face of the earth.
or: Alleluia!**

Bless the Lord, O my soul.
O Lord my God, you are very great.
O Lord, how manifold are your works!
The earth is full of your creatures.

When you take away their breath,
they die and return to their dust.
When you send forth your spirit, they
    are created;
and you renew the face of the earth.

May the glory of the Lord endure forever;
may the Lord rejoice in his works.
May my meditation be pleasing to him,
for I rejoice in the Lord.

READING II   1 Corinthians 12.3b–7, 12–13

A reading from the first Letter of Saint Paul to the Corinthians.

Brothers and **sisters**:
No one can say "**Jesus** is Lord" **except** by the Holy Spirit.
Now there are **varieties** of **gifts**, but the same **Spirit**;
and there are varieties of **services**, but the same **Lord**;
and there are varieties of **activities**,
but it is the **same** God who activates **all** of them in **everyone**.
To each is **given** the **manifestation** of the Spirit
    for the **common good**.
For just as the **body** is one and has many **members**,
and all the **members** of the body, though **many**, are one **body**,
so it is with Christ.
For in the one **Spirit** we were all **baptized** into one **body**
—**Jews** or **Greeks**, **slaves** or **free**—
and we were **all** made to **drink** of one **Spirit**.

Corinthians = kohr-IN-thee-uhnz

A didactic reading with claims of enduring force.
The invocation of the Holy Spirit is meant to echo the same in the first reading at Pentecost. Here the Holy Spirit is understood in terms of spiritual gifts.

Even stress on these five words: "so it is with Christ."

The vision of radical equality that Paul stresses in these lines is something the Church continues to aspire to.

different spirits to whom people can lay claim for their own benefit. Rather, it is the *one* Spirit who motivates and enlivens the life of the Christian community.

Further, Paul categorizes the manifestations of the Spirit, noting that there are different types of spiritual gifts, ways of service or ministering to others, and activities or workings or things wrought. All of these manifestations of the Spirit are necessary for healthy and fruitful communities of faith. Thus, Paul says elsewhere, "Do not quench the Spirit" (1 Thessalonians 5.19). The Greek word translated here as "quench"

also has the meaning of "extinguish, suppress, or stifle."

Finally, to reinforce the idea that the Spirit's role or mission is to foster unity, Paul uses the metaphor of a body. Just as the body has fingers and toes, a heart and a nose, each with different functions for the benefit of the body, so too does the Christian community, which is the body of Christ, have different manifestations of the Spirit. It does not matter who we are or what is our status in life; we all have been "made to drink of one Spirit."

| GOSPEL |

The setting for today's Gospel reading is described as "evening on the day Jesus rose from the dead." A lot has happened already on that day. Before dawn, Mary Magdalene had been to the garden tomb where Jesus was buried and found it empty. Peter and the Beloved Disciple ran to the tomb to find it empty. Mary met the risen Jesus and then told the disciples about Jesus' Resurrection. Despite all of this, we still find them hiding behind locked doors "for fear of the Jews." Most frequently in John's Gospel, "the Jews" is used interchangeably with references to

SEQUENCE

Holy Spirit, Lord divine,
Come, from heights of heav'n and shine,
Come with blessed radiance bright!

Come, O Father of the poor,
Come, whose treasured gifts ensure,
Come, our heart's unfailing light!

Of consolers, wisest, best,
And our soul's most welcome guest,
Sweet refreshment, sweet repose.

In our labour rest most sweet,
Pleasant coolness in the heat,
Consolation in our woes.

Light most blessed, shine with grace
In our heart's most secret place,
Fill your faithful through and through.

Left without your presence here,
Life itself would disappear,
Nothing thrives apart from you!

Cleanse our soiled hearts of sin,
Arid souls refresh within,
Wounded lives to health restore.

Bend the stubborn heart and will,
Melt the frozen, warm the chill,
Guide the wayward home once more!

On the faithful who are true
And profess their faith in you,
In your sev'nfold gift descend!

Give us virtue's sure reward,
Give us your salvation, Lord,
Give us joys that never end!

GOSPEL   John 20.19–23

A reading from the holy Gospel according to John.

It was **evening** on the day Jesus **rose** from the dead,
the first **day** of the week,
and the **doors** of the house where the **disciples** had met
were **locked** for fear of the **Jews**.
Jesus **came** and stood among them and **said**,
"**Peace** be with you."
After he said this, he **showed** them his hands and his side.
Then the **disciples** rejoiced when they **saw** the Lord.
Jesus said to them again,
"**Peace** be with you.
As the **Father** has sent me, so **I** send you."
When he had **said** this, he **breathed** on them and **said** to them,
"**Receive** the Holy Spirit.
If you **forgive** the sins of any, they are **forgiven** them;
if you **retain** the sins of any, they are **retained**."

A narrative reading that depicts the transmission of the Holy Spirit through Jesus himself to his disciples.

Jesus enters the scene with the word "Peace."

Breath is the most ancient sign of life in Scripture. Here, Jesus' powers are transmitted directly through his breath.

Note the parallel construction: forgive/forgiven; retain/retained.

the religious authorities in Jerusalem, so we must be careful not to assume that this mention of Jews applies to our Jewish brothers and sisters today or even to Jews in Jesus' time.

This story of the appearance of the risen Jesus to his disciples bears some similarities with Luke 24.36–40, in which the risen Jesus appears suddenly and shows his hands and feet to the disciples to allay their fears and show that he is truly alive. However, there are some important differences, as well. The greeting Jesus gives them, "Peace be with you," reminds us of

Jesus' words to the disciples earlier in John's Gospel, when during the farewell discourse and before his arrest and crucifixion he says, "Peace I leave with you; my peace I give to you. . . . Do not let your hearts be troubled" (John 14.27).

John's version of the story also has the detail about Jesus breathing upon the disciples and saying, "Receive the Holy Spirit." This statement should recall for us the second creation story of Genesis, when God creates a man, Adam, and breathes into him the breath of life and he "became a living being" (Genesis 2.7). When Jesus

breathes on the disciples, they become "new" living beings insofar as they have a new mission, which is to continue the work that God had given to Jesus to do—to be the light that casts out darkness (John 8.12; see also John 1.5; 3.19–21). When we hear the command "If you forgive the sins of any, they are forgiven; if you retain the sins of any, they are retained," we can see how it fits in as part of this larger mission of Jesus' disciples to be light in darkness. C.C.

JUNE 4, 2023

THE SOLEMNITY OF THE MOST HOLY TRINITY

LECTIONARY #164

Exodus = EK-suh-duhs

Moses = MOH-zihz or MOH-zihs

Sinai = Sī-nī

The tone of this reading is both powerful and intimate.

God is speaking this exhortation to Moses.

"Stiff-necked people": Moses is speaking for all of us in our stubbornness when he uses these words.

READING I   Exodus 34.4b–6, 8–9

A reading from the book of Exodus.

Moses rose **early** in the **morning** and went **up** on Mount **Sinai**,
as the **Lord** had **commanded** him,
and **took** in his **hand** the **two tablets** of **stone**.
The Lord **descended** in the **cloud** and **stood** with him there,
and **proclaimed** the **name**, "The **Lord**."
The **Lord** passed before **Moses**, and **proclaimed**,
"The **Lord**, the **Lord**,
a **God merciful** and **gracious**,
slow to **anger**, and **abounding** in **steadfast love**
    and **faithfulness**."
And **Moses** quickly **bowed** his **head** toward the **earth**,
    and **worshipped**.
He said, "If **now** I have found **favour** in your **sight**, O **Lord**,
I **pray**, let the **Lord** go **with** us.
Although **this** is a **stiff-necked people**,
pardon our **iniquity** and our **sin**,
and **take** us for your **inheritance**."

READING I Our first reading is part of the story about God restoring the tablets of the Law that Moses broke when he came down the mountain and saw the Israelites engaged in worshipping a golden calf (Exodus 32.19). The Book of Exodus describes Moses as having an intimate relationship with God, and the narrator of Exodus 33.11 tells us, "the LORD used to speak to Moses face to face, as one speaks to a friend." At one point, Moses asks to see God's glory, and God consents, saying, "I will . . . proclaim before you the name, 'The LORD.' . . . But . . . you cannot

see my face; for no one shall see me and live" (Exodus 33.19–20).

This is where today's reading begins. God tells Moses to prepare to return to the top of the mountain with two new stone tablets so that God can remake the tablets of the covenant with the Israelites. God comes down to the mountain to meet Moses and "proclaimed the name, 'The Lord.'" What is the significance of this action? If we look at the description of God's covenant with Moses and the Israelites in Exodus 20, we will find an important clue. There, too, God proclaims his name, that is,

identifies himself, as the one making the covenant. God does so by saying, "for I the LORD your God am a jealous God, punishing children for the iniquity of parents, to the third and the fourth generation of those who reject me, but showing steadfast love to the thousandth generation of those who love me and keep my commandments" (Exodus 20.5–6).

However, in this story of the restoration of the tablets of the Law, God proclaims his name differently. Here, God says, "The Lord, the Lord, a God merciful and gracious, slow to anger, and abounding in steadfast

198

For meditation and context:

RESPONSORIAL PSALM   Daniel 3.52, 53, 54, 55, 56 (R.52)

R. Glory and praise for ever!

Blessed are you, O Lord, God of our fathers
and blessed is your glorious and holy name.

Blessed are you in the temple of your
holy glory,
and to be extolled and highly glorified
forever.

Blessed are you on the throne of your
kingdom,
and to be extolled and highly exalted forever.

Blessed are you who look into the depths
from your throne on the cherubim.

Blessed are you in the firmament of heaven,
to be sung and glorified forever.

Corinthians = kohr-IN-thee-uhnz

This reading comes from the conclusion
of Paul's second letter to the Corinthians,
the so-called valediction. Its tone is
encouraging and uplifting, meant to
convey Paul's conclusive feelings of hope.

READING II   2 Corinthians 13.11–13

A reading from the second Letter of Saint Paul to the Corinthians.

Brothers and **sisters**,
put things in **order**, **listen** to my **appeal**,
agree with one another,
live in **peace**;
and the **God** of **love** and **peace** will **be** with you.
Greet one another with a **holy kiss**.
All the **saints greet** you.
The **grace** of the Lord **Jesus Christ**,
the **love** of **God**,
and the **communion** of the **Holy Spirit**
be with **all** of you.

love and faithfulness." Immediately Moses bowed his head—the Hebrew word suggests worship or submission—and asks God to be with them. All that remains is for God to deliver the Law, the Israelites' obligation to the covenant.

READING II Today's second reading is the conclusion of Paul's Second Letter to the Corinthians. Paul's exhortations to good behaviour are general in nature—like what a parent might say to an adolescent child before leaving them alone—but Paul's big concern is peace within the community. If we could reconstruct the life of this Christian community at Corinth based on Paul's two letters, we would be amazed at this colourful and unruly group of Christians. Their story would make a great soap opera! But the reason that this reading is noteworthy, especially today, on the solemnity of the Most Holy Trinity, is the final sentence. It is the clearest and most illuminating acclamation of the trinitarian God in the entire New Testament.

GOSPEL John's Gospel provides us with an equally beautiful and profound statement about Jesus, his relationship with the Father, and his role in the salvation of the world. The verbs in the phrases "he gave his only-begotten Son" and "God did not send the Son" have related meanings. Likewise, the verbs "to perish" and "to condemn" have related meanings, as do "to have eternal life" and "to be saved." But there is even more going on here. There are several Greek words for love, including sexual attraction, friendship love, and unconditional love without

GOSPEL John 3.16–18

A reading from the holy Gospel according to John.

Jesus said to **Nicodemus**:
"God **so loved** the **world** that he gave his **only-begotten Son**,
so that **everyone** who **believes** in him **may not perish**
but may have **eternal life**.
Indeed, **God** did not **send** the **Son** into the **world** to **condemn**
    the **world**,
but in **order** that the **world** might be saved **through** him.
The **one** who **believes** in him is **not condemned**;
but the **one** who does not believe is **condemned already**,
for **not** having **believed**
in the **name** of the **only-begotten Son** of **God**."

Nicodemus = nihk-uh-DEE-muhs

Note the repetition and the inversion: "believes" and "not condemned"; "does not believe" and "already condemned."

expectation for return. The Greek word for this third kind of love is *agapaó*. Although the author of John's Gospel is not entirely consistent regarding the use of these synonyms for love, clearly, in this instance, John has in mind unconditional love. Also, the author of this Gospel has what we call a "realized eschatology," meaning that he understands himself and his community to be already in the throes of the end time.

Why would early Christians think this way? Among first-century Jewish views about what happens after death, there was a segment of the population who believed that resurrection of the dead was a sign of the end time. Therefore, when people began to proclaim Jesus Christ raised from the dead, these same people thought that the end time was already underway. This is why there is no "in between" in the talk about salvation and condemnation. Either you are already committed to God and his Son Jesus or you are already condemned. Today, most Christians who anticipate an end-time return of Christ have a future eschatology, which significantly defers people's anxiety about the end time. Regardless, the point of this reading for today's believers is that God is so generous and unconditional with divine love that he is willing to give his only Son to effect salvation for the whole world. How else can we respond but in gratitude? C.C.

THE SOLEMNITY OF THE MOST HOLY BODY AND BLOOD OF CHRIST

LECTIONARY #167

READING I   Deuteronomy 8.2–3, 14–16

A reading from the book of Deuteronomy.

Moses spoke to the **people**:
"**Remember** the **long way** that the **Lord** your **God** has **led** you
these **forty years** in the **wilderness**,
in **order** to **humble** you, **testing** you to **know** what was
    in your **heart**,
whether or not you would **keep** his **commandments**.
He **humbled** you by letting you **hunger**,
then by **feeding** you with **manna**,
with which neither you nor your **ancestors** were **acquainted**,
in **order** to make you **understand** that **man does not live**
    by **bread alone**,
but by **every word** that **comes** from the **mouth** of the **Lord**.
Do not exalt yourself, **forgetting** the **Lord** your **God**,
who **brought** you out of the **land** of **Egypt**,
out of the **house** of **slavery**,
who **led** you through the **great** and **terrible wilderness**,
an **arid wasteland** with **poisonous snakes** and **scorpions**.
He made **water flow** for you from **flint rock**,
and fed you in the **wilderness** with **manna**
that your **ancestors** did not **know**,
to **humble** you and to **test** you,
and in the **end** to do you **good**."

Deuteronomy = doo-ter-AH-nuh-mee

Moses = MOH-zihz or MOH-zihs

This reading consists of two parts, the first introduced by "Remember," recalling the past of the Israelites, the second introduced by "Do not exalt yourself," offering advice about how to proceed.

manna = MAN-uh
Manna is a focus of this reading.

Note the rhythm of the second part of the reading, in which the verb in the phrase is emphasized to lead to a noun related to the Israelites' desert exile.

Once again, manna is mentioned.

READING I The first reading for today's feast is part of a unit that begins with the words "This entire commandment that I command you today you must diligently observe" (Deuteronomy 8.1). It provides a recollection of the past to urge obedience to the covenant. The recollection is of the manna that God provided to the Israelites in their sojourn in the wilderness (Exodus 16.4–15) and the water from the rock that God provided when the Israelites were thirsty (Exodus 17.1–7). The

reward associated with observing the commandments is to live and prosper in the land that was promised to their ancestors.

But Moses observes that the commandments are God's way of teaching discipline to God's people, like a father would teach his son (see Deuteronomy 8.5). And what does God want to teach the people? He wants them to learn reliance on God so that they never assume that their prosperity comes from their own hands.

READING II Our second reading is an excerpt from a section of the First Letter to the Corinthians in which Paul warns the community about the dangers of overconfidence, telling them that even God's chosen ones can fall into idolatry (1 Corinthians 10.1–13).

Transitioning from this general warning about overconfidence, Paul addresses the problem of idolatry more directly. Major social gatherings and other forms of entertainment in Corinth would have involved

For meditation and context:

RESPONSORIAL PSALM   Psalm 147.12–13, 14–15, 19–20 (R.12)

R. Praise the Lord, Jerusalem.
or: Alleluia!

Praise the Lord, O Jerusalem!
Praise your God, O Zion!
For he strengthens the bars of your gates;
he blesses your children within you.

He grants peace within your borders;
he fills you with the finest of wheat.
He sends out his command to the earth;
his word runs swiftly.

He declares his word to Jacob,
his statutes and ordinances to Israel.
He has not dealt thus with any other nation;
they do not know his ordinances.

READING II   1 Corinthians 10.16–17

A reading from the first Letter of Saint Paul to the Corinthians.

Brothers and **sisters**:
The **cup** of **blessing** that we **bless**,
is it not a **sharing** in the **Blood** of **Christ**?
The **bread** that we **break**,
is it not a **sharing** in the **Body** of **Christ**?
Because there is **one bread**,
we who are **many** are **one body**,
for we **all partake** of the **one bread**.

Corinthians = kohr-IN-thee-uhnz

An elegantly simple reading that condenses into its few lines a whole theology of the Eucharist. Emphasis throughout, especially on "body," "blood," "bread," and "cup."

sacrifices to idols, and these early Christians would have felt compelled to participate if they wanted to be part of the social scene. But Paul is asking, which is more fulfilling: idol worship or the Eucharist? To make his case, he uses two rhetorical questions that anticipate a response of "Yes, of course!" The Greek word translated here as "sharing" is *koinonia*, which also means "fellowship or partnership." Paul uses it frequently to refer to the communion of believers. Paul later says, "You cannot drink the cup of the Lord and the cup of demons. You cannot

partake of the table of the Lord and the table of demons" (1 Corinthians 10.21). In other words, you must choose!

GOSPEL   The Gospel reading for today is part of the "Bread of Life" discourse from the Gospel of John, which is often described as a midrash on the sentence "He gave them bread from heaven to eat" (John 6.31), a paraphrase and conflation of Exodus 16.4 and Psalm 78.24. A midrash is a type of Jewish literature in which the author provides commentary on a Scripture text, sometimes taking

it apart phrase by phrase or word by word and giving it a new contemporary meaning.

As a preface to this midrash, the narrator tells us that the crowds try to follow Jesus after he performs a miracle of multiplying loaves and fishes (John 6.1–15). They ask Jesus for a sign, like the manna their ancestors received in the desert. In the midrash that follows, Jesus clarifies that God, not Moses, was (and is) the giver of the sign. Also, "bread from heaven" is no longer manna but rather Jesus, who comes from the Father to do God's work.

A reading that draws out the potent metaphor of Jesus as the "living bread."

Do not sell the strangeness of this promise short. Eating flesh and drinking blood together were strictly forbidden in Jewish dietary laws (and still are for those who keep kosher). In those terms, what Jesus is saying here is appalling.

GOSPEL John 6.51–59

A reading from the holy Gospel according to John.

Jesus said to the **people**:
"I am the **living bread** that came **down** from **heaven**.
Whoever **eats** of this **bread** will live **forever**;
and the **bread** that I will **give** for the **life** of the **world**
is my **flesh**."
The **people** then **disputed** among **themselves**, saying,
"**How** can this man give us his **flesh** to **eat**?"
So **Jesus** said to them,
"**Very truly**, I **tell** you,
unless you **eat** the **flesh** of the **Son** of **Man** and **drink** his **blood**,
you have **no life** in you.
Whoever **eats** my **flesh** and **drinks** my **blood** has **eternal life**,
and I will raise them **up** on the **last day**;
for my **flesh** is **true food** and my **blood** is **true drink**.
Whoever **eats** my **flesh** and **drinks** my **blood abides** in me,
and **I** in **them**.
Just as the **living Father sent** me,
and **I live** because of the **Father**,
so whoever **eats** me will **live because** of me.
This is the **bread** that came **down** from **heaven**,
not like that which your **ancestors** ate, and they **died**.
But the **one** who **eats** this **bread** will **live forever**."
Jesus **said** these things
while he was **teaching** in the **synagogue** at **Capernaum**.

Today's Gospel is the last part of this midrash, where Jesus explains what "to eat" means. John's Gospel does not have a Last Supper/institution of the Eucharist narrative, but here we have lots of Eucharistic imagery. When Jesus declares that he is the living bread and that "whoever eats of this bread will live forever," "the Jews" (i.e., Jewish religious authorities) argue about what this means. In the simplest of terms, they think Jesus is inviting the crowd to be cannibals! The author of John's Gospel regularly uses this literary technique, in which Jesus says something deliberately ambiguous, and characters in the story understand only the plain meaning of his words, which allows Jesus to explain further. But, in this case, the Johannine Jesus piles on even more offensive language. No wonder people were upset!

The Greek verb *trógó*, translated here as "to eat," more often means "to gnaw on or to crunch on." Elsewhere, in this reading, the less repulsive *phago*, meaning "to eat," is used. Consider how these passages read with this understanding of the difference in "to eat": "Whoever eats (*phago*) my flesh and drinks my blood has eternal life." "Whoever gnaws on (*trógó*) my flesh and drinks my blood abides in me and I in them." "Whoever feeds on (*trógó*) me will live because of me." "Whoever crunches on (*trógó*) this bread will live forever."

Although we cannot fully know what the author intended to say with the use of such graphic language, at the very least we can say that Jesus was not a phantom; he was truly incarnated in flesh and blood, which he gave up for our salvation. Through the Eucharistic experience, we can remain in him and he in us. This is the fullness of life! C.C.

THE SOLEMNITY OF THE MOST SACRED HEART OF JESUS

LECTIONARY #170

READING I   Deuteronomy 7.6–11

A reading from the book of Deuteronomy.

Moses spoke to the **people**:
"**You** are a **people holy** to the **Lord** your **God**;
the **Lord** your **God** has **chosen** you
out of **all** the **peoples** on **earth** to be
his people, his **treasured possession**.
It was **not** because you were more **numerous**
        than a**ny other people**
that the **Lord** set his **heart** on you and **chose** you—
for you were the **fewest** of all **peoples**.
It was because the **Lord loved you**
and kept the **oath** that he **swore** to your **fathers**,
that the **Lord** has **brought** you out with a **mighty hand**,
and **redeemed** you from the **house** of **slavery**,
from the **hand** of **Pharaoh king** of **Egypt**.
Know therefore that the **Lord** your **God** is God,
the **faithful God**
who maintains **covenant loyalty** with **those** who **love** him
and **keep** his **commandments** to a **thousand generations**,
and who **directly repays** with **destruction**
the **one** who **rejects** him.
He **does not delay**
but **repays directly** the **one** who **rejects** him.

Deuteronomy = doo-ter-AH-nuh-mee or dyoo-ter-AH-nuh-mee

The tone of this declarative reading is forceful, almost like a persuasive legal argument.

Emphasis on "you."

Pharaoh = FAYR-oh

Even emphasis on "Know therefore."

READING I Our first reading is taken from the Book of Deuteronomy. The title of the book means "second law," and it presents Moses as the great law giver, who reiterates the Law to the Israelites before entering the Promised Land. This book was written over several centuries, starting in the eighth century BC and possibly extending to the exile in the sixth century BC.

After Moses tells the people that God wants them to purify the land of Canaan by defeating its inhabitants in battle, refusing to make covenant or intermarry with them, and destroying their sacred places, he describes how God views the Israelites as the chosen ones. God calls them his holy ones, meaning "separate and set apart" for God. They are also described as God's own valued property or unique treasure. It is not because of the Israelites' prominence that God "set his heart" on the Israelites—the Hebrew word also means "to be attached to"—but because they were a tiny and unprotected minority, and because God made a covenant with their ancestors. Moses goes on to say that God "maintains covenant loyalty," as is evidenced in the Exodus story, even to the thousandth generation for those who love him. But this covenant goes both ways. They must obey the laws of the covenant as their primary expression of love and faithfulness to God who loves them without end.

READING II Biblical scholars have investigated the relationship between the First Letter of John and the Gospel of John. Without going into all of the intricacies of this, we can say that the First Letter of John uses some of the same vocabulary as the Gospel of John and shares

Moses concludes by driving home his point.

Therefore, **observe diligently** the **commandment**—
the **statutes**, and the **ordinances**—
that I am **commanding** you **today**."

For meditation and context:

RESPONSORIAL PSALM PSALM 103.1–2, 3–4, 6–7, 8+10 (R.17)

R. The steadfast love of the Lord is everlasting on those who fear him.

Bless the Lord, O my soul,
and all that is within me, bless his holy name.
Bless the Lord, O my soul,
and do not forget all his benefits.

It is the Lord who forgives all your iniquity,
who heals all your diseases,
who redeems your life from the Pit,
who crowns you with steadfast love
    and mercy.

The Lord works vindication
and justice for all who are oppressed.
He made known his ways to Moses,
his acts to the people of Israel.

The Lord is merciful and gracious,
slow to anger and abounding in
    steadfast love.
He does not deal with us according to
    our sins,
nor repay us according to our iniquities.

READING II   1 John 4.7–16

A reading from the first Letter of Saint John.

The tone of this reading is passionate and intimate.

Beloved,
let us **love** one **another**,
because **love** is from **God**;
everyone who **loves** is **born** of **God** and **knows** God.
Whoever **does not love** does not **know** God,
for **God** is **love**.

This powerful declaration, that "God is love," focuses this reading. However, don't overdo it in your proclamation. Let its truth ring out from its simple, straightforward expression.

God's love was **revealed** among us in this **way**:
God sent his **only-begotten Son** into the **world**
so that we might live **through** him.
In **this** is **love**,

Emphasis on "us."

not that we **loved God** but that he **loved us**
and **sent** his **Son** to be the **atoning sacrifice** for our **sins**.
Beloved, since God loved us **so much**,
we also ought to **love one another**.
No one has **ever seen God**;
if we **love** one **another**, God **lives** in us,
and his **love** is **perfected** in **us**. »

some of its themes, especially around the commandment to love one another (for example, see 15.9–13).

This reading is especially appropriate for the solemnity of the Most Sacred Heart of Jesus because of its focus on the love of God—not our love of God, but God's love of us. But to fully appreciate its message, there are some terms and concepts that we need to understand. First, 1 John has some of the same dualism that we find in the Gospel of John, such as being born of God and not children of the devil. Also, both 1 John and the Gospel of John use the word

"to know" and "to see" in the deeper sense of "to experience or believe in." Another important term is "abiding." The Greek word is *menein*, which can also be translated as "to remain, to dwell in, to tarry, or to continue to be present." Theologically, it carries the sense of in-dwelling, such as how the Father dwells in the Son and the Son in the Father. The author of the First Letter of John wants us to understand that God's very being is love. Evidence of the extent of God's love is that he gave his only Son as "the atoning sacrifice for our sins," and therefore our most fitting response is

to love one another. When we experience and believe that God is love and that Jesus is God's Son and respond accordingly, then we also abide in God. How amazing!

GOSPEL Today's Gospel reading is Jesus' prayer to the Father, taken from the Gospel of Matthew, after Jesus scolded the cities where his mighty deeds had been manifested and still the people did not repent.

The opening of this prayer sounds like a typical Jewish prayer, except for the addition of the word "Father," which speaks to

Take note of the rhythm of this verse.

By **this** we **know** that we **abide** in **him** and **he** in **us**,
because he has **given** us of his **Spirit**.
And we have **seen** and do **testify**
that the **Father** has sent his **Son** as the **Saviour** of the **world**.
Whoever **confesses** that **Jesus** is the **Son** of **God**,
God **abides** in them, and **that person** in **God**.
So we have **known** and **believe** the **love** that God **has** for us.
God is **love**,
and the **one** who **abides** in **love abides** in **God**,
and **God** abides in **them**.

A repetition of the claim that "God is love" concludes this beautiful reading.

GOSPEL   Matthew 11.25–30

A reading from the holy Gospel according to Matthew.

Begin with an even emphasis on all of these words: "At that time Jesus said."

At that time Jesus said,
"I **thank** you, **Father**, **Lord** of **heaven** and **earth**,
because you have **hidden** these **things** from the **wise**
        and the **intelligent**
and have **revealed** them to **infants**;
yes, Father, for **such** was your **gracious will**."
He **continued**:

The reading begins with Jesus addressing the Father directly.

Here, Jesus addresses the multitudes to whom he is preaching.

"**All things** have been **handed over** to me by my **Father**;
and **no one knows** the Son except the **Father**,
and **no one knows** the Father except the **Son**
and **anyone** to whom the **Son chooses** to **reveal** him.
Come to **me**,
all you that are **weary** and are **carrying heavy burdens**,
and I will **give** you **rest**.
Take my **yoke upon** you, and **learn** from me;
for I am **gentle** and **humble** in heart,
and you will find **rest** for your **souls**.
For my **yoke** is **easy**, and my **burden** is **light**."

The image of the yoke focuses this reading.

Jesus' special relationship with God. The Greek word which is translated as "to thank" can also mean "to praise, to acknowledge joyfully, or to profess." Jesus is presented here as the revealer of God's wisdom, which is made known to the simple and uneducated—translated here as "infants"—but hidden from the so-called learned. The hidden things to which Jesus refers are (1) everything Jesus says and does comes from the Father or Jesus is the agent of God in all things, and (2) Jesus is the distinctive or exclusive revealer of God in that only the Father knows the Son and only the Son

knows the Father, except also those "to whom the Son chooses to reveal" the Father.

Moreover, as personified Wisdom, Jesus invites the weary or exhausted and heavily burdened to come to him so that he can give them rest. The Greek word translated here as "rest" can also mean "refreshment or calm." The word "yoke" has several connotations in this text. These include (1) a wooden beam designed to join two work animals to pull a heavy load or a single animal to pull a farming implement, (2) a symbol of slavery, and (3) obedience to the Torah or Jewish Law. However, here Jesus

invites people to take up his yoke, i.e., his example, and become his disciples. The word disciple means "learner." Finally, Jesus assures his listeners that his yoke is easy (Greek, *chréstos*, meaning "useful, virtuous, manageable, pleasant") and his burden light (Greek, *elaphros*, meaning "light in weight or easy to keep"). Come to him and you will find rest! C.C.

ELEVENTH SUNDAY IN ORDINARY TIME

LECTIONARY #91

READING I   Exodus 19.1–6a

A reading from the book of Exodus.

On the **third month**
after the **children** of **Israel** had gone **out** of the land of **Egypt**
they **came** to the **wilderness** of **Sinai**.
They had **journeyed** from **Rephidim**,
entered the **wilderness** of **Sinai**,
and **camped** in the **wilderness**;
Israel **camped** there in **front** of the **mountain**.
Then **Moses** went **up** to **God**;
the **Lord called** to him from the **mountain**, saying,
"**Thus** you shall **say** to the **house** of **Jacob**,
and tell the **children** of **Israel**:
'You have **seen** what I **did** to the **Egyptians**,
and how I bore you on **eagles' wings** and **brought** you to **myself**.
Now **therefore**, if you **obey** my **voice** and **keep** my **covenant**,
you shall be my **treasured possession** out of **all** the **peoples**.
Indeed, the **whole earth** is **mine**,
but you shall **be** for me a **priestly kingdom** and a **holy nation**.'
These are the **words** that you shall **speak** to the **children**
        of **Israel**."

Exodus = EK-suh-duhs

Visually, the focus in this reading is Moses' ascent of the holy mountain to speak to God.

Sinai = SĪ-nī

Rephidim = REF-ih-dim

The content of the reading is focused on the promise of God conveyed in his speech to Moses. God's promise is uplifting and encouraging.

READING I   Chapter 19 of the Book of Exodus, which we hear the beginning of today, begins the third part of Exodus and tells the story of God establishing a covenant with the children of Israel and bestowing upon them a code of law. It has taken the newly released exiles three months to journey out of Egypt beyond the Red Sea through the desert wilderness to finally arrive and set up camp at Mount Sinai, the holy mountain of God.

Upon their arrival, the first order of business is for God to speak individually to Moses. In revealing his covenant to the people, God will proceed to call Moses apart from them to instruct him and to foster the development of a relationship that symbolizes the one God will come to establish with the Israelite nation as a whole. The words God speaks to Moses here are meant to serve as a personal introduction that will remind the former slaves of how God has acted in the past on their behalf in order that they might expect his divine assistance in the future. God highlights his actions against the Egyptians as the care he showed the Israelites by stating that he "bore you on eagles' wings and brought you to myself." Instead of belonging to Pharaoh and all of Egypt, they are now God's "treasured possession." God demonstrates here a preferential option for Israel, as he desires to make them a people set apart. The notion of being separated from other nations is made clear in choosing them to be a holy people. It is not simply that Israel is made sacred to God but that they are to perform the role of mediating on behalf of other peoples, as priests are set apart to minister to others and be in God's presence.

For meditation and context:

PSALM PSALM   100.1–2, 3, 4, 5 (R.3c)

R. We are his people: the sheep of his pasture.

Make a joyful noise to the Lord, all
 the earth.
Worship the Lord with gladness;
come into his presence with singing.

Know that the Lord is God.
It is he that made us, and we are his;
we are his people, and the sheep of
 his pasture.

Enter his gates with thanksgiving,
and his courts with praise.
Give thanks to him, bless his name.

For the Lord is good;
his steadfast love endures forever,
and his faithfulness to all generations.

READING II   Romans 5.6–11

A reading from the Letter of Saint Paul to the Romans.

Paul's letter makes a complex argument about reconciliation. Proclaim at an even pace to allow its subtleties to register with the assembly.
Slight pause between "Christ" and "died."

Brothers and **sisters**:
While we were **still weak**,
at the **right time Christ died** for the **ungodly**.
Indeed, **rarely** will **anyone** die for a **righteous person**—
though **perhaps** for a **good person** someone might **actually** dare
  to **die**.
But **God proves** his **love** for us
in that while we still were **sinners** Christ **died** for us.
Much more **surely** then,
now that we have been **justified** by his **blood**,
will we be **saved** through him from the **wrath** of God.
For if while we were **enemies**,
we were reconciled to **God** through the **death** of his **Son**,
much more **surely**, having been **reconciled**,
will we be **saved** by his **life**.
But **more** than **that**,
we even **boast** in **God** through our **Lord Jesus Christ**,
through whom we have **now received reconciliation**.

Even emphasis on "now received reconciliation."

READING II This passage from Romans comes immediately after Paul's declaration of the justification by faith that Christians have through the grace of God. This is cause for the faithful to be filled with hope, even in times of persecution. Thus, Paul sets out to answer why Christians have reason to be hopeful. He begins by acknowledging that Christ chose to die for sinners, not the righteous. The decision not to die for only the holy ones demonstrates God's immense love, since it would be far easier to die for those who do not dwell in sin.

Thus, for Paul, justification is the reconciliation of sinners to Christ through his death on the cross. But salvation is a different thing. Sin must first be remitted before salvation can be given. Paul will go on to say that this is precisely what baptism will ensure (Romans 6.1–11). Having been reconciled to God by the blood of the cross, Christians are baptized into Christ in order to look forward in hope to the fullness of the gift that is salvation.

GOSPEL Jesus' words that "the harvest is plentiful, but the labourers are few" serve as a transition between several public cures and demonstrations of Jesus' authority and his commissioning of the twelve Apostles. Jesus has discovered in a very short time of proclaiming the kingdom of God that the people in the countryside are in desperate need of spiritual leadership. Matthew states quite clearly that Jesus "had compassion" for the people because they were "like sheep without a shepherd." He turns to his disciples and acknowledges the great amount of work that needs to be done. They are to

GOSPEL   Matthew 9.36—10.8

A reading from the holy Gospel according to Matthew.

Jesus uses the image of sheep without a shepherd to instruct his disciples. Not only is Jesus their shepherd but the disciples themselves are shepherds as they go out.

When **Jesus** saw the **crowds**, he had **compassion** for them,
because they were **harassed** and **helpless**,
like **sheep** without a **shepherd**.
Then he **said** to his **disciples**,
"The **harvest** is **plentiful**, but the **labourers** are **few**;
therefore ask the **Lord** of the **harvest**
to send out **labourers** into **his** harvest."
Then Jesus **summoned** his **twelve disciples**
and gave them **authority** over **unclean spirits**,
to **cast** them **out**,
and to **cure every disease** and **every sickness**.
These are the **names** of the **twelve Apostles**:
first, **Simon**, also known as **Peter**, and his brother **Andrew**;
James son of **Zebedee**, and his brother **John**;
Philip and **Bartholomew**;
Thomas and **Matthew** the **tax** collector;
James son of **Alphaeus**, and **Thaddaeus**;
Simon the **Cananaean** and **Judas Iscariot**,
the one who **betrayed** him.
These twelve Jesus sent **out** with the **following instructions**:
"Go **nowhere** among the **Gentiles**,
and enter **no town** of the **Samaritans**,
but go **rather** to the **lost sheep** of the **house** of **Israel**.
As you **go**, **proclaim** the **good news**,
'The **kingdom** of **heaven** has come **near**.'
Cure the **sick**, **raise** the **dead**,
cleanse the **lepers**, **cast** out **demons**.
You **received** without **payment**;
give without **payment**."

Don't rush through these names of the disciples. And don't give unnecessary emphasis to the name of Judas Iscariot.

Zebedee = ZEB-uh-dee
Bartholomew = Bahr-THAHL-uh-myoo

Alphaeus = AL-fee-uhs
Thaddeus = THAD-ee-uhs
Cananaean = kay-nuh-NEE-uhn
Iscariot = ih-SKAYR-ee-uht

Samaritans = suh-MAYR-uh-tuhnz
Here the image of the lost sheep returns.

Jesus provides instruction as clear and direct as possible as to what his disciples are to do. Proclaim these tasks forcefully.

pray for more people to assist with bringing people into the fold, or into God's kingdom.

After his honest assessment that the work to come will be arduous, Jesus gives authority to the twelve disciples—who are referred to by Matthew here as Apostles, meaning those who are sent out—to heal people and combat the works of evil. Essentially, Jesus invites these disciples to share in his ministry in a particular way. He then names them, and from this we have a list of the twelve Apostles. Earlier in Matthew we have heard the names of five of them: Peter, Andrew, James, and John were

mentioned when Jesus called these fishermen away from their father, their boats, and their nets (Matthew 4.18–22) and Matthew was called away from his post as a tax collector (Matthew 9.9); the remaining seven names are listed here for the first time.

Before releasing the disciples into the world, Jesus provides them with instructions that begin with a caution to avoid the territory of the Gentiles and Samaritans and to focus exclusively on "the lost sheep of the house of Israel." Remember that Jesus has been ministering among this people and has come to pity them. For Matthew's audience,

primarily a community of Jewish Christians struggling to understand their faith in a rapidly changing society where they are no longer accepted by the Jewish community, and in the wake of the Temple's destruction, this command by Jesus to minister within given boundaries would have been reassuring. But this is only the beginning of the work of the kingdom, as Jesus instructs them to announce that "the kingdom of heaven has come near." This work of the harvest is still ongoing today as we take up the Christian mission and give in abundance without expecting to be repaid. S.W.

THE NATIVITY OF SAINT JOHN THE BAPTIST (VIGIL MASS)

LECTIONARY #586

READING I Jeremiah 1.4–10

A reading from the book of the Prophet Jeremiah.

The **word** of the Lord **came** to me saying,
"Before I **formed** you in the **womb** I **knew** you,
and before you were **born** I **consecrated** you;
I appointed you a **Prophet** to the nations."
Then I said, "**Ah**, Lord **God**!
Truly I do not **know** how to **speak**,
for I am only a **boy**."
But the Lord **said** to me,
"Do not say, 'I am only a **boy**';
for you shall go to **all** to whom I **send** you,
and you shall **speak** whatever I **command** you.
Do not be **afraid** of them,
for I am **with** you to **deliver** you,
says the Lord."
Then the **Lord** put out his **hand** and touched my **mouth**;
and the Lord **said** to me,
"**Now** I have put my **words** in your **mouth**.
See, today I appoint you over **nations** and over **kingdoms**,
to pluck **up** and to pull **down**,
to **destroy** and to **overthrow**,
to **build** and to **plant**."

Jeremiah = jayr-uh-Mĭ-uh

A reading that consists mainly of exhortations, in which God reassures Jeremiah of the importance of his prophetic calling.

God says "Do not" twice as a way of framing who Jeremiah is to him.

The reading concludes with three contrasts you can emphasize: up/down; destroy/overthrow; build/plant.

READING I The first reading for the vigil of the Nativity of St. John the Baptist is part of a dialogue between God and Jeremiah in which Jeremiah is called to be a Prophet. The reference to God forming Jeremiah in the womb recalls the second creation story in Genesis, where God is described as forming *adam*, the man, out of the dust of the ground. The Hebrew word translated here as "to form" is almost always used to describe the work of a potter or carver.

Jeremiah's protest of his calling is relatively common in call narratives of this sort (see also Isaiah 6.5–7; Daniel 10.4–21), but it can be helpful to recognize that it is not about his unwillingness to serve but rather the fear that the task is too big. Thus, God's response should be seen as encouragement to a person who is unsure of his ability to fulfill his mission. The gesture of God touching Jeremiah's mouth to place God's words in him is a symbol of God doing what God promised: that God would give him the words to speak and be with him to deliver him from those who would do him harm. The cluster of verbs in the last sentence of this reading is typical of the Book of Jeremiah, indicating the dual role of the Prophet to condemn and to console or build up the nations.

For meditation and context:

RESPONSORIAL PSALM Psalm 71.1–2, 3, 5–6, 15+17 (R.6)

R. From my mother's womb, you have been my strength.

In you, O Lord, I take refuge;
let me never be put to shame.
In your righteousness deliver me and
    rescue me;
incline your ear to me and save me.

Be to me a rock of refuge,
a strong fortress, to save me,
for you are my rock and my fortress.
Rescue me, O my God, from the hand
    of the wicked.

For you, O Lord, are my hope,
my trust, O Lord, from my youth.
Upon you I have leaned from my birth;
from my mother's womb you have been
    my strength.

My mouth will tell of your righteous acts,
of your deeds of salvation all day long.
O God, from my youth you have taught me,
and I still proclaim your wondrous deeds.

READING II   1 Peter 1.8–12

A reading from the first Letter of Saint Peter.

Beloved:
Although you have not seen Jesus Christ, you **love** him;
and even though you do not see him **now**, you **believe** in him
and **rejoice** with an indescribable and glorious **joy**,
for you are receiving the **outcome** of your **faith**,
the **salvation** of your **souls**.
The **Prophets** who prophesied of the **grace**
that was to be **yours**
concerning this **salvation** made **careful search** and **inquiry**,
inquiring about the **person** or **time**
that the **Spirit** of Christ **within** them indicated
when he **testified** in **advance**
to the **sufferings** and the subsequent **glory** destined for **Christ**.
It was **revealed** to the **Prophets**
that they were serving not **themselves** but **you**,
in regard to the **things** that have now been **announced** to you
through **those** who brought you good **news**
by the **Holy Spirit** sent from **heaven**
—**things** into which **Angels** long to **look!** »

A reading of subtle argument and passionate feeling about the revelatory nature of the love of Jesus.

"Love" is the word that guides this reading. All of the things Peter sees revealed arise from the love he ascribes to his audience, whom he addresses tenderly throughout this reading in the second person.

READING II Our second reading comes from the First Letter of Peter. Most biblical scholars consider it to be a pseudonymous work, written in approximately AD 70–90 to honour Peter and continue his ministry into the next generation.

When the author of this document says, "Although you have not seen Jesus Christ," he is acknowledging the difference between Peter, who was an eyewitness to Jesus' ministry, and the recipients of this letter, who did not know Jesus in the flesh but who believe in him now. The statement

about the joy that will come to them when they receive the outcome of their faith is a reference to the end time. Because resurrection of the dead was one of the signs of the end time, many early Christians believed that they were already on the cusp of this joyous and glorious end time, when Christ would return and God's reign would be established on earth.

But the author of 1 Peter has some interesting things to say about the Prophets of the Old Testament. He says that they searched out diligently and inquired into the salvation that the recipients of this let-

ter were awaiting. This salvation he calls "grace," also translated as "favour or loving-kindness." He also suggests that these Prophets were possessed by the Spirit of Christ—most likely the Holy Spirit—and that the Holy Spirit testified in advance to the Prophets about the suffering, death, and exaltation of Jesus Christ, so that the recipients of this letter could receive the good news of Jesus Christ through the Holy Spirit. This good news is so delightful that even the Angels want to peer through the windows of heaven to see!

At "Therefore," Peter expresses his wishes. Stress "action" as well as "revealed" at the end.

Therefore prepare your **minds** for **action**;
discipline yourselves;
set all your **hope** on the **grace**
that **Jesus Christ** will bring you when he is **revealed**.

GOSPEL   Luke 1.5–17

A reading from the holy Gospel according to Luke.

A reading from the beginning of Luke's Gospel telling the dramatic and anticipatory tale of the coming of John the Baptist. The drama of the story is so ingrained in the language that it requires only your proclamation of it.

In the **days** of King Herod of **Judea**,
there was a **priest** named **Zechariah**,
who belonged to the **priestly order** of Abijah.
His **wife** was a descendant of **Aaron**,
and her **name** was **Elizabeth**.
Both of them were **righteous** before God,
living **blamelessly** according to all the **commandments**
and **regulations** of the **Lord**.
But they had no **children**, because **Elizabeth** was **barren**,
and **both** were getting **on** in years.
Once when Zechariah was serving as **priest** before God
and his **section** was on **duty**,
he was chosen by **lot**,
according to the **custom** of the **priesthood**,
to enter the **sanctuary** of the Lord and offer **incense**.
Now at the time of the **incense offering**,
the whole assembly of the **people** was praying **outside**.
Then there **appeared** to him an Angel of the **Lord**,
standing at the right side of the **altar** of incense.
When Zechariah **saw him**, he was **terrified**;
and **fear overwhelmed** him.
But the Angel **said** to him,
"Do **not** be **afraid**, Zechariah,
for your **prayer** has been **heard**.

Zechariah's terror is essential to the story. It's useful to be reminded that Angels, as Rilke insisted, are terrifying.

GOSPEL   The Gospel reading is the story of the Angel Gabriel's appearance to Zechariah to announce the birth of John the Baptist. The form or structure of the story is very similar to the story of Gabriel's appearance to Mary announcing the birth of Jesus (Luke 1.26–38). Both stories are found only in Luke's Gospel, and both begin with a statement about a woman who should not be pregnant.

Elizabeth is too old and Mary is not yet married. Both stories describe the Angel announcing the birth of a baby, in one case to Zechariah and the other to Mary. In both stories, the Angel tells them not to be afraid, provides the name of the child, and explains his destiny. In both stories, the recipient of the Angel's message protests, with Zechariah saying, "How will I know that this is so?" (Luke 1.18). And in both

stories, a sign is given, but here is where the two stories diverge. The Angel tells Zechariah that he will not be able to speak until everything the Angel told him comes to completion, because he did not believe the Angel's words (Luke 1.18–20).

But what did the Angel say about John's destiny? He will be great in God's sight, he will be consecrated to God from birth (that is what refraining from alcohol is

"He must never drink wine . . ." From here, we get a foretaste of the character of John the Baptist as foreseen by the Angel describing him to his father, Zechariah.

Your wife **Elizabeth** will bear you a **son**,
and you will name him **John**.
You will have **joy** and **gladness**,
and many will **rejoice** at his **birth**,
for he will be **great** in the sight of the **Lord**.
He must never **drink wine** or strong **drink**;
even before his **birth** he will be **filled** with the Holy **Spirit**.
He will turn **many** of the people of **Israel** to the Lord their **God**.
With the **spirit** and power of **Elijah** he will go **before** him,
to turn the **hearts** of parents to their **children**,
and the **disobedient** to the wisdom of the **righteous**,
to make **ready** a people **prepared** for the **Lord**."

referencing), and he will be possessed by the Holy Spirit before he is born. Finally, Luke includes a paraphrase of Malachi 3.23–24, which describes how the Prophet Elijah is supposed to appear before the day of God's judgment. But the evangelist reinterprets the text to indicate John the Baptist as the new Elijah, who comes before the day of the Lord Jesus Christ. Thus, he will be the source of great joy. C.C.

THE NATIVITY OF SAINT JOHN THE BAPTIST (MASS ON THE DAY)

LECTIONARY #587

READING I   Isaiah 49.1–6

A reading from the book of the Prophet Isaiah.

Listen to me, O **coastlands**,
pay **attention**, you **peoples** from far **away**!
The **Lord** called me before I was **born**,
while I was in my mother's **womb** he **named** me.
He made my **mouth** like a sharp **sword**,
in the **shadow** of his hand he **hid** me;
he made me a polished **arrow**,
in his **quiver** he hid me **away**.
And the Lord **said** to me,
"You are my **servant**, Israel, in whom I will be **glorified**."
But I said, "I have **laboured** in vain,
I have spent my strength for **nothing** and **vanity**;
yet **surely** my cause is with the **Lord**,
and my **reward** with my **God**."
And now the **Lord** says,
who **formed** me in the **womb** to be his **servant**,
to bring Jacob **back** to him,
and that **Israel** might be **gathered** to him,
for I am **honoured** in the sight of the **Lord**,
and my **God** has become my **strength**.

Isaiah = ī-ZAY-uh

A reading that rehearses the prophetic authority of Isaiah in powerful poetic language. You can treat the proclamation like a poem.

There is a certain amount of boastfulness in Isaiah's claim, which the Prophet himself will modify as the reading continues. Allow for both boastfulness and modesty in your proclamation.

READING I Today's first reading is the second of four servant songs from Second Isaiah (Isaiah 40–55), written during the Babylonian Exile. The exile was a very dark time in the history of God's people. Thus, we can expect that many of the oracles of Second Isaiah are oracles of consolation, and this one is no exception.

The oracle begins with an invitation to distant lands and peoples to hear the Prophet's declaration. He identifies himself as the servant, called by name from his mother's womb for his special mission and as the representative of Israel itself. The sharp-edged sword and the sharpened arrow are symbols of the Prophet's effectiveness in delivering God's word. Most likely, the references to God shielding the Prophet and hiding him in God's quiver are metaphors for God's protection of his servant. Although King Cyrus of Persia would be the one to allow the exiles to return to Judea, God speaks in the last section of this reading and says that the servant's mission is so much greater. He is to be a light to the nations to make God's salvation known to the whole world.

READING II Today's second reading is an excerpt from Acts of the Apostles, in which Paul is presented as giving a speech in a synagogue in Antioch of Pisidia on a Sabbath—Luke is the actual author of this speech—to an audience that includes fellow Jews as well as Gentiles who attended synagogue and participated in religious activities that were open to Gentiles.

Beginning with the Israelites' time in the wilderness, Paul talks about how God chose the Israelites while they lived in Egypt and how God lifted them up (or made them prosper) during that time. He also

He says,
"It is too small a thing that you should be my **servant**
to **raise up** the tribes of **Jacob**
and to **restore** the survivors of **Israel**;
I will give you as a **light** to the **nations**,
that my salvation may **reach** to the end of the **earth**."

Emphasis on "reach," "end," and "earth."

For meditation and context:

RESPONSORIAL PSALM   Psalm 139.1–3, 13–14a, 14b–15 (R.14)

R. I praise you, for I am wonderfully made.

O Lord, you have searched me and
    known me.
You know when I sit down and when I
    rise up;
you discern my thoughts from far away.
You search out my path and my lying down,
and are acquainted with all my ways.

For it was you who formed my inward parts;
you knit me together in my mother's womb.
I praise you,
for I am fearfully and wonderfully made.

Wonderful are your works; that I know
    very well.
My frame was not hidden from you,
when I was being made in secret,
intricately woven in the depths of the earth.

READING II   Acts 13.22–26

A reading from the Acts of the Apostles.

In **those** days, Paul said:
"God made **David** king of our **ancestors**.
In his **testimony** about him God said,
'I have found **David**, son of **Jesse**,
to be a **man** after my **heart**,
who will carry **out** all my **wishes**.'
Of **this man's** posterity
God has brought to **Israel** a **Saviour**, Jesus, as he **promised**;
before his **coming**
John had **already** proclaimed a **baptism** of **repentance**
to all the **people** of Israel.
And as John was **finishing** his work, he said,
'**What** do you suppose that I **am**?
I am not he. »

A reading that consists entirely of an exhortatory speech of Paul's, one in which he quotes God speaking (a nested exhortation). Paul is asserting his own acceptance of God's authority.

"I am not he." Even emphasis on each of these words.

---

talked about how God led them out of Egypt and endured their ways, like a mother cares for a child, for forty years in the wilderness, until they were able to enter the land of Canaan that God gave to them. Then God gave them judges to rescue them from their enemies and finally a king, as they requested.

This is where our reading begins. When Saul proved to be a bad king, Paul says that God raised up David and testified to David's worthiness with an allusion to Scripture, which appears to be a conflation of Psalm 89.20 and 1 Samuel 13.14. Further,

Paul talks about the promise made to David concerning one of his descendants, whom God will raise up and will give him an everlasting kingdom. Luke now turns to the Gospel tradition about John the Baptist proclaiming a baptism of repentance before the coming day of the Lord and responding to people's query about whether he might be the messiah. John rejects this idea by saying, "One is coming after me; I am not worthy to untie the thong of the sandals on his feet" (see Luke 3.1–18).

GOSPEL   Today's Gospel reading is the story of the birth, circumcision, and naming of John the Baptist, which is told only in Luke's Gospel. In some respects, the story is rather straightforward. We hear that Elizabeth gave birth to a baby boy, and friends and family rejoiced with her. However, since she was not expected to be able to get pregnant due to her old age, those around her attributed this marvellous event to God's mercy toward her. During this time period, it was believed that a woman's barrenness was the consequence of God withholding blessings from

No, but one is coming **after** me;
I am not **worthy** to untie the **thong** of the **sandals** on his **feet**.'
You **descendants** of Abraham's **family**,
and **others** who fear **God**,
to us the **message** of this **salvation** has been **sent**."

Paul concludes with conviction. Emphasis on "message," "salvation," and "sent."

GOSPEL   Luke 1.57–66, 80

A reading from the holy Gospel according to Luke.

The time came for **Elizabeth** to give **birth**,
and she bore a **son**.
Her **neighbours** and **relatives** heard
that the **Lord** had shown his great **mercy** to her,
and they **rejoiced** with her.
On the **eighth day** they came to **circumcise** the child,
and they were going to name him **Zechariah** after his **father**.
But his mother said, "**No**; he is to be called **John**."
They said to her, "None of your **relatives** has this name."
Then they began **motioning** to his father
to find out what **name** he wanted to **give** him.
He asked for a writing tablet and wrote,
"His **name** is **John**."
And **all** of them were **amazed**.
Immediately his mouth was **opened** and his tongue **freed**,
and he began to **speak**, praising **God**.
Fear came **over** all their **neighbours**,
and all these things were **talked** about
throughout the entire **hill** country of **Judea**.
All who **heard** them **pondered** them and **said**,
"**What then** will this child **become**?"
For, **indeed**, the hand of the **Lord** was **with** him.
The child **grew** and became **strong** in spirit,
and he was in the **wilderness**
until the day he appeared **publicly** to Israel.

A reading about the birth of John the Baptist, filled with inherent drama. This story never grows old.

The insistence on the name "John," which came from the Angel who announced Elizabeth's pregnancy, is presented in defiance of custom. Something will change because of this child John. The name can be spoken with familiarity and tenderness. The repetition of the name John. (Interestingly, here it is written rather than spoken.)

Emphasize "wilderness," a term with which John the Baptist is forever associated.

her. However, the Bible also contains several stories about once-barren women giving birth to great leaders in the tradition. For example, we hear of Sarah, the once-barren wife of Abraham who gave birth to Isaac; of Rebecca, the wife of Isaac, who gave birth to Esau and Jacob; and of Rachel, the wife of Jacob, who gave birth to Joseph. And now, Elizabeth, the once-barren wife of Zechariah, gives birth to John. Thus, the promise that the Angel made to Zechariah is fulfilled.

Likewise, it would have been typical for family and friends to gather on the eighth day after the baby's birth for the circumcision, which is the ritual of inclusion into Judaism. However, as the story suggests, there were traditional practices around the naming of a child, which neither Elizabeth nor Zechariah intended to follow. And when Zechariah wrote, "His name is John," the sign given to him by the Angel was lifted and he was able to speak again. Moreover, his first words were of blessing to God. The name "John" means "God has

shown favour." As for the response of family and friends, the Greek word *phobos*, translated here as "fear," also means "reverence or respect." Thus, they wondered over this child in awe, knowing that he was destined to be special. Finally, Luke expertly changes scenes by retiring John to the desert, until he appears later to preach his baptism of repentance in Luke 3.1–20. However, many details of John's birth and circumcision serve as a precursor to Jesus' birth, circumcision, and naming. C.C.

TWELFTH SUNDAY IN ORDINARY TIME

LECTIONARY #94

READING I   Jeremiah 20.10–13

A reading from the book of the Prophet Jeremiah.

Jeremiah = jer-uh-Mī-uh

The tone that opens this reading is fearful. Jeremiah is terrified.

Jeremiah cried **out**:
I hear **many whispering**:
"**Terror** is all **around**!
Denounce him! Let us **denounce** him!"
All my **close friends**
are **watching** for me to **stumble**.
"Perhaps he can be **enticed**,
and we can **prevail against** him,
and take our **revenge** on him."

Here, with "But," the tone shifts, becoming more hopeful. Jeremiah is talking himself into persevering.

But the **Lord** is **with** me like a **dread** warrior;
therefore my **persecutors** will **stumble**,
and they **will not prevail**.
They will be **greatly shamed**,
for they **will not succeed**.
Their **eternal dishonour**
will **never** be **forgotten**.

"O Lord" begins a petition, one in which Jeremiah asks to witness the vengeance God will take on his persecutors, a common enough request but nevertheless worth noting.

With this conclusion, Jeremiah shifts into the imperative voice: Jeremiah is speaking to the assembly through these words.

O **Lord** of **hosts**, you **test** the **righteous**,
you **see** the **heart** and the **mind**;
let me **see** your **retribution upon** them,
for to **you** I have **committed** my **cause**.
Sing to the **Lord**;
praise the **Lord**!
For he has delivered the life of the needy
from the hands of evildoers.

READING I This passage is a portion of one of Jeremiah's "confessions," a term scholars use to describe passages of Jeremiah in which the Prophet reveals personal anguish and lament to God. This confession follows Jeremiah's encounter with the priest Pashhur, who was one of the Temple priests who persecuted Jeremiah for his prediction of the destruction of Jerusalem by the Babylonians. In hearing Jeremiah's distress, it is important to keep in mind that he never sought the life of a Prophet and even, in this moment of lamentation, considers himself deceived by God to accept this life as a Prophet (Jeremiah 20.7).

Our reading begins with the announcement "Terror is all around!" Jeremiah uses these words to foretell the destruction of Jerusalem, but they also come from the lips of those who oppose the Prophet. Like Job, Jeremiah believes that his friends have turned against him (Job 19.19). What acts of "revenge" they plot for the demise of the Prophet we can only imagine. However, Jeremiah confronts fear and turns to the Lord, who will act as a hero on his behalf and cause his enemies to "stumble."

Jeremiah counts himself among the just whose mind and heart is known well by God, and he prays that he will be able to witness the power of the Lord bringing Jeremiah's enemies to shame.

The final words of Jeremiah's "confession" turns from lament to praise. He commands that songs of praise ring out before the Lord because he has defended the poor—who may be understood as the lowly ones of Israel—from the "hands of evildoers." It is clear that God defends the poor not because of their economic status but rather because of their dependence

For meditation and context:

RESPONSORIAL PSALM   Psalm 69.7–9, 13+16, 32–33, 35ab+36 (R.13)

R. Lord, in your steadfast love, answer me.

It is for your sake that I have borne reproach,
that shame has covered my face.
I have become a stranger to my kindred,
an alien to my mother's children.
It is zeal for your house that has
    consumed me;
the insults of those who insult you have
    fallen on me.

But as for me, my prayer is to you, O Lord.
At an acceptable time, O God,
in the abundance of your steadfast love,
    answer me.

With your steadfast help, rescue me.
Answer me, O Lord, for your steadfast
    love is good;
according to your abundant mercy,
    turn to me.

Let the oppressed see it and be glad;
you who seek God, let your hearts revive.
For the Lord hears the needy,
and does not despise his own that are
    in bonds.
Let heaven and earth praise him,
the seas and everything that moves in them.

READING II   Romans 5.12–15

A reading from the Letter of Saint Paul to the Romans.

Paul uses the example of Adam to make a complex argument about sin and sinfulness, especially its durability in Scripture. Like reading a nuanced legal argument aloud, proclaim at a slow and even pace to allow its contents to register with your assembly.

Brothers and **sisters**:
Just as **sin** came into the **world** through **one man**,
and **death** came through **sin**,
so **death spread** to **all people** because **all** have **sinned**.
Sin was **indeed** in the **world** before the **law**,
but **sin** is not **reckoned** when there **is** no **law**.
Yet **death** exercised **dominion** from **Adam** to **Moses**,
even over **those** whose **sins** were **not** like the **transgression**
    of **Adam**,
who is a **type** of the **one** who was to **come**.
But the **free gift** is not like the **trespass**.
For if the **many died** through the **one man's trespass**,
much more **surely** have the **grace** of **God**
and the **free gift** in the **grace** of the **one man**, **Jesus Christ**,
abounded for the **many**.

Note the inversion that concludes the reading: "many died" and "one man's trespass"; the "free gift" of "one man" benefiting the "many."

upon him. Although the Prophet did not ask for this task of proclaiming the word of God, he never falters in his obedience and his dependence on the goodness of God.

READING II | These verses from the fifth chapter of the Letter to the Romans serve as part of the prelude to Paul's foundational theology of baptism. Baptism is participation in Christ's death and burial so that sin can reign in the body no more and we will have life in Christ (Romans 6). The passage we read today provides the background as to why baptism is necessary.

Sin entered the world through the disobedience of Adam, and this resulted in the dawning of death. Adam brings about a universal predicament for all humans, namely that all participate in sin and will experience death.

The appearance of Moses in this passage is important for Paul's theology. Moses represents the giving of the Law by God. Thus, from the time between Adam and Moses, humanity was without the direction of the Law. This means that humanity could not be (legally) responsible for sin during this time since it did not have an understanding

of the Law. Nevertheless, sin did exist at this point because death had already entered the world. Sin cannot be separated from death; death is the result of sin.

Paul's major point here is that God provides a gift in the death of his Son that far outweighs the consequences of Adam's disobedience. By his own death, Jesus destroys death once and for all. With the destruction of death comes the banishment of all sin. The grace of God that is provided in this gift is to be accessed by baptism into Christ Jesus.

Jesus is speaking to his disciples and offering them advice. There is a somewhat stern and mysterious tone that prevails.

The example of the sparrows at first seems to be out of context with what comes before, yet Jesus persists in the example, connecting it with his message about overcoming fear.

Note the inversion Matthew uses to conclude Jesus' speech in this passage, contrasting acknowledgement and denial.

GOSPEL   Matthew 10.26–33

A reading from the holy Gospel according to Matthew.

Jesus said to his **Apostles**:
"**Fear no** one;
for **nothing** is covered **up** that will **not** be **uncovered**,
and nothing **secret** that will **not** become **known**.
What **I say** to you in the **dark**, **tell** in the **light**;
and what you hear **whispered**, **proclaim** from the **housetops**.
Do not **fear** those who **kill** the **body**
but cannot **kill** the **soul**;
rather **fear him** who can **destroy** both **soul** and **body** in **hell**.
Are not **two sparrows sold** for a **penny**?
Yet not **one** of them will **fall** to the **ground**
apart from your **Father**.
And even the **hairs** of your **head** are all **counted**.
So **do not** be **afraid**;
you are of **more value** than **many sparrows**.
Everyone **therefore** who **acknowledges** me before **humans**,
I **also** will **acknowledge** before my **Father** in **heaven**;
but whoever **denies** me before **humans**,
I **also** will **deny** before my **Father** in **heaven**."

GOSPEL   Jesus' instructions to the twelve Apostles as he sends them out to gather the harvest of the kingdom speak of the necessary boldness of discipleship that will turn whispers into a message shouted from the housetops. Jesus has just finished informing his disciples that when he sends them into the world, they can expect to be persecuted by those who refuse to listen to them. Their response to such persecution must be quite simply "Fear no one." In fact, in this one reading, Jesus tells them three times that fear is not an acceptable attitude for disciples.

The quiet nature of the message of the kingdom by which Jesus instructs his disciples, spoken in "the dark" and heard "whispered," also calls our attention to the commission of the disciples after the Resurrection. The fullness of Jesus' message can't be proclaimed yet, even by the those closest to Jesus, because the disciples lack a full understanding of the kingdom and what Jesus' death and Resurrection will mean; at the end of Matthew's Gospel, the disciples are called to share the Good News with all peoples. Returning our attention to this moment, the disciples do go out and proclaim it as they can at that time.

The dire warning that death is a possible outcome of this mission is cause for fear, yet Jesus helps the disciples to shift their focus from the fear of bodily harm and death to the importance of preserving one's soul in the face of the wicked. Because of their identity as followers of God, they are cared for by God. They must act in a manner that illustrates this, trusting in God and remaining in him. S.W.

SAINTS PETER AND PAUL, APOSTLES (VIGIL MASS)

LECTIONARY #590

READING I   Acts 3.1–10

A reading from the Acts of the Apostles.

One day **Peter** and **John** were going up to the **temple**
at the hour of **prayer**, at three o'clock in the **afternoon**.
A man **lame** from birth was being carried **in**.
People would lay him **daily** at the gate of the **temple**
called the **Beautiful Gate**
so that he could **ask** for alms from those entering the **temple**.
When he saw **Peter** and **John** about to go into the temple,
he **asked** them for **alms**.
Peter looked intently at him, as did John, and said,
"**Look at us**."
He fixed his attention on them,
expecting to receive something from them.
Peter said, "I have **no silver** or **gold**,
but what I **have** I **give** you;
in the name of **Jesus Christ** of **Nazareth**, stand up and **walk**."
And he **took** him by the **right hand** and raised him **up**;
and **immediately** his feet and ankles were made **strong**.
Jumping **up**, the man **stood** and began to **walk**,
and he entered the temple **with** them,
walking and **leaping** and **praising** God.

A compelling reading that depicts the healing power provided to the Apostles, presented from the perspective of the person who is healed. The dramatic quality of the narrative speaks for itself; your proclamation, guided by attention to the rhythms of the reading, will allow it to speak.

Even stresses on all three words, almost: "Look. At. Us."

Notice the effective use of participles in these two lines, "walking," "leaping," "praising," with "walking" and "praising" repeated. Allow the stresses of these words (DAH-dah, poetically speaking) to guide the rhythm of these lines when you proclaim them.

READING I On this vigil of the solemnity that commemorates the life and martyrdom of Sts. Peter and Paul, we celebrate the audacity of love in action. Our first reading, from the Acts of the Apostles, tells the story of Peter and John encountering a beggar at one of the city gates of Jerusalem. For those of us who live in urban areas, this is a rather familiar scene and one from which we often prefer to avert our eyes. It is easier simply not to look at our modern-day beggars than to reckon with the complexities of life that result in this kind of suffering.

This is the first miracle story of the Acts of the Apostles, and, in many respects, it reads like a miracle story from the Gospels. It has a description of a problem, the miracle worker's word or deed, and evidence that the miracle took place. Notice, however, the amount of dialogue between the beggar and Peter. Notice, also, how Peter is very deliberate about encountering the beggar. He seems to recognize what the beggar wants—a handout of some sort—but he gives him so much more, namely, the ability to walk and even to jump for joy! How did Peter effect this miracle? The narrator tells us that it was because of Jesus' power working in and through him to liberate this poor beggar. As people of faith, let us pray that we can be so bold as to make an audacious act of love for someone we meet today.

READING II In this reading from the Letter to the Galatians, Paul tells us a bit about his own life story, but the context is important. In the preceding verses, he fiercely scolds the churches of Galatia, because they abandoned the Gospel—literally, good message—of Jesus

All the people saw him **walking** and **praising** God,
and they **recognized** him as the one who used to **sit**
and ask for **alms** at the Beautiful **Gate** of the **temple**;
they were **filled** with wonder and **amazement**
at what had **happened** to him.

For meditation and context:

RESPONSORIAL PSALM   Psalm 19.1–2, 3–4 (R.4a)

R. Their voice goes out through all the earth.

The heavens are telling the glory of God;
and the firmament proclaims his handiwork.
Day to day pours forth speech,
and night to night declares knowledge.

There is no speech, nor are there words;
their voice is not heard;
yet their voice goes out through all the earth,
and their words to the end of the world.

READING II   Galatians 1.11–20

A reading from the Letter of Saint Paul to the Galatians.

Paul uses this letter to the members of the early Church in Galatia to present the story of his apostolic authority, providing a narrative of his experience as well as a sense of his difference from and connection to the Apostles in Jerusalem (specifically, to Peter).

Emphasize that Paul received the Gospel from an origin that was not human (by implication, divine).

From here, Paul rehearses his experience. Something like his resumé. Slight emphasis on "violently."

I want you to **know**, brothers and sisters,
that the Gospel that was proclaimed by **me** is not
of **human** origin;
for I did not **receive** it from a human **being**,
nor was I **taught** it,
but I **received** it through a **revelation** of Jesus **Christ**.
You have **heard**, no doubt, of my earlier **life** in Judaism.
I was **violently** persecuting the **Church** of God
and was **trying** to destroy it.
I advanced in Judaism
beyond **many** among my people of the same **age**,
for I was far more **zealous** for the **traditions** of my **ancestors**.
But when **God**, who had set me **apart** before I was **born**
and called me through his **grace**,
was pleased to **reveal** his **Son** to me,
so that I might **proclaim** him among the **Gentiles**,
I did not **confer** with flesh and **blood**, **»**

Christ that he proclaimed when he first visited them, and now they have taken up a different proclamation of faith. He is so offended by their action that he issues a curse on anyone who proclaims this other Gospel (Galatians 1.6–9).

Apparently, Paul was also deeply offended by some community members' suggestion that he was preaching the message of Jesus Christ for his own gain. Thus, he asserts that the message about Jesus Christ that he proclaims is sound and without bias or ulterior motives, because he did not receive it from any human source but

only through Jesus' own revelation to him. This is most likely an allusion to the story in Acts 9.1–30, in which Paul, then called Saul, was on the road to Damascus to hunt down and arrest followers of Jesus, whom he viewed as troublemakers within Jewish communities in the area.

Paul continues to assert his credibility as an Apostle by telling his life story, explaining that he was a learned and devout Jew, zealous to uphold the traditions of Judaism, but that the appearance of the risen Christ on the road to Damascus dramatically changed him. Although he never stopped

being a Jew, he now identifies himself as an Apostle of Jesus, because of his experience with the risen Christ, and as one called by God from birth to take up the mission of evangelization among the Gentiles (non-Jews), including their own churches in Galatia. We know from other sources that Paul's devotion to this mission and his love for the Gentile Christian communities that he serves will cost him greatly, ending in his martyrdom in Rome.

Emphasize "Arabia" and "Damascus." And then "three years." This provides a sense of Paul's distance from Jerusalem as he was beginning his ministry.

The implication of this last line is that someone, who has also been in contact with the members of the early Church in Galatia, has suggested that Paul has been lying. He is correcting this suggestion (or accusation) with this letter. This last line and the last word especially are therefore loaded.

An exquisite conversation between Jesus and Peter. Traditionally, this reading is believed to depict Jesus' forgiveness of Peter for the sin of denying knowledge of Jesus three times after he was arrested.

First expression of Peter's love. Emphasis on "know."

Second expression of Peter's love. Emphasis again on "know."

nor did I go **up** to Jerusalem
to those who were already Apostles **before** me,
but I went away at **once** into **Arabia**,
and afterwards I returned to **Damascus**.
Then after **three years**
I did go up to **Jerusalem** to visit **Cephas**
and **stayed** with him **fifteen days**;
but I **did not see** any other apostle
except **James** the Lord's brother.
In what I am **writing** to you, before God, I do not **lie**!

GOSPEL   John 21.15–19

A reading from the holy Gospel according to John.

For the **third time** after he was **raised** from the dead,
Jesus appeared to the disciples.
Just after daybreak, he stood on the beach
and said to them, "**Come** and **eat**."
When they had **finished** breakfast,
Jesus said to Simon **Peter**,
"**Simon** son of John, do you **love** me more than **these**?"
He said to him, "**Yes**, Lord; you know that I **love** you."
Jesus said to him, "**Feed** my lambs."
A **second** time he said to him,
"**Simon** son of **John**, do you **love** me?"
He said to him, "**Yes**, Lord; you **know** that I **love** you."
Jesus said to him, "**Tend** my **sheep**."
He said to him the **third** time,
"**Simon** son of **John**, do you **love** me?"
Peter felt **hurt** because he said to him the **third time**,
"Do you **love** me?"

GOSPEL This reading is taken from the epilogue of the Gospel of John. An epilogue is an afterword or a comment about the conclusion of a story: in this case, the story of Jesus' appearance to the disciples in the upper room where they had been hiding after his crucifixion. In the beginning of the epilogue (John 21.1–13), we learn that Peter decides to go fishing, and six other disciples go with him. After fishing all night and catching nothing, Jesus appears to them and directs them to put down their nets once again. When they catch so many fish that they cannot haul in

their nets, the Beloved Disciple recognizes the man standing on the shore as Jesus, and Peter jumps into the water to come to Jesus, who, by then, is preparing breakfast for them.

At the beginning of today's Gospel reading, the narrator tells us that this was the third time the risen Jesus had appeared to the disciples. The first was the night of his Resurrection, when the disciples had locked themselves in the upper room. The second was a week later, when Thomas was with the disciples, again in the locked room. Now, with the meal finished, Jesus

addresses Simon Peter three times with some form of "Do you love me more than these [other disciples]?" Peter answers, "Yes, Lord; you know that I love you," and Jesus responds with a version of "Feed/tend my lambs/sheep." Scholars of John's Gospel have speculated at length about the author's intent in this scene. Is he wishing to reinstate Peter as a genuine disciple of Jesus by reversing his three denials of Jesus in the courtyard of the high priest, Annas (John 18.15–18, 25–27)? Is this the Gospel writer's way of suggesting that Jesus commissioned Peter to be the shepherd or

Third expression of Peter's love. Emphasis on "everything" and on "love."

The reading concludes with Jesus suggesting the way his death (which has already happened; this reading takes place after the Resurrection) will glorify God. Emphasis on "Follow."

And he **said** to him,
"**Lord**, you know **everything**; you **know** that I **love** you."
Jesus said to him, "**Feed** my **sheep**.
Very truly, I **tell** you,
when you were **younger**,
you used to **fasten** your own belt and to go **wherever**
     you **wished**.
But when you grow **old**, you will stretch out your **hands**,
and someone **else** will fasten a belt **around** you
and **take you** where you do not wish to **go**."
(He **said** this to indicate the kind of **death**
by which he would glorify **God**.)
After this he **said** to him,
"**Follow** me."

PRAYERFUL READING, OR *LECTIO DIVINA*

1. *Lectio:* Read a Scripture passage aloud slowly. Notice what phrase captures your attention and be attentive to its meaning. Silent pause.

2. *Meditatio:* Read the passage aloud slowly again, reflecting on the passage, allowing God to speak to you through it. Silent pause.

3. *Oratio:* Read it aloud slowly a third time, allowing it to be your prayer or response to God's gift of insight to you. Silent pause.

4. *Contemplatio:* Read it aloud slowly a fourth time, now resting in God's Word.

---

overseer of the Church, even though the Beloved Disciple is the local spiritual leader? Is the author intending to show Peter as the inheritor of Jesus' role as the good shepherd (John 10.11–18, 25–28)? When Jesus asks, "Do you love me?" is he inviting Peter to take a special role in executing the words that Jesus gave to his disciples on the night of his arrest: "This is my commandment, that you love one another as I have loved you. No one has greater love than this, to lay down one's life for one's friends" (John 15.12–13).

Earlier in John's Gospel, at the Last Supper, Peter insisted that he would lay down his life for Jesus, even as Jesus prophesied that Peter would soon deny him (John 13.37–38). Now Jesus declares that Peter will indeed fulfill his promise to lay down his life for Jesus. Jesus makes this rather cryptic saying of Peter that one day "you will stretch out your hands, and someone else will fasten a belt around you and take you where you do not wish to go." This saying refers to Peter's martyrdom, which took place in approximately AD 64, some

twenty-five to thirty-five years before the Gospel of John was written. It is not certain whether "you will stretch out your hands" refers to crucifixion or to arrest more generally. However, the narrator adds that this saying indicates the way Peter would die and thus "glorify God" or fulfill God's will. C.C.

SAINTS PETER AND PAUL, APOSTLES (MASS ON THE DAY)

A visionary scene of Peter's rescue from imprisonment by help from an Angel. The reading has a supernatural, vividly highlighted quality, like a painting by El Greco, that comes through directly. A straightforward style of proclamation serves this reading best.

The reading begins by setting up the narrative, providing lots of details that lead to Peter's arrest by Herod and his henchmen. You can move through these details at a decent clip.

Emphasize the "chains," which play a role in Peter's miraculous rescue.

LECTIONARY #591

READING I   Acts 12.1–11

A reading from the Acts of the Apostles.

In those days,
King **Herod** laid violent **hands** upon some who **belonged**
    to the Church.
He had **James**, the brother of **John**, **killed** with the **sword**.
After he **saw** that it **pleased** some of the **people**,
he proceeded to arrest **Peter** also.
This was during the **festival** of Unleavened **Bread**.
When he had **seized** him, he put him in **prison**
and handed him over to **four squads** of soldiers to **guard** him,
intending to bring him **out** to the people after the **Passover**.
While **Peter** was kept in **prison**,
the Church prayed **fervently** to **God** for him.
The **very night** before Herod was going to **bring him out**,
Peter, bound with two **chains**, was **sleeping** between
    two **soldiers**,
while **guards** in front of the door were keeping **watch**
over the **prison**.
Suddenly an Angel of the Lord **appeared**
and a **light** shone in the **cell**.

READING I On this solemnity of Sts. Peter and Paul, our first reading tells a story about Peter being rescued from the clutches of Herod Agrippa, who reigned as king of Judea in AD 41–44. Apparently to curry favour with Jewish religious authorities in Jerusalem, Herod had James, an Apostle and one of the sons of Zebedee, put to death by the sword, and went on to arrest Peter as well.

Because it was the feast of Passover, Herod had Peter put in jail until the week-long spring pilgrimage festival was over, probably out of fear of the large number of visitors in Jerusalem at the time. Luke, the author of Acts of the Apostles, heightens the drama of this story by indicating that four "squads," or four sets of four soldiers, were assigned to guard him, and that he was doubly chained between two soldiers even at night. But Luke's story becomes even more spectacular as he tells his readers about how an Angel surrounded by light awakens Peter, tells him to get dressed, and leads him out of the prison. Inexplicably, the chains fall off and the gate of the prison opens on its own power and without attracting the attention of the guards.

While the Angel led him out of the prison complex and onto a lane that led to the city, Peter thought he was having a nighttime vision. Suddenly Peter comes to his senses, acknowledging that he had been under God's protection and that God's Angel released him from prison. The phrase "from all that the people were expecting" (literally, "from the expectation of the people of the Jews") probably refers to Luke's overarching plan to show how the Jesus movement shifted from its Jewish origins to the Gentile world.

He tapped **Peter** on the side and **woke** him,
saying, "Get up **quickly**."
And the **chains** fell off his **wrists**.
The Angel said to him,
"**Fasten your belt** and **put on** your **sandals**."
He **did** so. Then he said to him,
"**Wrap** your cloak **around** you and **follow** me."
Peter went out and **followed** him;
he did not **realize**
that what was **happening** with the Angel's **help** was **real**;
he thought he was seeing a **vision**.
After they had passed the **first** and the **second** guard,
they **came** before the iron **gate** leading into the **city**.
It **opened** for them of its own **accord**,
and they went **outside** and walked along a **lane**,
when **suddenly** the Angel **left** him.
Then **Peter** came to himself and said,
"**Now** I am sure that the **Lord** has sent his **Angel**
and **rescued** me from the hands of **Herod**
and from **all** that the people were **expecting**."

Emphasize "chains" and "wrists."

The visionary quality of this scene is what makes it so arresting. Don't overplay Peter's evident confusion (is it a dream, a vision, something else?). Instead, allow the scene to play out as you proclaim it.

When Peter comes to himself, he is asserting the truth, in part, of visionary experience. State these last three lines straightforwardly.

For meditation and context:

RESPONSORIAL PSALM   Psalm 34.1–2, 3–4, 5–6, 7–8 (R.4b)

R. The Lord set me free from all my fears.

I will bless the Lord at all times;
his praise shall continually be in my mouth.
My soul makes its boast in the Lord;
let the humble hear and be glad.

O magnify the Lord with me,
and let us exalt his name together.
I sought the Lord, and he answered me,
and delivered me from all my fears.

Look to him, and be radiant;
so your faces shall never be ashamed.
The poor one called, and the Lord heard,
and saved that person from every trouble.

The Angel of the Lord encamps
around those who fear him, and
    delivers them.
O taste and see that the Lord is good;
blessed is the one who takes refuge in him.

READING II   Today's second reading is another account of God's protective care for a martyred minister of the early Church. The author of this letter assumes the voice of Paul at the end of his life. However, most New Testament scholars consider the pastoral letters (1 and 2 Timothy and Titus) to be pseudepigraphic, that is, written in Paul's name by a later disciple to continue his memory into a later generation. These pastoral letters are usually assigned a date of approximately AD 100. Like Peter, Paul's martyrdom is thought to have taken place in Rome in approximately AD 64. Timothy, who is identified as the recipient of 2 Timothy, was a companion of Paul on his missionary journeys and is depicted in this letter as bishop or overseer of the Christians in Ephesus.

Writing in the name of Paul, this author uses beautifully poetic words to describe his preparedness for death in terms of a sacrificial offering and winning a boxing match or running a race. The Greek word for "libation" describes a drink offering poured out in a sacred place or on a sacred object to honour the deity. Thus, the libation mentioned here is Paul's blood that was shed in martyrdom. Likewise, ancient public games like the Olympics serve as background for understanding the author's reference to the judge and the crown. The judge of the public games was responsible for ensuring that the rules were followed, and the crown, usually made of olive leaves, was the award for winning. Here, the judge of righteousness is the risen Christ, and the crown is admission to God's kingdom in the end time, when Christ returns in glory.

libation = lī-BAY-shuhn

One of the pastoral letters, whose authorship scholars continue to debate, the context of this reading is that Paul, who is depicted as imprisoned and dying, is writing a letter to Timothy summarizing his life.

Note the repetition of the "have" phrases. These will provide you with a rhythm to follow in this poetic text as you proclaim.

Emphasize the inclusion here, "not *only* to me but also to *all* . . ."

The two uses of "rescue" in these two lines are important (and echo the use of this word in the first reading).

READING II   2 Timothy 4.6–8, 17–18

A reading from the second Letter of Saint Paul to Timothy.

Beloved:
I am **already** being poured **out** as a libation,
and the **time** of my **departure** has **come**.
I have **fought** the good fight,
I have **finished** the race,
I have **kept** the faith.
From **now on**
there is **reserved** for me the **crown** of **righteousness**,
which the **Lord**, the righteous **judge**,
will **give me** on that **day**,
and not **only** to me
but also to **all** who have **longed** for his **appearing**.
The Lord stood **by** me and gave me **strength**,
so that **through** me the message might be **fully** proclaimed
and **all** the Gentiles might **hear** it.
So I was **rescued** from the lion's **mouth**.
The Lord will **rescue** me from every evil **attack**
and **save** me for his heavenly **kingdom**.
To **him** be the **glory forever** and **ever**. Amen.

GOSPEL   Today's Gospel reading presents Peter as a most earnest but somewhat flawed disciple of Jesus. The Gospel begins with Jesus posing a question about his honour status among the people. Unlike people of the modern Western world who focus on individuality, people of the ancient Mediterranean world paid more attention to the social status of groups of people or their family of origin. Thus, the likely response of Jesus' disciples would be to say, "Well, you're from Nazareth," with the understanding that all inhabitants of Nazareth are small-town folk from the mixed Jewish/Gentile countryside. Likewise, to say that Jesus was the son of a carpenter would be to label him with all the attributes of a woodworker. Consider, then, the significance of the responses that Jesus' disciples give to his question: John the Baptist, Elijah, Jeremiah, or one of the Prophets, all spokespersons of God.

But when Jesus asks about his honour status among his group of disciples, Peter speaks up: "You are the Christ, the Son of the living God." What a radical statement, especially coming from a fisherman from Galilee! Matthew portrays Jesus as attribut-ing this statement to a revelation from God, thereby raising Peter's honour status among the disciples. He is not just one of the disciples; rather, he is now someone with authority. Thus, Jesus gives him a new name to signify his new role. "You are Peter [Greek, *Petros*]," he says, "and on this rock [Greek, *petra*, meaning also "cliff or rocky ground"] I will build my Church [Greek, *ecclēsia*, meaning "assembly" of believers]." In Matthew's time, Hades was understood to be the realm of the dead. Thus, Jesus' words about the gates of Hades not prevail-ing against the Church is a promise of the

Elijah = ee-Lī-juh

Jeremiah = jayr-uh-Mī-uh

This reading depicts a set piece, a version of which appears in each of the synoptic Gospels, in which Jesus asks his disciples to tell him what people are saying he is like.

Give emphasis to each of these three figures: John the Baptist, Elijah, and Jeremiah.

Emphasize "Christ," "Son," and "God."

In Matthew's Gospel, this scene concludes with Jesus indicating Peter as the rock upon which the Church will be built. No need to overplay this indication.

Note the repetitions, which signal Peter's power: bind/bound; loose/loosed.

GOSPEL Matthew 16.13–19

A reading from the holy Gospel according to Matthew.

When Jesus came into the district of **Caesarea Philippi**,
he asked his **disciples**,
"**Who** do people say that the Son of Man **is**?"
And they said, "**Some** say John the **Baptist**,
but others **Elijah**,
and still **others Jeremiah** or one of the **Prophets**."
He said to them, "But who do **you** say that I am?"
Simon Peter answered,
"You are the **Christ**, the **Son** of the living **God**."
And Jesus answered him,
"**Blessed** are you, **Simon** son of **Jonah**!
For **flesh** and **blood** has not **revealed** this to you,
but my **Father** in heaven.
And I **tell** you, you are **Peter**,
and on this **rock** I will build my **Church**,
and the gates of **Hades** will not prevail **against** it.
I will **give** you the keys of the **kingdom** of heaven,
and whatever you **bind** on earth will be **bound** in heaven,
and whatever you **loose** on earth will be **loosed** in heaven."

durability or permanence of the believing community. Finally, Jesus gives to Peter, and later to all the disciples (Matthew 18.18), the authority to bind and loose. Biblical scholars have long debated exactly what this binding and loosing refers to, but the main point is that the authority comes from God and is conferred on the disciples. The verb phrases "will be bound in heaven" and "will be loosed in heaven" are called divine passives; the unnamed actor is God.

Thus, in this Gospel reading, the Matthean Jesus gives tremendous honour and responsibility to Peter on behalf of the Christian community. However, it is also important for us to recognize that Peter is not without shortcomings. In this same chapter of Matthew's Gospel, though not in today's reading, Jesus tells the disciples that it will be necessary for him to go to Jerusalem, where he must suffer, be killed, and be raised from the dead (Matthew 16.21–23). In response, Peter pulls Jesus aside and scolds him, saying that it shouldn't happen. Against Peter's scolding, Jesus calls him Satan and a stumbling block, because he thinks like humans think and not like God thinks. We should be consoled that, like Peter, we will fall short of our earnest devotion to Christ, but he will never abandon us. C.C.

THIRTEENTH SUNDAY IN ORDINARY TIME

LECTIONARY #97

READING I   2 Kings 4.8–12a, 14–16

A reading from the second book of Kings.

Elisha = ee-LĪ-shuh
Shunem = SHOO-nuhm

Slight pause between "day" and "Elisha." This reading recounts a powerful narrative of generosity and reward. It's almost like a fable and can be proclaimed with that sense of wonder.

One day Elisha was passing through **Shunem**,
where a **wealthy woman lived**,
who urged him to have a **meal**.
So **whenever** he **passed** that way,
he would **stop** there for a **meal**.
She **said** to her **husband**,
"**Look**, I am **sure** that this **man** who **regularly passes** our **way**
is a **holy** man of **God**.
Let us make a **small roof chamber** with **walls**,
and **put** there for him a **bed**, a **table**, a **chair**, and a **lamp**,
so that he can **stay** there **whenever** he **comes** to us."
One day when **Elisha came** there,
he went **up** to the **chamber** and lay **down** there.

Gehazi = geh-HAY-zī

He said to his servant **Gehazi**,
"**What then** may be done for the **woman**?"
Gehazi **answered**,
"**Well**, she has **no son**, and her **husband** is **old**."
Elisha said, "**Call** her."
When the **servant** had **called** her, she **stood** at the **door**.
Elisha said,

Even emphasis on "this season" and "due time."

"At **this season**, in **due time**, you shall **embrace** a **son**."

READING I On this Thirteenth Sunday of Ordinary Time, we are invited to reflect on the gifts that come to us when we practise hospitality with no strings attached. Today's first reading tells the story of the Prophet Elisha, who regularly stopped at the home of a wealthy couple when he was passing through Shunem, located approximately 50 kilometres northeast of Samaria, in the land given to the tribe of Issachar, one of the twelve tribes of Israel. The woman remains unnamed, but she is the one who first invited Elisha to dinner, and she is the one who told her husband that they should prepare a room for him to stay when he comes to Shunem, for no other reason than she believed him to be a holy man. Perhaps her wealth gave her privilege, but we should not ignore the fact that most women in the ancient world did not enjoy such power or influence. In response to her generous hospitality, Elisha asks his servant what he might offer as a gift of gratitude, and he learns that she has no son.

This is a very serious problem. Without a son, there was no one to take care of the couple in their old age and no way to pass on the husband's legacy to the next generation. Ancients thought that the woman determined the gender of their child, so it was her responsibility and shame that they had no son. Therefore, Elisha's prophecy is a huge gift to the couple.

We learn from the verses that follow this reading that the woman is skeptical and pleads with him not to give her false hope (2 Kings 4.16), and Elisha does not disappoint. Just as he prophesied, in the following year she had a healthy son, but tragedy struck when the son complained of a headache and died later that day (2 Kings

228

For meditation and context:

RESPONSORIAL PSALM   Psalm 89.1–2, 15–16, 17–18 (R.1a)

R. Forever I will sing of your steadfast love, O Lord.

I will sing of your steadfast love,
    O Lord, forever;
with my mouth I will proclaim your
    faithfulness to all generations.
I declare that your steadfast love is
    established forever;
your faithfulness is as firm as the heavens.

Blessed are the people who know the
    festal shout,
who walk, O Lord, in the light of
    your countenance;
they exult in your name all day long,
and extol your righteousness.

For you are the glory of their strength;
by your favour our horn is exalted.
For our shield belongs to the Lord,
our king to the Holy One of Israel.

READING II   Romans 6.3–4, 8–11

A reading from the Letter of Saint Paul to the Romans.

Brothers and **sisters**:
All of us who have been **baptized** into **Christ Jesus**
were **baptized** into his **death**.
Therefore we have been **buried** with him by **baptism** into **death**,
so that, just as **Christ** was **raised** from the **dead**
by the **glory** of the **Father**,
so **we too** might **walk** in **newness** of life.
But if we have **died** with **Christ**,
we **believe** that we will also **live** with him.
We **know** that **Christ**, being **raised** from the **dead**,
will **never** die **again**;
death no **longer** has **dominion** over him.
The **death** he **died**, he **died** to **sin**, **once** for **all**;
but the **life** he **lives**, he **lives** to **God**.
So **you also** must **consider** yourselves **dead** to **sin**
and **alive** to **God** in **Christ Jesus**.

Paul's argument is staged in two parts. In the first part, he introduces his argument about baptism, death, and life with a question. The question allows the argument to proceed.

Paul's argument concludes with the application of the example of Christ to our own lives. It's a complex argument that deserves to be stated slowly and clearly.

4.18–20). This brave and determined woman seeks out Elisha to bring her dead son back to life, which he does, thus rewarding her doubly for her hospitality (2 Kings 4.22–37).

READING II As in the most recent Sundays in Ordinary Time, our second reading comes from Paul's Letter to the Romans. Today's reading is an excerpt from his teaching on baptism. Water is a fitting element to be associated with the ritual of baptism, since the Greek word *baptizó* means "to dip, submerge, or immerse." Paul describes baptism as a participation in the death of Jesus Christ "so that, just as Christ was raised from the dead," we can enter into newness of life and live with Christ. Further, because he understood that death entered the world because of sin, Jesus' Resurrection was a triumph over sin *and* death. Therefore, being submerged in the water is an apt symbol for going into death and emerging from the water is a symbol for coming into new life. Paul goes on to assure his audience that Jesus, now resurrected, will never die again.

So, too, we are "dead to sin," that is, to our old way of life, and should consider ourselves "alive to God in Christ Jesus."

GOSPEL Today's Gospel reading is taken from a section of Matthew's Gospel sometimes called the "mission discourse." The mission discourse begins with the narrator listing the twelve disciples (Matthew 10.1–4) and describing how Jesus commissioned them to go out among the people of the house of Israel and to teach and heal (Matthew 10.5–15).

GOSPEL Matthew 10.37–42

A reading from the holy Gospel according to Matthew.

Jesus said to his **Apostles**:
"Whoever loves **father** or **mother more** than **me**
is not **worthy** of me;
and whoever loves **son** or **daughter more** than **me**
is not **worthy** of me;
and whoever does **not** take **up** their **cross** and **follow** me
is not **worthy** of me.
Whoever **finds** their life will **lose** it,
and whoever **loses** their **life** for **my sake** will **find** it.
Whoever welcomes **you** welcomes **me**,
and whoever welcomes **me**
welcomes the **one** who **sent** me.
Whoever welcomes a **prophet** in the **name** of a **prophet**
will receive a **prophet's reward**;
and whoever welcomes a **righteous person**
in the name of a **righteous person**
will receive the **reward** of the **righteous**;
and whoever gives even a **cup** of **cold water**
to one of these **little ones** in the **name** of a **disciple**—
truly I tell you—
that **person** will not **lose** their **reward**."

The words of Jesus in this reading, divided into two parts, are challenging. In this first part, Jesus argues for worthiness in his followers based on how they feel about their family members. Then as now, these are hard words to reconcile to the ways we actually feel about our family members. Though unstressed, let the repetitions of "whoever" anchor your proclamation.

The second part of the reading focuses on the spiritual and moral sense of reward that Jesus wants to impart on his disciples and those who would heed his teachings.

TO KEEP IN MIND
Pause to break up separate thoughts, set apart significant statements, or indicate major shifts. Never pause in the middle of a thought. Your primary guide for pauses is punctuation.

But before they depart on their mission, Jesus prepares them for what they might face along the way; they will face persecution and must muster their courage, but they should also be encouraged because God protects even the sparrows, so why would he not protect them? He also warns them that they will experience Jesus as a source of division in the communities they visit and among families (Matthew 10.16–36).

This is the background for today's Gospel teaching on discipleship. It is a call to radical discipleship! We are told that we must love Jesus more than father or mother

and son or daughter. We must be willing to take up our crosses and follow Jesus even to death. But as radical as this call to discipleship is, its success depends on a corresponding ministry of hospitality. Ancient cultures of the Near East operated on the patronage system. Patrons were responsible for providing certain protections or resources for their clients, and clients performed certain services for their patron. In some cases, this meant that the client would serve as an agent of the patron such that whatever he said or did in the name of his patron had the power and authority of

the patron himself. Thus, the disciples are about to be sent out to be Jesus' presence among the people they meet and, as Jesus' representatives, they are likewise agents of God. Similarly, if we insist on holding onto what we value in our daily lives, Jesus says that we will lose it. But if we perform acts of hospitality, even if only a cup of water for the least of God's children, we will receive God's reward. C.C.

FOURTEENTH SUNDAY IN ORDINARY TIME

LECTIONARY #100

READING I   Zechariah 9.9–10

A reading from the book of the Prophet Zechariah.

Thus says the **Lord**:
Rejoice greatly, O **daughter Zion**!
Shout aloud, O **daughter Jerusalem**!
Lo, your **king comes** to you;
triumphant and **victorious** is **he**,
humble and **riding** on a **donkey**,
on a **colt**, the **foal** of a **donkey**.
He will cut **off** the **chariot** from **Ephraim**
and the war **horse** from **Jerusalem**;
and the **warrior's bow** shall be **cut off**,
and he shall **command peace** to the **nations**;
his **dominion** shall be from **sea** to **sea**,
and from the **River** to the **ends** of the **earth**.

Zechariah = zek-uh-Rī-uh

Zion = Zī-uhn or Zī-ahn

A rich and exhortatory reading, in which the words of the Lord ring out joyfully and forcefully. Let your tone be guided by the joy and force that come through this reading, as much like a poem as it is Scripture.

Ephraim = EE-fray-im; EF-r*m

READING I   Today's readings invite us to consider God's benevolence as we face the challenges of our daily lives. We can reimagine what our life is like when God's promise of salvation is fulfilled and we accept its grace into our lives.

The Book of Zechariah is a collection of two or perhaps three smaller prophetic units written by different authors but having somewhat similar themes. Although parts of this book are more universal in tone, it was probably compiled after the return from the Babylonian Exile in the sixth century BC. This period of rebuilding the Jerusalem Temple and re-establishing a working society in Judea was a perilous time, so messages of consolation would have been most welcome.

This first reading is the second oracle in the second section (chapters 9 through 11) of the Book of Zechariah. Its interpretation depends on the meaning of the first oracle. Briefly, the first oracle describes how God, the great warrior, will take sides on behalf of Judea and against its neighbours and enemies. Some will be assimilated into Judea and others will be destroyed. God will protect Judea by setting up his home in the Jerusalem Temple and establishing his garrison there, not because Judea has earned God's protection, but because God has seen their affliction.

Subsequently, in this second oracle, which is today's first reading, God urges Jerusalem to rejoice, because God is sending a king who is just—in right relationship to God—and humble. This one who is to come will be a king of peace, riding on a donkey, an animal used for farming and commerce, and vanquishing the implements of war (bows and arrows, chariots and horses). The Hebrew word translated

For meditation and context:

RESPONSORIAL PSALM   Psalm 145.1–2, 8–9, 10–11, 13cd–14 (R.1b)

R. I will bless your name for ever, my King and my God.
or:
Alleluia!

I will extol you, my God and King,
and bless your name forever and ever.
Every day I will bless you,
and praise your name forever and ever.

The Lord is gracious and merciful,
slow to anger and abounding in
    steadfast love.
The Lord is good to all,
and his compassion is over all that he
    has made.

All your works shall give thanks to you,
    O Lord,
and all your faithful shall bless you.
They shall speak of the glory of
    your kingdom,
and tell of your power.

The Lord is faithful in all his words,
and gracious in all his deeds.
The Lord upholds all who are falling,
and raises up all who are bowed down.

READING II   Romans 8.9, 11–13

A reading from the Letter of Saint Paul to the Romans.

Brothers and **sisters**:
You are **not** in the **flesh**;
you are in the **Spirit**,
since the **Spirit** of **God dwells** in you.
Anyone who **does not have** the **Spirit** of **Christ**
does not **belong** to **him**.
If the **Spirit** of **God** who raised **Jesus** from the **dead dwells**
    in you,
he who raised **Christ** from the **dead**
will give **life** to your **mortal bodies also**
through his **Spirit** that **dwells** in you.
So then, **brothers** and **sisters**, we are **debtors**,
not to the **flesh**, to live **according** to the **flesh**—
for if you **live according** to the **flesh**, you will **die**;
but if by the **Spirit** you put to **death** the **deeds** of the **body**,
    you will **live**.

In this portion of his letter to the Romans, Paul instructs his audience about the nature of life in the Spirit. His watchwords are "death" and "life," the "body" and "flesh," and "spirit." Less does he contrast these terms than he works them into his argument like ingredients into dough, in which the Spirit is the leavening agent. Read slowly and carefully, to allow the terms of Paul's argument to sink into your assembly.

Slight pause between "God" and "dwells."

Slight pause between "dead" and "dwells."

"humble" to describe the king also has the connotation of "poor," "weak," or "lowly." Thus, we can surmise that this king will come from among his own people. But when God establishes him in power, he will have dominion over all the peoples of the world. As you can imagine, the early Church associated this prophecy with Jesus and his entrance into Jerusalem on a donkey (see Matthew 21.1–11).

READING II | Today's second reading is a continuation of our recent Sunday readings from Paul's Letter to the Romans. It is part of a longer section that began in chapter 5, in which Paul expounds on the nature of Christian life for those who have been justified by faith. Justification can be a difficult concept to understand, but, briefly, Paul asserts that fallen humanity has been set right with God through the death and Resurrection of Jesus. This justification is available to all who open themselves in faith to receive this free gift. Further, he argues that the lives of the justified are transformed insofar as they are now free from sin and death (Romans 5), free from their old selves (Romans 6) and

free from the belief that Jewish law will put them right with God (Romans 7). Finally, as we see in this reading, Paul asserts that the Christian life is lived in the Spirit. We leave behind our old way of life—what Paul calls living "according to the flesh"—and now live in the Spirit of God who dwells in us. And because the Spirit of God dwells in us, we can be assured that we will be raised from the dead, just as Jesus was raised from the dead. But this is not our doing. It is God's free gift. Therefore, we should live as joyful and grateful believers in Jesus Christ.

Though all the words in this opening line are evenly emphasized, there is a slight pause between "time" and "Jesus."

The first half of this reading has Jesus directly addressing God the Father. It has a quality of public intimacy.

The second half of this reading begins with these familiar and comforting words of Jesus. Imagine they are being said for the first time as you proclaim them.

Beautiful and reassuring.

GOSPEL Matthew 11.25–30

A reading from the holy Gospel according to Matthew.

At that time Jesus **said**,
"**I thank** you, **Father**, **Lord** of **heaven** and **earth**,
because you have **hidden** these **things** from the **wise**
     and the **intelligent**
and have **revealed** them to **infants**;
yes, **Father**, for **such** was your **gracious will**."
He continued:
"**All things** have been handed **over** to me by my **Father**;
and **no one knows** the **Son** except the **Father**,
and **no one knows** the **Father** except the **Son**
and **anyone** to whom the **Son chooses** to **reveal** him.
Come to me,
all you that are **weary** and are **carrying heavy burdens**,
and **I** will give you **rest**.
Take my **yoke upon** you, and **learn** from me;
for I am **gentle** and **humble** in **heart**,
and you will find **rest** for your **souls**.
For my **yoke** is **easy**, and my **burden** is light."

GOSPEL | This reading from Matthew's Gospel is an example of the wisdom teachings of Jesus. Something similar can be found in Sirach 51.23–30. In keeping with Matthew's Jewish-Christian audience, Jesus begins with a traditional Jewish blessing formula—"I thank you, Father, Lord of heaven and earth"—but with the addition of the divine attribute "Father." He is offering praise and thanks for God's revelation, which will be channelled through Jesus according to God's "gracious will." The Greek *eudokia* here expands our understanding of God's attitude; it includes the notion that these actions are taken with "good will, kindly intent, or benevolence." Moreover, it is not something that can be attained through superior intellect. Rather, it is revealed to "infants," metaphorically speaking, the simple and uneducated. And what is this revelation? It is knowledge or experience of God's very self, to which Jesus has unique access as Son of the Father. In other words, we come to know God through the person of Jesus.

Thus, Jesus, like personified Wisdom in Sirach, invites all of us who are exhausted and weighed down to come to him and to take rest in him and be refreshed. The reference to taking on Jesus' yoke is probably in juxtaposition to the obligations of Torah law, since first- and second-century rabbis used the term in the phrases "yoke of the Torah" and "yoke of the kingdom of heaven" with a similar meaning. The words translated here as "gentle" and "humble of heart" have similar meanings and can be translated, respectively, as "gentle or humble" and "lowly or deferring oneself as a servant to others." Let us ask ourselves, then, what does it mean to say that Jesus' yoke is easy and his burden light? C.C.

FIFTEENTH SUNDAY IN ORDINARY TIME

LECTIONARY #103

READING I   Isaiah 55.10–11

A reading from the book of the Prophet Isaiah.

Thus says the **Lord**:
"As the **rain** and the **snow** come **down** from **heaven**,
and **do not return there** until they have **watered** the **earth**,
making it **bring forth** and **sprout**,
giving **seed** to the **sower** and **bread** to the **one** who **eats**,
so shall my **word** be that goes **out** from my **mouth**;
it shall not **return** to me **empty**,
but it shall **accomplish that** which I **purpose**,
and **succeed** in the **thing** for which I **sent** it."

Isaiah = ī-ZAY-uh

A simple and elegant reading in poetic language that makes a direct and powerful comparison between nourishing water and the word of God.

purpose = per-POSE
Slight pause between "accomplish" and "that."

For meditation and context:

RESPONSORIAL PSALM   Psalm 65.9abcd, 9e–10, 11–12, 13 (R. Lk 8.8)

R. The seed that fell on good soil produced a hundredfold.

You visit the earth and water it,
you greatly enrich it;
the river of God is full of water;
you provide the people with grain.

For so you have prepared the earth:
you water its furrows abundantly,
settling its ridges, softening it
    with showers,
and blessing its growth.

You crown the year with your bounty;
your pathways overflow with richness.
The pastures of the wilderness overflow,
the hills gird themselves with joy.

The meadows clothe themselves with flocks,
the valleys deck themselves with grain,
they shout and sing together for joy.

READING I | Today's readings invite us to reflect on the full flourishing of God's word in the world and the way it bears fruit in our lives.

The first reading comes from the section of the Book of Isaiah referred to as Second Isaiah (Isaiah 40–55), which is generally understood to have been written by a disciple of the eighth-century BC Prophet during the time of the Babylonian Exile.

This short reading is part of the last oracle of consolation in Second Isaiah, which begins with an invitation from God to come to the one who nourishes all of life. In the first part of the oracle, God acknowledges that Israel has sinned but invites them to turn to him for mercy (Isaiah 55.7). God also tells them that he will make a covenant with them and be steadfast and loyal to them (Isaiah 55.3). This is where we pick up today's reading. The Prophet, speaking for God, says that God's word is not out in the ether somewhere. Rather, it comes gently to earth like rain or snow that nourishes the earth and makes it sprout with new growth that returns to God as plants and trees. Think of this as a metaphor for the human experience of the divine. Like gentle rain or sparkling snow, God's word comes down upon us and infuses our being with God's life-giving Spirit, and we can trust that God will make his word fruitful in us to the praise and glory of God.

READING II   Romans 8.18–23

A reading from the Letter of Saint Paul to the Romans.

Brothers and **sisters**:
I consider that the **sufferings** of this **present time**
are **not worth comparing** with the **glory**
about to be **revealed** to us.
For the **creation waits** with **eager longing**
for the **revealing** of the **children** of **God**;
for the **creation** was **subjected** to **futility**,
not of its **own will**
but by the **will** of the **one** who **subjected** it,
in **hope** that the **creation itself**
will be **set free** from its **bondage** to **decay**
and will **obtain** the **freedom** of the **glory** of the **children** of **God**.
We **know** that the whole **creation**
has been **groaning** in **labour pains** until **now**;
and **not only** the **creation**,
but **we ourselves**, who have the **first fruits** of the **Spirit**,
groan **inwardly** while we **wait** for **adoption** to **sonship**,
the **redemption** of our **bodies**.

GOSPEL   Matthew 13.1–23

A reading from the holy Gospel according to Matthew.

[**Jesus** went **out** of the **house** and **sat** beside the **sea**.
Such **great crowds gathered around** him
that he got into a **boat** and **sat** there,
while the **whole crowd stood** on the **beach**.
And he **told** them **many things** in **parables**.
"**Listen!** A **sower** went out to **sow**.
And as he **sowed**, some **seeds fell** on the **path**,
and the **birds came** and **ate** them **up**. »

In this letter, Paul discusses the role of suffering as a metaphysical condition that defines life. It's a challenging argument he is making. Proclaim slowly and carefully so that his words can sink in.

"Longing" is a focal word in this reading.

One of the more powerful images in Paul's letters. Emphasis on "whole creation."

Slight pause between "crowds" and "gathered." The first part of this reading relates a well-known parable, as straightforward as it is compelling.

Slight pause between "seeds" and "fell."

READING II Today's second reading continues our recent Sunday readings from Paul's Letter to the Romans. Here Paul is writing about the destiny that awaits Christians in the end time. He uses the metaphor of a woman having labour pains to describe the "sufferings of this present time." The pain is great in the moment, but so is the hope of a glorious new life. Paul recognizes that all of creation was negatively affected by humanity's first sin, but that creation has within it a deep longing to share in humanity's redemption in Christ. Paul says that human sin subjects all of creation to the slavery of corruption or decay. But we have hope because humanity possesses "the first fruits of the Spirit." In the Jewish sacrificial system, the first fruits were the first and best of the harvest offered to God as a pledge of what is to come for the entire harvest. And so, we groan as we await the full flourishing of the harvest or what Paul calls "the redemption of our bodies." To redeem is to "buy back," in this case, from the forces of sin and evil. As our bodies are redeemed through the death and Resurrection of Jesus, we become fully children of God.

GOSPEL The short form of today's Gospel is the very familiar parable of the sower and the seed. The long form includes Jesus' explanation for why he teaches in parables, as well as an interpretation of this parable. Parables are riddles that take the form of fictional

Other seeds fell on rocky ground,
where they did not have much soil,
and they sprang up quickly,
since they had no depth of soil.
But when the sun rose, they were scorched;
and since they had no root, they withered away.
Other seeds fell among thorns,
and the thorns grew up and choked them.
Other seeds fell on good soil and brought forth grain,
some a hundredfold, some sixty, some thirty.
Let anyone with ears listen!"]
Then the disciples came and asked Jesus,
"Why do you speak to them in parables?"
He answered,
"To you it has been given to know the secrets of the kingdom
	of heaven,
but to them it has not been given.
For to those who have, more will be given,
and they will have an abundance;
but from those who have nothing,
even what they have will be taken away.
The reason I speak to them in parables
is that 'seeing they do not perceive,
and hearing they do not listen, nor do they understand.'
With them indeed is fulfilled
the prophecy of Isaiah that says:
'You will indeed listen, but never understand,
and you will indeed look, but never perceive.
For this people's heart has grown dull,
and their ears are hard of hearing,
and they have shut their eyes;
so that they might not look with their eyes,
and listen with their ears,

Here, speaking to his disciples about the parable he has spoken, Jesus initiates them into the mysteries of the kingdom of heaven. A revelatory tone pervades.

Jesus uses Scripture to underscore the mysteries he is revealing. They are ancient mysteries.

stories designed to engage the listener in active thought. This parable is about a farmer who goes out to sow seed, which falls on four different types of soil and bears fruit in proportion to the type of soil on which it falls. The riddle or surprising element of this parable is the bountiful harvest that the good soil produces. Even today, with our advanced techniques of farming, a hundredfold yield is impossible! Hence, we need to look more deeply into the message of the parable.

Gospel parables often do not include an interpretation, but this one does. The seed is the "word of the kingdom" or message about the reign of God. The four types of soil represent the categories of people who are invited to respond to the Word. The path is so hard that the seed cannot penetrate the soil or begin to germinate, so the evil one is able to steal it away. The rocky soil receives the Word and quickly responds, but, as the plants begin to grow, the heat and lack of moisture—i.e., persecutions—

cause the produce to wither and die. Likewise, the thorny soil does not produce results because "the cares of the world" keep us from responding to God's word. The questions for us, then, are "What kind of soil am I?" and "How do I open myself to be like the good soil that receives it and produces more?"

The longer form of today's Gospel also has a section that explains why Jesus taught in parables, and it is not what you might expect. First, he offers a proverb that

Here, he boosts the confidence of his disciples. By extension, this boosts our own confidence that we, too, are being initiated into these mysteries.

The explanation of the parable begins with "Hear."

and **understand** with their **heart** and **turn**—
and I would **heal** them.'
But **blessed** are your **eyes**, for they **see**,
and your **ears**, for they **hear**.
Truly I tell you,
many **Prophets** and **righteous people**
longed to **see** what you **see**, but **did not see** it,
and to **hear** what you **hear**, but **did not hear** it.
Hear then the **parable** of the **sower**.
When **anyone** hears the **word** of the **kingdom**
and **does not understand** it,
the **evil one comes** and **snatches away** what is **sown**
        in the **heart**;
this is what was **sown** on the **path**.
As for what was **sown** on **rocky ground**,
this is the **one** who **hears** the **word**
and **immediately** receives it with **joy**;
yet such a **person** has no **root**,
but **endures** only for a **while**,
and when **trouble** or **persecution arises**
on **account** of the **word**,
that person **immediately** falls **away**.
As for what was **sown** among **thorns**,
this is the **one** who **hears** the **word**,
but the **cares** of the **world** and the **lure** of **wealth**
choke the **word**, and it yields **nothing**.
But as for what was **sown** on **good soil**,
this is the one who **hears** the **word** and **understands** it,
who **indeed** bears **fruit**
and **yields**, in **one case** a **hundredfold**,
in another **sixty**, and in another **thirty**."

[Shorter: Matthew 13.1–9 (see brackets)]

still holds true today; some have been given more than others, and the ones who have more will receive more. Second, he quotes from Isaiah 6.9–10, essentially saying that God ordained it that some would accept God's word and others would not. As Christianity began to separate itself from Judaism in the second century AD, Christians used this text to argue that the Jews' refusal to accept Jesus as the Messiah resulted in God's covenant being extended to Gentile believers (see Acts 28.23–28). C.C.

SIXTEENTH SUNDAY IN ORDINARY TIME

LECTIONARY #106

READING I Wisdom 12.13, 16–19

A reading from the book of Wisdom.

A poetic and forceful reading with an uplifting message and a somewhat complex delivery. Proclaim with care to let its language settle on your assembly.

There is **no god besides** you, **Lord**,
whose **care** is for all **people**,
to whom you should **prove** that you have not **judged unjustly**.
For your **strength** is the **source** of **righteousness**,
and your **sovereignty** over **all** causes you to **spare all**.
For you **show** your **strength**
when **people doubt** the **completeness** of your **power**,
and you **rebuke** any **insolence** among **those** who **know** it.
Although you are **sovereign** in **strength**,
you **judge** with **mildness**,
and with **great forbearance** you **govern** us;
for you have power to **act whenever** you **choose**.
Through such **works** you have **taught** your **people**
that the **righteous** must be **kind**,
and you have **filled** your **children** with **good hope**,
because you give **repentance** for **sins**.

READING I Our first reading is taken from the Book of Wisdom, also called the Wisdom of Solomon. Although the author is anonymous, we can surmise that he was a well-educated, Greek-speaking Jew, possibly from Alexandria, Egypt. Biblical scholars are divided about its date of composition, but sometime between the end of the first century BC and the beginning of the first century AD is reasonable. Catholics classify this book as deuterocanonical, meaning "second list of authoritative books," and part of the Bible, but most of our Protestant brothers and sisters consider it to be apocryphal, meaning "of doubtful authenticity," and include it in a separate section of the Bible.

To best appreciate this reading, we should try to get a sense of the big picture. It is part of a lengthy reflection on God's faithfulness and providential care of the Israelites during the Exodus, which begins at Wisdom 11.2 and extends to Wisdom 19.22. The first element of this reflection is a brief retelling of the Exodus narrative based on Psalm 107. Second, the author introduces the theme of his reflection: the Israelites benefited from the very things that God did to punish the Egyptians. Third, the author presents five examples, each in the form of a diptych, that is, a text in two related parts. The five diptychs appear in this order: the miracle of water from the rock as compared to the plague of blood in the Nile; the miracle of quail in the wilderness as compared to the plagues of locusts and flies; the miracle of manna in the wilderness as compared to the plague of storms; the miracle of the column of fire as compared to the plague of darkness; and the tenth plague that brought freedom to the

For meditation and context:

RESPONSORIAL PSALM Psalm 86.5–6, 9–10, 15–16 (R.5)

R. Lord, you are good and forgiving.

You, O Lord, are good and forgiving,
abounding in steadfast love to all who
    call on you.
Give ear, O Lord, to my prayer;
listen to my cry of supplication.

All the nations you have made shall come
and bow down before you, O Lord,
and shall glorify your name.
For you are great and do wondrous things;
you alone are God.

But you, O Lord, are a God merciful
    and gracious,
slow to anger and abounding in steadfast
    love and faithfulness.
Turn to me and be gracious to me.
Give your strength to your servant.

READING II Romans 8.26–27

A reading from the Letter of Saint Paul to the Romans.

Brothers and **sisters**:
The **Spirit helps** us in our **weakness**;
for we d**o not know** how to **pray** as we **ought**,
but that **very Spirit intercedes** with **sighs** too **deep** for **words**.
And **God**, who **searches** the **heart**,
knows what is the **mind** of the **Spirit**,
because the **Spirit intercedes** for the **saints**
according to the **will** of **God**.

A brief and incisive reading from Paul in which he offers up a challenging teaching, that our ignorance might be interceded upon by the Spirit. The emphasis is on our weakness.

Slight pause between "Spirit" and "intercedes."

Israelites and death to the Egyptians' first born.

The second of these diptychs is interrupted by several digressions, including the one from which today's reading is taken. The topic of this digression is God's power and mercy. Our author begins by praising God who is all-powerful and who cares for the needs of everyone; there is no other god who can accuse God of dealing unjustly with his people. The author argues further that God's power is the "source of righteousness," which also allows God to be lenient, balancing justice with mercy.

Although the author's comparison is not obvious in this short excerpt, we should be reminded of the words of the wicked expressed earlier in the book, "But let our might be our law of right, for what is weak proves itself to be useless" (Wisdom 2.11). The wicked are the ones who, by their words and deeds, bring about their own destruction (Wisdom 1.12). The author of this excerpt concludes by saying that, just as God tempers justice with mercy, so too we must be kind in our dealings with others. Knowing that God allows for repentance of sin gives us hope for ourselves and all of humanity.

READING II Once again, our second reading is a continuation of recent Sunday readings from Paul's Letter to the Romans. In the verses that immediately precede this reading, Paul writes about how Jesus' followers await with great hope the birth of a new creation. In today's reading, he explains that having been made children of God, "the Spirit helps us in our weakness." Implied here is the recognition that human aspirations will

GOSPEL   Matthew 13.24–43

A reading from the holy Gospel according to Matthew.

[**Jesus** put **before** the **crowds** a **parable**:
"The **kingdom** of **heaven** may be **compared**
to **someone** who **sowed good seed** in his **field**;
but while **everybody** was **asleep**,
an **enemy came** and **sowed weeds** among the **wheat**,
     and then **went away**.
So when the **plants** came **up** and **bore grain**,
then the **weeds appeared** as **well**.
And the slaves of the **householder came** and **said** to him,
'**Master**, did you not **sow good seed** in your **field**?
Where, then, did **these weeds come** from?'
He answered, 'An **enemy** has **done** this.'
The slaves **said** to him,
'Then do you **want** us to **go** and **gather** them?'
But he replied, '**No**;
for in **gathering** the **weeds** you would **uproot** the **wheat** along
     with them.
Let **both** of them **grow together** until the **harvest**;
and at **harvest** time I will **tell** the **reapers**,
Collect the **weeds** first and **bind** them in **bundles** to be **burned**,
but **gather** the **wheat** into my **barn**.'"
Jesus put **before** them **another parable**:
"The **kingdom** of **heaven** is like a **mustard seed**
that **someone took** and **sowed** in his **field**;
it is the **smallest** of **all** the **seeds**,
but when it has **grown**
it is the **greatest** of **shrubs** and **becomes** a **tree**,
so that the **birds** of the **air come** and make **nests**
     in its **branches**."

A lengthy reading that consists of three different parables and the explanation of the first. The tone is instructive, of course, but also mysterious. The first parable is the most detailed.

This second parable involves a very familiar teaching. Proclaim it as if for the first time.

Slight pause between "air" and "come."

---

never reach their mark without assistance, because of the limitations brought on by sin. But the Spirit will intercede for us over and above our human limitations, with "sighs too deep for words." The phrase "who searches the heart" is a reference to God, who can understand what the Spirit says, as it intercedes on our behalf. What a wondrous mystery! And what consolation to know that God hears us through the agency of the Spirit, even when we are unable to pray as we want.

GOSPEL   Today's Gospel reading consists of a collection of three parables from Matthew's Gospel. The longer form of this Gospel reading also includes an interpretation of the first of these parables. Parables are puzzles that take the form of fictional stories designed to engage the listener in active thought. Most, though not all, begin with a phrase like "the kingdom of heaven is like . . . ." In other words, parables are comparisons. Also, "the kingdom of heaven" is not heaven. Rather, it describes the anticipated reality in which God's authority will mani-

fest itself fully in creation and rid the world of discord, pain, and suffering.

The first of these parables is often referred to as the Parable of the Weeds and Wheat. However, on a deeper level, it should be called the Parable of Feuding Farmers, because the weeds are merely instruments designed to dishonour one's enemy. In the ancient Near East and in many parts of the world even today, societies operated on the notion that the enemies of one's grandparents and parents are your enemies as well. To maintain your family's honour, you were obligated to challenge

The third parable consists of a powerful image.

He **told** them **another parable**:
"The **kingdom** of **heaven** is like yeast
that a **woman took** and mixed in with **three measures** of **flour**
until **all** of it was **leavened**."]
Jesus **told** the **crowds all** these things in **parables**;
without a **parable** he told them **nothing**.
This was to **fulfill** what had been **spoken** through the **Prophet**:
"I will **open** my **mouth** to **speak** in **parables**;
I will **proclaim** what has been **hidden** from the **foundation**
        of the **world**."
Then **Jesus** left the **crowds** and **went** into the **house**.
And his **disciples approached** him, **saying**,
"**Explain** to us the **parable** of the **weeds** of the **field**."
He **answered**,
"The **one** who sows the **good seed** is the **Son** of **Man**;
the **field** is the **world**,
and the **good seed** are the **children** of the **kingdom**;
the **weeds** are the **children** of the **evil one**,
and the **enemy** who **sowed** them is the **devil**;
the **harvest** is the end of the **age**,
and the **reapers** are **Angels**.
Just as the **weeds** are **collected** and **burned up** with **fire**,
so will it **be** at the **end** of the **age**.
The **Son** of **Man** will send his **Angels**,
and they will **collect out** of his **kingdom**
all **causes** of sin and **all evildoers**,
and they will **throw** them into the **furnace** of **fire**,
where there will be **weeping** and **gnashing** of **teeth**.
Then the **righteous** will **shine** like the **sun** in the **kingdom**
        of their **Father**.
Let **anyone** with **ears listen**!"

[Shorter: Matthew 13:24–33 (see brackets)]

When the disciples ask for an explanation, they are asking Jesus to deepen their initiation into the mysteries he is revealing to them. That Jesus complies eagerly is part of the excitement of this Gospel reading.

The tone that concludes this reading is decidedly apocalyptic.

the social status of those enemies in some way—even if meant introducing weeds into your enemy's field! The typical farmer would have felt obligated to respond in kind, but this farmer does not retaliate and instead allows his honour to be compromised for an entire season until harvest, which is a symbol of God's end time judgment, when the instruments of hatred can be destroyed in fire.

The second and third parables in this reading compare the kingdom of heaven to something that begins its existence very small but becomes very large when it comes to completeness. The mustard seed is very small, though in fact not the smallest seed found in Israel and elsewhere, and it can grow to as much as six feet. However, it is not a tree. Rather, it is a gangly bush that sways easily in the wind, so it is unlikely to hold a bird's nest. Anyone walking the villages and fields of the time would know that this is hyperbole, but it clearly makes the point: the reign of God will surely grow, and it will grow beyond imagining. Likewise, the parable about the yeast is surprising, but this time it is because of the enormous amount of flour involved.

Biblical scholars do not have consensus about how big a measure was in first-century Palestine, but three measures likely would have amounted to 18 to 27 kilograms of flour, which, when leavened, would create an enormous amount of bread! But such is the coming reign of God, encompassing all and being the source of nourishment for all. C.C.

SEVENTEENTH SUNDAY IN ORDINARY TIME

LECTIONARY #109

READING I   1 Kings 3.5–12++

A reading from the first book of Kings.

At **Gibeon** the **Lord** appeared to **Solomon** in a **dream** by **night**;
and **God said**, "**Ask** what I should give you."
And **Solomon** said,
"You have shown **great** and **steadfast** love
to your **servant** my **father David**,
because he walked **before** you in **faithfulness**,
in **righteousness**, and in **uprightness** of **heart toward** you;
and you have **kept** for him this **great** and **steadfast** love,
and have **given** him a **son** to **sit** on his **throne** today.
And **now**, O **Lord** my **God**,
you have made your **servant king** in place of my **father David**,
although I am **only** a little **child**;
I d**o not know** how to go out or come **in**.
And your **servant** is in the **midst** of the **people**
whom you have **chosen**, a great **people**,
so **numerous** they cannot be **numbered** or **counted**.
Give your **servant therefore** an **understanding mind**
to **govern** your **people**,
able to **discern** between **good** and **evil**;
for **who** can **govern this**, your **great people**?"
It **pleased** the **Lord** that **Solomon** had **asked** this.
God **said** to him,
"**Because** you have **asked** this,
and **have not asked** for **yourself long** life or **riches**,

Solomon = SOL-uh-muhn
Gibeon = GIB-ee-uhn

A reading like a fairy tale, in which a request is granted, as instructive as it is full of wonder.

Part of the power of the reading comes from the way that Solomon draws out his request. Allow it to unfold in your proclamation.

Slight pause between "heart" and "toward."

Slight pause between "yourself" and "long."

READING I Our first reading comes from the First Book of Kings. It tells the story about how King Solomon had a powerful night-time vision of a conversation with God. In the chapter and verses that precede this reading, we learn that Solomon ascended the throne of Israel in Jerusalem after his father David died. Before David died, he instructed Solomon to follow God's ordinances in the law of Moses. David tells his son to settle scores with some of his enemies, which he does. Solomon also had his brother Adonijah killed, because he perceived him to be a threat to his kingship. Finally, when he had established his kingdom, he began to build his home and the Temple in Jerusalem.

The narrator of the story tells us that Solomon "loved the Lord, walking in the statutes of his father David" (1 Kings 3.3). This is why God said to Solomon, "Ask what I should give you." Solomon's response is comprised of three statements. The first is about God's past relationship with his father, David, who was loved by God for his faithfulness (literally, walking in truth), his righteousness as a ruler, and the upright nature of his heart. Ancients believed that the heart was associated with emotions but also thought, insight, discernment, and will. The second statement is about Solomon's present relationship with God. He describes himself as God's servant, chosen to be king in his father's place, even though he feels greatly inadequate to the job. The third statement is a request for the future that he be given "an understanding mind," literally, "a listening heart," so that he can govern well and act with proper discernment toward God's people. God responds by praising him for not asking for things that kings typically wanted and by

Slight pause between "yourself" and "understanding."

or for the **life** of your **enemies**,
but have **asked** for **yourself understanding**
        to **discern** what is **right**,
I now **do according** to your **word**.
Indeed I give you a **wise** and **discerning mind**;
no one like **you** has been **before** you
and **no one** like **you** shall **arise after** you."

For meditation and context:

RESPONSORIAL PSALM   Psalm 119.57+72, 76–77, 127–128, 129–130 (R.97)

R. Lord, how I love your law!

The Lord is my portion;
I promise to keep your words.
The law of your mouth is better to me
than thousands of gold and silver pieces.

Let your steadfast love become my comfort
according to your promise to your servant.
Let your mercy come to me, that I may live;
for your law is my delight.

Truly I love your commandments more
        than gold,
more than fine gold.
Truly I direct my steps by all your precepts;
I hate every false way.

Your decrees are wonderful;
therefore my soul keeps them.
The unfolding of your words gives light;
it imparts understanding to the simple.

READING II   Romans 8.28–30

A reading from the Letter of Saint Paul to the Romans.

Paul's teaching in this letter is complex and challenging. Read it with care because its content might easily be misconstrued.

Brothers and **sisters**:
We **know** that **all things** work **together** for **good**
for **those** who love **God**,
who are **called according** to his **purpose**.
For **those** whom **God foreknew**
he also **predestined** to be **conformed** to the **image** of his **Son**,
in **order** that he might be the **firstborn**
among **many brothers** and **sisters**.
And **those** whom **God predestined** he **also called**;
and **those** whom he **called** he **also justified**;
and **those** whom he **justified** he **also** glorified.

TO KEEP IN MIND
Read the Scripture passage and its commentary in Workbook. Then read it from your Bible, including what comes before and after it, so that you understand the context.

---

granting Solomon's request for wisdom and discernment, adding that Solomon is unique among the kings of Israel. Sadly, Solomon's reign would end much differently than it began, because he stopped observing God's commandments (see 1 Kings 11.1–13).

READING II   Today's second reading follows immediately after last Sunday's reading from Paul's Letter to the Romans, in which Paul explained how the Spirit would come to our aid in our weakness and intercede for us before God when we do not know how to pray. In this read-

ing, Paul goes on to assure his readers that God is in control and everything that we experience is part of God's plan. And what is God's plan for those who love God? Paul is thinking of the community as a whole here, not individuals on their own merit. But notice that Paul does not use the term "predestined," as modern theologians do, suggesting that God has determined beforehand who would be saved and who would not. Rather, it means something like "God decided beforehand" that he wanted humanity to be formed in a way similar to the image or likeness of Christ. Thus, God

called us and justified us—put us in right relationship with God—so that we can also be glorified with Christ. Essentially, Paul is talking about the invitation God has given us to participate in the Paschal Mystery, dying with Christ so that we can come to fullness of life in Christ.

GOSPEL   Matthew 13.44–52

A reading from the holy Gospel according to Matthew.

This reading consists of a series of vivid comparisons and likenesses to the kingdom of heaven that Jesus provides for his disciples.

[**Jesus spoke** to the **crowds**:
"The **kingdom** of **heaven** is like **treasure hidden** in a **field**,
which someone **found** and **hid**;
then in his joy he **goes** and **sells all** that he **has**
and **buys** that **field**.
Again, the **kingdom** of **heaven** is like a **merchant**
in **search** of **fine pearls**;
on finding **one pearl** of **great value**,
he **went** and sold **all** that he **had** and **bought** it.
Again, the **kingdom** of **heaven** is **like** a **net**
that was **thrown** into the **sea** and **caught fish** of **every kind**;
when it was **full**, they drew it **ashore**, sat **down**,
and put the **good** into **baskets**
but **threw out** the **bad**.]

After providing the likenesses, Jesus' tone becomes more pointedly apocalyptic.

So it will **be** at the **end** of the **age**.
The **Angels** will **come out**
and **separate** the **evil** from the **righteous**
and **throw** them into the **furnace** of **fire**,
where there will be **weeping** and **gnashing** of teeth.
Have you **understood all this**?"
They answered, "**Yes**."

With this question, Jesus concludes the initiation into the mysteries of heaven he has undertaken with the disciples.

And he **said** to them,
"**Therefore every scribe** who has been **trained** for the **kingdom of heaven**
is like the **master** of a **household**

Let the strangeness of this imagery abide with the members of your assembly.

who brings **out** of his **treasure** what is **new** and what is **old**".

[Shorter: Matthew 13.44–48 (see brackets)]

GOSPEL | Today's Gospel provides us with three more parables about the reign of God or what Matthew calls "the kingdom of heaven." The first two—the parable of the treasure and the parable of the pearl of great price—have some important similarities, and therefore most likely are intended to have a similar message. In both cases, the values of the treasure and the pearl are noted. Such is the reign of God; it is a treasure of immeasurable value. Nothing can compare to it anywhere on earth. And what about the person who seeks out the treasure or pearl? Having found this object of great price, the person goes off and sells everything he has in order to secure it. Again, such is the reign of God; the wise person recognizes it in joy and commits to it so fully that he gives up everything he has to participate in it.

The third parable sounds a lot like the parable of the weeds and wheat from the previous Sunday's Gospel reading. The sea is filled with good fish and bad fish. Likewise, the field has wheat and weeds growing together until harvest. Thus, the netting and sorting of fish in this parable serves the same purpose as the gathering of the harvest and burning of the weeds in the previous parable. Both are symbols of God's end time judgment, when the righteous will be separated from the wicked. But to be clear, God is the judge. It is not our place to judge others but to act with patience and charity. God will judge when the time is right. Moreover, there is hope for all of us because God's judgment is best described as justice tempered with mercy. C.C.

THE TRANSFIGURATION OF THE LORD

LECTIONARY #614

READING I   Daniel 7:9–10, 13–14

A reading from the book of the Prophet Daniel.

As I **watched**,
thrones were **set** in **place**,
and the **One** who is **Ancient** of **Days** took his **throne**.
His **clothing** was **white** as **snow**,
and the **hair** of his **head** like **pure wool**.
His **throne** was **fiery flames**,
and its **wheels** were **burning** fire.
A **stream** of fire **issued**
and **flowed out** from his **presence**.
A t**housand thousands served** him,
and **ten thousand** times **ten thousand** stood **attending** him.
The **court** sat in **judgment**,
and the **books** were **opened**.
As I **watched** in the **night visions**,
I saw **one** like a **son** of **man** coming with the **clouds** of **heaven**.
And he **came** to the **One** who is **Ancient** of **Days**
and was **presented before** him.
To **him** was given **dominion** and **glory** and **kingship**,
that **all peoples**, **nations**, and **languages** should **serve** him.
His **dominion** is an **everlasting dominion**
that **shall not pass away**,
and his **kingship** is **one** that shall **never** be **destroyed**.

A powerful, visionary reading that is a thrill to proclaim. The images are so vivid and the language so exciting and strange, be careful not to get carried away. Proclaim in a firm and steady voice and let the contents of the reading come through in your clarity.

The focus of the reading shifts with this new vision of Daniel's, one that foretells the coming of Jesus, lending this vision a special power.

READING I In the verses preceding today's reading, the Prophet receives a vision of four great beasts that emerge from the sea, which are thought to represent four great empires in succession: the Babylonians, the Medes, the Persians, and the Greeks. Each beast has a number of horns that represent kings associated with that dynasty. As Daniel's vision continues, a tiny horn sprouts on the fourth beast, replacing three of its ten horns. This is the Seleucid King Antiochus IV Epiphanes, who was notorious for his violence and who launched a persecution of the Jews in the mid-second century BC. He took the name "Epiphanes," which means "god manifest," but his eccentric behaviour earned him the name Epimanes, meaning "the mad one," among his contemporaries.

This background about Antiochus IV is important for understanding today's reading because it explains the expansiveness and elegance of Daniel's vision of God's throne room. The "One who is Ancient of Days" is God, and the details of his appearance speak to his divine status of wisdom and purity. The throne and river of fire suggest God's supremacy over cosmic phenomena. Daniel sees that God has so many court ministers and such a large number of subjects that it was impossible to count them. So much for Antiochus claiming to be Epiphanes, "god manifest!" In contrast to Antiochus' tiny horn with eyes and a mouth (Daniel 7.8), the Ancient of Days is what a real God looks like! Also, in contrast to whatever power Antiochus IV might have, there is "one like a son of man," or someone in human form, who is presented before the Ancient of Days to receive "dominion and glory and kingship" from God. Moreover, his kingship will last forever.

R. The Lord is king, the most high over all the earth.

The Lord is king! Let the earth rejoice;
let the many coastlands be glad!
Clouds and thick darkness are all
    around him;
righteousness and justice are the
    foundation of his throne.

The mountains melt like wax before
    the Lord,
before the Lord of all the earth.
The heavens proclaim his righteousness;
and all the peoples behold his glory.

For you, O Lord, are most high over all
    the earth;
you are exalted far above all gods.

READING II   2 Peter 1.16–19

A reading from the second Letter of Saint Peter.

We **did not follow cleverly devised myths**
when we **made known** to **you**
the **power** and **coming** of our **Lord Jesus Christ**,
but we had been **eyewitnesses** of his **majesty**.
For he received **honour** and **glory** from **God** the **Father**
when that **voice** was **conveyed** to him by the **Majestic Glory**,
saying, "**This** is my **Son**, the **Beloved**.
With **him** I am **well pleased**."
We ourselves heard this **voice come** from **heaven**,
while we were **with** him on the **holy mountain**.
So we have the **prophetic message** more **fully confirmed**.
You will **do well** to be **attentive** to this
as to a **lamp shining** in a **dark place**,
until the **day dawns**
and the **morning star rises** in your **hearts**.

Even emphasis on "did not follow cleverly devised myths," with a slight pause between "follow" and "cleverly."

Slight pauses between "ourselves" and "heard" and between "voice" and "come."

Slight pause between "star" and "rises."

Most likely Daniel understood this one like a son of man to be a representative of God's chosen people (see Daniel 7.18) or Israel's messiah. Early Christians associated this text with Jesus, and the Gospels use Son of Man as a title for Jesus, though the origin of that title is unclear.

READING II Our second reading is from the Second Letter of Peter. Although attributed to Peter, this work is most likely pseudonymous, written in approximately AD 100–125, by a disciple or admirer of Peter to keep his memory alive some forty to fifty years after his martyrdom.

One of the topics that this document addresses is the delay of the parousia, the return of Christ at the end time. Because resurrection from the dead was one of the signs of the end time, the earliest Christians believed that the Christ's return would happen very soon. In fact, Paul thought it would be within his lifetime (1 Thessalonians 4.13–18). Now, some seventy to ninety years after Jesus' Resurrection, early Christians were still waiting for the parousia. The reference to "cleverly devised myths" appears to be a response to an accusation that was levelled against people who made up stories about rewards and punishment in the end time in order to control people's behaviour. This writer asserts that he does not spout such myths. Rather, writing as if he were Peter, he declares that he actually witnessed Jesus' prophecy about the end time in the power and glory of his transfigured appearance and in the voice from heaven. This prophecy we can rely on, he says.

GOSPEL The story of Jesus' transfiguration on a high mountain

GOSPEL Matthew 17.1–9

A reading from the holy Gospel according to Matthew.

Jesus took with him **Peter** and **James** and his brother **John**
and **led** them **up** a **high mountain**, by **themselves**.
And he was **transfigured before** them,
and his **face shone** like the **sun**,
and his **clothes** became **dazzling white**.
Suddenly there **appeared** to them **Moses** and **Elijah**,
    talking with him.
Then **Peter** said to **Jesus**,
"**Lord**, it is **good** for us to **be** here;
if you **wish**, I will make **dwellings** here,
one for you, one for **Moses**, and one for **Elijah**."
While he was **still speaking**,
suddenly a **bright cloud overshadowed** them,
and from the **cloud** a **voice** said,
"**This** is my **Son**, the **Beloved**;
with **him** I am **well pleased**;
listen to him!"
When the disciples **heard** this,
they **fell** to the **ground** and were **overcome** by fear.
But **Jesus** came and **touched** them, **saying**,
"Get **up** and do **not** be **afraid**."
And when they **looked up**,
they saw **no one** except **Jesus himself alone**.
As they were **coming down** the **mountain**, Jesus **ordered** them,
"Tell **no one** about the **vision**
until **after** the **Son** of **Man** has been **raised** from the **dead**."

"Transfigured" focuses this reading, sets its tone. This is a celestial event.

Moses = MOH-zihz or MOH-zihs
Elijah = ee-Lī-juh
Initially, the appearance of Moses and Elijah intensifies the focus.
But then Peter humanizes things in his desire to set up a shrine.

At "suddenly," the focus shifts back to a heavenly perspective that overwhelms the earthly perspective.

The mystery of this final command of Jesus is worth lingering over as you conclude your proclamation.

is included in all three of the synoptic Gospels. The mountain that provides the setting for this story is unnamed, but tradition has identified it with Mount Tabor, though Mount Carmel or Mount Hermon is also a possibility. However, the precise location does not matter. More important to know is that ancient peoples believed mountains to be the site of divine revelations. Jesus is radiant with light, which is how ancients would have understood a divine presence. Moses and Elijah, who appear with Jesus, represent the Law and the Prophets, respectively.

Though this is a familiar story, there are several things that we can learn anew. Peter's desire to put up tents for the three heavenly beings suggests the Feast of Tabernacles, which is a commemoration of the giving of the Law on Sinai and an anticipation of the coming reign of God at the end time. The tents are a reminder of the forty years living in temporary dwellings in the wilderness. Today, this Jewish feast is usually celebrated at the end of September.

God's voice from heaven announcing that Jesus is God's beloved Son is similar to the words that came from heaven at Jesus' baptism (see Matthew 3.13–17), except that now the words are addressed to the disciples. Only Matthew includes the detail about the disciples bowing down in fear and adoration. But their fear is reasonable, because many ancient peoples believed that humans could not see God face to face and remain alive. Matthew has Jesus describe this event as a vision, suggesting that it symbolizes an event that will happen later, though it can be helpful to remember that the Gospel was written after the Resurrection of Jesus and with the after-the-fact insight that goes with the experience. C.C.

NINETEENTH SUNDAY IN ORDINARY TIME

LECTIONARY #115

READING I   1 Kings 19.9, 11–13

A reading from the first book of Kings.

When **Elijah** reached **Horeb**, the **mountain** of **God**,
he **came** to a **cave**, and spent the **night** there.
Then the **word** of the **Lord came** to him, saying,
"Go **out** and **stand** on the **mountain before** the **Lord**,
for the **Lord** is about to **pass by**."
Now there was a **great wind**,
so **strong** that it was **splitting mountains**
and **breaking rocks** in **pieces** before the **Lord**,
but the **Lord** was **not** in the **wind**;
and after the **wind** an **earthquake**,
but the **Lord** was **not** in the **earthquake**;
and after the **earthquake** a **fire**,
but the **Lord** was not in the **fire**;
and after the **fire** a **sound** of **sheer** silence.
When Elijah **heard** it,
he **wrapped** his **face** in his **mantle** and **went out**
and **stood** at the **entrance** of the **cave**.

Elijah = ee-Lī-juh
Horeb = HOHR-eb

A bracing and poetic reading, with the quality of both a myth and a parable. There is a magical clarity that defines it.

The rhythm here is important, especially the "*Lord* was *not* . . ."

READING I Today's first reading is the story of Elijah's encounter with God. To better understand this reading, we should know that Elijah was a Prophet of God in the time of King Ahab, whose wife was Jezebel, a foreigner and worshipper of Baal. After Elijah slayed the Prophets of Baal in the Wadi Kishon in Galilee, Jezebel vowed to kill him, so he ran all the way to Beer-sheba, a distance of more than 150 kilometres. He escaped into the wilderness, where he lay down under a broom tree and prayed for death. Miraculously, an Angel came to wake him and tell him to eat and drink what was left for him. When the Angel came again to waken him, Elijah was told again to eat and drink in preparation for a journey, which takes him to Mount Horeb, also known as Sinai (1 Kings 19.1–8).

When he arrived at Horeb, God asks Elijah what he's doing there. Elijah responds with a complaint about how God's people had abandoned the covenant, destroyed God's altars, and killed his Prophets. Elijah adds, "I alone am left, and they are seeking my life, to take it away" (1 Kings 19.10). Arriving at the beginning of our first reading, we hear God telling Elijah to go out and stand on the mountain before God. The phrase "stand before the Lord" is another way of saying that Elijah is being called to service. The fierce wind, earthquake, and fire are all accompaniments to a theophany—a manifestation of the divine—but it is only in the "sound of sheer silence" that Elijah knows God's presence. Thus, he emerged from the cave but hid his face because ancients believed that no one could see God face to face and live. Today, too, we might not see God face to face, but we can see God's activity in the world if we look attentively. Where is God at work in your life?

248

For meditation and context:

RESPONSORIAL PSALM   Psalm 85.8ab+9, 10–11, 12–13 (R.7)

R. Show us your steadfast love, O Lord, and grant us your salvation.

Let me hear what God the Lord will speak,
for he will speak peace to his people.
Surely his salvation is at hand for those
    who fear him,
that his glory may dwell in our land.

Steadfast love and faithfulness will meet;
righteousness and peace will kiss each other.

Faithfulness will spring up from the ground,
and righteousness will look down from
    the sky.

The Lord will give what is good,
and our land will yield its increase.
Righteousness will go before him,
and will make a path for his steps.

READING II   Romans 9.1–5

A reading from the Letter of Saint Paul to the Romans.

Brothers and **sisters:**
I am **speaking** the **truth** in **Christ.**
I **am not lying;**
my **conscience confirms** it by the **Holy Spirit.**
I have **great sorrow** and **unceasing anguish** in my **heart.**
For I could **wish** that I **myself** were **accursed**
and **cut off** from **Christ** for the **sake** of my **own people,**
my **kindred according** to the **flesh.**
They are **children** of **Israel,**
and to **them belong** the **adoption,** the **glory,** the **covenants,**
the **giving** of the **law,** the **worship,** and the **promises;**
to **them** belong the **patriarchs,**
and **from** them, **according** to the **flesh,** comes the **Christ,**
who is **over all,**
God be **blessed forever. Amen.**

Even emphasis on "am not lying."

Note the unusual rhythm/rhetoric of the phrases beginning with "to them."

Strong emphasis on the whole phrase, "over all, God be blessed forever."

READING II   Our second reading is a continuation of Paul's Letter to the Romans, which we have been hearing during recent Sundays in Ordinary Time. This reading is the opening section of a long diatribe that extends from Romans 9.1 through 11.36. Although our modern understanding of diatribe usually has negative connotations and anger associated with it, in literature and during the time period of Paul, a diatribe is a type of argument in which the speaker, or writer in this case, imagines a hypothetical respondent who challenges the speaker or asks questions of him at different points in the argument. The speaker or writer's responses then become the starting point for another section of the argument. Paul's concern is immediately evident. He is worried about his fellow Jews who have not accepted Jesus Christ as the Messiah and have not joined the Jesus movement. Hopefully you can get a sense of the profound grief and anguish that he carries in his heart. He says that he would rather be cut off from Christ—the worst possible thing that Paul could imagine—for the sake of his people. He also lists seven privileges that God has given to the chosen people and adds an eighth—the sending of Christ, the pre-eminent descendant of the patriarchs—whom some of his Jewish brethren refuse to accept. At the end of Paul's diatribe, he will conclude that the reason for his Jewish brethren's rejection of Jesus is to make it possible for the expansion of God's covenant to include the Gentiles.

GOSPEL   Matthew 14.22–33

A reading from the holy Gospel according to Matthew.

Immediately after **feeding** the **crowd**
with the **five loaves** and **two** fish,
Jesus made the **disciples** get into the boat
and go on **ahead** to the other side,
while he **dismissed** the **crowds**.
And after he had **dismissed** the **crowds**,
he went **up** the **mountain** by **himself** to **pray**.
When **evening came**, he was **there alone**,
but by **this time** the **boat**, **battered** by the **waves**,
was **far** from the **land**,
for the **wind** was **against** them.
And **early** in the **morning**
Jesus came **walking toward** them on the **sea**.
But when the **disciples saw** him **walking** on the **sea**,
they were **terrified**, saying,
"It is a **ghost!**"
And they cried **out** in **fear**.
But **immediately** Jesus **spoke** to them and **said**,
"Take **heart**, it is **I**;
do **not** be **afraid**."
Peter **answered** him, "**Lord**, if it is **you**,
command me to **come** to you on the **water**."
Jesus said, "**Come**."
So **Peter** got **out** of the **boat**,
started **walking** on the **water**, and came toward **Jesus**.
But when he **noticed** the **strong wind**,
he became **frightened**, and **beginning** to **sink**,
he cried **out**, "**Lord**, **save** me!"

This reading depicts such a vivid scene, it's like a short film.

That Jesus is alone suggests something of the power he is feeling/gathering.

Seeing Jesus, the disciples are truly frightened. Fear is the mood of this reading.

The disciples' fear is contrasted by Jesus telling them not to be afraid.

Once again, fright.

GOSPEL   Today's Gospel reading tells the story of another theophany or manifestation of the divine. In Matthew's Gospel, this story appears immediately after the first of two miracles of the multiplication of loaves and fishes (Matthew 14.13–21 and 15.32–39). In this reading, Jesus first directs his disciples to go to the other side of the Sea of Galilee, away from the crowds that had gathered in the wilderness and were fed from the five loaves and two fish. Then he goes off by himself to pray. The Sea of Galilee is a large freshwater lake measuring approximately 53 kilometres in circumference. Because of its geography, night-time storms on the lake are common even today.

The narrator of this story tells us that the boat that holds the disciples is already a few kilometres offshore when Jesus observes their predicament, presumably because of the high winds that they are encountering. He went out to them very early in the morning, likely before or close to dawn. The disciples must have been exhausted after fighting the storm all night. But then they see a figure walking toward them on the water and are beside themselves with fear. Stormy water suggested that its monsters were exerting their powers. They thought this figure was a ghost or a haunting spirit, but when Jesus spoke, they realized it was Jesus.

The scene in which Peter asks Jesus to have him come to Jesus across the water is only in Matthew's Gospel (compare it with

When Jesus rebukes Peter for his doubt, he seems especially to be calling him out for letting his fear master him.

Slight pause between "boat" and "worshipped."

Jesus **immediately reached out** his **hand** and **caught** him, **saying** to him, "**You** of little **faith**, **why** did you **doubt?**" When they **got** into the **boat**, the **wind ceased**. And **those** in the **boat worshipped** him, **saying**, "**Truly** you are the **Son** of **God**."

Mark 6.45–52). Peter is extremely enthusiastic at first, but he quickly doubts and begins to sink into the water. Finally, when Jesus calms the storm, they know his true identity, because only God can control the forces of nature. Thus, the disciples bow down in worship and acknowledge him as the Son of God. C.C.

THE ASSUMPTION OF THE BLESSED VIRGIN MARY (VIGIL MASS)

LECTIONARY #621

READING I   1 Chronicles 15.3–4, 15–16; 16.1–2

A reading from the first book of Chronicles.

Chronicles = KRAH-nih-k*ls

A reading that describes the preparation and then the activities of a celebration ordained by King David.

Aaron = AYR-uhn
Levites = LEE-vĭts

Don't rush through the details. These—including the musical instruments—signify the nature and quality of the celebration.

Note the parallel emphases on "burnt offerings" and "offerings of well-being."

David assembled **all Israel** in **Jerusalem**
to bring up the **ark** of the **Lord** to its **place**,
which he had **prepared** for it.
Then David gathered together
the **descendants** of **Aaron** and the **Levites**.
The **Levites** carried the **ark** of God
on their **shoulders** with the **poles**,
as **Moses** had **commanded** according to the **word** of the Lord.
David also commanded the **chiefs** of the **Levites**
to **appoint** their **kindred** as the **singers**
to play on **musical** instruments,
on **harps** and **lyres** and **cymbals**,
to raise **loud sounds** of **joy**.
They brought in the **ark** of **God**,
and set it **inside** the **tent** that **David** had **pitched** for it;
and they offered **burnt offerings**
and offerings of **well-being** before **God**.
When **David** had finished offering the **burnt offerings**
and the offerings of **well-being**,
he **blessed** the people in the **name** of the **Lord**.

The feast of the Assumption of Mary is both ancient and new. It has been celebrated as part of the Christian tradition since the fifth century, but the Catholic dogma (doctrine) of the assumption of Mary did not become official until 1950, under Pope Pius XII. The readings for the vigil Mass point to the holiness of those objects or people that bear the presence of God; Mary is honoured by God for her discipleship and holiness in bearing Christ into the world, and so we believe she was taken up, body and soul, into heaven.

READING I | Our first reading is a narrative account of King David bringing the ark of God into Jerusalem. This is the ark that had travelled with the Israelites from the time of the Exodus. It was said to have contained the tablets of the Ten Commandments and to have special powers of protection for the Israelites. Except for the times that their warriors carried it into battle, it was kept in a special tent attended by Israelite priests and Levites, the tribe of Jacob that was set aside for religious service.

When David first rose to power, the ark was housed at Kirjath-jearim, but after he built his palace in Jerusalem, he ordered that the ark be brought to Jerusalem, where it continued to reside in a tent, as it had throughout the Exodus. This reading gives us a glimpse into the honour and splendour associated with the ark of God. The descendants of Aaron, whom David gathered for the transport of the ark, are the priests. The Levites, who carried the ark over its 14-kilometre journey to Jerusalem, did so with poles on their shoulders in order not to touch the ark itself. The event was so sacred that the musical instruments could only be played by members of the

For meditation and context:

RESPONSORIAL PSALM Psalm 132.6–7, 9–10, 13–14 (R.8)

R. Rise up, O Lord, and go to your resting place, you and the ark of your might.

We heard of the ark in Ephrathah;
we found it in the fields of Jaar.
"Let us go to his dwelling place;
let us worship at his footstool."

Let your priests be clothed with
    righteousness,
and let your faithful shout for joy.
For your servant David's sake
do not turn away the face of your
    anointed one.

For the Lord has chosen Zion;
he has desired it for his habitation.
"This is my resting place forever;
here I will reside, for I have desired it."

READING II 1 Corinthians 15.54–57

Corinthians = kohr-IN-thee-uhnz

A reading in which Paul insists on the victory over death that results from the defiance of sin gained through Christ's sacrifice.

In this quotation, emphasis on the first and last word in each line in quotation marks.

Note the rhythm of these two lines, each of which has three beats: sting, death, sin, and power, sin, law.

A reading from the first Letter of Saint Paul to the Corinthians.

Brothers and **sisters**:
When this **perishable** body puts on **imperishability**,
and this **mortal** body puts on **immortality**,
then the **saying** that is **written** will be **fulfilled**:
"**Death** has been swallowed up in **victory**."
"**Where**, O death, is your **victory**?
Where, O death, is your **sting**?"
The **sting** of **death** is **sin**,
and the **power** of **sin** is the **law**.
But **thanks** be to **God**,
who gives us the **victory** through our **Lord** Jesus **Christ**.

> **TO KEEP IN MIND**
> Make eye contact with the assembly. This helps keep the assembly engaged with the reading.

tribe of Levi, and David himself offered the offerings of well-being before the ark. The offering of well-being was a burnt offering, part of which was given to God and part to the people, thus establishing communion with God. What a splendid affair!

READING II In today's second reading, Paul completes his lengthy teaching on the resurrection of the body with a powerful exclamatory statement about what it will be like to inherit the kingdom of God at the end time. He has already made the point that the corruptible body,

that is, the physical body which decays, cannot inherit the kingdom of God. Rather, at the end time, a trumpet will sound, and the dead will be raised incorruptible, that is, with an immortal spiritual body. When this happens, Paul says, the words of Scripture will be fulfilled. Paul's quotation is a loose conflation of Isaiah 25.8 and Hosea 13.14, which results in a beautifully poetic statement about death being swallowed up in victory.

In his Letter to the Romans, Paul states even more clearly than in today's reading that death came into the world through sin (see Romans 5.12) and that humanity did

not know sin except through Jewish law, but that sin took advantage of the law to make us want what we should not have (Romans 7.7–13). This is what Paul means here, when he says, "the sting of death is sin" and "the power of sin is the law." But just as God raised Jesus from the dead in triumph over sin and death, we too, with our transformed bodies, will be raised in victory over death.

GOSPEL Our Gospel reading is very short but certainly relevant for this feast. It is part of a longer segment

A short but intense Gospel reading in which an exhortation is embedded in a brief narrative. This reading can seem like a rebuke or at least a correction on Jesus' part. Instead, consider it an intensification of the excited statement made by the woman in the crowd.

Don't change your tone at "rather." Instead, treat what Jesus says as an affirmation and furthering of what the woman has said.

GOSPEL   Luke 11.27–28

A reading from the holy Gospel according to Luke.

As **Jesus** was **speaking** to the people,
a **woman** in the crowd **raised** her **voice** and **said** to him,
"**Blessed** is the **womb** that **bore** you
and the **breasts** that **nursed** you!"
But Jesus said,
"Blessed rather are **those** who **hear** the **word** of **God**
      and **obey** it!"

of Luke's Gospel in which Jesus responds to the accusation from some in the crowd that he drives out demons by the power of Satan (Luke 11.14–26) and to their demand for a sign from heaven before they will accept his testimony (Luke 11.29–36). In the first response, Jesus argues that he is actually the enemy of Satan and that he drives out demons by the power of God. In the second response, he turns the tables on his accusers, calling them an evil generation and telling them that the only sign he will give them is the sign of Jonah—a reference to how the people of Nineveh repented

when they heard Jonah's preaching—and the great distance from which the queen of the south came to hear Solomon's words. Finally, Jesus delivers the decisive blow against his opponents by saying that they have someone greater than Solomon or Jonah in their midst and they do not see him because their bodies are filled with darkness. Ancients believed that people were able to see because of the light that radiated out from within them. To call someone "blind" was to say that they were entirely unenlightened and incapable of serving as light to those around them.

This is the backdrop for today's Gospel reading. Against Jesus' opponents who refuse to acknowledge the power of his word, a woman in the crowd shouts out "Blessed is the womb that bore you." In so doing, she is defending Jesus' honour and countering the charge that his power comes from Satan. Jesus' response to her encapsules all that needs to be said about discipleship—"Blessed are those who hear the word of God and obey it." Thankfully, we can call on Mary to be our guide in our journey of discipleship, because she is blessed on both counts! C.C.

THE ASSUMPTION OF THE BLESSED VIRGIN MARY (MASS ON THE DAY)

LECTIONARY #622

READING I   Revelation 11.19a; 12.1–6a; 10ab

A reading from the book of Revelation.

God's **temple** in **heaven** was **opened**,
and the **ark** of his **covenant** was **seen** within his **temple**.
A great **portent** appeared in **heaven**:
a **woman clothed** with the **sun**,
with the **moon** under her **feet**,
and on her **head** a crown of **twelve stars**.
She was **pregnant** and was **crying out** in **birth pangs**,
in the **agony** of giving **birth**.
Then another **portent** appeared in **heaven**:
a **great red dragon**, with seven **heads** and ten **horns**,
and seven **diadems** on his **heads**.
His **tail** swept down a **third** of the **stars** of **heaven**
and **threw** them to the **earth**.
Then the **dragon** stood before the **woman**
who was **about** to bear a **child**,
so that he might **devour** her **child**
as soon as it was **born**.
And she gave **birth** to a **son**, a **male child**,
who is to **rule** all the **nations** with a rod of **iron**.
But her **child** was **snatched** away
and **taken** to **God** and to his **throne**; »

A reading full of vivid depictions and visionary intensity. Avoid the temptation to exaggerate your tone; instead, proclaim this text directly and straightforwardly, allowing its inherent drama to ring out to your assembly. Proclaim at an even pace so that the extraordinary details can be clearly imagined.

Slight pause between "woman" and "clothed."

Note the repeated use of the word "birth" in this reading. Themes and visualizations of birth dominate the details.

Once again, the theme of birth.

READING I   A brief history of the origin of the feast of the Assumption of Mary and the doctrine associated with the feast is provided in the preface to the commentary on the readings for the vigil of this feast. In 1950, when Pope Pius XII defined the doctrine of the Assumption of Mary in the apostolic constitution *Munificentissimus Deus*, he noted many Scripture passages that theologians have used to contribute to our understanding of this teaching of Mary's assumption. Two Scripture texts that are part of the liturgy for the vigil of this feast, namely, 1 Corinthians 15.54–57 and Psalm 132, are referenced in his writing. He also mentions the vision of the woman clothed with the sun from the Book of Revelation (chapter 12), which is our first reading for today's feast. The identity of this woman is not evident from the text, but some Christian theologians in the early Church understand her to be Mary. Over time, this became the traditional Catholic interpretation of our text, but other suggestions include the Church, the heavenly Jerusalem, the people of Israel, and personified wisdom.

In this vision, John, the author of the Book of Revelation, saw a pregnant woman, who was adorned as a goddess, hovering in the sky. Her labour pains are a reminder of the consequences of Adam and Eve's fall (see Genesis 3.16), suggesting to some that she is the new Eve. He also saw a great red dragon waiting to devour her child when it was born. The dragon is a reminder of the serpent in the Adam and Eve story (Genesis 3.1–7), who is later identified with Satan. The dragon's ten horns introduce a detail from Daniel's vision of the four great oppressive empires of the world (Daniel 7.7). In

Be sure to observe the commas with slight pauses.

and the **woman fled** into the **wilderness**,
where she has a **place prepared** by **God**,
so that **there** she can be **nourished**
for **one thousand two hundred sixty days**.
Then I heard a **loud voice** in heaven, **proclaiming**,

The loud voice indicates the Anointed One. You don't need to raise your voice any more than you already have. Instead, you can slow your pace just slightly.

"**Now** have come the **salvation** and the **power**
and the **kingdom** of our **God**
and the **authority** of his **Christ**."

For meditation and context:

RESPONSORIAL PSALM   Psalm 45.9–10, 11+12c+14, 15 (R.9b)

R. At your right hand stands the queen in gold of Ophir.

Daughters of kings are among your ladies
   of honour;
at your right hand stands the queen in gold
   of Ophir.
Hear, O daughter, consider and incline
   your ear;
forget your people and your father's house.

The king will desire your beauty.
Since he is your lord, bow to him;
The princess is decked with golden robes;
in many-coloured robes she is led
   to the king;
behind her the virgins, her companions,
   follow.

With joy and gladness they are led along
as they enter the palace of the king.

READING II   1 Corinthians 15.20–26

Corinthians = kohr-IN-thee-uhnz

A reading from the first Letter of Saint Paul to the Corinthians.

A reading in which Paul makes a set of forceful claims he wants the members of the early Church in Corinth to understand.

Brothers and **sisters**:
Christ has been **raised** from the **dead**,
the **first fruits** of **those** who have fallen **asleep**.
For since **death** came through a **man**,
the **resurrection** of the **dead** has **also** come through a **man**;
for as all **die** in **Adam**,

Paul uses analogy here to contrast the original sin of Adam to the redemption from sin of Christ.

so **all** will be made **alive** in **Christ**.
But **each** in his own **order**:
Christ the **first fruits**,

Note the repetition of the biblical term "first fruits."

then at his **coming those** who belong to **Christ**.

---

general, horns represented power, and ten was the number representing fullness in the Greco-Roman world. Also, the detail about the dragon throwing down stars from the sky recalls a myth about a rebellious chaos monster that went so far as to attack the stars (see Daniel 8.10).

   Likewise, the detail about the dragon waiting to devour the woman's baby would have reminded the initial readers of this text of the Greco-Roman myth of the birth of Apollo, whose mother Leto was attacked by the mythical dragon Python in order to kill the child and preserve his power over

the oracle at Delphi. But Apollo's father, Zeus, intervened to secure protection for Leto, and after Apollo was born, the child killed Python. It appears that John used these cultural images to depict the birth of the Messiah, who was destined to rule with "a rod of iron." Finally, the detail about the woman escaping to the desert, there to be taken care of by God, is a reminder of the Exodus. The length of her stay—one thousand two hundred sixty days—is about three and a half years. Half of seven, a number of fullness, this number represents a limited time.

Our first reading ends with a heavenly voice declaring that God's salvation and his kingdom have arrived, and Christ's authority is made known. This saying makes a beautiful *inclusio* with the opening sentence of the reading (a literary device used to frame a portion of text). Also, because this reading is intended to honour Mary's heavenly reality, the lectionary leaves out the intercalated vision of how the archangel Michael defeated the dragon and its minions (Revelation 12.7–9). This, too, is cause for rejoicing.

Then comes the **end**,
when he hands **over** the **kingdom** to **God** the **Father**,
after he has **destroyed** every **ruler** and every **authority**
    and **power**.
For he must **reign** until he has put all his **enemies** under
    his **feet**.
The **last** enemy to be **destroyed** is **death**.

The conclusion of this reading is quite forceful; note the emphatic connection between "enemies" and "death."

GOSPEL Luke 1.39–56

A reading from the holy Gospel according to Luke.

Judah = JOO-duh
Zechariah = zek-uh-Rī-uh

A reading from Luke's Gospel included in the Nativity story. Its familiarity to your assembly will not diminish its power. No need to over-dramatize it; let the words of the reading convey its power.

The focus of this reading is on sound, especially of Mary's voice. Let that voice ring out.

Words at the core of one of our most familiar prayers.

Mary set **out** and went with **haste**
to a **Judean** town in the **hill** country,
where she **entered** the house of **Zechariah** and greeted **Elizabeth**.
When Elizabeth heard Mary's **greeting**,
the child **leaped** in her **womb**.
And **Elizabeth** was **filled** with the **Holy Spirit**
and **exclaimed** with a **loud cry**,
"**Blessed** are **you** among **women**,
and **blessed** is the **fruit** of your **womb**.
And **why** has this happened to **me**,
that the **mother** of my **Lord comes** to me?
For as **soon** as I heard the **sound** of your **greeting**,
the **child** in my **womb** leaped for **joy**.
And **blessed** is **she** who **believed**
that there would be a **fulfilment**
of what was **spoken** to her by the **Lord**."
And Mary said,
"My **soul magnifies** the **Lord**,
and my **spirit** rejoices in **God** my **Saviour**,
for he has **looked** with **favour** on the **lowliness** of his **servant**. »

Once again, the emphasis is on the sound of Mary's voice and the joy it brings.

Here, Mary proclaims the words of the Magnificat, one of the most solemn hymns in the Church. These are the words of a joyful affirmation the Gospels uniquely possess.

READING II Our second reading comes from the same section of the First Letter to the Corinthians as did the second reading for the vigil of this feast. Paul has been making the argument that Christians who believe that Jesus was raised from the dead must also believe that they will be raised bodily from the dead—not with our present, physical bodies but with our new, transformed bodies. If we believe otherwise, then Jesus did not triumph over sin and death.

In this reading, Paul writes about Christ as the first fruits, the first and best of the harvest offered to God as a symbol and consecration of all God's chosen ones who have fallen asleep. Paul also uses a method of interpretation called typology, an investigation of patterns of persons or events from the Old Testament that are fully realized in the New Testament. Here, Adam, who brought death into the world, is a type of Christ, who brings fullness of life. The "coming" of Christ is a reference to the parousia at the end time when Christ returns and God's reign is fully manifest to the world.

GOSPEL Today's Gospel reading is the beautiful story of Mary's visitation to her cousin Elizabeth's home, after she learns that Elizabeth, who was old and barren, is six months pregnant and Mary herself is newly pregnant. This story is told only in Luke's Gospel.

On the surface of this story, it could appear that there is little to say beyond the fact that Mary is presented as a charitable young Jewish girl who is concerned for the welfare of her aged relative. However, let's dig a little deeper. Why does the narrator say that Mary travelled in haste? Also, was

"He has shown," "He has brought down," "He has filled," "He has helped": these phrases drive the rhythm of the Magnificat as it is proclaimed in this Gospel reading.

Surely, from now **on** all **generations** will call me **blessed**;
for the **Mighty One** has done great **things** for me,
and **holy** is his **name**.
His **mercy** is for those who **fear** him
from **generation** to **generation**.
He has shown **strength** with his **arm**;
he has scattered the **proud** in the **thoughts** of their **hearts**.
He has brought down the **powerful** from their **thrones**,
and **lifted up** the **lowly**;
he has filled the **hungry** with **good things**,
and sent the **rich** away **empty**.
He has **helped** his servant **Israel**,
in **remembrance** of his **mercy**,
according to the **promise** he made to our fathers,
to **Abraham** and to his **descendants** forever."
And Mary **remained** with Elizabeth about three **months**
and then **returned** to her **home**.

she travelling alone or with a caravan? Why would she have been allowed to make this approximately 145-kilometre, four-day journey alone? The chances of being raped or killed along the way would have been extremely high. Though we don't have the details of her journey, the manner in which she undertook it is significant.

Perhaps Luke's intention in having Mary travel "with haste" was to maintain a close connection between the announcement of the conception of these women's children and the acclamation of their sons' relationship to one another. Both the narra-

tor and Elizabeth comment on her unborn baby leaping in her womb when she hears Mary's greeting, further suggesting that her child, John, recognized Jesus even before either was born. In all four Gospels, John is the one who precedes Jesus and paves the way for his ministry in the world. Elizabeth also acclaims Mary's blessedness and the blessedness of her unborn baby. She is the mother of their Lord! She is also the model of faith for all believers.

Mary responds with words that have come to be known as the Magnificat or the Canticle of Mary. It is patterned after the

Song of Hannah (1 Samuel 2.1–10), which Hannah prayed to God when she brought her son Samuel to the house of the Lord in Shiloh to dedicate him to God, after she had endured years of bullying and shame because of her barrenness. Here, in the Magnificat, Mary attributes her blessedness to God, who in his mercy has raised up the lowly and brought down the proud of heart. Luke highlights this reversal theology throughout his Gospel. C.C.

TWENTIETH SUNDAY IN ORDINARY TIME

LECTIONARY #118

READING I   Isaiah 56.1, 6–7

Isaiah = ī-ZAY-uh

A reading charged with poetry. Be attentive to its rhythms, which convey a lot of its power.

A reading from the book of the Prophet Isaiah.

Thus says the **Lord**:
"Maintain **justice**, and **do** what is **right**,
for **soon** my **salvation** will **come**,
and my **deliverance** be **revealed**.
And the **foreigners** who **join** themselves to the **Lord**,
to **minister** to him, to love the **name** of the **Lord**,
and to be his **servants**,
all who keep the **Sabbath**, and do not **profane** it,
and hold **fast** my **covenant**—
these I will **bring** to my **holy mountain**,
and make them **joyful** in my **house** of **prayer**;
their **burnt offerings** and their **sacrifices**
will be **accepted** on my **altar**;
for my **house** shall be **called** a **house** of **prayer**
for **all peoples**."

The conclusion shifts into an uplifting register.

READING I Chapters 55–66 of Isaiah constitute the section known as Trito-Isaiah, a collection of prophetic material spoken to the Israelites after their return to Jerusalem following the Babylonian Exile. By the time this portion of Isaiah had been written, the Temple has been rebuilt and there needed to be a rethinking as to what constitutes the true nature of the religion. Sacrifice in the Temple was an established means of expressing fidelity to the covenant, but in the time that passed during the absence of the Temple, the people deepened their understanding of what God truly looks for in choosing them as his beloved possession.

The primary theme of this passage is that the covenant is about justice, especially demonstrated in the acceptance of outsiders. The Lord's voice speaks to the people, reminding them that his justice will dawn very soon. Furthermore, the Israelites must not see themselves as having exclusive access to the fruits of God's justice. Instead, all those who love the Lord and find a way to serve him will be welcomed on God's mountain. The Lord suggests that those who have been gifted with the law ought to teach those who do not know the law how to serve God, as well as how to keep the covenant and honour the Sabbath. Undoubtedly, those who have returned from exile rejoice in the restoration of God's house in the city of Jerusalem, but now they must extend God's household far beyond the Temple precincts. The truly acceptable sacrifice is to participate in the construction of a unity among all peoples so that God's house may become "a house of prayer for all peoples."

For meditation and context:

RESPONSORIAL PSALM   Psalm 67.1–2, 4–5, 6–7 (R.5)

R. Let the peoples praise you, O God, let all the peoples praise you!

May God be gracious to us and bless us
and make his face to shine upon us,
that your way may be known upon earth,
your saving power among all nations.

Let the nations be glad and sing for joy,
for you judge the peoples with equity
and guide the nations upon earth.
Let the peoples praise you, O God;
let all the peoples praise you.

The earth has yielded its increase;
God, our God, has blessed us.
May God continue to bless us;
let all the ends of the earth revere him.

READING II   Romans 11.13–15, 29–32

A reading from the Letter of Saint Paul to the Romans.

An uplifting message that Paul addresses directly to the Gentiles.

Brothers and **sisters**:
Now I am **speaking** to you **Gentiles**.
Inasmuch then as I am an **Apostle** to the **Gentiles**,
I **glorify** my **ministry**
in **order** to make my **own flesh** and **blood jealous**,

Slight pause between "save" and "some."

and **thus** save **some** of them.
For if their **rejection** is the **reconciliation** of the **world**,
what will their **acceptance** be but **life** from the **dead**!
The **gifts** and the **calling** of God are **irrevocable**.

irrevocable = ir-REV-uh-kuh-b*l

Just as **you** were once **disobedient** to God
but have now received **mercy because** of their **disobedience**,
so **they** have **now** been **disobedient**

Slight pause between "mercy" and "because."

in order that, by the **mercy shown** to you,
they too may **now** receive **mercy**.
For **God** has **imprisoned** all in **disobedience**
so that he may be **merciful** to **all**.

READING II   In addressing his fellow Christians in Rome, whom he identifies as Gentiles or outsiders, Paul refers to himself as their Apostle. Beginning in chapter 9, Paul begins a long exhortation regarding the privilege granted to the people of Israel as well as their responsibility to see that the law is fulfilled in Christ (Romans 10.4). It is Paul's hope that Israel will accept the mercy of God and choose to recognize Jesus as their saviour. In today's reading, we see that Paul hopes that his ministry to the Gentiles will make his own people "jealous" and lead at least some of them to

seek the way of conversion. Paul acknowledges that just as Israel's rejection of the Christian way has led to the blossoming of the Church in foreign lands, the opportunity for them to embrace Christ will be a great sign of resurrected life in the world.

In the second half of this reading, Paul illuminates the triumphant power of God's mercy. Both the gifts of God and his call are "irrevocable." This is certainly true for the mercy of God. The Gentiles did not ask for mercy, but because the Jews rejected the Gospel, Paul has preached God's merciful word to them. The "disobedience" of some

has allowed others to benefit from God's forgiveness. The bottom line is that sin and disobedience become the means by which God is able to display his very nature to the world, for he is a God that desires to "be merciful to all."

GOSPEL   Take note that all three readings today deal with Gentiles, or outsiders. Given the fact that Matthew is writing to a community primarily composed of Jewish Christians, it is not surprising that the tenor of this encounter between Jesus and the Canaanite woman

GOSPEL   Matthew 15.21–28

A reading from the holy Gospel according to Matthew.

Jesus went away to the **district** of **Tyre** and **Sidon**.
A **Canaanite woman** from that region came **out**,
and started **shouting**,
"Have **mercy** on me, **Lord**, **Son** of **David**;
my **daughter** is **tormented** by a **demon**."
But he did not **answer** her at **all**.
And his **disciples** came and **urged** him, saying,
"**Send** her **away**, for she keeps **shouting** after us."
He **answered**,
"I was sent **only** to the **lost sheep** of the **house** of **Israel**."
But the **woman came** and **knelt before** him,
saying, "**Lord**, **help** me."
He **answered**, "It **is not fair** to take the **children's food**
and **throw** it to the **dogs**."
She said, "**Yes, Lord**, yet even the **dogs** eat the **crumbs**
that **fall** from their **masters' table**.
"Then Jesus **answered** her,
"**Woman, great** is your **faith**!
Let it be **done** for you as you **wish**."
And her **daughter** was healed **instantly**.

Tyre = tīr
Sidon = Sī-duhn
Canaanite = KAY-nuh-nīt

A straightforward and instructive reading, with suggestive drama, despite its relatively short length.

Jesus' refusal to answer the Canaanite woman, and his subsequent responses, may seem startling to us.

At last, Jesus' mood changes when he recognizes the depth of the Canaanite woman's faith.

seems to display exclusion. We may even wonder why Jesus would want to find seclusion in this northern region near the border of Phoenicia. He will announce that his mission is "only to the lost sheep of the house of Israel," and yet he has placed himself squarely in foreign territory.

Nevertheless, the location has a great surprise in store for Jesus. He is able to discover an outsider to the Jewish world who has incredible faith. Three times the Canaanite woman begs Jesus to release her daughter from the torment of a demon. After the first request, Jesus simply ignores her, while the disciples beg him to send her away. This gives Jesus the opportunity to announce the parameter of his mission as extending only for the people of Israel. In turn, the woman seems to ignore Jesus, as she performs some act of homage and states boldly, "Lord, help me." Now, Jesus replies with a rather startling comment, comparing her to a dog. Even in the face of this insult, the woman does not relent, but instead suggests that even dogs are worthy of table scraps. Her persistent pleading now causes Jesus to appreciate the depths of her faith, and he cures the daughter from a distance at that very moment. Matthew uses the story to demonstrate an expansion of the mission in the vision of Jesus himself. S.W.

TWENTY-FIRST SUNDAY IN ORDINARY TIME

LECTIONARY #121

READING I   Isaiah 22.15, 19–23

Isaiah = ī-ZAY-uh

A poetic reading in whose rhythms express the powers and convictions of the Lord.

Shebna = SHEB-nah

Eliakim = ee-Lī-uh-kim
Hilkiah = hil-Kī-uh

Take note of the inversion: "open"/"shut"; "shut"/"open." Give them emphasis.

A reading from the book of the Prophet Isaiah.

Thus says the **Lord God** of **hosts**:
Go to the **steward**, to **Shebna**,
who is **master** of the **household**, and **say** to him:
"I will **thrust** you from your **office**,
and you will be **pulled down** from your **post**.
On **that day** I will call my **servant Eliakim** son of **Hilkiah**,
and will **clothe** him with your **robe** and bind your **sash** on him.
I will commit your **authority** to his **hand**,
and he shall be a **father**
to the **inhabitants** of **Jerusalem** and to the **house** of **Judah**.
I will **place** on his **shoulder** the **key** of the **house** of **David**;
he shall **open**, and no one shall **shut**;
he shall **shut**, and no one shall **open**.
I will **fasten** him like a **peg** in a **secure place**,
and he will become a **throne** of **honour** to the **house**
        of his **ancestors**."

TO KEEP IN MIND
If you are assigned to proclaim the first reading, read the Gospel for that week as well. They are connected in thematic ways.

READING I | This reading exhibits a popular literary theme based on the "keeper of the keys," wherein someone has power and insider knowledge because of the responsibility given to them to control entry into the place. Here we have Shebna, who holds the keys that will allow the king entrance, being replaced by a new steward named Eliakim. This exchange takes place during the reign of Hezekiah, the thirteenth king of Judah who ruled in the late eighth to early seventh century BC. The Lord has determined that the king's chief steward must be replaced because he has become prideful by building a tomb for himself and taking pride in his chariots, among other things that might bring shame to the king (Isaiah 22.16–18).

The Lord describes the confidence he has in selecting Eliakim to replace Shebna by the vesture of his office. He will be clothed with Shebna's own robe and sash, which serves to mark the transition of authority from Shebna to Eliakim. Unlike Shebna's display of infidelity, Eliakim will be like a "father" to the people. This means that he will not take advantage of the role entrusted to him. Finally, Eliakim will be given the "key of the house of David." Keys are often used as a symbol of authority. It will be Eliakim's decision whom to admit to the king's palace and whom to reject. He is not to be understood as any mere doorkeeper, but he is to be a steward who has great care and concern for all in his responsibility. Because the Lord's confidence in this servant is so great, he will become an honour for his family.

READING II | Paul's hymn of wonder over the wisdom revealed in God's plan must be read within the frame-

For meditation and context:

RESPONSORIAL PSALM   Psalm 138.1–2a, 2b–3, 6+8b (R.8b)

R. Your steadfast love, O Lord, endures forever.
Do not forsake the work of your hands.

I give you thanks, O Lord, with my
    whole heart;
before the Angels I sing your praise;
I bow down toward your holy temple,
    and give thanks to your name
for your steadfast love and your faithfulness.

For you have exalted your name
and your word above everything.
On the day I called, you answered me,
you increased my strength of soul.

For though the Lord is high, he regards
    the lowly;
but the haughty he perceives from far away.
Your steadfast love, O Lord, endures forever.
Do not forsake the work of your hands.

READING II   Romans 11.33–36

A reading from the Letter of Saint Paul to the Romans.

O the **depth** of the **riches** and **wisdom** and **knowledge** of **God**!
How **unsearchable** are his **judgments**
and how **inscrutable** his **ways**!
"For **who** has known the **mind** of the **Lord**?
Or **who** has been his **counsellor**?"
"Or **who** has given a **gift** to him,
to **receive** a **gift** in **return**?"
For **from** him and **through** him and **to** him are **all things**.
To **him** be the **glory forever**. **Amen**.

A short and powerful reading from Paul, expressed with great passion.

inscrutable = in-SKROO-tuh-b*l (unknowable)

Note how the prepositions supply the power: "from," "through," and "to."

work of the Apostle's overall mission to the Gentiles. Paul himself surely must have been utterly amazed at the work of God in his own conversion from being a strident persecutor of the Christian way to leading the charge to spread the Gospel to peoples far removed from Jerusalem. Paul has just reminded the Romans that while the Jewish people continue to receive God's favour, the conversion of the Gentiles to Christ has allowed God to display the gift of his mercy, which the chosen people of Israel are invited to accept (Romans 11.1–29).

This brief hymn proclaims there is no wisdom and knowledge comparable to God's. This theme of praise can be seen in Old Testament texts that champion God's wisdom (for example, Wisdom 17.1). For Paul, it is simply impossible to plumb the depths of God's knowledge. Furthermore, the hymn proclaims that God acts alone and has no need of advice in carrying out his plan for creation. Though human beings may not understand God's ways, God is the beginning, the sustainer, and the end of all that is. As the conclusion of Paul's exhortation on the place of the people of Israel in

God's plan of salvation, this hymn conveys the message that it would be utter foolishness to do anything but cooperate fully with God's wisdom and thus work toward a bond of unity between Jews and Gentiles.

GOSPEL   Today's reading from Matthew is generally considered to be the chief evangelical text for our understanding of the Church's foundation. While the story of Peter's profession of faith is recorded in Mark 8.27–30 and in Luke 9.18–21, it is only in Matthew that Jesus calls Simon "Peter," or "the Rock"

GOSPEL   Matthew 16.13–20

A reading from the holy Gospel according to Matthew.

When **Jesus** came into the **district** of **Caesarea Philippi**,
he **asked** his **disciples**,
"**Who** do people **say** that the Son of **Man is**?"
And they said, "**Some** say **John** the **Baptist**,
but **others Elijah**,
and **still others Jeremiah** or one of the **Prophets**."
He **said** to them, "But who do you say that I am?"
Simon Peter answered,
"**You** are the **Christ**, the **Son** of the **living God**."
And Jesus **answered** him,
"**Blessed** are **you**, **Simon** son of **Jonah**!
For **flesh** and **blood** has not **revealed** this to you,
but my **Father** in **heaven**.
And I **tell** you, you are **Peter**,
and **on this rock** I will **build** my **Church**,
and the **gates** of **Hades** will **not** prevail **against** it.
I will give you the **keys** of the **kingdom** of **heaven**,
and whatever you **bind** on **earth** will be **bound** in **heaven**,
and whatever you **loose** on **earth** will be **loosed** in **heaven**."
Then Jesus **sternly ordered** the **disciples**
not to tell **anyone** that he was the **Christ**.

Caesarea Philippi = sez-uh-REE-uh fih-LIP-ī

This reading is a set piece in which Jesus, in asking the disciples to tell him what people are saying about him, designates Peter as the one to receive the keys to his kingdom. As such, it has a vivid narrative quality.

Slight pause between "others" and "Jeremiah."

Even emphasis on "on this rock."

Note the parallel: bind-earth-bound-heaven || loose-earth-loosed-heaven.

The conclusion is mysterious. You can allow some of that mystery and slight confusion to slip into your tone.

(from the Greek, *petra/Petros*; and the Aramaic, *kēpā′/Kēphas*), and gives him the power to forgive sins. What is evident here is the influence of the early Church, which presents itself as solid, authoritative, and clearly organized.

The location for this story, in the land north of Galilee, very near to Gentile territory, is important. Matthew designs his Gospel so that the first profession of faith is uttered not in Jerusalem but in a place some distance from the centre. When asked by Jesus "Who do people say that the Son of Man is?" the disciples reply with a variety of well-known figures in the Hebrew faith—John the Baptist, Elijah, and Jeremiah—but the follow-up question, "But who do you say that I am?" suggests that the disciples are more insiders than these classic figures. Furthermore, Peter's profession of Jesus' identity being both "the Christ" and "the Son of the living God" suggests divine wisdom. True knowledge of Jesus can only be granted by God himself. "Flesh and blood" alone, meaning human knowledge, is incapable of grasping the mystery of God revealed in Jesus; this gift comes from above.

At such a profound statement of faith and openness to the Spirit, Jesus does not simply offer words of praise but instead grants Peter complete authority over his future mission. "The Rock" is to provide a firm foundation for the earthly Church and to make heavenly entrance possible by the forgiveness of sins. The Church is completely life-giving, with no power of death able to conquer it. Like Eliakim being in charge of the keys to the palace in the first reading, Peter is a righteous steward called to manage well the affairs of God's household. S.W.

TWENTY-SECOND SUNDAY IN ORDINARY TIME

LECTIONARY #124

READING I Jeremiah 20.7–9

Jeremiah = jayr-uh-Mī-uh

A reading from the book of the Prophet Jeremiah.

O **Lord**, you have **enticed** me,
and I was **enticed**;
you have **overpowered** me,
and you have **prevailed**.

"Enticed": it's a seductive word, one that adds another layer to the tone of this reading, which is one of weariness and frustration.

I have become a **laughingstock all day long**;
everyone **mocks** me.

Slight pause between "laughingstock" and "all."

For whenever I **speak**, I must **cry out**,
I must **shout**, "**Violence** and **destruction**!"
For the **word** of the **Lord** has **become** for me
a **reproach** and **derision all day long**.

Slight pause between "derision" and "all."

Take care not to over-dramatize Jeremiah's frustration. It will come through clearly in the words themselves as you proclaim them.

If I say, "I **will not mention** him,
or **speak** any more in his **name**,"
then within me there is **something** like a **burning fire**
shut up in my **bones**;
I am **weary** with **holding** it in,
and I **cannot**.

Extra emphasis on "cannot."

READING I The words that we read from Jeremiah today are some of the strongest words of lamentation found in the Old Testament. The Prophet has just completed three forecasts of Jerusalem's downfall (Jeremiah 19.1–3, 14–15, and 20.1–5). The most recent prediction of the city's demise was made to the Temple priest Pashhur, who had placed him in the stocks outside of the Temple's gate (Jeremiah 20.2). After announcing that Pashhur and all his family will die in captivity in Babylon, Jeremiah turns his attention to God and calls out in his agony.

Jeremiah claims that God had "enticed" him by calling him into service as a Prophet. The Hebrew word *pātâ* may also be translated as "seduced," thereby making the accusation more comparable to sexual allurement. The Prophet's point is to address God as boldly as possible, revealing the frustration he has internalized for a long period of time. Jeremiah complains that his work as a Prophet has been met with utter rejection, as the people treat him with "reproach and derision."

However, in the final verse, Jeremiah seems to surrender to God once more. While he would like to forget God, refusing to bring him to mind or utter his name, God's call surges up in him again "like a burning fire shut up in my bones." Although he knows he will make every attempt to contain this fire within, it must be released. The language of this passage of lament suggests that to attempt to restrain the Word of God that must be spoken is simply impossible.

For meditation and context:

RESPONSORIAL PSALM   Psalm 63.1, 2–3, 4–5, 7–8 (R.1a)

R. My soul thirsts for you, O Lord my God.

O God, you are my God, I seek you,
my soul thirsts for you;
my flesh faints for you,
as in a dry and weary land where there
         is no water.

So I have looked upon you in the sanctuary,
beholding your power and glory.
Because your steadfast love is better
         than life,
my lips will praise you.

So I will bless you as long as I live;
I will lift up my hands and call on your name.
My soul is satisfied as with a rich feast,
and my mouth praises you with joyful lips.

For you have been my help,
and in the shadow of your wings I sing
         for joy.
My soul clings to you;
your right hand upholds me.

READING II   Romans 12.1–2

A reading from the Letter of Saint Paul to the Romans.

A short and potent reading whose urgency presents a challenge to your assembly.

I **appeal** to you, **brothers** and **sisters**,
by the **mercies** of **God**,
to **present** your **bodies** as a living **sacrifice**,
holy and **acceptable** to **God**,
which is your **spiritual worship**.
Do not be **conformed** to this **world**,

As challenging a teaching today as it was when Paul made it.

but be **transformed** by the **renewing** of your **minds**,
so that you may **discern** what is the **will** of **God**—
what is **good** and **acceptable** and **perfect**.

READING II Chapter 12 of Romans contains an exhortation on humility and charity. Paul has just finished proclaiming a hymn honouring the wisdom of God's mercy (Romans 11.33–36), and now he wishes to impress upon the Romans the need to live and to behave in a manner appropriate to the Christian way. In keeping with the mercy freely given by God, Paul opens this part of the letter by suggesting that God's grace makes it possible for one to offer the entirety of oneself (one's "body") "as a living sacrifice." The use of sacrificial language underscores that Paul is demand-

ing complete and total surrender of the self. This is conversion not only of the mind and heart but of the way in which the body is used as well.

To accomplish this conversion—always to be done in cooperation with God's will—disciples are urged to resist conforming to the world. Since the transformation of a Christian into the life of Christ is an ongoing process, the mind must be constantly discerning what is "good and acceptable and perfect." Before Paul outlines concretely the ways in which disciples must live in this world with humil-

ity and charity, he prevails upon the Christians in Rome to envision life as constant transformation. Even though the world in which human beings live is temporary (see 1 Corinthians 7.31), Paul wants believers to understand the hard work of Christian life as a sacrifice pleasing to God.

GOSPEL This passage marks a shift in the structure of Matthew's Gospel. Immediately prior to today's reading, Jesus asks his disciples about his identity, and Peter offers his great profession of faith (Matthew 16.13–20, see

GOSPEL   Matthew 16.21–27

A reading from the holy Gospel according to Matthew.

Jesus began to show his **disciples**
that he must **go** to **Jerusalem** and undergo **great suffering**
at the **hands** of the **elders** and **chief priests** and **scribes**,
and be **killed**,
and on the third **day** be **raised**.
And **Peter** took **Jesus aside** and began to **rebuke** him, saying,
"God **forbid** it, **Lord**!
This must **never happen** to you."
But he **turned** and said to **Peter**,
"Get **behind** me, **Satan**!
You are a **stumbling block** to me;
for you are thinking **not** as **God** does,
but as **humans** do."
Then **Jesus** told his **disciples**,
"If **anyone** wants to **become** my **follower**,
let him **deny** himself
and **take up** his **cross** and **follow** me.
For whoever wants to **save** their life will **lose** it,
and whoever **loses** their **life** for **my sake** will **find** it.
For what will it **profit** anyone
to gain the **whole world** but **forfeit** their **life**?
Or what will **anyone give** in **return** for their **life**?
For the **Son** of **Man** is to **come** with his **Angels**
in the **glory** of his **Father**,
and then he will repay **each according** to their **work**."

The tone of this Gospel reading begins gloomily, even apocalyptically.

"Rebuke": This is a strong word. Peter is upset.

But Jesus is bothered, even more so than Peter is upset.

Familiar though Jesus' command may be, it is challenging, something even the most devout Christian might not be able to live up to.

Note the inversion: wants-life-lose compared to loses-life-find.

Slight pause between "each" and "according."

last week's Gospel reading). Matthew's Gospel now turns to focus on the cross. While Peter is able to identify Jesus as the Christ, he is unwilling to accept Jesus' humble acceptance of God's will, which would lead to his suffering and eventual death. Thus, the juxtaposition of these two passages demonstrates the difficulty of holding together the horror of the cross with the messianic nature of the person Jesus.

In his private rebuke of Peter (Peter had taken Jesus aside) for attempting to shield him from suffering, Jesus reminds Peter that he is failing to discern the will of God. Peter is viewing power and authority as humans naturally would. However, Jesus turns to his disciples as a whole and tells them the true nature of power and authority, namely, what will come to be celebrated in the Church as the Paschal Mystery. Discipleship involves the willingness to die to self in order to find life again in service of others. Jesus outlines this as a threefold movement: denial of self, taking up the cross, and following after him. Far from seeking the reward of glory, the very purpose of following Jesus is the carrying of the cross. Profit and gain are overturned in Christian discipleship; Christians are to give themselves away in order to receive all that Christ will have in store for them when he returns in glory. The final verse of the reading foreshadows Matthew's story of the Son of Man separating the sheep from the goats on the day of his return (25.31–46). S.W.

TWENTY-THIRD SUNDAY
IN ORDINARY TIME

Ezekiel = ee-ZEE-kee-uhl

An ominous reading in which God makes a challenging command. God speaks directly to the assembly through Ezekiel.

Emphasis on "you."

TO KEEP IN MIND

As you prepare your proclamation, make choices about what emotions need to be expressed. Some choices are evident from the text, but some are harder to discern. Understanding the context of the Scripture passage will help you decide.

LECTIONARY #127

READING I   Ezekiel 33.7–9

A reading from the book of the Prophet Ezekiel.

Thus says the **Lord**:
"So **you**, O **son** of **man**, I have made a **watchman** for the **house**
    of **Israel**;
whenever you hear a **word** from my **mouth**,
you shall give them **warning** from me.
"If I **say** to the **wicked**,
'O **wicked** one, you shall **surely die**,'
and you **do not speak** to **warn** the **wicked** to **turn**
    from their **ways**,
the **wicked person** shall **die** in their **iniquity**,
but their **blood** I will **require** at your **hand**.
But if you **warn** the wicked **person** to turn from their **ways**,
and they **do not turn** from their **ways**,
they shall **die** in their **iniquity**,
but **you** will have saved your **life**."

READING I The Prophet Ezekiel experienced the forced exile of the Israelites by the Babylonians. During that time, he received his call by God to watch over Israel and to challenge the ways of the wicked. Ezekiel was one of the few Old Testament Prophets who received his calling outside the land of Israel, which can shed light on his understanding of God's universal judgment—in Ezekiel, God judges not only the deeds of his chosen people but those of all the nations.

Foretelling the impending destruction of Jerusalem, the voice of the Lord summons Ezekiel to be a "watchman" during the time of conflict. He is to provide a warning to the wicked to renounce their ways. Ezekiel is told quite clearly that failing to enact this task will result in his own demise. This is the second instance of Ezekiel being called to be a watchman and communicate God's message to those who sin, the first being in Ezekiel 3.17–21. The reading we hear today takes place after the Prophet has called many nations to conversion and has prophesied the eventual restoration of Israel. Once again, like a trustworthy sentinel who is to protect the people, Ezekiel receives the call to address the ways of the wicked with challenging words. As watchman, Ezekiel is to make very clear the seriousness of failing to turn from evil in order to pursue the way of righteousness. While Israel has certainly suffered from their deportation to Babylon, they ought to be bolstered in God's care and concern for them by his placing such great responsibility in Ezekiel, a trustworthy and vigilant Prophet.

For meditation and context:

RESPONSORIAL PSALM   Psalm 95.1–2, 6–7ab, 7c–9 (R.7c+8a)

R. O that today you would listen to the voice of the Lord.
Do not harden your hearts!

O come, let us sing to the Lord;
let us make a joyful noise to the rock
    of our salvation!
Let us come into his presence with
    thanksgiving;
let us make a joyful noise to him with
    songs of praise!

O come, let us worship and bow down,
let us kneel before the Lord, our Maker!
For he is our God, and we are the people
    of his pasture,
and the sheep of his hand.

O that today you would listen to his voice!
Do not harden your hearts, as at Meribah,
as on the day at Massah in the wilderness,
when your ancestors tested me,
and put me to the proof,
though they had seen my work.

READING II   Romans 13.8–10

A reading from the Letter of Saint Paul to the Romans.

The reading begins with a potent exhortation that shifts into a more subtle teaching.

The recitation of these commandments has a rote quality . . .

. . . which leads to this distillation of the wisdom of the Scriptures.
Even emphasis on "Love does no wrong."

Brothers and **sisters**:
Owe no one **anything**, except to **love** one **another**;
for the one who loves **another** has **fulfilled** the **law**.
The **commandments**, "You **shall not** commit **adultery**;
You **shall not murder**;
You **shall not steal**;
You **shall not covet**";
and **any** other **commandment**,
are **summed up** in **this word**,
"**Love** your **neighbour as** yourself."
Love does no wrong to a **neighbour**;
therefore, love is the **fulfilling** of the **law**.

READING II | This reading on the commandment to love follows Paul's instruction to the Romans to obey the rule of civil authorities. Paul understands all civil authority as subject to the law of God. Thus, since God is the ultimate authority, obedience ought to be given to the law of the land since rupture in society is ultimately in conflict with the unity God desires.

Paul tells the Romans that the only debt they are to incur is "to love one another." While the foundation of Hebrew law is based on the command to avoid certain wrongdoings such as murder, theft, and lust (see Exodus 20.13–17), Paul speaks of the law's foundation in a proactive manner. Love is not simply avoiding actions that are evil, but love involves moving outside of oneself in order to support the lives of others. The command to love by no means replaces the ancient law, but instead, it buffers it and demands more than mere passivity. In the next chapter, Paul will provide concrete examples as to how love unfolds in charitable outreach to others. We see him begin to explore this idea at the end of this reading by bringing together the law and the life of the Christian: "Love does no wrong to a neighbour; therefore, love is the fulfilling of the law."

GOSPEL | In the verses preceding today's Gospel passage, Jesus tells his disciples the parable of the lost sheep among the flock of one hundred. Great effort is expended by the caring shepherd who leaves the ninety-nine in order to seek out the one who has gone astray. Jesus then likens the Father to the shepherd who is vigilant in guarding his flock and making sure that none are lost.

A reading that demonstrates, in part, the way that Jesus sequences his thoughts, one following from another, building his argument. Slight pause between "sister" and "sins."

Slight pause between "others" and "along."

Note the parallel: bind-earth-bound-heaven || loose-earth-loosed-heaven.

Try to proclaim this familiar insistence as if saying these words for the first time.

GOSPEL   Matthew 18.15–20

A reading from the holy Gospel according to Matthew.

Jesus spoke to his **disciples**.
"If your **brother** or **sister** sins **against** you,
go and **point out** the **fault** when the **two** of you are **alone**.
If **he** or **she listens** to you,
you have **regained** your **brother** or **sister**.
But if the person **does not listen**,
take **one** or **two others along** with you,
so that **every word** may be **confirmed**
by the **evidence** of **two** or three **witnesses**.
If the person **refuses** to **listen** to them,
tell it to the **Church**;
and if that person **refuses** to **listen even** to the **Church**,
let such a **one** be to **you** as a **Gentile** and a **tax collector**.
Truly I **tell** you,
whatever you **bind** on **earth** will be **bound** in **heaven**,
and whatever you **loose** on **earth** will be loosed in **heaven**.
Again, **truly** I **tell** you,
if **two** of you **agree** on **earth** about **anything** you **ask**,
it will be **done** for you by my **Father** in **heaven**.
For where **two** or **three** are **gathered** in my **name**,
I am **there among** them."

It is in this context that we are to read today's teaching on how disputes within the community are not to lead to permanent division but must be resolved through a process of forgiveness. Jesus tells his disciples that the first step in this process is to confront the one responsible for a "fault." If this private encounter proves unsuccessful, several witnesses may assist in exposing the culpability of the one who denies his sin. The authority of the Church is to be consulted as a third option to correct the wrongdoing, and if this fails, the sinner is to be treated as "a Gentile and a tax collector."

In other words, the person is to be treated as someone who is outside the faith of the Church.

All of this culminates in Jesus alluding to the ministry of reconciliation as carried out by the Church. The Church as a whole is given the authority to determine what sins are to be "bound" and "loosed." This is an authority that was earlier handed over by Jesus to Peter alone (Matthew 16.19). Furthermore, Jesus concludes the instruction by ensuring his disciples of the efficacy of prayer and the importance of community. When two or more come together to

pray, they must believe that the Father will hear their prayer. The source of this confidence is found in the presence of the Lord in the midst of his assembled Church. Thus, in their ministry of forgiveness and in their petition of the Lord's aid, the community of believers experiences the presence of Jesus in their midst. S.W.

TWENTY-FOURTH SUNDAY IN ORDINARY TIME

LECTIONARY #130

READING I   Sirach 27.30—28.7

A reading from the book of Sirach.

Anger and **wrath**, **these** are **abominations**,
yet a **sinner** holds **on** to them.
The **vengeful person** will **face** the Lord's **vengeance**,
for he keeps a **strict account** of their sins.
Forgive your **neighbour** the **wrong** that is **done**,
and then your **sins** will be **pardoned** when you **pray**.
Does anyone harbour **anger** against **another**,
and expect **healing** from the **Lord**?
If one has **no mercy** toward **another** like **oneself**,
can one then seek **pardon** for one's own **sins**?
If one who is but **flesh** harbours **wrath**,
who will make an **atoning sacrifice** for **that person's sins**?
Remember the **end** of your **life**,
and set **enmity aside**;
remember **corruption** and **death**,
and be **true** to the **commandments**.
Remember the **commandments**,
and **do not** be **angry** with your **neighbour**;
remember the **covenant** of the **Most High**,
and o**verlook faults**.

Sirach = SEER-ak or Sī-ruhk

A poetic reading drawn along by its powerful rhythm.

These emphatic questions set the tone of the reading.

The reading concludes with an exhortation whose timeliness remains relevant.

READING I The wisdom of the Hebrew scribe Ben Sira is believed to have been compiled between the years 200 and 175 BC. As a collection of ethical instructions, this book attempts to provide practical advice on primary relationships, such as those with mother and father, siblings, the rich and the poor. Today's reading offers wisdom on the issue of holding a grudge against others. Ben Sira opens this section with the image of the sinner hugging tightly "anger and wrath."

He proceeds to instruct his hearers that those who inflict vengeance upon others will in turn receive the Lord's vengeance. In order to be forgiven by God, one must extend forgiveness to others. The same is true with anger; if one harbours anger in one's heart, then one should not be surprised when God will not heal the situation. In the final portion of his instruction on why a person should avoid hatred and vengeance, the author employs the image of death. The threat of death is indeed the gravest of all of his warnings. By remembering the last moments of life, a person ought to recognize that it would be ultimate destruction to die in a state of holding hatred against another. Ben Sira's message is abundantly clear: live constantly the virtue of dismissing the faults of others, and God will respond in kind.

For meditation and context:

RESPONSORIAL PSALM   Psalm 103.1–2, 3–4, 9–10, 11–12 (R.8)

**R. The Lord is merciful and gracious;
slow to anger, and abounding in steadfast love.**

Bless the Lord, O my soul,
and all that is within me, bless his
    holy name.
Bless the Lord, O my soul,
and do not forget all his benefits. R.

It is the Lord who forgives all your iniquity,
who heals all your diseases,
who redeems your life from the Pit,
who crowns you with steadfast love
    and mercy.

He will not always accuse,
nor will he keep his anger forever.
He does not deal with us according to
    our sins,
nor repay us according to our iniquities.

For as the heavens are high above the earth,
so great is his steadfast love toward those
    who fear him;
as far as the east is from the west,
so far he removes our transgressions from us.

READING II   Romans 14.7–9

A reading from the Letter of Saint Paul to the Romans.

A short and potent reading that makes use of the opposition of "live" to "die," using these words to drive home its insistence that Jesus embodies both "the dead" and "the living."

Brothers and **sisters**:
We **do not live** to **ourselves**,
and we **do not die** to **ourselves**.
If we **live**, we **live** to the **Lord**,
and if we **die**, we **die** to the **Lord**;
so then, whether we live or whether we **die**,
we are the **Lord's**.
For to **this end** Christ **died** and **lived again**,
so that he might be **Lord** of both the **dead** and the **living**.

READING II The wisdom of Ben Sira flows nicely into today's reading from Romans. Paul has just cautioned the Romans against judging one another, and now he tells them quite clearly that the nature of the Christian life is to live totally and completely for the Lord. In other words, as love and mercy flow from the heart of God, so too must all Christians embody these key virtues.

For Paul, conforming oneself to Christ is a matter of life and death. In life, a Christian lives "to the Lord," and in death, a Christian dies "to the Lord." Paul presents such absolute commitment in the framework of belonging. Christians live and die for Christ because they belong completely to him. We know that Paul's understanding of belonging is rooted in baptism. Through baptism, Christians are immersed into his death in order to have new life in him (Romans 6.1–11). Freedom is based no longer on a law written upon a scroll but rather on a relationship of complete allegiance. This cove- nantal relationship applies not only to the living but to the dead as well. Those who have already died belong to Christ as much as those who live. Jesus, who experienced both human life and human death, will give life to all who belong to him.

A very challenging Gospel reading in which a quite descriptive parable is used to illuminate Jesus' extravagant teaching about forgiveness.

Here begins the parable, which proceeds in an understandable way.

It is useful to keep in mind that the slaves are subject to the king, their master.

Note the differences between interactions in the scenes: the king toward the slave, the slave toward the other slave, and once again the king toward the first slave.

GOSPEL Matthew 18.21–35

A reading from the holy Gospel according to Matthew.

Peter came and **said** to **Jesus**,
"**Lord**, how **often** should I **forgive**
my **brother** or **sister** if they **sin against** me?
As many as **seven times**?"
Jesus **said** to him,
"Not **seven** times,
but, I tell you, **seventy-seven times**.
For **this** reason the **kingdom** of heaven may be **compared**
        to a **king**
who wished to **settle accounts** with his **slaves**.
When he **began** the **reckoning**,
one who owed him **ten thousand talents** was **brought** to him;
and, as he **could not pay**,
his lord **ordered** him to be **sold**,
together with his **wife** and **children** and **all** his **possessions**,
and **payment** to be **made**.
So the **slave** fell on his **knees before** him, saying,
'Have **patience** with me,
and I will pay you every**thing**.'
The lord of that **slave released** him
and **forgave** him the **debt**.
But that **same slave**, as he **went out**,
came upon one of his **fellow slaves**
who owed him a **hundred denarii**;
and **seizing** him by the **throat**, he said,
'Pay what you owe.'
Then his **fellow slave** fell **down** and **pleaded** with him,
'Have **patience** with me, and I will **pay** you.'
But he **refused**;
then he went and **threw** him into **prison**
until he would **pay** the **debt**. »

GOSPEL Jesus has just finished instructing his disciples on the important role of forgiveness and prayer in uniting the community of disciples when Peter asks him how far a person should go in being willing to forgive. Peter attempts to provide a potential answer to his own question, suggesting seven times, or the biblical number of perfection. However, the saying uttered by Jesus transcends even perfection, as he contends that there must be no end to a disciple's willingness to forgive another. Thus, the number seventy-seven.

This discussion on forgiveness allows Jesus to tell the parable of the unforgiving debtor. While not exactly revealing the limitless need to forgive, the story certainly underscores the importance of developing an attitude of empathy and being ready to forgive the one who sins. Jesus likens the kingdom of heaven to a king who wants his slaves to pay back what they owe him. The first slave has accumulated a great debt of "ten thousand talents" that he owes the king. When the king threatens to balance the debt by selling the slave along with his entire household, the slave begs the king to treat him with patience. Jesus says that this request caused the king to act with compassion, as he released the slave and forgave the debt.

But we quickly discover the lack of gratitude on the part of this slave, as he leaves the king's presence and demands that a fellow servant pay off the debt that

The master's wrath is tangible.

The reading concludes on a challenging note: If you don't forgive, the heavenly Father will be wrathful and punish you like the master punishes his ungrateful slave!

When **his fellow slaves** saw what had **happened**,
they were **greatly distressed**,
and they went and **reported** to their **lord**
all that had taken **place**.
Then his lord summoned him and said to him,
'You **wicked slave**!
I forgave you **all that debt** because you **pleaded** with me.
Should you not have had **mercy** on your **fellow slave**,
as **I** had **mercy** on **you**?'
And in **anger** his lord handed him **over** to be **tortured**
until he would **pay** his entire **debt**.
So my heavenly Father will **also do** to **every one** of **you**,
if you **do not forgive** your **brother** or **sister** from your **heart**."

he owed him. This second slave utters to his debtor the same plea as the first: "Have patience with me, and I will pay you." However, unlike the compassionate king, the slave is not moved with pity, nor does he forgive the debt. Instead, he has the slave thrown in prison. Clearly, this man represents the contrasting attitude to that of the king; he learns nothing from the king's kindness.

In a way that corresponds to the method for brotherly correction in last week's Gospel reading of Matthew 18.15–18, the parable continues by introducing other "fellow slaves" who witness the injustice and approach the king with the story of the servant's sin. The king summons the slave before him and pronounces him "wicked." Thus, forgiveness is to be returned to the one who extends forgiveness, but to the one who fails to forgive, no mercy will be shown in return. S.W.

TWENTY-FIFTH SUNDAY IN ORDINARY TIME

LECTIONARY #133

READING I Isaiah 55.6–9

Isaiah = ī-ZAY-uh

An intense and poetic reading. Let its language carry your proclamation.

A reading from the book of the Prophet Isaiah.

Seek the **Lord** while he may be **found**,
call upon him while he is **near**;
let the **wicked person forsake** their **way**,
and the **unrighteous person** their **thoughts**;
let that person **return** to the **Lord** that he may have **mercy**
    on them,
and to our **God**, for he will **abundantly pardon**.
For my thoughts are not **your** thoughts,
nor are **your ways** my **ways**, says the **Lord**.
For as the **heavens** are **higher** than the **earth**,
so are **my ways higher** than your **ways**
and **my thoughts** than your **thoughts**.

Slight pause between "ways" and "my."

In these last three lines, the Lord is presumably speaking, through Isaiah.

For meditation and context:

RESPONSORIAL PSALM Psalm 145.2–3, 8–9, 17–18 (R.18)

R. The Lord is near to all who call on him.

Every day I will bless you,
and praise your name forever and ever.
Great is the Lord, and greatly to be praised;
his greatness is unsearchable.

The Lord is gracious and merciful,
slow to anger and abounding in
    steadfast love.
The Lord is good to all,
and his compassion is over all that he
    has made.

The Lord is just in all his ways,
and kind in all his doings.
The Lord is near to all who call on him,
to all who call on him in truth.

READING I | This reading comes from the final chapter of the second portion of Isaiah known as "Deutero-Isaiah." Chapters 40 to 55 were most likely written after Israel had been exiled to Babylon. The basic warning found in today's reading focuses on the temptation to make God operate in a way that corresponds to human understanding. God's ways do not always correspond with ours.

The reading opens with the command to "seek the Lord." Searching for the Lord is possible because he allows himself to be found, and the author says that God is indeed "near." Recall that the pattern of seeking God for the Israelites was generally found in the sacrifices offered in the Temple, now destroyed by the Babylonians. Because of their exile, the Israelites had to find a new way to seek the Lord, one that was more personal in nature. Isaiah suggests that the Lord can be found when one turns from evil and seeks the Lord's mercy. Because God "will abundantly pardon," one can trust that the past will be overturned as new way of living begins.

It is in the context of assuring Israel that the repentant sinner will be restored to relationship with God that Deutero-Isaiah cautions against trying to overly scrutinize God's ways. Searching for the Lord does not mean imposing human standards upon him. While the mercy of God is abundant, one should not attempt to measure it according to the world's sense of justice. The Lord transcends all human thought. Even though God's ways and wisdom are mysterious and beyond us, true worship of God demands conversion of life and constant journeying to find and follow the way of the Lord.

READING II   Philippians 1.20–24, 27

A reading from the Letter of Saint Paul to the Philippians.

Brothers and **sisters**:
Christ will be **exalted now** as **always** in my **body**,
whether by **life** or by **death**.
For to **me**, **living** is **Christ** and **dying** is **gain**.
If I am to **live** in the **flesh**,
that means **fruitful labour** for **me**;
and I do not **know** which I **prefer**.
I am **hard pressed** between the **two**:
my **desire** is to **depart** and be with **Christ**,
for **that** is far **better**;
but to **remain** in the **flesh** is more **necessary** for **you**.
Live your **life** in a manner **worthy** of the **Gospel** of **Christ**.

Philippians = fih-LIP-ee-uhnz

A passionate exhortation, expressed in a tone of vulnerability.

Slight pause between "exalted" and "now."

Paul expresses a moving thought here: Though he longs to be united with Christ in heaven, he recognizes the value of remaining in the flesh to do God's work.

GOSPEL   Matthew 20.1–16

A reading from the holy Gospel according to Matthew.

Jesus spoke this **parable** to his **disciples**.
"The **kingdom** of **heaven** is like a **landowner**
who went out **early** in the **morning**
to hire **labourers** for his **vineyard**.
After **agreeing** with the **labourers** for the **usual daily wage**,
he **sent** them into his **vineyard**.
When he went **out** about **nine o'clock**,
he saw **others standing idle** in the **marketplace**;
and he **said** to them,
'**You also go** into the **vineyard**,
and I will pay you whatever is **right**.'
So they **went**.

A long parable but one told with a clear-eyed economy whose message is crystal clear.

Slight pause between "also" and "go."

READING II At the beginning of the Letter to the Philippians, Paul greets them with thanksgiving and a prayer for the fruition of the community before he turns to a lengthy description of his state of imprisonment. Given the backdrop of prison, it is no wonder that Paul ruminates on the possibility of death in today's reading. Paul begins by acknowledging his body as a means of glorifying Christ. The analogy of the body suggests that Paul is totally dedicated to the Lord. Every part of his being, in life and in death, functions to serve Christ.

Paul continues by exploring the possible outcomes for himself, the value of his life versus the value of his death. On the one hand, continuing to live, even from the confines of jail, allows Paul the opportunity to spread the message of the Gospel. On the other hand, if Paul were put to death, he would enter into an even deeper relationship with Christ. While Paul assesses that the latter option of death and eternal union with Christ is far more valuable, he knows that it is better for the infant Church that he continue to live.

Omitted from our reading are verses 25 and 26, in which Paul announces that he will renew his commitment to encourage the community and will one day return to them. In the meantime, he expects that they will behave "in a manner worthy of the Gospel of Christ." He has provided them with all the tools they need to live in Christ.

GOSPEL It is important to notice that the parable begins with the kingdom of heaven being likened to the "landowner" and not to the vineyard. In fact, for those who heard this parable from the

When he went **out again** about noon and about **three o'clock**,
he did the **same**.
And about **five o'clock** he went **out** and found **others**
        standing **around**;
and he **said** to them,
'Why are you standing here **idle all day**?'
They **said** to him,
'Because **no one** has **hired** us.'
He **said** to them,
'**You also go** into the **vineyard**.'
When **evening** came,
the owner of the **vineyard** said to his **manager**,
'Call the **labourers** and **give** them their **pay**,
beginning with the **last** and then **going** to the **first**.'
When **those hired** about **five o'clock** came,
each of them received the **usual daily wage**.
Now when the **first** came,
they thought they would **receive more**;
but **each** of them **also received** the **usual daily wage**.
And when they **received** it,
they **grumbled** against the **landowner**, saying,
'**These last** worked **only one hour**,
and you have made them **equal** to us
who have **borne** the **burden** of the **day** and the **scorching heat**.'
But he **replied** to one of them,
'**Friend**, I am **doing** you **no wrong**;
did you **not agree** with me for the **usual daily wage**?
Take what **belongs** to you and **go**;
I **choose** to give to this **last** the **same** as I give to **you**.
Am I not allowed to **do** what I choose
with what **belongs** to me?
Or are you **envious** because I am **generous**?'
So the **last** will be **first**,
and the **first** will be **last**."

Slight pause between "also" and "go."

Don't overdo the workers' grumbling tone.

Likewise, don't overdo the landowner's pedantic tone. Allow his equanimity to all the workers he hired to characterize your tone.

mouth of Jesus, the image of the vineyard most likely conjured up the idea of Israel. Isaiah 5 foretells the future of Israel as a vineyard that produced bad fruit and which God judged. The point of this parable is that the landowner's method of care is quite unlike anything we may expect.

The parable suggests that those who are waiting to be hired are loafing around rather than being proactive in their pursuit of work. When the landowner returns for a final time at five o'clock, he appears to be perplexed at their ongoing inactivity, as he asks them, "Why are you standing here idle all day?" Their simple excuse that no one has hired them does not dissuade the landowner from sending these men into the vineyard. But what could they possibly accomplish with such a short time left in the day?

This question does not seem to cross the landowner's mind as he instructs his foreman to begin paying those who began their work at the end of the day with the same "usual daily wage" that is due those who started work at nine in the morning. We are likely to relate to those first employed who initially see this generosity as a good thing, believing they will receive more. However, that is not the way this landowner does business. When they get nothing more than those who arrived last in the vineyard, their excitement turns to resentment, as they grumble and complain that they deserve more.

The generosity of the landowner does not pair with typical human understanding of justice, but that is the very point of this parable on the kingdom of heaven. God's invitation to share in the kingdom is far more universal than we might think. What matters most is responding to the call of discipleship, no matter the time in one's life. S.W.

TWENTY-SIXTH SUNDAY IN ORDINARY TIME

Ezekiel = ee-ZEE-kee-uhl

The expression that begins this reading is familiar to anyone who has parented young children. There is a little of the petulance of a child in the house of Israel's complaint.

God's argument is to turn the tables; he's not unfair but instead the house of Israel behaves unfairly toward him.

LECTIONARY #136

READING I   Ezekiel 18.25–28

A reading from the book of the Prophet Ezekiel.

Thus says the **Lord**:
"You object, O **House** of **Israel**!
You say, 'The **way** of the Lord is **unfair**.'
Hear now, O **house** of **Israel**:
Is my **way unfair**?
Is it not **your ways** that are **unfair**?
When the **righteous person** turns **away** from their **righteousness**
and **commits iniquity**,
they shall **die** for it;
for the **iniquity** that they have **committed** they shall die.
Again, when the **wicked person turns away**
from the **wickedness** they have **committed**
and does what is **lawful** and **right**,
they shall **save** their **life**.
Because that person **considered** and turned **away**
from all the **transgressions** that they had **committed**,
they shall **surely live**;
they **shall not die**."

READING I   The chapter of Ezekiel from which our reading comes deals with individual responsibility. Written during the time of Babylonian captivity, the mandates represented here reveal a new chapter in Israelite law. Up to this point, the emphasis was placed on corporate responsibility. Sins committed by parents were understood to be passed on to their children. However, the strong sense of guilt brought about by the destruction of Jerusalem and the exile to Babylon gave rise to a new sense of individual responsibility, whereby each person could develop a rela-

tionship with God and was responsible for maintaining that relationship.

This reading deals with the consequences of departing from a virtuous way of life in order to pursue some form of wickedness. Speaking the Lord's own words to the people of Israel, Ezekiel begins by challenging them to adjust their understanding of fairness. While they may perceive a certain punishment given by the Lord to be unfair, it is really the actions of people themselves that are unfair. Ezekiel raises the topic of the punishment of death that is given to the one who turns from virtue to

wickedness. Death is deemed quite fair for this failure to act responsibly. Similarly, God's fairness will be executed in the life of the one who turns from wickedness to doing what is "lawful and right." That person's reward shall be the preservation of life. Thus, we see that God's justice—both punishment and reward—is not passed down through the generations; instead, it is a matter of personal culpability.

READING II   After reminding the Philippians of his imprisonment and of the need to persevere in faith,

For meditation and context:

RESPONSORIAL PSALM   Psalm 25.4–5a, 6+7b, 8–9 (R.6)

R. Lord, be mindful of your mercy.

Make me to know your ways, O Lord;
teach me your paths.
Lead me in your truth, and teach me,
for you are the God of my salvation.

Be mindful of your mercy, O Lord, and of
your steadfast love,
for they have been from of old.

According to your steadfast love
remember me,
for the sake of your goodness, O Lord!

Good and upright is the Lord;
therefore he instructs sinners in the way.
He leads the humble in what is right,
and teaches the humble his way.

READING II   Philippians 2.1–11

A reading from the Letter of Saint Paul to the Philippians.

[**Brothers** and **sisters**:
If there is **any encouragement** in **Christ**,
any **consolation** from **love**,
any **sharing** in the **Spirit**,
any **compassion** and **sympathy**,
then **make** my **joy complete**:
be of the **same mind**,
having the **same love**,
being in **full accord** and of **one mind**.
Do **nothing** from **selfish ambition** or **conceit**,
but in **humility** regard **others** as **better** than **yourselves**.
Let **each** of you look **not** to your **own interests**,
but to the **interests** of **others**.
Let the **same mind be** in **you**
that was in **Christ Jesus**,]
who, though he was in the **form** of **God**,
did not regard **equality** with **God** as **something** to be **exploited**,
but **emptied** himself, taking the **form** of a **slave**,
being born in human likeness.
And being found in human form,
he **humbled** himself
and became **obedient** to the **point** of **death**—
even **death** on a **cross**. »

Philippians = fil-LIP-ee-uhnz

A reading of great and solemn mystery, offering a glimpse into the beliefs and expressions of the members of the early Church.

Slight pause between "mind" and "be."

In this expression lies one of the mystical cores of Christian beliefs, Christ's self-emptying (kenosis). Proclaim it solemnly.

Paul turns to the topic of the Church's pursuit of unity in a spirit of humility. Employing the evidence of an early Christological hymn in which Christ's exaltation is revealed as a reward for his humility, Paul encourages Christians to have the "the same mind" as Christ.

This reading opens with the reason Christians must pursue the way of unity. Because they belong to Christ and participate in the Spirit, they ought to consider themselves as sharers in the "same mind" and the "same love" that flow from Christ. The way this oneness is most concretely displayed is in the way in which Christians reject any form of selfishness and consider the needs of others as more important than their own.

Halfway into this reading, Paul introduces what was an early Christian hymn the community might have been aware of to portray the humility of Christ. The first half of the hymn reveals Christ's humble attitude displayed in his rejection of divine power in order to share in the lot of humanity. Instead of grasping at or exploiting his divine nature, Christ became as lowly as a "slave." His humility continues to the cross, where he becomes perfectly "obedient" by accepting his death as part of God's will.

The second half of the hymn praises Christ and describes the reward bestowed upon him by God. God exalts him, places his name over all things in the cosmos, and moves every being to proclaim that "Jesus Christ is Lord!" While this reading does not provide a suggestion as to how to put this hymn into practice, Paul's intention is very clear: Christ's humility and obedience ought to guide all Christian living.

These words probably belong to an ancient hymn Paul records in this letter. Allow for their musical quality to echo in your speech.

Therefore God highly exalted him
and gave him the name that is **above every name**,
so that at the **name** of **Jesus** every **knee** should **bend**,
in **heaven** and on **earth** and **under** the **earth**,
and **every tongue** should **confess** that **Jesus Christ** is **Lord**,
to the **glory** of **God** the **Father**.

[Shorter: Philippians 2.1–5 (see brackets)]

GOSPEL   Matthew 21.28–32

A reading from the holy Gospel according to Matthew.

In this reading, Jesus uses the techniques of a rabbi to demonstrate to the rabbis the weakness of their own understanding. It's as subtle as it is striking.

First, Jesus sets up a position of defiance followed by compliance.

Next, Jesus sets up compliance followed by defiance.

When Jesus says "Truly," he brings home his parable to the present situation, speaking with the chief priests and elders.

Jesus said to the **chief priests** and the **elders** of the **people**:
"What do you **think**?
A **man** had **two sons**;
he went to the **first** and **said**,
'Son, **go** and **work** in the **vineyard** today.'
He answered, 'I **will not**';
but **later** he changed his **mind** and **went**.
The father went to the **second** and said the **same**;
and he **answered**, 'I am **going**, sir';
but he **did not go**.
Which of the **two** did the will of his **father**?"
They said, "The **first**."
Jesus **said** to them,
"**Truly** I **tell** you,
the **tax collectors** and the **prostitutes**
are **going** into the **kingdom** of **God ahead** of you.
For John **came** to you in the way of **righteousness**
and you **did not believe** him,
but the **tax collectors** and the **prostitutes believed** him;
and even after you **saw** it,
you **did not change** your **minds** and **believe** him."

GOSPEL ┃ This encounter between Jesus and powerful religious leaders takes place in the Jerusalem Temple. These authorities have been questioning Jesus on the source of his authority to teach. Rather than providing a solid answer, Jesus tells them the parable of the two sons in order to point out their stubbornness in failing to recognize and respond to God's will when it ought to be fully apparent before their very eyes (that is, in the teaching and ministry of Jesus himself).

Jesus employs the image of a vineyard, which is a popular metaphor for the nation of Israel (Isaiah 5.1–7) as well as for the kingdom of God (Matthew 20.1; 21.33). However, the focus of this parable is not on the vineyard but on the attitude of the two sons. The first son, who blatantly tells his father that he will not work in the vineyard, changes his mind and responds obediently to his father's summons. This first son represents the "tax collectors" and "prostitutes," who are deemed sinners, and yet prove themselves open to conversion. The second son, who tells his father that he will work in the vineyard but does not go, represents those who have been questioning the authority of Jesus. They appear to be righteous, but they fail to be open to the coming of God's kingdom (alluded to here in the ministry of John the Baptist). This parable, which is unique to Matthew, clearly speaks to the infant Church of the constant need for conversion in carrying out the will of God; discipleship must involve no sense of hesitancy or complacency. S.W.

TWENTY-SEVENTH SUNDAY IN ORDINARY TIME

LECTIONARY #139

READING I   Isaiah 5.1–7

A reading from the book of the Prophet Isaiah.

Let me **sing** for my **beloved**
my **love song concerning** his **vineyard**:
"My **beloved** had a **vineyard** on a **very fertile hill**.
He **dug** it and **cleared** it of **stones**,
and **planted** it with **choice vines**;
he built a **watchtower** in the **midst** of it,
and **hewed out** a **wine** vat in it;
he **expected** it to yield **grapes**,
but it yielded **wild grapes**.
And **now**, **inhabitants** of **Jerusalem** and **people** of **Judah**,
judge between **me** and my **vineyard**.
What more was there to **do** for my **vineyard**
that **I have not done** in it?
When I **expected** it to yield **grapes**,
why did it **yield wild grapes**?
And **now** I will tell you what I will **do** to my **vineyard**.
I will **remove** its **hedge**, and it shall be **devoured**;
I will **break down** its **wall**, and it shall be **trampled down**.
I will make it a **waste**;
it shall not be **pruned** or **hoed**,
and it shall be **overgrown** with **briers** and **thorns**; »

Isaiah = ī-ZAY-uh

A lengthy, rich, and poetic reading whose point is the condemnation of the house of Israel for its wildness.

Even emphasis on "What more."

Even emphasis on "yield wild grapes."

READING I   Isaiah's prophecy takes the form of a poetic song in today's first reading and reads as a parable for those in Israel who hear Isaiah's words. Using the image of a beautiful vineyard that will be made "a waste," Isaiah addresses Israel's failure to remain faithful to the covenant. In the preceding chapters, Isaiah has revealed to the people that Jerusalem will soon be torn apart by great destruction. Although some inhabitants will survive as a remnant, the nation as a whole has gone astray from the way of God and will be dispersed from the land. Thus, the lamentation that follows in the song of the vineyard.

Isaiah states that the song is sung about his "beloved" who, in reality, is God. Isaiah labours at length to describe the way in which this friend has invested his energy and his livelihood into his vineyard. First, the vineyard owner chooses the most fertile land on which to plant his grape vines. He spades the land, removes stones, and plants "choice vines." He constructs a tower from which he can watch over his vineyard, and he readies for a fruitful harvest by preparing a wine press. Undoubtedly, this is a project of great pride for Isaiah's "beloved."

With all the construction complete, he now waits for the growth of the vines and hopes for an abundant crop of beautiful sweet grapes. But, alas, all this grand vineyard yields are "wild grapes" that are rotten. Still speaking from the viewpoint of the vineyard owner, Isaiah calls the people of Israel to pass judgment on the predicament presented in the song. What is the owner to do? Has he not done all that he can to assure a good harvest? At this point in the

I will also **command** the **clouds**
that they rain **no rain upon it**.
For the **vineyard** of the **Lord** of **hosts** is the **house** of **Israel**,
and the **people** of **Judah** are his **pleasant planting**;
he expected **justice**, but saw **bloodshed**;
righteousness, but heard a **cry!**"

For meditation and context:

RESPONSORIAL PSALM   Psalm 80.8+11, 12–13, 14–15, 18–19 (R. Isa 5.7)

R. The vineyard of the Lord is the house of Israel.

You brought a vine out of Egypt;
you drove out the nations and planted it.
It sent out its branches to the sea,
and its shoots to the River.

Why then have you broken down its walls,
so that all who pass along the way pluck
    its fruit?
The boar from the forest ravages it,
and all that move in the field feed on it.

Turn again, O God of hosts;
look down from heaven, and see;
have regard for this vine,
the stock that your right hand planted.

Then we will never turn back from you;
give us life, and we will call on your name.
Restore us, O Lord God of hosts;
let your face shine, that we may be saved.

READING II   Philippians 4.6–9

A reading from the Letter of Saint Paul to the Philippians.

Philippians = fih-LIP-ee-uhnz

This reading begins with an exhortation that seems easy to make but hard to believe—is it really possible to have no anxiety at all? Paul wants to encourage you that it might be so.

Brothers and **sisters**:
Do not worry about **anything**,
but in **everything**
by **prayer** and **supplication** with **thanksgiving**
let your **requests** be made **known** to **God**.
And the **peace** of **God**,
which **surpasses all understanding**,
will **guard** your hearts and your **minds in Christ Jesus**.
Finally, **brothers** and **sisters**,
whatever is **true**, whatever is **honourable**,
whatever is **just**, whatever is **pure**,
whatever is **pleasing**, whatever is **commendable**,

A really compelling rhythm picks up here.

story, what might the hearers of this be thinking? What is the lesson to be learned?

While the "beloved" asked the people to decide the fate of the vineyard for themselves, the speaker then tells the listeners exactly what he intends to do with his failed project. The tone of the story builds with intensity as he begins to describe in detail how he will destroy his vineyard. He will begin by dismantling hedges and walls so that other may trample upon it. He will not care for it in any way, neither pruning the vines nor hoeing the soil, but instead will allow it to be "overgrown with briers

and thorns." He will go so far as to pray that no rain will fall upon it to keep it alive. It will become thoroughly lifeless. It is only here at the end of the song that Isaiah clearly identifies the vineyard as the "house of Israel," and the "pleasant planting" is "the people of Judah." The Lord did all that he could to provide for Israel; his sense of justice leaves no other choice than to dismantle what he once favoured.

READING II   Before Paul closes his letter to the Philippians, he imparts further advice on living the Christian

life. First, he upholds the importance of prayer as a means of conquering all forms of anxiety. He contends that when one turns to God with "prayer and supplication with thanksgiving," making one's needs known to him, that the "peace of God" will fill believers. Prayer is the way believers communicate all things to God and express their complete dependence upon him. The divine peace that flows from prayer is the foundation of their Christian life and keeps them in Christ.

This leads Paul to his second piece of advice for the Christians at Philippi. He

if there is **any excellence**
and if there is anything **worthy** of **praise**,
think about **these things**.
Keep on doing the **things** that you have **learned**
and **received** and **heard** and **seen** in me,
and the **God** of **peace** will be **with** you.

GOSPEL   Matthew 21.33–43

A reading from the holy Gospel according to Matthew.

Jesus said to the **chief priests** and the **elders** of the **people**:
"**Listen** to **another parable**.
There was a **landowner** who planted a **vineyard**,
put a **fence** around it, dug a **wine press** in it,
and built a **watchtower**.
Then he **leased** it to **tenants** and went to **another country**.
When the **harvest time** had **come**,
he sent his **slaves** to the **tenants** to **collect** his **produce**.
But the **tenants** seized his **slaves**
and **beat** one, **killed** another, and **stoned** another.
Again he sent **other slaves**, **more** than the **first**;
and they **treated** them in the **same way**.
Finally he sent his **son** to them, saying,
'They will respect my **son**.'
But when the **tenants** saw the **son**,
they **said** to **themselves**,
'**This** is the **heir**;
come, let us **kill** him and get his **inheritance**.'
So they **seized** him,
threw him out of the **vineyard**, and **killed** him. »

The conclusion is especially uplifting.

Clear-eyed as many of Jesus' parables are, it must be admitted that some of them are completely opaque. This is one of the more challenging ones to fathom.

Don't be afraid to stress the viciousness of the tenants. It's part of the parable's power.

Likewise, the brutality of the tenants.

proceeds to list several virtues that he connects with the gift of God's peace. These virtues are truth, honour, justice, purity, beauty, and graciousness. Some similar values are found in the philosophical movement of stoicism, which was prevalent during that time period and in that community. Their culture was very skilled at celebrating core human values that would ensure happiness in this life. Thus, Paul challenges the Philippians to strive for "excellence" in living out these virtues in their Christian life. Paul tells them that what they have "learned and received and

heard and seen" from his teaching and his actions is all that they need to follow the path of discipleship. In the end, Paul assures them that lives lived virtuously in Christ are sure to be filled with the grace of the "God of peace." Once again, there is no room for anxiety in the life of a Christian who has the mind and the heart of Christ.

GOSPEL   Just as in the story of the vineyard in the first reading from Isaiah, today's Gospel text from Matthew also considers the owner of a vineyard. The landowner plants a vineyard,

surrounds it with a hedge, digs a wine press, and constructs a watchtower. However, rather than caring for this vineyard on his own as in Isaiah, the landowner entrusts its care to several tenants. Because he is confident that they will watch over it with the same level of care and concern that he put in to create it, he departs on a journey.

We can assume that an entire growing season has passed when the landowner sends his slaves to the vineyard to collect his share of the harvest. However, the tenants, who have been watching over the vineyard, have no intention of sharing with

The parable pivots when Jesus quotes Scripture, as much to change its tone as to offer understanding.

This is a hard conclusion to a disturbing parable.

Now when the owner of the **vineyard comes**,
what will he **do** to those **tenants**?"
They **said** to him,
"He will **put** those **wretches** to a **miserable death**,
and **lease** the **vineyard** to **other tenants**
who will give him the **produce** at the **harvest time**."
Jesus **said** to them,
"Have you **never read** in the **Scriptures**:
'The **stone** that the **builders rejected**
has **become** the **cornerstone**;
this was the Lord's **doing**,
and it is **amazing** in our **eyes**'?
Therefore I **tell** you,
the **kingdom** of God will be **taken away** from you
and **given** to a **people** that **produces** the **fruits** of the **kingdom**."

the landowner. Instead, they beat and kill the slaves that the landowner sends them. As a final means of attempting to secure his portion of the harvest, the landowner sends his son to the tenants, thinking, "They will respect my son." Seeing the son as the heir to all that belongs to the landowner, they put him to death as well.

When Jesus asks the chief priests and elders, who have been listening to the parable, what will happen to the wicked tenants, they reply that the landowner will put them to death and hand the vineyard over to the care of responsible tenants. Jesus responds by reminding them of Psalm 118, which the early Church understood as a prophetic allusion to Jesus being rejected by his own people. Although rejected, the "cornerstone" of the Church, namely Christ himself, was deemed "amazing" in the eyes of those who received him and cared for his Father's vineyard. Matthew's Jesus ends the passage by suggesting that God will not look so favourably upon those who reject the gift that has been sent specifically to them, and that gift is his very Son.
S.W.

TWENTY-EIGHTH SUNDAY IN ORDINARY TIME

LECTIONARY #142

READING I Isaiah 25.6–10a

A reading from the book of the Prophet Isaiah.

On **this mountain** the **Lord** of **hosts** will make for **all peoples**
a **feast** of **rich food**, a **feast** of **well-aged wines**,
of **rich food filled** with **marrow**,
of **well-aged wines strained clear**.
And he will **destroy** on this **mountain**
the **shroud** that is **cast** over **all peoples**,
the **sheet** that is **spread** over **all nations**;
he will swallow up **death forever**.
Then the **Lord God** will **wipe away** the **tears** from all **faces**,
and the **disgrace** of his **people**
he will **take away** from **all** the **earth**,
for the **Lord** has **spoken**.
It will be **said** on that **day**,
"**Lo**, **this** is our **God**;
we have waited for him, so that he might **save** us.
This is the Lord for **whom** we have **waited**;
let us be **glad** and **rejoice** in his **salvation**.
For the **hand** of the **Lord** will rest on this **mountain**."

Isaiah = ī-ZAY-uh

A luminously poetic and uplifting reading offering a powerful vision of eternal life.
Slight pause between "food" and "filled."
Slight pause between "wines" and "strained."

An intoxicating promise.

Let the image with which the reading concludes linger with your assembly by pausing for a long moment before saying, "The word of the Lord."

READING I Isaiah 24 to 27 constitutes what scholars call the "Apocalypse of Isaiah," which concludes ten chapters of prophesies on the future of various nations. Although Isaiah has prophesied that Israel has lost favour with God and will witness the destruction of Jerusalem, he is clear that nations at odds with Israel will also be subject to God's judgment. Chapter 24 compares Jerusalem to a vine that is withering away (Isaiah 24.7), and yet there is the hope that Israel's repentance will result in God's forgiveness.

In chapter 25, which our reading is from today, we read about a sense of universal eschatology. The Lord will welcome people from every nation to his mountain with a feast of abundant joy. After the Lord has destroyed all that is evil in the world, including the ultimate enemy found in death, he will gather to his holy place all those who heard his voice and turned from their wicked ways.

Isaiah says that God will destroy "the shroud that is cast over all peoples." This "shroud," that he also calls "the sheet," is an allusion to death. In the past, all peoples were tangled in the powers of death, but now God "will swallow up death forever." God will not only destroy death, but he will take away all pain and suffering; all the toils and struggles, the "tears" and the "disgrace" experienced by his people will be no more. We may assume that the words "his people" has expanded to include representatives from every nation and not simply from Israel alone.

The passage concludes with a chorus of voices heralding the presence and power of God "for whom we have waited." At the end of time, when this power of God is

For meditation and context:

RESPONSORIAL PSALM   Psalm 23.1–3a, 3b–4, 5, 6 (R.6cd)

R. I shall dwell in the house of the Lord my whole life long.

The Lord is my shepherd, I shall not want.
He makes me lie down in green pastures;
he leads me beside still waters;
he restores my soul.

He leads me in right paths for his
    name's sake.
Even though I walk through the darkest
    valley, I fear no evil;
for you are with me;
your rod and your staff—they comfort me.

You prepare a table before me
in the presence of my enemies;
you anoint my head with oil;
my cup overflows.

Surely goodness and mercy shall follow me
all the days of my life,
and I shall dwell in the house of the Lord
my whole life long.

Philippians = fih-LIP-ee-uhnz

A conclusive reading that records the
sentiments near the end of Paul's letter
to the members of the early church at
Philippi. Its tone is personal and thankful.

READING II   Philippians 4.12–14, 19–20

A reading from the Letter of Saint Paul to the Philippians.

Brothers and **sisters**:
I **know** what it is to have **little**,
and I **know** what it is to have **plenty**.
In **any** and **all circumstances** I have learned the **secret**
of being **well-fed** and of going **hungry**,
of having **plenty** and of being in **need**.
I can do **all things through** him who **strengthens** me.
In **any** case, it was **kind** of you to share my **distress**.
My God will **fully satisfy every need** of yours
according to his **riches** in **glory** in **Christ Jesus**.
To our **God** and **Father** be glory **forever** and **ever**. **Amen**.

revealed, it will indeed be a cause for joy
among all peoples who have recognized
the truth of God and followed him.

READING II | In the verses immediately
prior to this passage, Paul
praises God for the support given to him by
the Philippians, both for their monetary
support and their spiritual growth that is a
testament to the continued spread of the
Good News. The latter, more than donations
sent to him, is sure to bolster his spirit during his time of imprisonment and be a
greater witness to the truth of his preaching.

Paul uses this as an opportunity to
remind the Philippians of a Christian's true
source of support: God. While striving to be
self-sufficient in his own ministry, and having experienced both times of having "little" and "plenty," Paul has come to learn
true dependence on God. Today's reading
omits verses 15–18, which comment on the
previous generosity of the Philippians to
Paul when he was just beginning to preach
the Gospel. These verses lead into a final
statement by Paul regarding his confidence
that God will provide the Christian community with whatever it needs. In all things,

they are to look to Christ, as Paul has done
throughout his own ministry.

GOSPEL | Today's parable is addressed
to the chief priests and
elders gathered within the Temple precincts. Jesus opens the parable with the
king's method of summoning guests to the
wedding banquet for his son: slaves are
sent to extend the invitation. However, all
the invited guests decline the invitation.
The king tries a second time by sending
other slaves, who are not just to invite
guests but are to lure them with words of

GOSPEL   Matthew 22.1–14

A reading from the holy Gospel according to Matthew.

[**Once more Jesus spoke** to the **chief priests** and **Pharisees**
in **parables**:
"The **kingdom** of **heaven** may be **compared** to a **king**
who gave a **wedding** banquet for his **son**.
He sent his **slaves** to call **those**
who had been invited to the **wedding** banquet,
but they **would not come**.
Again he sent **other slaves**, saying,
'**Tell those** who have been **invited**:
"**Look**, I have **prepared** my **dinner**,
my **oxen** and my **fat calves** have been **slaughtered**,
and **everything** is **ready**;
come to the **wedding** banquet."'
But they made **light** of it and went **away**,
one to his **farm**, **another** to his **business**,
while the rest **seized** his **slaves**,
mistreated them, and **killed** them.
The **king** was **enraged**.
He sent his **troops**, **destroyed** those **murderers**,
and **burned** their **city**.
Then he **said** to his **slaves**,
'The **wedding** is **ready**,
but **those invited** were not **worthy**.
Go **therefore** into the **main streets**,
and invite **everyone** you **find** to the **wedding** banquet.' ❯❯

Slight pause between "Jesus" and "spoke."

This parable seems straightforward but takes an unexpected turn, ending with a somewhat disturbing message. It could also be interpreted as having an ironic tone when one compares those who were invited originally with those who ended up actually celebrating with the king.

Even emphasis on "Tell those."

Don't overdo the king's rage.

bounty, describing what they would otherwise be missing. This time the rejection of the invitation is more forceful; while some are simply indifferent to it, others capture the slaves and kill them.

The king's reaction is swift and severe. He sends an army to destroy the city of the guests who had been invited. Scholars believe this to be an allusion to the recent destruction of the Temple and the city of Jerusalem in AD 70, which the Matthean community would have experienced, since this Gospel was compiled after that time.

Nevertheless, the king is unwilling to allow the abundant feast that he has prepared go to waste. Thus, he instructs his slaves to go out "into the main streets" in order to invite whomever they might find. Jesus tells his listeners that these slaves succeed in filling the hall with guests, both wicked and good. Here we are meant to understand that God, like this king, is willing to welcome anyone into his kingdom.

For this reason, the king's entrance into the hall and his reaction to the guest who is not dressed in the appropriate attire for a wedding feast is quite shocking. When

the king asks the man to explain himself for his attendance at the wedding feast, the man can give no reply. In response to his lack of "a wedding robe," the king has the man bound and thrown out into the darkness "where there will be weeping and gnashing of teeth." This final portion of the parable is filled with symbols pertaining to eschatological judgment. The king's entrance into the wedding hall represents God's entrance into the world for its final judgment. The wedding garment is the sign of a person's repentance and participation in the Church; the man improperly dressed

The king's fixation on how this presumably vagrant wedding guest is dressed is yet another disturbing reaction, out of context and unrealistic to what the listeners expected to hear.

Those slaves went out into the streets
and gathered all whom they found, both good and bad;
so the wedding hall was filled with guests.]
But when the king came in to see the guests,
he noticed a man there who was not wearing a wedding robe,
and he said to him,
'Friend, how did you get in here without a wedding robe?'
And he was speechless.
Then the king said to the attendants,
'Bind him hand and foot,
and throw him into the outer darkness,
where there will be weeping and gnashing of teeth.'

This conclusion reinforces that sense of irony.

For many are called, but few are chosen."

[Shorter: Matthew 22:1–10 Insert: (see brackets)]

stands for those outside the Church's membership who have not turned their hearts to God. While the kingdom may be open to both the good and the bad, only those dressed in the garment of salvation will avoid being banished from the feast. Finally, the last line from the parable suggests that being called or invited does not necessarily mean being chosen among the elect. Matthew's theology suggests that salvation depends upon some level of transformation in Christ; responding to the invitation requires a sign of belonging. S.W.

TWENTY-NINTH SUNDAY IN ORDINARY TIME

LECTIONARY #145

READING I   Isaiah 45.1, 4–6

A reading from the book of the Prophet Isaiah.

Thus says the **Lord** to his **anointed**,
to **Cyrus**, whose **right hand** I have **grasped**
to subdue **nations before** him
and strip **kings** of their **robes**,
to open **doors before** him—
and the **gates** shall **not** be **closed**:
"For the **sake** of my servant **Jacob**,
and **Israel** my **chosen**,
I **call** you by your **name**,
I **surname** you, though you **do not know** me.
I am the **Lord**, and there **is no other**;
besides me there **is no** god.
I **arm** you, though you do not **know** me,
so that **all** may **know**,
from the **rising** of the **sun** and from the **west**,
that there is **no one besides** me;
I am the **Lord**, and there **is no other**."

Isaiah = ī-ZAY-uh

A forceful reading whose tone is stern.

Cyrus = SĪ-ruhs

These lines, echoing the first of the Ten Commandments, is the heart of this reading.

The concluding repetition requires emphasis on "is no other."

TO KEEP IN MIND
Read the Scripture passage and its commentary in Workbook. Then read it from your Bible, including what comes before and after it, so that you understand the context.

READING I Today's readings illustrate an interesting theme, namely, "How can God work for good in a world that does not believe in God?" This first reading is an example. King Cyrus was a Persian king who reigned in 559–530 BC and who created the largest empire known to date. Part of his success in managing his vast empire was allowing conquered peoples to have some governing powers at the regional level and respecting the religions and customs of his subjects. An edict by King Cyrus in 538 BC allowed the Judean exiles to return from Babylon to Jerusalem, and the author of Second Isaiah says this is God's doing.

In this first reading, God is speaking through the Prophet, and he identifies Cyrus as God's anointed. The Hebrew word is *mashiach*, meaning "anointed" or messiah in English. Kings were anointed, so in some sense this title is not surprising, but the Prophet goes on to describe Cyrus as chosen to advance his conquest of other nations on God's behalf and to demonstrate to the world that there is no god other than the God of Jacob and Israel. Moreover, he says that God called Cyrus by name and gave him a title—probably referring to his messiahship—even though Cyrus did not know the God of the Israelites. What a stunning declaration! God can work even through people who do not know God or acknowledge God as their saviour.

READING II Our second reading is the opening section of Paul's First Letter to the Thessalonians. Here we see the standard letter opening of first-century Hellenistic writers: sender, recipients, greeting, and thanksgiving. Only Paul's letter to the Galatians deviates from

For meditation and context:

RESPONSORIAL PSALM   Psalm 96.1+3, 4–5, 7–8, 9+10ac (R.7b)

R. Ascribe to the Lord glory and strength.

O sing to the Lord a new song;
sing to the Lord, all the earth.
Declare his glory among the nations,
his marvellous works among all the peoples.

For great is the Lord, and greatly
   to be praised;
he is to be revered above all gods.
For all the gods of the peoples are idols,
but the Lord made the heavens.

Ascribe to the Lord, O families of
   the peoples,
ascribe to the Lord glory and strength.
Ascribe to the Lord the glory due his name;
bring an offering, and come into his courts.

Worship the Lord in holy splendour;
tremble before him, all the earth.
Say among the nations, "The Lord is king!
He will judge the peoples with equity."

READING II   1 Thessalonians 1.1–5ab

A reading from the first Letter of Saint Paul to the Thessalonians.

From **Paul**, **Silvanus**, and **Timothy**,
to the **Church** of the **Thessalonians**
in **God** the **Father** and the **Lord Jesus Christ**:
Grace to you and peace.
We **always** give **thanks** to **God** for **all** of you
and **mention** you in our **prayers**,
constantly remembering before our **God** and **Father**
your **work** of **faith** and **labour** of **love**
and **steadfastness** of **hope** in our **Lord Jesus Christ**.
For we **know**, **brothers** and **sisters beloved** by **God**,
that he has **chosen** you,
because our **message** of the **Gospel**
came to you not in **word only**,
but **also** in **power** and in the **Holy Spirit**
and with **full conviction**.

Thessalonians = thes-uh-LOH-nee-uhnz

Silvanus = sil-VAY-nuhs

This reading comes from the opening of Paul's first letter to the members of the early church in Thessalonica. In effect, it is the salutation, which is meant to have a rousing, even cheerful quality.

This thanks being given is sincere; let your tone reflect that sincerity. Slight pause between "remembering" and "before."

A rousing and spirited conclusion.

this pattern, and that is because he was too mad at the Galatian churches and the people who were leading them astray to pray in thanksgiving to God for them. Instead, he gives them a good scolding (see Galatians 1.6–7)! Turning our attention back to today's reading, we see that Timothy, who was Paul's constant companion for much of his ministry, is mentioned here and in several other letters as a co-sender. Likewise, Silvanus is mentioned; he is most likely the one identified as Silas in Acts of the Apostles (e.g., Acts 15.22, 40). Paul's thanksgiving is in the form of a prayer to

God as he remembers the community's exercise of the theological virtues of faith, hope, and love. Notice that Paul does not view these virtues as abstractions, since he ties them to nouns that suggest activity: work, labour, and steadfastness, respectively. Finally, he identifies the source and sustainer of this activity, namely, the Holy Spirit. Notice also the affection that Paul has for this community. He calls them God's beloved and God's chosen ones.

| GOSPEL | Today's Gospel reading is found in all three of the synoptic Gospels with slight variations. It is a story about some Pharisees, teachers of the Law, teaming up with some Herodians to entrap Jesus so that they could make a formal complaint against him. The Herodians are often paired with the Pharisees in the synoptic Gospels as groups who were opposed to Roman rule, but the Herodians are so named because they wanted someone from the lineage of Herod the Great to be their ruler. Herod the Great was origi-

GOSPEL   Matthew 22.15–21

A reading from the holy Gospel according to Matthew.

The **Pharisees** went and **plotted**
to **entrap Jesus** in **what** he **said**.
So they **sent** their **disciples** to him,
along with the **Herodians**, saying,
"**Teacher**, we **know** that you are **sincere**,
and teach the **way** of God in **accordance** with **truth**,
and show **deference** to **no one**;
for you **do not regard people** with **partiality**.
Tell us, then, what you **think**.
Is it **lawful** to pay **taxes** to the **emperor**, or **not**?"
But **Jesus**, **aware** of their **malice**, said,
"**Why** are you putting me to the **test**, you **hypocrites**?
Show me the **coin used** for the **tax**."
And they **brought** him a **denarius**.
Then he **said** to them,
"**Whose head** is **this**, and **whose title**?"
They **answered**, "**Caesar's**."
Then he **said** to them,
"Give **therefore** to **Caesar** the **things** that are **Caesar's**,
and to **God** the **things** that are **God's**."

Pharisees = FAYR-uh-seez

This reading consists of a set-up that backfires on the Pharisees. Its drama is inherent. No need to overplay it.

Especially, the wickedness of the Pharisees: Don't overplay it. It will come through in your steady proclamation.

Consider that Jesus' tone here is exasperation.

Pause before "Caesar's" to suggest the Pharisees' recognition that their plan to entrap Jesus has backfired.

---

nally from Edom, south of Judea, and was raised as a Jew by his parents.

As the scene unfolds, the Pharisees and Herodians heap (false) praise on Jesus for being impartial and sincere in his efforts to teach the way of God. This is their set-up to ensnare Jesus by flattery, but he recognizes their evil intent. They ask him whether it is lawful for Jews to pay taxes to the emperor. But Jesus calls them out as the hypocrites they are by demanding that they show him the coin used for paying the tax, a Roman denarius, and asking whose image is on the coin and what is written on it. The image is that of the emperor, and its inscription would read something like "Tiberius Caesar, Augustus, son of divine Augustus." Jews who were strict observers of Jewish law would not admit to being in possession of a denarius because of their strong belief that there is no god except the God of Israel. But someone in the group pulls out the coin, probably with great embarrassment when they realize that Jesus has defeated them in this confrontation. Some interpreters of Jesus' response—"Give therefore to Caesar the things that are Caesar's, and to God the things that are God's"—suggest that it is an argument for the separation of church and state. However, in first-century Palestine, no such division existed. Rather, his words more likely reflect the notion that kinship is more important—in this case, kinship with God—than polity, what we might call civil entities, though it has a place in society and should be respected as such. Thus, the second half of Jesus' statement is an accusation directed at the Pharisees and Herodians: they do not pay to God the honour that is due to God. C.C.

THIRTIETH SUNDAY IN ORDINARY TIME

LECTIONARY #148

READING I Exodus 22.21–27

A reading from the book of Exodus.

Thus says the **Lord**:
"You shall **not wrong** or **oppress** a **resident** alien,
for you were **aliens** in the **land** of **Egypt**.
You shall not **abuse** any **widow** or **orphan**.
If you **do abuse** them, when they **cry out** to me,
I will **surely** heed their **cry**;
my **wrath** will **burn**,
and I will **kill** you with the **sword**,
and your **wives** shall become **widows** and your
      children orphans.
If you lend **money** to my **people**, to the **poor one among** you,
you **shall not deal** with them as a **creditor**;
you **shall not exact interest** from them.
If you take your **neighbour's cloak** in **pawn**,
you shall **restore** it to that **person** before the **sun** goes **down**;
for it may be their **only clothing** to **use** as **cover**;
in **what else** shall that **person sleep**?
And if that **person** cries **out** to me,
I will **listen**, for I am **compassionate**."

Exodus = EK-suh-duhs

The tone of this powerful reading is unusually stern.

Note the violence of the Lord's wrath, flaring up. Give slight emphasis to "kill."

Even emphasis on "shall not deal" and "shall not exact interest."

The reading concludes with a note of contrast on the word "compassionate."

READING I Our first reading comes from a larger section of Exodus that biblical scholars call the Covenant Code (Exodus 20.22—23.33), which consists of a collection of case law, pronouncements, commands, and prohibitions. The Covenant Code follows immediately after God's appearance on Mount Sinai and delivery of the Ten Commandments. With the thunder, lightning, and smoke on the mountain, the Israelites became afraid and told Moses to speak God's commands to them instead of them directly encountering God. Thus, Moses became the mediator of God's covenant law to the people.

Today's reading provides us with two of these commands from the Covenant Code. Both fall into a category that today we might call social justice teaching. The first command is to protect and not abuse the resident alien. The Hebrew word is *ger*, meaning "stranger, temporary dweller, or sojourner." The reason given for this mandate is that God did the same for them when they were sojourners in the land. In the Old Testament especially, resident aliens are regularly grouped with widows and orphans as the poorest and most vulnerable in society. The punishment due to those who do not observe this command speaks to its importance.

The second command has to do with money lending, which, in the ancient world, was more like the pawnbroker today than our modern banking system. Only poor people who had no other access to financial resources used moneylenders, who charged high interest and demanded significant collateral. This command forbids charging interest, and it places substantial limitations on what constitutes collateral.

For meditation and context:

RESPONSORIAL PSALM   Psalm 18.1–2, 3+6b, 46+50ab (R.1)

R. I love you, O Lord, my strength.

I love you, O Lord, my strength.
The Lord is my rock, my fortress,
    and my deliverer.
My God, my rock in whom I take refuge,
my shield, and the source of my salvation,
    my stronghold.

I call upon the Lord, who is worthy
    to be praised,
so I shall be saved from my enemies.
From his temple he heard my voice,
and my cry to him reached his ears.

The Lord lives! Blessed be my rock,
and exalted be the God of my salvation.
Great triumphs he gives to his king,
and shows steadfast love to his anointed.

READING II   1 Thessalonians 1.5c–10

Thessalonians = thes-uh-LOH-nee-uhnz

Paul is heaping praise in this reading onto the Thessalonians for how impressively they have become models for believers. His praise is as sincere as it is motivating, which you can convey to your assembly as you proclaim.

Macedonia = mas-eh-DOH-nee-uh
Achaia = uh-KAY-uh

Slight pause between "regions" and "report."

A reading from the first Letter of Saint Paul to the Thessalonians.

Brothers and **sisters**:
You **know** what kind of **persons** we **proved** to be
among you for your **sake**.
And you became **imitators** of us and of the **Lord**,
for in **spite** of **persecution**
you received the **word** with joy **inspired** by the **Holy Spirit**,
so that you became an **example**
to **all** the **believers** in **Macedonia** and in **Achaia**.
For the **word** of the **Lord** has **sounded forth** from you
not **only** in **Macedonia** and **Achaia**,
but in **every place** your **faith** in **God** has become **known**,
so that we have **no need** to **speak** about it.
For the **people** of those **regions report about** us
what **kind** of **welcome** we **had among** you,
and **how** you turned to **God** from **idols**,
to serve a **living** and **true God**,
and to **wait** for his **Son** from **heaven**,
whom he **raised** from the **dead**—
Jesus, who **rescues** us from the **wrath** that is **coming**.

For example, you cannot keep a person's cloak as collateral, because it likely serves as his bedding at night. Notice that God calls the poor "my people." How can we deny God's people the protections they need?

READING II Today's second reading is the second half of the thanksgiving section of the First Letter to the Thessalonians, which we began reading last week. The thanksgiving sections of Paul's letters are interesting because they often contain the major themes of the letter. This one is no exception. One of his favourite

themes is captured in the phrase "And you became imitators of us and of the Lord." It might sound arrogant to modern listeners, but Paul repeatedly tells the communities that he founded to imitate him. He can say this because he sees his own life as imitating Christ, that is, dying with him so that he can come to new life in Christ (see Philippians 3.7–11). All of this is by God's grace.

A related theme that Paul previews in this thanksgiving is the persecution that they share. The Greek word for this is *thlipsis*, and it means "oppression, affliction, tribulation, or distress." Paul intends it to

refer to the tribulations that were expected to accompany the parousia, the return of the risen Christ in the end time. Although he was mistaken about the timing of the parousia—he thought it would be in his lifetime (1 Thessalonians 4.14–18)—his message is sound. Despite afflictions, Christians should receive God's word with joy and live out their faith in service so that they can be an example to others until the coming of the risen Lord. Moreover, we can live in hope because, just as God raised Jesus, Jesus will rescue us at the end time.

GOSPEL   Matthew 22.34–40

A reading from the holy Gospel according to Matthew.

When the **Pharisees** heard that **Jesus** had silenced
     the **Sadducees**,
they **gathered together**,
and **one** of them, a **lawyer**, asked him a **question** to **test** him.
"**Teacher**, which **commandment** in the **Law** is the **greatest**?"
Jesus **said** to him,
"'You shall **love** the **Lord** your **God** with all your **heart**,
and with all your **soul**, and with all your **mind**.'
This is the **greatest** and **first commandment**.
And a **second** is **like** it:
'You shall love your **neighbour** as **yourself**.'
On t**hese two commandments** hang **all** the **Law**
     and the **Prophets**."

Pharisees = FAYH-uh-seez

Sadducees = SAD-yoo-seez

The greatest commandment; this reading is as consequential to Christian belief as it is powerful and concise. Its clarity is that of water from the clearest spring.

The emphases on the words in this line are worth practising to get right.

GOSPEL   Our Gospel reading picks up the subject of the Covenant Code in today's first reading. In the preceding verses, the Sadducees challenged Jesus with an issue related to teachings about resurrection of the dead, but Jesus bested them with his response (Matthew 22.23–33). The Sadducees were theologically conservative and did not accept the possibility of resurrection. They were also part of the leadership in Jerusalem and Judea, though they were not well liked by the Jewish population because they colluded with the Romans to maintain their positions of power.

Knowing that the Sadducees failed in trying to bring Jesus down, now the Pharisees, who were scholars and interpreters of Jewish Law, try to challenge Jesus. Their designated speaker, a lawyer (Greek, *nomikos*, meaning someone who was an expert in the law), asks this question: "Teacher, which commandment in the Law is the greatest?" In essence, they are testing Jesus on what he thinks makes all of Jewish law meaningful and relevant. This is a monumental question fraught with potential landmines, but Jesus answers beautifully, quoting Deuteronomy 6.5 and Leviticus 19.18. To love God with all your heart, soul, and mind describes fidelity to God and to the covenant that God made with his people. To love your neighbour as you might love yourself is to abandon any tendency toward narcissism and to be focused on others in all you say and do. C.C.

ALL SAINTS

LECTIONARY #667

READING I   Revelation 7.2–4, 9–14

A reading from the book of Revelation.

I, **John**, saw an **Angel**
ascending from the **rising** of the **sun**,
having the **seal** of the living **God**,
and he **called** with a **loud voice** to the four **Angels**
who had been given **power** to **damage earth** and **sea**, saying,
"Do not **damage** the **earth** or the **sea** or the **trees**,
until we have **marked** the **servants** of our **God**
with a **seal** on their **foreheads**."
And I heard the **number** of those who were **sealed**,
one **hundred** forty-four **thousand**,
sealed out of **every** tribe of the **people** of Israel.
After **this** I **looked**, and there was a great **multitude**
	that **no one** could **count**,
from every **nation**, from all **tribes** and **peoples** and **languages**,
standing before the **throne** and before the **Lamb**,
robed in white, with palm branches in their hands.
They cried out in a **loud voice**,
"**Salvation** belongs to our **God** who is **seated** on the **throne**,
and to the **Lamb**!" »

A reading of visionary power and enticing detail. Revelation has inherent drama in its language and imagery. You only need to proclaim the passage with clarity and directness; its power will express itself through your voice

Note the repetitions: damage, earth, sea.

Even stresses on the words in this line.

Emphasis on Lamb, which will be repeated at the end of the passage.

READING I   The first reading for this feast is taken from the Book of Revelation, specifically from two visions that are inserted between the vision of the opening of the sixth seal of the Book of Life, which the risen Christ holds in his hands (Revelation 6.12–17) and the introduction of the vision of the seventh seal (Revelation 8.1–5). Seals were used by powerful people in the ancient world to mark their property and lend authority to their communications.

These two inserted visions are triumphant in tone, the first being a vision of the sealing of God's elect (Revelation 7.1–8) and the second being the vision of the multitude singing in praise of God's salvation (Revelation 7.9–17). Ancients believed that Angels or spirit beings controlled the activities of cosmic phenomena like winds and planets. Thus, the four Angels represent the winds at the four corners of the world who stand at the ready to exact God's judgment on the earth. The Angel who holds God's seal commands them to wait until God's holy ones are marked with his seal. This seal will not save them from death, because, as we learn toward the end of the

second vision, they are the martyrs who went through the great ordeal. Having gone through death, the martyrs will be able to participate in the unending heavenly liturgy before God's throne. The author likely has in mind Rome's persecution of Christians under Emperor Domitian (reigned AD 81–96) and might also harken back to the persecutions under Emperor Nero (reigned AD 54–68).

The number who are marked with God's seal is 144,000. However, we should be careful not to take this number literally. Mathematically, it is 12 multiplied by 12 and multiplied again by 1,000, but 12 is symbolic

Note the heavy emphases on the words in this exclamation.

And all the **Angels** stood around the **throne**,
around the **elders** and the **four** living **creatures**;
they **fell** on their **faces** before the **throne**
and worshipped **God**, singing,
"**Amen**! **Blessing** and **glory** and **wisdom**
and **thanksgiving** and **honour** and **power** and **might**
be to our **God** forever and **ever**! **Amen**."
Then one of the **elders addressed** me,
"**Who** are these, **robed** in **white**,
and **where** have they **come** from?"
I said to him, "**Sir**, **you** are the **one** that **knows**."
Then he said to me,
"**These** are **they** who have come **out** of the **great ordeal**;
they have **washed** their robes
and made them **white** in the **blood** of the **Lamb**."

Allow this image to expand in your proclamation of it. Emphasis on *Lamb*.

For meditation and context:

RESPONSORIAL PSALM　Psalm 24.1–2, 3–4ab, 5–6 (R.6)

R. Lord, this is the company of those who seek your face.

The earth is the Lord's and all that is in it,
the world, and those who live in it;
for he has founded it on the seas,
and established it on the river.

Who shall ascend the hill of the Lord?
And who shall stand in his holy place?
Someone who has clean hands and a
　　pure heart,
who does not lift up their soul to what
　　is false.

That person will receive blessing from
　　the Lord,
and vindication from the God of
　　their salvation.
Such is the company of those who seek him,
who seek the face of the God of Jacob.

TO KEEP IN MIND

As you prepare your proclamation, make choices about what emotions need to be expressed. Some choices are evident from the text, but some are harder to discern. Understanding the context of the Scripture passage will help you decide.

of fullness (and recalls the twelve tribes of Israel) and 1,000 represents an incalculably large number. Hence, John says that he could see, before God's throne, "a great multitude that no one could count" from everywhere on earth. They are dressed in white, a symbol of victory in the Book of Revelation, because they were washed "in the blood of the Lamb," meaning that these holy ones share in Jesus' suffering to death. Likewise, the palm fronds that they carry are symbols of victory.

And what a beautiful song! It is introduced by the martyrs who cry out, "Salvation belongs to our God." The Greek word *sōtēria*, which is translated here as "salvation," can also mean "deliverance or safety," which has led some translators to use "victory" instead of "salvation" in this sentence. Immediately, those stationed around God's throne—the four living creatures that watch over it, the twenty-four elders who sit on thrones surrounding God's throne, and the Angels—join the martyrs in singing a victory song to God. Notice that there are exactly seven attributions given to God in this song. Seven is a number symbolizing perfection. Finally, the Hebrew word *amēn* means "truly, or so be it." Although Christians use it now to conclude their prayers, it was first used in the synagogue as a way for those in attendance to affirm the words of the leader of prayer.

This reading paints a vivid picture of what the experience of the saints at this moment might look like: all in heaven glorifying God and singing songs of praise. We are invited to rejoice as well, knowing that these holy men and women have reached their reward and the suffering of the saints and martyrs has passed into the glory of God.

READING II   1 John 3.1–3

A reading from the first Letter of Saint John.

A reading proclaiming the mysterious nature of God's revelation.

Beloved:
See what **love** the **Father** has **given** us,
that we should be **called** children of **God**;
and **that** is what we **are**.
The **reason** the world does not **know** us
is that it did not know **him**.

Emphasis on "know." In the next line, on "him."

Beloved, we are **God's** children now;
what we will **be** has not yet been **revealed**.
What we **do** know is **this**:
when he is **revealed**, we will be **like** him,
for we will **see** him as he **is**.

Note the interplay between "revealed" and "see."

And **all** who have this **hope** in **God purify** themselves,
just as **he** is pure.

READING II Our second reading comes from the First Letter of John, which is thought by most scholars to have been written by someone from the Johannine Christian community in a decade or so after the Gospel of John was written. If you know John's Gospel, you will quickly see that the vocabulary of this document is like the vocabulary of the Gospel, though it is not always used in the same way. The author of this document expresses frustration with members of the community who caused harm by separating from his group, even while they claim to love God and love the brothers and sisters (see 1 John 2.18–23).

With this background in mind, we can understand that the author of this document identifies his community as "children of God," which is an expression of God's love for them. Further, he addresses the problem of the world's refusal to acknowledge them as such by saying that it is because they do not know God. From the tone of this document, we can assume that the author is including the schismatics in this group that he identifies as "the world."

A defection from one's own community hurts much more than rejection by strangers. Perhaps to console his community or at least himself, the author adds, "what we will be has not yet been revealed." What follows is a profound theological teaching. Our author says, "when he is revealed, we will be like him." Grammatically, the pronoun "he" should refer to God, but it is possible that the referent is Christ, since he is God's agent, whose identity is one with God. Regardless, our author is saying that, when the divine power is revealed, we will

A reading whose expressions are familiar but whose specifics are helpfully reintroduced to your assembly. This Gospel reading is an opportunity to teach the beatitudes anew.

Note the rhythmical emphases. The first word in each beatitude is stressed, as is the last word in each line. Let that rhythm guide your proclamation.

GOSPEL   Matthew 5.1–12a

A reading from the holy Gospel according to Matthew.

When **Jesus** saw the **crowds**, he went up the **mountain**;
and after he sat **down**, his disciples **came** to him.
Then he began to speak, and **taught** them, saying:
"**Blessed** are the poor in **spirit**,
for **theirs** is the **kingdom** of **heaven**.
Blessed are those who **mourn**,
for **they** will be **comforted**.
Blessed are the **meek**,
for they will **inherit** the **earth**.
Blessed are those who **hunger** and **thirst** for **righteousness**,
for they will be **filled**.
Blessed are the **merciful**,
for they will receive **mercy**.
Blessed are the pure in **heart**,
for they will see **God**.
Blessed are the **peacemakers**,
for they will be called **children** of God.
Blessed are those who are **persecuted** for **righteousness**' sake,
for **theirs** is the **kingdom** of **heaven**.
Blessed are **you** when people **revile** you and **persecute** you
and utter all kinds of evil **against** you falsely on **my** account.
Rejoice and be **glad**,
for your **reward** is **great** in **heaven**."

TO KEEP IN MIND
Smile when you share good news. Nonverbal cues like a smile help the assembly understand the reading.

be divinized (not that we will become God, but that "we will be like him" when he transforms us at the end of time)! Thus, the author's exhortation is to purify ourselves now so that, when the time comes, we will be worthy to see God as God is, when we join the communion of saints.

GOSPEL   Today's Gospel is a familiar one for most of us. The sayings in this reading are called beatitudes because of the Greek word *makarios*, which stands at the beginning of each saying and which means "happy or blessed," as in congratulations. To whom are these beatitudes addressed? They are addressed to the poor in spirit, i.e., those who are generous with what they have and care for the poor; those who mourn, i.e., people who go beyond themselves to give proper burial for the dead; those who are meek, i.e., people who are slow to anger and treat others with kindness; those who act justly and mercifully, as God is just and merciful; and so on. The last two beatitudes—some describe them as one long beatitude in two parts—are different in style and tone from the others and probably reflect the situation of the early Church where local persecutions of Christians were commonplace. But if you do these things, be glad. God's kingdom is near at hand! C.C.

THE COMMEMORATION OF ALL THE FAITHFUL DEPARTED (ALL SOULS' DAY)

LECTIONARY #668

READING I   Wisdom 3.1–9

A reading from the book of Wisdom.

The **souls** of the **righteous** are in the **hand** of **God**,
and **no torment** will **ever touch** them.
In the **eyes** of the **foolish** they **seemed** to have **died**,
and their **departure** was thought to be a **disaster**,
and their **going** from us to be their **destruction**;
but **they** are at **peace**.
For though in the **sight** of **others** they were **punished**,
their **hope** is full of **immortality**.
Having been **disciplined** a **little**,
they will receive **great good**,
because **God tested** them
and found them **worthy** of **himself**;
like **gold** in the **furnace** he **tried** them,
and like a **sacrificial burnt offering** he **accepted** them.
In the **time** of their **visitation** they will **shine forth**,
and will run like **sparks** through the **stubble**.
They will **govern nations** and **rule** over **peoples**,
and the **Lord** will reign **over** them **forever**.
Those who **trust** in him will **understand truth**,
and the **faithful** will **abide** with him in **love**,
because **grace** and **mercy** are upon his **holy ones**,
and he **watches** over his **elect**.

---

righteous = Rī-chuhs
An exhortatory reading, one whose tone is conciliatory and hopeful.

Emphasize "peace."

Emphasize "himself." God gathers all the souls offered to him, transforming them.

Emphasize "grace," "mercy," and "holy ones."

There are options for today's readings. Contact your parish staff to learn which readings will be used.

READING I The readings for today offer the encouragement of hope and trust in God to those who hear them proclaimed, which is why they are chosen for this celebration of the Commemoration of All the Faithful Departed (All Souls). By digging deep into questions of suffering and salvation, these readings show us how God's overwhelming love draws us to himself and is expressed in the Paschal Mystery of Christ, which we join in through our sacramental participation.

The Wisdom of Solomon, from which our first reading comes, is one of several books known to Catholics as deuterocanonical or belonging to a second canon of the Bible. However, because of theological debates that arose during the Reformation, Protestant reformers decided to count them as apocryphal, meaning "of doubtful authenticity." Nevertheless, it is included in the Catholic Bible. Its author (not King Solomon, though the attributions to him in the book lend value to the teachings in the book) writes of many important themes that reveal the nature of God and encourage readers to trust in God.

Today's first reading is part of a longer section of the Book of Wisdom that addresses the question of the vindication of the righteous (Wisdom 3.1—4.19). Briefly, Jewish and Christian theologies express the question this way: If God is sovereign and just, how are the righteous rewarded and the wicked punished? The author of Wisdom addresses the question by commenting on three scenarios in which it might appear that the righteous are being

For meditation and context:

RESPONSORIAL PSALM   Psalm 103.8+10, 13–14, 15–16, 17 (R.8 or Ps 37.39)

R. The Lord is merciful and gracious.
or: The salvation of the righteous is from the Lord.

The Lord is merciful and gracious,
slow to anger and abounding in
    steadfast love.
He does not deal with us according
    to our sins,
nor repay us according to our iniquities.

As a father has compassion for his children,
so the Lord has compassion for those who
    fear him.
For he knows how we were made;
he remembers that we are dust.

As for mortals, their days are like grass;
they flourish like a flower of the field;
for the wind passes over it, and it is gone,
and its place knows it no more.

The steadfast love of the Lord
is from everlasting to everlasting
on those who fear him,
and his righteousness to children's children,
to those who keep his covenant
and remember to do his commandments.

READING II   Romans 6.3–9

A reading from the Letter of Saint Paul to the Romans.

Brothers and **sisters**:
Do you **not know**
that all of us who have been **baptized** into Christ **Jesus**
were **baptized** into his **death**?
Therefore we have been **buried** with him by baptism into **death**,
so that, just as **Christ** was raised from the **dead**
by the **glory** of the **Father**,
so we too might **walk** in newness of **life**.
For if we have been **united** with him in a death like **his**,
we will certainly be **united** with him in a resurrection like **his**.
We know that our old **self** was **crucified** with him
so that the **body** of sin might be destroyed,
and we might no longer be **enslaved** to **sin**.
For whoever has died is **freed** from sin.
But if we have **died** with **Christ**,
we **believe** that we will also **live** with him.

A didactic reading, somewhat dense in its considerations. Give them space in your proclamation to be heard. Don't rush through any portions of the reading.

Note the analogy, introduced here by "so that." Paul is connecting our eternal life to Jesus', prepared for us by his death and Resurrection.

From here until the end of the reading, Paul intensifies the analogy between us and Jesus, relating it to metaphors of life and death as well as the body and sinfulness. The material is dense; pace yourself as you proclaim it.

---

punished: human suffering, childlessness, and early death. This reading focuses on the suffering of the righteous. It begins by asserting that, whatever the foolish might think they perceive, the righteous have immortality or eternal life and peace with God. The beautiful image of being "in the hand of God" is about protection from the forces of evil. Notice, also, the author's belief that suffering can be educative—like a nanny teaching a child to do what is right and good—and that suffering can purify us—like fire can purify and separate precious metal from dross. Suffering can also

be like a sacrificial offering which God accepts to himself. The word "visitation" refers to God's intervention on behalf of the suffering righteous, and their shining and darting around "like sparks through stubble" is a reference to their resurrection or immortality (see Daniel 12.3). Finally, the truth that the faithful ones will come to know is who God is in Godself—something the mystics and saints long to experience!

READING II   Today's second reading is part of Paul's teaching on baptism from his Letter to the Romans,

which is part of a much larger section on the life of the justified (Romans 5.1—8.39). To be justified is to be put in right relationship with God. Justification is a legal term which can best be understood as acquittal in a court of law. God is the judge, and sinful humanity is the accused. God as judge decides to dismiss the charges as a free gift to humanity, effected through the death and Resurrection of Jesus for all who believe or trust in God. But Jesus' death and Resurrection is not simply a historical event that took place some two thousand years ago. Rather, if we understand Paul's

We know that **Christ**, being **raised** from the **dead**,
will never **die** again;
death no **longer** has **dominion** over him.

GOSPEL   John 6.37–40

A reading from the holy Gospel according to John.

Jesus said to the **crowds**:
"**Everything** that the Father **gives** me will **come** to me,
and **anyone** who **comes** to me I will never drive away;
for I have come **down** from heaven,
not to do my **own will**,
but the **will** of **him** who **sent** me.
And this is the will of him who sent me,
that I should lose **nothing** of all that he has **given** me,
but **raise** it up on the last **day**.
This is indeed the **will** of my **Father**,
that **whoever** sees the **Son** and **believes** in him
may have eternal **life**;
and I will raise them up on the **last day**."

A powerful and assertive exhortatory reading that expresses one of John's favourite themes, the will of the Father.

Will is the operative word in this reading. It is repeated four times (as a noun). Give it weight each time you say it.

For John, will is connected directly to the Father, toward which Jesus, as Son, is utterly obedient and which clearly empowers him. Emphasize "this," "will," and "Father."

teaching on baptism correctly, we continue to experience Jesus' death and Resurrection in our bodies. The Greek verb *baptizō* means "to dip, immerse, or submerge." Therefore, in baptism, we are immersed in Christ's death and subsequently also buried with Christ. And because baptized Christians are "dipped" into Christ's death, they can also hope to be raised from the dead "as Christ was raised from the dead by the glory of the Father." We leave behind our old way of life as if crucified with Christ and embrace our new life in Christ.

GOSPEL   Today's Gospel is part of the Bread of Life discourse, in which Jesus addresses a challenge made by the crowds who were chasing after him in hope of getting more food to eat, after the multiplication of loaves and fishes near the Sea of Galilee (John 6.1–15). When they caught up to him, they asked for a sign, one like the manna that God sent down from heaven during the time of Moses (John 6.30–31). Thus, Jesus declares that he is the bread from heaven, sent from God to give the world life. Coming to today's reading, we see that Jesus is the agent of God, who, in complete fidelity, receives everything he has from the Father and does only what the Father tells him to do. An integral aspect of his mission as the bread of life is described in this reading: that Jesus receives everyone the Father gives and will not lose any one of them. Not even death will separate Christ from the people; they will be raised up "on the last day." What sweet comfort to all who believe in Jesus' name! They will have everlasting life, that is, the fullness of life now, and be raised up on the last day. C.C.

THIRTY-FIRST SUNDAY IN ORDINARY TIME

LECTIONARY #151

READING I   Malachi 1.14—2.2, 8–10

Malachi = MAL-uh-kī

A poetic and heroic-sounding reading, with alluring oratorical overtones.

Emphasis on "curse," which focuses the drama of the reading.

Let the forcefulness of the questions that conclude this reading draw you to its end.

A reading from the book of the Prophet Malachi.

"I am a **great King**," says the **Lord** of **hosts**,
"and my **name** is **reverenced** among the **nations**.
And **now**, O **priests**, this **command** is for **you**.
If you **will not listen**,
if you **will not lay** it to **heart** to give glory to my **name**,"
says the **Lord** of **hosts**,
"then I will send the **curse** on you
and I will **curse** your **blessings**;
indeed I have **already cursed** them,
because you **do not lay** it to **heart**.
You have turned **aside** from the **way**;
you have caused **many** to **stumble** by your **instruction**;
you have **corrupted** the **covenant** of **Levi**,"
says the **Lord** of **hosts**,
"and so I make you **despised** and **abased before** all the **people**,
inasmuch as you **have not kept** my **ways**
but have shown **partiality** in your **instruction**."
Have we **not all one father**?
Has not one **God created** us?
Why then are we **faithless** to one **another**,
profaning the **covenant** of our **ancestors**?

READING I Today's first reading is from the Book of Malachi, which is believed to have been written after the Babylonian Exile. In the verses immediately preceding this reading, the Prophet describes God as feeling dishonoured and suggests that someone should just shut the gates to the Temple so that the priests cannot make defiling or imperfect offerings on the altar. He also casts blame on those who provide the animals for Temple sacrifice: they promise with a vow that an animal is appropriate for sacrifice and then, at the time of sacrifice, replace it with a defective one. How disingenuous!

With this context in mind, today's reading begins with the Prophet voicing God's assertion that he is a king whose "name is reverenced among the nations." Although this statement of universal reverence is an exaggeration, the claims of God's universal kingship are valid insofar as God is the creator and sustainer of all life and should be worshipped as such, especially by God's chosen people and by the priests who are charged with carrying out Levi's legacy. Levi was one of the sons of Jacob and founder of the tribe of Levi. The other tribes were allotted land as Moses had promised before they entered the Promised Land (Numbers 33—34), but the tribe of Levi was not given its own land, because "the Lord God of Israel is their inheritance, as he said to them" (Joshua 13.33). Malachi describes Levi as having integrity and as capable of turning people away from the ways of evil with his instruction (Malachi 2.6). By contrast, these Temple priests do not give God the honour that is due and use their teaching to advance their own desires. Therefore, God says that he will shame them

For meditation and context:

RESPONSORIAL PSALM Psalm 131.1, 2, 3 (R. see 2)

R. In you, Lord, I have found my peace.

O Lord, my heart is not lifted up,
my eyes are not raised too high;
I do not occupy myself with things
too great and too marvellous for me.

But I have calmed and quieted my soul,
like a weaned child with its mother;
my soul is like the weaned child
that is with me.

O Israel, hope in the Lord
from this time on and forevermore.

READING II   1 Thessalonians 2.7–9, 13

Thessalonians = thes-uh-LOH-nee-uhnz

A reading from the first Letter of Saint Paul to the Thessalonians.

Paul describes the trouble he has undergone to bring the Gospel to the Thessalonians as a way of praising them for receiving the Good News. In the first half, Paul describes his trouble. In the second half, he turns the description into praise.

Brothers and sisters:
Though we might have made **demands** as **Apostles** of **Christ**,
we were **gentle among** you,
like a nurse **tenderly caring** for her **own children**.
So **deeply** do we **care** for you
that we are **determined** to **share** with you
not only the **Gospel** of **God** but also our **own selves**,
because you have become **very dear** to us.
You **remember** our **labour** and **toil**,
brothers and **sisters**;
we worked **night** and **day**,
so that we **might not** burden **any** of you
while we **proclaimed** to you the **Gospel** of **God**.

Here the second half begins, and the tone becomes more uplifting.

We also **constantly** give **thanks** to **God** for this,
that when you **received** the **word** of **God**
that you **heard** from us,
you **accepted** it not as a **human word**
but as what it **really** is, the **word** of **God**,
which is also at **work** in you **believers**.

before the people. At the end of the reading, the Prophet speaks in his own words, using several rhetorical questions to make the point that Israel is different from other nations, who identify themselves merely by ethnicity or other human factors. In fact, Israel is one family, the children of God, and refusing to uphold the covenant of their ancestors, in essence, makes them "faithless to one another."

READING II In our second reading, Paul presents himself and his fellow missionaries in a way that is quite

different from the priests of Malachi's time. In the sentences that precede this reading, he writes about the indignities they faced in Philippi, which gave them courage to speak the Good News of God to the people of Thessalonica. They did so, Paul says, without deception or delusion or flattery or greed. Moreover, they did not push their weight around by claiming and exploiting their role as Apostles (1 Thessalonians 2.1–6a).

Our reading begins with Paul asserting that he and his comrades were gentle and affectionate with the Thessalonian community, acting as wet nurses among them.

The "nutrition" they share with the community is the Good News, of course, but also their very selves. Such is their love (literally, "yearning") for these Christians! By noting the sufferings that Paul and his co-missionaries endured on their behalf and explaining how they worked to avoid being a burden to them, Paul is again asserting that the community was not coerced in any way to receive the Good News. Instead, they knew it to be God's word, which they allow to work in them. For this reason, he continually gives thanks to God.

A scornful and critical reading that includes challenging imperatives.

phylacteries = fih-LAK-tuh-reez

Consider how strange it is for Jesus to tell the crowd not to call anyone "rabbi," a commonplace honorific for referring to a teacher.

Stranger still to tell the crowd not to call anyone "father." Same goes for "instructor."

The reading concludes with an inversion: exalts–humbled to humbles–exalted.

TO KEEP IN MIND
Recognize how important your proclamation of the Word of God is. Prepare well and take joy in your ministry.

GOSPEL   Matthew 23.1–12

A reading from the holy Gospel according to Matthew.

Then **Jesus** said to the **crowds** and to his **disciples**,
"The **scribes** and the **Pharisees** sit in **Moses' chair**;
therefore, do **whatever** they **teach** you and **follow** it;
but **do** not **do** as they **do**,
for they **do not practise** what they **teach**.
They **tie up heavy burdens**, **hard** to **bear**,
and **lay** them on the **shoulders** of **others**;
but they **themselves** are **unwilling** to lift a **finger** to **move** them.
They do **all** their **deeds** to be **seen** by **others**;
for they make their **phylacteries broad** and their **fringes long**.
They love to have the **place** of **honour** at **banquets**
and the **best seats** in the **synagogues**,
and to be **greeted** with **respect** in the **marketplaces**,
and to have **people** call them **rabbi**.
But you are **not** to be called **rabbi**,
for you have **one teacher**,
and you are all **brothers** and **sisters**.
And call **no one** your **father** on **earth**,
for you have **one Father**—the **one** in **heaven**.
Nor are you to be called **instructors**,
for you have **one instructor**, the **Christ**.
The **greatest** among you will be your **servant**.
Whoever **exalts** himself will be **humbled**,
and whoever **humbles** himself will be **exalted**."

GOSPEL   Today's Gospel is the introduction to Matthew's version of the woes that Jesus issues against the scribes and Pharisees. Among prophetic literary forms, a woe is a lamentation or expression of grief followed by charges issued against the persons to whom the woe is directed. Like Malachi's charges against the Temple priests in our first reading, Jesus' charges against the scribes and Pharisees highlight the human condition and the potential for people in positions of power to abuse their authority. Thus, in today's Gospel reading, Jesus advises his disciples and the crowd that had gathered around them that they should heed the teachings of the scribes and Pharisees, experts in the Law, because they hold "Moses' chair," that is, a symbol of Moses' authority, but they should not follow their example. He goes on to name practices that these people employ to bring attention to themselves and impose heavy religious burdens on those who have less power than themselves. Phylacteries, the small leather boxes worn on the forehead and left arm, and fringes are both intended to be reminders to follow covenant law (see Deuteronomy 11.18; Numbers 15.38–39) but making them bigger and longer is a violation of the spirit of the law. No matter a person's station on earth, even if they are in positions of honour or power or instruction, there is only one who deserves the full weight of those titles: God. The Matthean Jesus' message is that the greatest and most exalted should be a humble servant. C.C.

THIRTY-SECOND SUNDAY IN ORDINARY TIME

LECTIONARY #154

READING I   Wisdom 6.12–16

A reading from the book of Wisdom.

Wisdom is **radiant** and **unfading**,
and she is **easily discerned** by **those** who **love** her,
and is **found** by those who **seek** her.
She **hastens** to make herself **known** to those who **desire** her.
One who rises **early** to **seek** her will have **no difficulty**,
for she will be found **sitting** at the **gate**.
To **fix** one's **thought** on her is **perfect understanding**,
and one who is **vigilant** on her **account** will **soon** be
     free from **care**,
because she goes about **seeking** those **worthy** of her,
and she graciously **appears** to them in their **paths**,
and meets them in **every thought**.

A poetic reading. In Greek and Jewish cultures, Wisdom was traditionally feminized. In this reading, Wisdom is a personified woman who acts and responds and can even be observed.

For meditation and context:

RESPONSORIAL PSALM   Psalm 63.1, 2–3, 4–5, 6–7 (R.1a)

R. My soul thirsts for you, O Lord my God.

O God, you are my God, I seek you,
my soul thirsts for you;
my flesh faints for you,
as in a dry and weary land where there is
     no water.

So I have looked upon you in the sanctuary,
beholding your power and glory.
Because your steadfast love is better
     than life,
my lips will praise you.

So I will bless you as long as I live;
I will lift up my hands and call on your name.
My soul is satisfied as with a rich feast,
and my mouth praises you with joyful lips.

I think of you on my bed,
and meditate on you in the watches of
     the night;
for you have been my help,
and in the shadow of your wings I sing
     for joy.

READING I   Our first reading comes from the Book of Wisdom. When the author of this book writes about wisdom, he presents her as a personified, feminine power of God because the Greek word for wisdom is *sophia*, a feminine noun. Today's reading, which focuses on wisdom's accessibility, is part of a longer exhortation to those who wish to be wise. Wisdom is the speaker. She exhorts kings and princes to seek wisdom, because God will punish them harshly if they do not change their ways (Wisdom 6.1–11).

In today's reading, Wisdom's accessibility is described in terms of the theme of seeking and finding, which is also found in Proverbs 1.20–21; 3.13–18; and 8.1–36. Wisdom's unfading radiance is due to her connection to the divine. Elsewhere in Wisdom, she is described as reflecting divine light, as a mirror (Wisdom 7.26). The people who love her learn to be discerning and free from care because she is with them, appearing in their paths and meeting them "in every thought." What a beautiful message! If we seek wisdom in discerning love, we will find her and become like her.

READING II   One of the main topics of Paul's First Letter to the Thessalonians is how the community should deal with the delayed parousia, the return of the risen Christ at the end time. Apparently, they understood from Paul that the return of the risen Christ would happen very soon, since resurrection from the dead was thought to be a sign of the end time. Now, some twenty years later, the parousia has not yet happened. This young Christian community is deeply troubled because some of their members are dying. Paul's response is unequivocal! Since we

READING II   1 Thessalonians 4.13–18

A reading from the first Letter of Saint Paul to the Thessalonians.

We **do not want** you to be **uninformed**, **brothers** and **sisters**,
about **those** who have **died**,
so that you may not grieve as **others do** who **have no hope**.
For since we **believe** that **Jesus died** and **rose again**,
even **so**, through **Jesus**,
God will bring **with** him **those** who have **died**.
For **this** we **declare** to you by the **word** of the **Lord**,
that **we** who are **alive**,
who are **left** until the **coming** of the **Lord**,
will by **no means precede** those who have **died**.
For the **Lord himself**, with a **cry** of **command**,
with the **Archangel's call** and with the **sound** of **God's trumpet**,
will **descend** from **heaven**,
and the **dead** in **Christ** will **rise** first.
Then **we** who are **alive**, who are **left**,
will be **caught up** in the **clouds**
together with them to meet the **Lord** in the **air**;
and so we will **be** with the **Lord forever**.
Therefore **encourage** one another with **these words**.

Thessalonians = thes-uh-LOH-nee-uhnz

Emphasis on "not."

Slight pause between "Jesus" and "died."

archangel = AHRK-ayn-jihl

Paul's apocalyptic view reveals itself as the reading intensifies toward its conclusion. He's sharing a vision of end times with his fellow believers.

believe Jesus died and was raised from the dead, God will surely raise your beloved deceased from the dead. Paul continues in the style of a Prophet, declaring "by the word of the Lord" how this end time parousia will come about. The imagery is reminiscent of God's appearance to Moses on Sinai or a king's entrance into a heavenly throne room. The line about being "caught up in the clouds" refers to the ancient belief that spiritual beings used clouds as their vehicles to get around heaven. In the midst of this grand imagery, notice that Paul's message is one of consolation and encour-

agement. Their beloved dead are not lost. Indeed, they will be the first to enter into the divine presence!

GOSPEL Today's Gospel reading is about both seeking wisdom and anticipating the end time appearance of the risen Christ. It is the parable of the wise and foolish virgins, which is found only in Matthew's Gospel. Parables are fictional stories that establish a comparison— in this case, "the kingdom of heaven will be like . . ."—and that involve common, everyday images to communicate their meaning. The

phrase "kingdom of heaven" is often misunderstood to refer to heaven. However, it is better understood as the full manifestation of the reign of God and the dissolution of evil and suffering in the land.

Unfortunately, because wedding feasts were a common reality in first-century Jewish communities, the modern reader is given few details about what took place at these celebrations. Yet, from other contemporaneous sources we know that marriages were contractual relationships between families for the purposes of establishing alliances or protecting resources, so

GOSPEL Matthew 25.1–13

A reading from the holy Gospel according to Matthew.

A reading that consists of the telling of a straightforward parable whose message is for believers to be prepared.

Jesus spoke this **parable** to the **disciples**:
"The **kingdom** of **heaven** will **be** like **this**.
Ten bridesmaids took their **lamps**
and **went** to **meet** the **bridegroom**.
Five of them were **foolish**, and **five** were **wise**.
When the **foolish** took their **lamps**, they took **no oil** with them;
but the **wise** took **flasks** of oil with their **lamps**.
As the **bridegroom** was **delayed**,
all of them became **drowsy** and **slept**.
But at **midnight** there was a **shout**,
'**Look! Here** is the **bridegroom**!
Come out to **meet** him.'
Then **all those bridesmaids** got up and **trimmed** their **lamps**.
The **foolish** said to the **wise**,
'**Give** us some of your **oil**, for our **lamps** are going **out**.'
But the **wise replied**,
'**No**! There will **not** be **enough** for **you** and for **us**;
you had **better go** to the **dealers** and **buy some** for **yourselves**.'
And while they went to **buy** it, the **bridegroom** came,
and **those** who were **ready** went **with** him

Emphasis on "with."

into the **wedding** banquet;
and the **door** was **shut**.
Later the **other bridesmaids** came also, saying,
'**Lord, lord, open** to us.'
But he **replied**, '**Truly** I **tell** you, I **do not know** you.'
Keep **awake** therefore,
for you know neither the **day** nor the **hour**."

the betrothal contract was an important first step in the process. The wedding itself, which could go on for several days or even a week, was focused on the process of transferring the bride from her father's home to her husband's home, which was often somewhere near or even within his father's home. When the procession of the groom to the bride's home and back to his home was complete, the bride and groom would consummate their marriage, with the witnesses waiting outside to confirm the bride's virginity prior to consummation, after which the witnesses would accom-

pany the bride and groom into the banquet area for lots of feasting!

If we allow ourselves a bit of allegory, we can imagine the ten virgins (the bridesmaids)—young girls not yet eligible for marriage—as the witnesses to the consummation event. Five were not wise and did not prepare sufficiently for the delay of the bridegroom, the parousia of the risen Christ. Because they had to go and purchase more oil for their lamps, they missed the opportunity to accompany the bridal couple when they joined the wedding banquet, and they were not allowed into the

feast later, because the bridegroom did not know who they were. Although biblical scholars are divided about the significance of the wedding feast, in this context it likely represents the messianic banquet that is supposed to accompany the end time. The message of the parable is "If you are wise, you will stay alert and ready for the bridegroom's coming!" C.C.

THIRTY-THIRD SUNDAY IN ORDINARY TIME

LECTIONARY #157

READING I Proverbs 31.10–13, 16–18, 20, 26, 28–31++

A reading from the book of Proverbs.

A **capable wife**, **who** can **find** her?
She is **far more precious** than **jewels**.
The **heart** of her **husband trusts** in her,
and he will have **no lack** of gain.
She **does** him **good**, and not **harm**,
all the **days** of her **life**.
She seeks **wool** and **flax**,
and works with **willing hands**.
She considers a **field** and **buys** it;
with the **fruit** of her **hands** she **plants** a **vineyard**.
She **girds** herself with **strength**,
and makes her **arms strong**.
She perceives that her **merchandise** is **profitable**.
Her lamp does **not** go out at **night**.
She opens her **hand** to the **poor**,
and reaches out her **hands** to the **needy**.
She opens her **mouth** with **wisdom**,
and the teaching of **kindness** is on her **tongue**.
Her children rise **up** and call her **happy**;
her **husband too**, and he **praises** her:
"Many **women** have done **excellently**,
but you surpass them **all**."
Charm is **deceitful**, and **beauty** is **vain**,
but a **woman** who fears the **Lord** is to be **praised**.

Read this in light of these attributes being descriptive of wisdom. Consider how these everyday tasks take on new meaning when done for the glory of God and describe one who follows God closely. Let that understanding come through in your proclamation.

READING I On this Thirty-Third Sunday in Ordinary Time, only two weeks before the beginning of a new liturgical year, the First Sunday of Advent, today's readings bring us to thoughts about the fulfillment of the salvation story. We do not know when the time will come, whether it be for ourselves individually or for God's creation in totality, but, if we have responded to the grace that is given us in life, we have nothing to fear from a good and gracious God.

On the surface, at least, today's first reading from the Book of Proverbs might be difficult for some modern readers to embrace, because of what we might call gender stereotyping. However, a deeper look might prove beneficial for everyone. First, this entire section, Proverbs 31.10–31, is composed as an acrostic poem. Written in Hebrew, the first verse begins with the first letter of the Hebrew alphabet, *alef*. The second verse begins with *bet*, the second letter of the Hebrew alphabet, and so on until it arrives at the last letter of the Hebrew alphabet, *tav*. Despite the patriarchy of the time in which this masterpiece was created, it outlines the skills and virtues of a strong woman. It also picks up much of the feminine imagery that appears elsewhere in this book, which has led some biblical scholars to describe this woman as the concrete and visible image of Lady Wisdom as she is described in Proverbs 1—9. The wisdom literature of the Bible portrays Lady Wisdom as the power of God who is ever-present and active in the world, a radiant light, the source of insight, the bringer of peace, the breath of God's might, and the pure emanation of God's glory (see Wisdom 7.24–30; Proverbs 8.1–36; Sirach 24.1–33).

Give her a **share** in the **fruit** of her **hands**,
and let her **works praise** her in the **city gates**.

For meditation and context:

RESPONSORIAL PSALM   Psalm 128.1–2, 3, 4–5 (R.1)

R. Blessed is everyone who fears the Lord.

Blessed is everyone who fears the Lord,
who walks in his ways.
You shall eat the fruit of the labour of
    your hands;
you shall be happy, and it shall go well
    with you.

Your wife will be like a fruitful vine
within your house;
your children will be like olive shoots
around your table.

Thus shall the man be blessed who fears
    the Lord.
The Lord bless you from Zion.
May you see the prosperity of Jerusalem
all the days of your life.

READING II   1 Thessalonians 5.1–6

A reading from the first Letter of Saint Paul to the Thessalonians.

Now **concerning** the **times** and the **seasons**, **brothers** and **sisters**,
you **do not need** to have **anything written** to you.
For **you yourselves** know **very well**
that the **day** of the **Lord** will come like a **thief** in the **night**.
When they say, "There is **peace** and **security**,"
then **sudden destruction** will **come upon** them,
as **labour** pains come upon a **pregnant woman**,
and there will be **no escape**!
But **you**, **beloved**, are **not** in **darkness**
for **that day** to **surprise** you like a **thief**.
You are **all children** of **light** and **children** of the **day**;
we are **not** of the **night** or of **darkness**.
So then let us **not** fall **asleep** as **others** do,
but let us **keep awake** and be **sober**.

Thessalonians = thes-uh-LOH-nee-uhnz

A reading whose tone is urgent—Paul is imagining what the end of things will be like.

The core of the reading, the "thief in the night."

Emphasis on "not."

Note the contrasts between light and dark, day and night.

READING II Our second reading is from Paul's First Letter to the Thessalonians, which is believed to have been written around AD 51, only a couple of years after Paul established this community in Thessalonica. Based on Paul's teaching, they apparently believed that the parousia, the return of the risen Christ, was to take place soon after his Resurrection. But now it is twenty-five or more years later, and they are concerned that something is amiss. Some members of the community have died, and they fear that they are forever lost. In the section immediately preced-

ing this reading (1 Thessalonians 4.13–18), Paul gives them strong words of encouragement, saying that their deceased loved ones will actually be the first to join the risen Christ in the heavens, when he comes.

In today's reading, Paul picks up a topic that easily flows from this earlier concern. The heart of their unasked question is "If we have not missed Christ's second coming, when will it happen?" He begins by reminding the community that they already know the answer to this question, but by repeating his message, he offers further encouragement to the recipients of this let-

ter. The "day of the Lord" is a reference to God's end-time judgment of the world, borrowed from the prophetic literature of the Hebrew Scriptures (for example, Amos 5.18–20; Joel 2.1–11; Zephaniah 1.7–8). For those who are unaware and unprepared, the day of the Lord will come as if it were a disaster. The images of a night-time thief and sudden birth pangs are typical of this type of eschatological (i.e., end time) literature. But Paul departs from these themes and asserts, "you are all children of light," so there is no need to fear the things of darkness and the night, as long as you stay

A reading that consists of the telling of a lengthy parable, one whose meaning appears straightforward but whose content suggests something more ambiguous.

Pacing: It's important to keep the different numbers in mind.

GOSPEL   Matthew 25.14–30

A reading from the holy Gospel according to Matthew.

[**Jesus** spoke this **parable** to his **disciples**:
"For it is as if a **man**, **going** on a **journey**,
summoned his **slaves** and **entrusted** his **property** to them;
to **one** he gave **five talents**,
to **another two**, to **another one**,
to **each** according to his **ability**.
Then he **went away**.]
The one who had received the five **talents**
went **off** at **once** and **traded** with them,
and made **five more talents**.
In the **same way**,
the **one** who had the two **talents** made **two more talents**.
But the **one** who had received the one **talent**
went **off** and dug a hole in the **ground**
and hid his **master's money**.
[After a **long time** the **master** of those **slaves came**
and **settled accounts** with them.
Then the **one** who had received the five **talents** came forward,
bringing **five more talents**, saying,
'**Master**, you handed over to me **five talents**;
see, I have made **five more talents**.'
His master **said** to him,

Here, the master uses a formulaic phrase to praise the slave.

'**Well done, good** and **trustworthy slave**;
you have been **trustworthy** in a **few things**,
I will put you in **charge** of **many things**;
enter into the joy of your **master**.']
And the one with the **two talents** also came forward, saying,
'**Master**, you handed over to me **two talents**;
see, I have made **two more talents**.'

---

awake. Though it is not included in this reading, Paul ends this section of his letter by urging the Thessalonians to be an encouragement to each other, since all of them are on this journey of hope and expectation as they await Christ's second coming. This is our task as well, as we await the coming of our Lord Jesus Christ.

GOSPEL   Our Gospel reading for today is another parable about the end times. As a reminder, parables are fictional stories that establish a comparison—for example, "the kingdom of

heaven is like . . ."—and that involve common, everyday images to communicate their meaning. But parables are also riddles designed to make the reader think deeply about their meaning, and this parable of the talents has several details to make people shake their heads in amazement. For example, the amount of money trading hands in this parable is stupendous! In the ancient world, the value of a talent varied by location and composition, but one example of the estimated value of a talent was 36 kilograms of silver, which had an equivalent value of 6,000 denarii, where a denarius

was a full day's wages for most workers. Really! Who gives a servant or employee five talents or perhaps the equivalent of 83 years' wages to invest, while they go off on a journey to who-knows-where with no indication of when they will return?

One can imagine that the investment activities of the first and second servants were aggressive, even ruthless, because doubling investments as large as these by righteous means is highly unlikely. Why, then, does the master praise them? Perhaps it is because these two servants are like him. The third servant describes the master

Once again, the formulaic phrase.

His master **said** to him,
'**Well done**, **good** and **trustworthy slave**;
you have been **trustworthy** in a **few things**,
I will put you in **charge** of **many things**;
enter into the joy of your **master**.'
Then the one who had received the **one talent**
also came forward, saying,
'**Master**, **I knew** that you were a **harsh man**,
reaping where you did not **sow**,
and **gathering** where you did **not** scatter **seed**;
so I was **afraid**,
and I went and **hid** your **talent** in the **ground**.
Here you **have** what is **yours**.'
But his **master replied**,

The viciousness of the master, even though we expect it, is shocking.

'You **wicked** and **lazy slave**!
You **knew**, did you, that I **reap** where I did not **sow**,
and **gather** where I did not **scatter**?
Then you ought to have **invested** my **money** with the **bankers**,
and on my **return**
I would have **received** what was my **own** with **interest**.
So take the **talent** from him, and **give** it to **the** one with the
       ten talents.
For to **all those** who **have**,
more will be **given**, and they will have an **abundance**;
but from **those** who have **nothing**,
even what they have will be **taken away**.

Emphasis on "worthless."

As for this **worthless slave**,
throw him into the **outer darkness**,
where there will be **weeping** and **gnashing** of **teeth**.'"

[Shorter: Matthew 25.14–15, 19–21 (see brackets)]

as "a harsh man, reaping where you did not sow, and gathering where you did not scatter seed." In other words, the master's wealth comes from taking from others by force. In an honour/shame culture such as the first-century Mediterranean world in which this parable was created, an honourable person would not seek more than what was allotted to him because it meant taking away what belonged to another. Perhaps this is why the master directed his servants to do his dirty work while he was away.

And what about the third servant? This parable appears among a collection of parables about the end time and how we ought to behave as we await the parousia, the return of the risen Christ. In the context of this story, we can imagine that the third servant did what he thought was prudent, especially given his relatively low status in society. He could not afford to lose the money placed in his care, so he buried it for safekeeping. The master's response is fierce and punishing, but it is not for the servant's unwillingness to take risks. Rather, it is because he considered the servant to be lazy! Perhaps this is the message of this parable. We live in this in-between time still today, waiting for the master to return, and the worst thing we can do is sit around being lazy. What will you do to help advance the coming reign of God, until its full glory will be revealed in the end time? C.C.

NOVEMBER 26, 2023

THIRTY-FOURTH SUNDAY IN ORDINARY TIME: CHRIST THE KING

LECTIONARY #160

READING I   Ezekiel 34.11–12, 15–17

A reading from the book of the Prophet Ezekiel.

Thus says the **Lord God**:
"**I myself** will **search** for my **sheep**,
and will **seek** them **out**.
As a **shepherd** seeks out his **flock**
when he is **among** his **scattered sheep**,
so I will **seek** out my **sheep**.
I will **rescue** them from all the **places**
to which they have been **scattered**
on a **day** of **clouds** and **thick darkness**.
I myself will be the **shepherd** of my **sheep**,
and I will make them **lie down**,"
says the **Lord God**.
"I will **seek** the **lost**,
and I will **bring back** the **strayed**,
and I will **bind up** the **injured**,
and I will **strengthen** the **weak**,
but the **fat** and the **strong** I will **destroy**.
I will **feed** my sheep with **justice**.
As for **you**, my **flock**," **thus** says the **Lord God**:
"I shall **judge** between **one sheep** and **another**,
between **rams** and **goats**."

Ezekiel = ee-ZEE-kee-uhl

An expressive reading that elaborates the powerful metaphor of God as shepherd and believers as the sheep in his flock.

Note the emphatic repetitions of "I myself."

Note the rhythm of each line, beginning with a verb for what God will do and ending with a noun.

The reading concludes with a mysterious claim.

READING I There are many aspects of our culture that attempt to overshadow the sovereignty of Christ in the world, yet today's readings draw our attention to the true power of God that will shine forth in the second coming of Christ and the judgment that will be placed on all peoples. This is an important reminder for us who live in the world: we belong to Christ, not to the ever-changing whims of culture, and must live in a way that reflects our citizenship in his kingdom.

Today's first reading comes from the longer parable of the shepherds (Ezekiel 34.1–31) in the Book of Ezekiel. In the verses that immediately precede this reading, Ezekiel delivers a woe oracle, that is, a warning, against the shepherds of Israel who have been taking advantage of the sheep, ruling harshly against them and not caring for the sick, injured, or lost among them. The metaphor of kings and leaders as shepherds and their constituencies as sheep had long been in use in the Mediterranean world, so people knew well what Ezekiel was talking about. Here, Ezekiel is blaming the king and religious leaders of Judea for the fate of God's people, scat-tered about in exile and metaphorically eaten by wild animals.

As we pick up today's reading, we hear Ezekiel giving voice to God's word against the shepherds of Israel, who did such great harm to God's people. The imagery of God as shepherd is very evocative and can be seen in other Old Testament passages (for example, see Genesis 48.15; Psalm 23; Isaiah 40.11; Jeremiah 31.10). Imagine God collecting his scattered sheep that have been battered and bruised in exile, feeding the hungry ones, tending the sick among them, and providing a place for

For meditation and context:

RESPONSORIAL PSALM   Psalm 23.1–3a, 3b–4, 5, 6 (R.1)

R. The Lord is my shepherd; I shall not want.

The Lord is my shepherd, I shall not want.
He makes me lie down in green pastures;
he leads me beside still waters;
he restores my soul.

He leads me in right paths for his
    name's sake.
Even though I walk through the darkest
    valley, I fear no evil;
for you are with me;
your rod and your staff—they comfort me.

You prepare a table before me
in the presence of my enemies;
you anoint my head with oil;
my cup overflows.

Surely goodness and mercy shall follow me
all the days of my life,
and I shall dwell in the house of the Lord
my whole life long.

READING II   1 Corinthians 15.20–26, 28

Corinthians = kohr-IN-thee-uhnz

An urgent reading from Paul, no less complex for its urgency. Pace your proclamation; there is a lot to absorb here.

Emphasis in these two lines on "man."

Note the sequence of the order in which death will be defeated.

A reading from the first Letter of Saint Paul to the Corinthians.

Brothers and **sisters**:
Christ has been **raised** from the **dead**,
the **first fruits** of **those** who have **fallen asleep**.
For since **death came** through a **man**,
the **resurrection** of the **dead** has **also come** through a **man**;
for as **all die** in **Adam**,
so **all** will be made **alive** in **Christ**.
But **each** in his **own order**:
Christ the **first fruits**,
then at his **coming** those who belong to **Christ**.
Then comes the **end**,
when he **hands over** the **kingdom** to **God** the **Father**,
after he has **destroyed** every **ruler** and every **authority**
    and **power**.
For he must **reign** until he has put **all** his **enemies under**
    his **feet**.
The **last enemy** to be **destroyed** is **death**. »

Pause slightly after "death."

---

them to rest in safety after their long and harrowing ordeal. But not every sheep in a flock is good. The "the fat and the strong" is an allusion to members of the sheepfold who, like the bad shepherds, take advantage of the others for their own benefit. Immediately following this reading is an oracle about separating the bad sheep from the good, the rams from the goats (Ezekiel 34.17–24). Thus, this God who shepherds like a good and great king also judges justly. In summary, God says that he will take the sheep away from the bad shepherds and

take charge of the sheep himself, undoing the damage that the bad shepherds did.

READING II Our second reading is from Paul's First Letter to the Corinthians, and it is part of his much longer teaching on resurrection of the body (1 Corinthians 15.1–58). Briefly, he argues that Christians who believe in Christ's Resurrection must also believe that they will be resurrected bodily. Otherwise, there would be no triumph over death, and sin would not be defeated.

In this reading, Paul presents Jesus as the first fruits of those who are deceased. The term "first fruits" represents the first and best of the harvest offered to God as a sacrifice in consecration of the entire harvest to God. To further illustrate this theme, Paul uses a method of biblical interpretation called typology, which compares an Old Testament person or event with a New Testament person or event, the former being merely a blueprint of the latter. Here Paul describes Adam as a type of Jesus Christ: Adam brought sin and death into the

When **all things** are **subjected** to him,
then the **Son himself** will **also** be **subjected** to the **one**
who put **all things** in **subjection under** him,
so that **God** may be **all** in **all**.

GOSPEL   Matthew 25.31–46

A reading from the holy Gospel according to Matthew.

Jesus said to his **disciples**:
"When the **Son** of **Man comes** in his **glory**,
and **all** the **Angels with** him,
then he will **sit** on the **throne** of his **glory**.
All the **nations** will be **gathered before** him,
and he will **separate people one** from **another**
as a **shepherd separates** the **sheep** from the **goats**,
and he will put the **sheep** at his **right hand**
and the **goats** at the **left**.
Then the **king** will say to **those** at his **right hand**,
'**Come, you** that are **blessed** by my **Father**,
inherit the **kingdom prepared** for you
from the **foundation** of the **world**;
for I was **hungry** and you gave me **food**,
I was **thirsty** and you gave me **something** to **drink**,
I was a **stranger** and you **welcomed** me,
I was **naked** and you gave me **clothing**,
I was **sick** and you took **care** of me,
I was in **prison** and you **visited** me.'
Then the **righteous** will **answer** him,
'**Lord**, when **was** it that we saw you **hungry** and gave you **food**,
or **thirsty** and gave you **something** to **drink**?
And when **was** it that we saw you a **stranger** and **welcomed** you,
or **naked** and gave you **clothing**?

Slow your pace slightly at "all in all."

TO KEEP IN MIND
Use the pitch and volume of your voice to gain the attention of the assembly.

A reading in which, through a kind of visionary parable, Jesus reveals an apocalyptic vision of judgment. It involves repetitions that serve to reinforce the qualities of the vision.

Be attentive to the rhythms here.

These questions are asked in earnest.

---

world for all humankind, while Jesus Christ brought life into the world for all peoples. Paul explains that this sacrifice of first fruits begins with Jesus' Resurrection and comes to its fullness with his return as the exalted Lord. When he comes, all who belong to Christ will also be resurrected. Then, having assumed his role as king, the risen Christ will destroy all other sovereignties and subject competing authorities to his power, until he destroys death itself. Then he will turn over his kingdom to God who is Lord over all, so that "God may be all in all."

What a powerful image of God's peaceful kingdom to come!

GOSPEL   The Gospel reading for today gives us important insights into the nature of Christ's kingship and its relevance for our daily lives. This teaching is the last in a series of parables and teachings on the return of the risen Christ in the end time that are found in Matthew 24—25, after which Matthew unfolds for us the story of Jesus' arrest, crucifixion, death, and Resurrection.

This teaching, which biblical scholars categorize as an apocalyptic discourse, has no parallel in the other Gospels. The word apocalypse means "revelation," and it usually refers to the revelation of heavenly realities to a human recipient through visions or auditions. The heavenly reality being revealed here is judgment day, when the righteous are separated out for reward and the wicked are separated out for judgment. The phrase "Son of Man" possibly has its origins in Daniel 7 or Zechariah 14, but in the Gospels, it is spoken only by Jesus and

And when **was** it that we saw you sick or in **prison**
and **visited** you?'
And the king will **answer** them,
'**Truly** I **tell** you,
just as you **did** it to **one** of the **least** of these **brothers** and **sisters**
 of **mine**,
you **did** it to **me**.'
Then he will **say** to those at his **left hand**,
'**You** that are **accursed**,
depart from me into the **eternal fire**
prepared for the **devil** and his **angels**;
for I was **hungry** and you gave me **no food**,
I was **thirsty** and you gave me **nothing** to **drink**,
I was a **stranger** and you **did not welcome** me,
naked and you **did not give** me **clothing**,
sick and in **prison** and you **did not visit** me.'
Then they **also** will **answer**,
'**Lord**, **when was** it that we **saw** you **hungry** or **thirsty**
or a **stranger** or **naked** or **sick** or in **prison**,
and **did not** take **care** of you?'
Then he will **answer** them,
'**Truly** I **tell** you,
just as you **did not do** it to one of the **least** of **these**,
you **did not do** it to **me**.'
And **these** will go **away** into **eternal punishment**,
but the **righteous** into **eternal life**."

Once again, be attentive to the rhythms.

Once again, the question is asked in earnest.

Note the clear contrast between "eternal punishment" and "eternal life."

applied to himself. Thus, when Matthew describes Jesus as saying, "when the Son of Man comes in his glory," Jesus is talking about himself and referring to the parousia, his return in glory after his Resurrection.

The metaphors of the kingly Christ as both shepherd and judge are present in this text. The risen Christ comes to sit on his heavenly throne with all the nations—Jews and Gentiles—gathered around him, representing his universal kingship. Then, as a shepherd, he separates sheep from goats. The Greek word that is translated as sheep here can mean any small grazing animal, even small cattle. The Greek word that is translated here as goat is the diminutive of *erion*, meaning "wool," as in "little woolly creatures." Perhaps they are less desirable because they are not fully grown or have not reached their full potential. The sheep or the mature grazers are invited into the kingdom that has been prepared for them. The goats or "little woolly creatures" are told to depart from Christ's throne. Jesus even calls them "accursed," because, when it comes time for the final judgment, there are no do-overs; you are either mature and ready to enter God's kingdom or you are not. And what is the measure of readiness? It is that you perform the corporal works of mercy from your heart, with pure motive and without self-flattery or desire to curry favour with someone. Notice the similarities between Jesus' criteria for admission to the kingdom and the seven corporal works of mercy—feeding the hungry, giving drink to the thirsty, sheltering the homeless, visiting the sick and prisoners, burying the dead, and giving alms to the poor. C.C.